Collaborative Futures

Also published by The Graduate School Press of Syracuse University

Building Community
Stories and Strategies for Future Learning Community Faculty and Professionals

Pedagogy, not Policing
Positive Approaches to Academic Integrity at the University

Interrupting Heteronormativity
Lesbian, Gay, Bisexual and Transgender Pedagogy and Responsible Teaching at Syracuse University

Building Pedagogical Curb Cuts
Incorporating Disability in the University Classroom and Curriculum

Using Writing to Teach

COLLABORATIVE FUTURES

Critical Reflections on Publicly Active Graduate Education

Edited by
Amanda Gilvin
Georgia M. Roberts
and Craig Martin

The Graduate School Press
SYRACUSE UNIVERSITY

Library of Congress Cataloging-in-Publication Data

Collaborative futures : critical reflections on publicly active graduate education / Edited by Amanda Gilvin, Georgia M. Roberts, and Craig Martin.
pages cm
Includes bibliographical references and index.
ISBN 978-0-9777847-5-2 (pbk.) -- ISBN 0-9777847-5-4 (pbk.)
1. Universities and colleges--United States--Graduate work. 2. Public universities and colleges--United States. I. Gilvin, Amanda, editor of compilation. II. Roberts, Georgia M., editor of compilation. III. Martin, Craig, editor of compilation.
LB2371.4.C66 2012
378.1'550973--dc23
2012012781

For more information about this publication, please contact:

Graduate School Programs
220 Bowne Hall
Syracuse University
Syracuse, NY 13244

www.syr.edu/gradschool/gsprograms

Manufactured in the United States of America

Contents

Illustrations

Figures

Tables

CONTRIBUTORS

Victor Becerra directs the Community Outreach Partnership Center (COPC) at the University of California, Irvine, where he has worked since 2001. Located in the School of Social Ecology, COPC facilitates and supports engaged scholarship efforts around community development in Orange County and southern California. Mr. Becerra (C. Phil. in Urban Planning from UCLA) serves on the governing council of the Center for Collaborative Research for an Equitable California, a University of California Multi-Campus Research Program funded by the UC Office of the President.

Nicholas Behm, an assistant professor at Elmhurst College in Elmhurst, Illinois, studies composition pedagogy and theory, ancient rhetoric, postmodern rhetorical theory, and critical race theory. He teaches undergraduate and graduate courses in composition theory and rhetoric, and frequently leads workshops about composition theory, writing assessment, writing in the disciplines, and graduate education.

Linda Bergmann is a professor in the Rhetoric and Composition Program at Purdue University and directs the Purdue Writing Lab. She has published over 20 articles in such journals as *Language and Learning Across the Disciplines, Feminist Teacher,* and *A/B: Auto/Biography Studies,* and as chapters in edited collections. She is co-editor of *Composition and/or Literature: The End(s) of Education* (NCTE Press, 2006). Her textbook on research writing, *Academic Research and Writing: Inquiry and Argument in College* (Longman/Pearson), was released in the fall of 2009. She is an elected member of the Executive Council of the Conference on College Composition and Communication and of the Delegate Assembly of the Modern Language Association.

Kevin Bott is Associate Director of Imagining America: Artists and Scholars in Public Life and a part-time instructor at Syracuse University. Kevin designs and facilitates theater-based campus-community partnerships that seek to expand democratic participation. He currently leads The D.R.E.A.(M.)[3] Freedom Revival, an ongoing musical Tent Revival for Freedom and Democracy based in Syracuse, New York.

Ernest L. Boyer (1928–1995) was among the most influential figures in American higher education in the twentieth century. He served as chancellor of the State University of New York system (1970–77), U.S. Commissioner of Education (1977–79), and president of the Carnegie Foundation for the Advancement of Teaching (1979–95). His Carnegie report *Scholarship Reconsidered: Priorities of the Professoriate* (1990) helped set the stage for the emergence of the engaged scholarship movement.

Allen Brizee is an assistant professor in the Department of Writing at Loyola University Maryland and serves on the Department of English Distinguished Alumni Board at Virginia Tech. His scholarship focuses on civic engagement, empirical research, and rhetorical theory, and he has published in *Computers and Composition*, the *Journal of Technical Writing and Communication*, and edited collections. Currently he is working on an article titled, "Using Isocrates for Contemporary Civic Engagement."

Kristina Bross is an associate professor of English and American studies at Purdue University. She has authored books and articles on seventeenth-century European-Native contact, colonial American religious studies, and early Native literacy in New England. Together with Susan Curtis, she has been offering service-learning classes to graduate students since 2004.

Austin Bunn is an assistant professor in the Writing Department at Grand Valley State University in Grand Rapids, Michigan. His fiction and nonfiction have appeared in the *Atlantic Monthly*, the *New York Times Magazine*, *Best American Science and Nature Writing*, *The Pushcart Prize Anthology*, and elsewhere. He is a graduate of the Iowa Writers' Workshop and former Axton Fellow in Fiction and Michener-Copernicus Fellow.

Jan Cohen-Cruz is Director of Imagining America: Artists and Scholars in Public Life; author of *Engaging Performance: Theatre as Call and Response* (Routledge, 2010) and *Local Acts: Community-Based Performance in the United States* (Rutgers University Press, 2005); editor of *Radical Street Performance* (Routledge, 1998); and co-editor of *A Boal Companion* (Routledge, 2006) and *Playing Boal: Theatre, Therapy, Activism* (Routledge, 1993). Jan is a University Professor at Syracuse University and is currently evaluating 15 community-based visual arts diplomacy projects taking place in 15 countries through the State Department.

Susan Curtis is a professor of history and directs the American Studies Program at Purdue University. Her most recent book, *Colored Memories: A Biographer's Quest for the Elusive Lester A. Walton* (University of Missouri Press, 2008), reflects her involvement in a local engagement project involving community partners and local archival materials, a project that provides an interface between public memory, academic scholarship, and historical awareness.

Kristen Day is a professor and head of the Department of Technology, Culture and Society at the Polytechnic Institute of New York University in Brooklyn. She was previously a professor of urban planning and Director of Engagement for the University of California, Irvine. Her research focuses on planning and design to promote health and to support diverse communities.

Chris Dixon, originally from Alaska, is a longtime activist, writer, and educator who recently received his Ph.D. from the History of Consciousness Program at the University of California at Santa Cruz. He is currently completing a book, tentatively titled *Against and Beyond,* based on interviews with anti-authoritarian organizers across the U.S. and Canada involved in broader-based movements. Dixon serves on the board of the Institute for Anarchist Studies and the advisory board for the journal *Upping the Anti*. He can be reached at chrisd@resist.ca.

Timothy K. Eatman, an educational sociologist, is a faculty member in the Higher Education Department at Syracuse University and serves also as Director of Research for the consortium Imagining America: Artists and Scholars in Public Life, headquartered at Syracuse. Tim is co-author of *Scholarship in Public: Knowledge Creation and Tenure Policy in the Engaged University* (Imagining America, 2008), a report that has received widespread attention within higher education as a useful resource for conceptualizing a continuum of knowledge creation that acknowledges scholarly approaches and practices beyond conventional frames. He is currently developing a study of the aspirations and decisions of graduate students and early-career publicly engaged scholars—knowledge makers both inside and outside the academy.

Sylvia Gale is Associate Director of the Bonner Center for Civic Engagement at the University of Richmond. She received her Ph.D. in English with a concentration in rhetoric and writing from the University of Texas at Austin in 2008. She serves on the National Advisory Board of Imagining America and was the founding director of IA's Publicly Active Graduate Education (PAGE) initiative. She can be reached at sgale@richmond.edu.

Amanda Gilvin received her Ph.D. in the history of art at Cornell University, where she also completed a master's degree in Africana Studies. She is now a Five College Postdoctoral Fellow in African Art and

Architecture at Mount Holyoke College and Smith College. Her research interests include African art, the taxonomy of art and craft, museum studies, gender studies, and textiles.

Amanda Jane Graham is a doctoral candidate in the graduate program in visual and cultural studies at the University of Rochester. A former New York City public school teacher and community organizer, Graham has an M.A. in communication and culture from York University and an M.S. in education from Brooklyn College. Her essay "Abstract Division: Tracing Nadia Myre's Scar Trajectory" appears in *Nadia Myre: En[counter]s* (Éditions Art Mûr, 2011).

Ivan Illich (1926–2002) was an Austrian-born philosopher and social critic. He was ordained a Catholic priest in 1951. His work with Puerto Rican immigrants in Manhattan led to a position with the Catholic University of Puerto Rico. Illich founded the Centro Intercultural de Documentación (CIDOC) in 1961 and went on to forge an international reputation as a critic of "Third World" development programs and of Western institutions generally. His major work in the philosophy of education is *Deschooling Society* (1971).

Miranda Joseph is an associate professor of gender and women's studies at the University of Arizona. She is the author of *Against the Romance of Community* (University of Minnesota Press, 2002) as well as a number of essays, including "Accounting for Interdisciplinarity" (in *Interdisciplinarity and Social Justice,* SUNY Press, 2010) and, with Sandra K. Soto, "Neoliberalism and the Battle over Ethnic Studies in Arizona" (in *Thought and Action*, 2010). Her current project, *A Debt to Society*, explores techniques and sites of accounting as performative practices that attribute credits and debts and thus sustain or transform social relations.

Ron Krabill is an associate professor of interdisciplinary arts and sciences and faculty coordinator of the M.A. program in cultural studies at the University of Washington Bothell. He is also affiliated with the Department of Communication, the African Studies Program, and the Graduate Interdisciplinary Group on Public Scholarship at the University of Washington, Seattle. He is the author of *Starring Mandela and Cosby: Media and the End(s) of Apartheid* (University of Chicago Press, 2010).

Craig Martin is an assistant professor of religious studies at St. Thomas Aquinas College, editor of the *Bulletin for the Study of Religion*, and Executive Secretary of the North American Association for the Study of Religion. His books include *Masking Hegemony: A Genealogy of Liberal-*

ism, Religion and the Private Sphere (Equinox, 2010), *A Critical Introduction to the Study of Religion* (Equinox, forthcoming), and *Religious Experience: A Reader*, co-edited with Russell T. McCutcheon (Equinox, forthcoming). Craig's research interests concern social theories of religion and ideology, with a particular focus on how "religion" is imagined in modern thought and popular discourses.

Judith E. Meighan is an associate professor of the history of art in the College of Visual and Performing Arts at Syracuse University. Dr. Meighan is an expert in nineteenth- and twentieth-century art and specializes in the beginnings of modern art in Italy. She received her B.A. from Swarthmore College and her M.A., M.Phil., and Ph.D. degrees from Columbia University. Before joining the SU faculty in 1993, she worked at the Museum of Modern Art (MoMA) in New York. Dr. Meighan has been a curator, frequent advisor, and popular lecturer at Syracuse's Everson Museum of Art. A resident of Syracuse, she has forged links between SU's College of Visual and Performing Arts and the Syracuse City School District.

Ali Colleen Neff, a cultural studies Ph.D. student at the University of North Carolina, is committed to documenting, amplifying, and celebrating the musical creativity of young people throughout the Black Atlantic. Her work in Mississippi and Senegal is manifest in her book, *Let the World Listen Right: The Mississippi Delta Hip-Hop Story* (University Press of Mississippi, 2011) and her website, www.ethnolyrical.org.

Michael Powe is a postdoctoral research associate at the University of California, Irvine. His research explores the capacity of urban policy and planning to address issues of urban inequality and social exclusion in urban neighborhoods. He is currently developing a book, tentatively titled *Loft Living in Skid Row: The Contradictions of Planning in a Contested Community*, based on interviews with more than 70 city officials, business representatives, social service providers, and Skid Row residents.

Georgia M. Roberts is a Ph.D. candidate in English at the University of Washington, Seattle, and a predoctoral lecturer in interdisciplinary arts and sciences at UW Bothell. She has held several teaching positions across the humanities: in English, the comparative history of ideas, and as a director and instructor for the UW study abroad program in South Africa. Her research interests include global hip-hop culture, American and comparative cultural studies, critical race theory, and public scholarship.

Duane Roen is Assistant Vice Provost for University Academic Success

Programs at Arizona State University. In the School of Letters and Sciences at ASU, he serves as head of technical communication and head of interdisciplinary and liberal studies. Active in the field of rhetoric and composition, he currently serves as president of the Council of Writing Program Administrators.

Shirley K. Rose is a professor of English and directs Arizona State University Writing Programs in the English Department on the Tempe campus, where she has taught since 2009. She has published several book chapters on archival studies in rhetoric and composition, exploring topics such as writing program administrators as archivists, George Wykoff's professional narratives as representation of WPA intellectual work, and recognizing the rhetorical work of professional archivists. Professor Rose has taught graduate seminars in archival methodologies, team-teaching with colleagues in American studies and with professional archivists at the Tippecanoe County Historical Association and at the Purdue University Archives and Special Collections.

Vicki L. Ruiz is Dean of the School of Humanities and a professor of history and Chicano/Latino studies at the University of California, Irvine. An award-winning historian, she is the author of *From Out of the Shadows: Mexican Women in Twentieth-Century America* (Oxford University Press, 1998) and *Cannery Women, Cannery Lives* (University of New Mexico Press, 1987). She is past president of the Organization of American Historians and the American Studies Association.

George J. Sánchez is a professor of American studies and ethnicity and of history at the University of Southern California. He is the author of *Becoming Mexican American: Ethnicity, Culture and Identity in Chicano Los Angeles, 1900–1945* (Oxford University Press, 1993), and coeditor of *Civic Engagement in the Wake of Katrina* (University of Michigan Press, 2009) and *Los Angeles and the Future of Urban Cultures* (Johns Hopkins University Press, 2005). Past president of the American Studies Association in 2001–02, he currently serves as director of the Center for Diversity and Democracy and Vice Dean for Diversity and Strategic Initiatives at USC College of Letters, Arts, and Sciences.

Marcy H. Schnitzer is a research associate at the Virginia Tech Institute for Policy and Governance. She holds a Ph.D. in government and international affairs from Virginia Tech, where she was formerly Assistant Director of the Service-Learning Center. She has conducted research in intergenerational engagement, nonprofit philanthropy, peacebuilding, and disaster management.

Damien M. Schnyder completed his degree in anthropology with a concentration in the African diaspora from the University of Texas at Austin. Damien is currently working on a book manuscript that analyzes prisons, education, masculinity, resistance movements, and Black culture. In addition to serving on the board of the Southern California Library, Damien is a member of Critical Resistance and sits on the editorial board of *Black California Dreamin': Social Vision and the Crisis of California's African American Communities.*

Timothy J. Shaffer is a Ph.D. candidate studying adult and extension education at Cornell University. His research focuses on historical and contemporary examples of higher education's public purposes and work, primarily within the land-grant system. Specifically, he is interested in questions about democracy, expertise, knowledge, and passion—both for academic professionals and for citizens.

Alexis Shotwell is an assistant professor in philosophy and English at Laurentian University in Sudbury, Ontario. Her academic work addresses racial formation, unspeakable and unspoken knowledge, gender, and political transformation. Her engagement in political struggle focuses on indigenous solidarity, ending war, and feminist community education. She has recently completed a book entitled *Knowing Otherwise: Race, Gender, and Implicit Understanding* (Penn State University Press, 2011). She can be reached at ashotwell@laurentian.ca.

Max Stephenson Jr. directs the Institute for Policy and Governance and is an associate professor in the School of Public and International Affairs at Virginia Tech. He is the author of more than 40 articles and book chapters in his areas of research interest, as well as three monographs and several edited published symposia. He and Professor Laura Zanotti (also of Virginia Tech) will publish a book and an edited volume in the coming year: *Community-Based NGOs, Peacebuilding and the Challenges of Post-Conflict Governance* (Kumarian Press, 2012) and *Building Walls and Dissolving Borders: Alterity, Community and Securitizing Space* (Ashgate, 2012).

Jaclyn M. Wells is an assistant professor of English and directs the River Bend Writing Project at the University of Southern Indiana. She received a Ph.D. in English from Purdue University. Wells has published and presented in the areas of community engagement, public rhetoric, and writing program administration. She is currently working on a project about military veterans in the writing classroom, as well as a collaborative book with Allen Brizee about the CWEST project.

FOREWORD

Kevin Bott

> I call the distribution of the sensible the system of self-evident facts of sense perception that simultaneously discloses the existence of something common and the delimitations that define the respective parts and positions within it.
>
> – Jacques Rancière, *The Politics of Aesthetics*

> Publicly engaged academic work is scholarly or creative activity integral to [one's] academic area. It encompasses different forms of making knowledge about, for, and with diverse communities. Through a coherent, purposeful sequence of activities, it contributes to the public good and yields artifacts of public and intellectual value.
>
> – Tenure Team Initiative, *Scholarship in Public*

THE HAND-WRINGING that resurfaced in the mid-1980s about the woeful state of the civic identities of undergraduate students, and typified by the creation of and enthusiastic response to organizations like Campus Compact, exists within a contemporary context that too frequently ignores the roots of modern civic engagement in higher education. These roots are traceable to the disciplinary formation of cultural studies in the 1960s, a formation itself existing in dialogic relationship with the larger, cultural emancipatory movements in the U.S. and abroad. People of color, women, gays and lesbians, and working-class and economically poor people brought with them social and political identities that they would not, and perhaps could not, dis-integrate from their professional selves in the name of a detached and objective pursuit of knowledge. Rather, the pursuit of knowledge was seen, by necessity, as emerging from and ultimately directed toward the real-world issues and lived experiences of "ordinary" people.

The immediate and vigorous cry from some quarters about the politicization of higher education that this purportedly agenda-driven phenomenon represented was a tactic for maintaining the "value-neutral," "agenda-free," and positivist reality of the dominant paradigm. The inconvenient assertion of different kinds of knowledge, of different voices and perspectives by those traditionally excluded from the academy, brought with it, first, a denunciation of the interlopers and, from some, a denunciation of higher education itself. These attacks, which would prove impressively durable, were intended to make the culture and purpose of higher education alien to those very same "ordinary" individuals and communities who had become, for many scholars, the subject rather than the object of inquiry. By turning the spotlight away from the broader, emergent inclusiveness of higher education and instead toward the complex methods of linguistic and cultural deconstruction being used to understand difference and the subtleties of hegemony, conservative critics were quite successful in framing academe as a home to Lefty ideologues, radicals, and "elites."

But in fact, long before the cultural turn of the twentieth century, higher education in the United States could claim a legacy of thought about its democratic role reaching back to the colonial colleges of the eighteenth century through the land-grant movement of the nineteenth. Running counter to the post-sixties corporatization of education at all levels, which focused on testing, "empty vessel" pedagogy, and individual gain while eschewing notions of the common good, the late twentieth and early twenty-first centuries have seen those invested in the civic mission of higher education expand the political and democratic dimensions of the academy and its practices. The organization for which I currently serve as associate director, Imagining America: Artists and Scholars in Public Life, emerged in the late 1990s and early 2000s, in part to assert the value of artists, humanists, and designers whose scholarship and creative activity are intimately linked to addressing real-world issues. It also extended arguments famously asserted by Ernest Boyer in his 1990 report, *Scholarship Reconsidered: Priorities of the Professoriate*, in which he called for an expansion of higher education's understanding of "scholarship" to include "discovery, integration, application, and teaching."

By "application," Boyer refers to scholarly practice that extends beyond campuses to address public concerns, though critics rightly point out the top-down connotation of the term and the inherent simplification it expresses in regard to how real-world issues are understood and addressed: the privileged academic coming down from the hill to "apply" his or her knowledge and skill to the messy problems of the community, which exists without agency or ingenuity of its own.

Many individuals and organizations have since expanded this idea of "application" with terms such as "public" or "engaged" scholarship, "scholarship in action," or "civically engaged" practice, each having slightly different emphases and meanings among researcher-practitioners. While undergraduate student success understandably continues to drive much engagement work, more intentional focus continues to be placed on faculty who undertake and mentor others in this work, on graduate students, and, increasingly, on the processual and ethical dimensions of engaged practices—for example, how such work may be practiced equitably and to the benefit of all participants, rather than relying on a unidirectional flow of power and capital from campus to community. Emphasis, too, is increasingly placed on the importance of adjusting, and in some cases overhauling, the means and methods by which we can understand, value, and reward the artifacts produced and the pedagogy undertaken by those who consider themselves "engaged" artists and scholars. Imagining America (IA) offers one definition of this kind of work:

> Publicly engaged academic work is scholarly or creative activity integral to [one's] academic area. It encompasses different forms of making knowledge about, for, and with diverse communities. Through a coherent, purposeful sequence of activities, it contributes to the public good and yields artifacts of public and intellectual value.

This definition provides a broad platform for students and advanced scholars, one grounded in a notion of the academy as purposed toward both knowledge creation and the common good.

In the second decade of the twenty-first century many within the movement to change higher education continue to push the boundaries of engaged practice. Perhaps as a result of professional and civic identities becoming more fluid for those who place their own work on a part of the scholarly continuum that emphasizes engagement, many recognize that the community, rather than campus, is the true center of their work. Without strong and robust communities and community organizations, the civically minded scholar has no partner. And without community partners, community-focused scholarly and creative practice can only be a one-way street, a form of traditional scholarship in which the community is either studied or "improved." I can say that at Imagining America at least, there is a deep awareness about the truly desperate financial times in which community-based arts and direct service organizations find themselves. Positioning ourselves as a higher education consortium at the forefront of elevating and disseminating community strengths and knowledge points toward a critical responsibility to leverage the academy's resources to strengthen those communities. Otherwise, there will truly be "no there there."

Questions abound, too, about access and diversity in higher education, and the implications for democracy when the demographic landscape of higher education is increasingly at odds with that of the nation as a whole. For example, what does it mean for a democracy that, according to a November 2005 policy alert from the National

Center for Public Policy and Higher Education, the "greatest increase in population growth in the U.S. workforce is occurring among those racial/ethnic groups with the lowest level of education," and that the latest census data shows the U.S. on course to have a so-called "minority-majority" by the year 2050? If, as our colonial forebears believed, an educated citizenry is foundational to a thriving democracy, what will it mean when higher education becomes increasingly unattainable for the majority? We must recognize that those who perform work undertaken with community partners to address concrete community issues do so not simply or solely as a professional preference. Many do so out of morally and personally grounded conviction. For some, such convictions are in the DNA, so to speak; they derive from longstanding family and community histories. Others, like me, learn our convictions and our ethics over time, sometimes with difficulty as we confront assumed privilege and grapple for language to make sense of our own contradictions and hypocrisies. Like many of the contributors to this volume, I found my language and my education in graduate school, a fact for which I am profoundly grateful. Thus, like many scholars who critique higher education in the United States, just as with the many American citizens who critique United States policies, my critique comes not from a lack of love. Rather it comes from a deep desire to see both the nation and the academy live up to the more inclusive, receptive, creative, and democratic ideals that provide my own frame of reference for each.

I am a first generation-college graduate. Growing up I was taught that a college education was a path away from the family trade of boilermaking. And while the combination of a) a liberal arts undergraduate education, b) my particular temperament, and c) a lifetime interest in acting and singing led me first toward a lengthy career in the field of waiting tables, I have since come to understand that the ideas and experiences I had in college have proven far more lasting and important than the jobs I did or didn't get after graduation. (And I have yet to make a boiler.)

Still, my return to graduate school after almost ten years was, at root, an attempt at a career shift. The intellectual, political, and creative seeds that were planted in me during high school and college eventually drove me from my pursuit of becoming a stage actor and back to school, where I hoped to connect my social and political commitments to my interest in and talent for theater. Perhaps the most fruitful seed was also the most unexpected: my involvement, first as a young actor and then as a teenage and young adult director, with my local community theater on Long Beach Island, New Jersey. It was as an aspiring young theater director that I came to understand how powerful art-making could be for young people, especially when the achievement of rehearsing and staging a play was explicitly linked to kids' essential value and goodness. Working so intensely for several years with teens—both those who came from truly broken and/or violent homes and those simply experiencing typical teenage doubts and insecurities—changed my worldview and aspirations. I just didn't know it for another few years.

When I finally gave up on my acting career in New York City, the result of finding the commercial theater world increasingly unsatisfying vis-à-vis my social and political interests, I was urged by a friend who knew me during my community theater days not to also give up on my theater career. Upon reflection, it seemed so obvious that the commitments I wanted to honor could be connected, quite easily I thought, to the dormant knowledge of how to use my talents and training to "make a difference" in other people's lives. I decided I wanted (using the language I employed then) "to serve underserved youth" through theater. Mind you, I didn't know what this meant exactly: I had notions about "empowerment" and "giving voice to" and "opening space for" young people. The way I saw myself as a potential "savior" to poor city kids, the way my ego was wrapped up in the ostensibly charitable act, the top-down, empty-vessel approach to teaching and learning: all of these were assumed and unconscious at the time. I also knew that to do all of these things—to get a *job* working with young people through art and theater—it helped to have credentials. So I went back to school. Despite my nascent political consciousness, my hardwiring told me that higher education remained, essentially, a place to go when you wanted to get a better job.

But graduate school turned out to be so much more than I could have expected. The opportunity—the space and time—to immerse myself in the world and history of thought and reason was an unexpected gift and treasure. My introduction to and immersion in Freirean pedagogy, performance art, and participatory theater oriented my aspirations toward creating my own art and scholarship in partnership with communities outside of higher education. I was also fortunate to have immediately found an intellectual and creative home in the Imagining America consortium. My formal introduction to IA happened to coincide with my first week of doctoral courses. I attended the 2006 IA conference in Columbus, Ohio, as a PAGE (Publicly Active Graduate Education) Fellow the weekend before classes were to begin.

As a pre-Ph.D. experience—truly my introduction to higher education—attending this unusually energetic conference of very spirited, very talented artists, humanists, and designers whose work intentionally pointed toward equity, democracy, and justice shaped the immediate lens through which I saw graduate school. The conference launched me into my studies with the notion that higher education in the United States has a living heritage that includes a civic and democratic purpose—a thought I couldn't remember having ever been exposed to at any level of my previous schooling. In retrospect, I think of that 2006 conference as having left a very powerful initial imprint, the kind of imprinting that happens among ducks and geese. The imprint overrode the assumed idea of schooling as individually focused and instrumental. It also simply convinced me that higher education was about civic identity and existed to fulfill, in part, a democratic purpose. Engaged scholarship became my "mother" as it were, and I've been following it ever since.

Fortunately, my doctoral program, in educational and applied theater at NYU, was specifically tailored toward and encouraging of project-oriented dissertations. It was common for students' and professsors' scholarship and creative practice to bridge campus and community, and for people to frame their work in terms of its social or political impact. When I began my doctoral studies, I was also working as a theater facilitator in New York State prisons; thus, the kind of work IA supported made immediate sense to me. Overall, I took legitimization of and support for campus-community partnerships for granted.

It was only after becoming more involved with IA that I started to understand that for many graduate students such supportive, resistance-free structures didn't exist. I found incredibly talented scholars-in-training, those who wanted to integrate their academic knowledge with their desire to contribute to the public good, living a kind of double existence. They were lying to the advisors whom they knew didn't support public scholarship. They were doing their "proper" research—the research that would earn them their PhDs—while they spent their "free" time trying to create programs and initiatives that satisfied their need to use their intellectual and creative capacities in service to the greater good. Most had more or less resigned themselves to a dis-integration between their work in the academy and their work in the world. The importance of a volume like this one, then, cannot be overstated. Great courage and strength is derived from knowing one is not alone in this work, and that many others are facing—and finding ways to overcome—similar challenges within the academy. This book offers important perspectives to the many early-career scholars committed to asserting the coherence between their scholarly and public passions.

What I've come to understand are the political implications of publicly engaged art and scholarship in higher education and the importance of excellent community-based work in regard to the civic mission of the academy. Within this political context, I've come to view the experiences of would-be publicly engaged scholars through the lens of social movements (and in fact many in the field refer to public scholarship in terms of a "movement" and "movement building") insofar as the personal and the political are connected through individual acts of courage intended to open new spaces and opportunities for oneself and for people involved in a larger struggle for equity and opportunity. If, from the outside, these efforts can seem to be an exercise in small *p* politics, in which self-interested white-collar workers are fighting to do the kind of work they want to do within the academy, in fact many recognize that their institutional struggles are directly related to the leveraging of institutional capital toward the strengthening of community, and to broader ideas about fairness, equity, and legitimization, both on campus and within communities not affiliated with higher education. In other words, to return to the epigraph by Jacques Rancière with which I began, those who undertake the struggle for legitimacy, and the struggle to perform engaged scholarship and practice within the academy are, quite consciously, engaged in a more meaningful capital *P* political mission.

To the many for whom active, participatory engagement with communities is the primary medium through which their art and scholarship occurs, and for whom skepticism about the rigor and legitimacy of their work is still the norm in higher education, the sense of being engaged in a kind of political movement is concrete. It is directed both inward, toward one's professional life, and outward, linking to the communities and struggles that have catapulted so many of us into the academy to begin with. Despite the increasing rhetoric about higher education's civic mission, many who would teach, model, and study this work within the academy continue to be punished for attempting to do so. As noted in *Scholarship in Public*, a 2008 report by IA's Tenure Team Initiative, "a university's strong commitment to its public mission does not guarantee a strong commitment to the civic potential of its faculty" (xii). The report goes on to quote Craig Calhoun's observation that many schools

> are doing a lot of work to reach parts of the public, open up access to higher education, shape what a variety of different constituencies will know about important issues for public debate.... But [faculty on these campuses] don't have much prospect of tenure. (xii, brackets in original)

Many experience their position in higher education as a very real struggle in which they are asked, for the sake of professional advancement, to set aside central convictions and modes of pedagogy, scholarship, and creativity. With the dangling carrot of professional stability and the stick of threatened banishment as incentives, scholars are asked to delay doing the work they're passionate about for six years or more as they work to achieve tenure. (And for those increasing ranks of clinical and contingent faculty for whom no such support is promised or forthcoming, linking one's professional role to larger commitments is virtually unthinkable.) They are often asked to cleave themselves in two, as if their means for enacting citizenship within the wider world were incompatible with their professional context—even if that context increasingly touts its civic mission as foundational. Thus, the decision to be forthright about one's professional and epistemological beliefs cannot be made lightly, for it involves real risk. It is a highly personal act, situated within a complex web of competing allegiances: to personal integrity, to a concern for professional reputation and longevity, to daily professional responsibilities, and to the desire for security for oneself and one's family.

On the front lines where these issues are playing out—in the classroom, in department meetings, in dissertation committee meetings, in tenure and promotion dossiers and IRB applications, in front of tenure committees—it is natural for artists and scholars to see themselves fighting for their professional lives, and making decisions informed at least in part by fear and self-preservation. Perhaps these fights have become more apparent as the diversity of graduate students and early-career faculty within the academy has increased, and with them a concomitant diversity of perspectives, commitments, and allegiances. But again, the alignment with other historical movements is apropos. In seeking to fundamentally challenge the status quo within a traditionally conservative and exclusive institution, acts of individual courage are crucial, unnerving though they may be; change simply does not occur without struggle involving tangible risks. To sustain oneself through the work of effecting change, one must connect the individual acts that attempt to alter departmental and institutional stances toward engagement to the larger goals and ideals of democratic renewal, civic agency, and higher education's role in a democracy. Such a connection broadens one's perspective beyond self-interest and provides nourishment and support by helping scholars identify themselves within intellectual and moral traditions linking higher education's purpose to democratic citizenship.

More importantly, to speak and engage seriously about the civic and democratic purposes of higher education is first and foremost to identify and respond to crises of democracy in this particular historical moment. If proponents and practitioners of public scholarship continue to focus most of their attention inward—on the positive outcomes for students and the new possibilities for knowledge generation, as well as on the challenges of effecting institutional change and professional sustainability—without being prepared to concretely address, beyond discrete projects and initiatives, the increasingly dire systemic challenges facing community-based artists, cultural workers, and cultural organizations, higher education can only set itself up for more of the same old kinds of skepticism, cynicism, and distrust it has often faced, and by the very groups and individuals with whom engaged scholars would propose to partner. As argued in the chapters that follow, it is necessary for those of us within higher education to continue working for a more expansive institution that reclaims and re-embraces its democratic and civic mission. But it is equally important to frame that work within a broader theory of change related to the revival of robust participatory democracy at large. By directing the vast stores of American higher education's financial, intellectual, and creative resources toward our resource-poor and economically victimized communities, and to work in equitable partnership with community leaders to address and solve real-world issues that threaten the great democratic experiment, the academy has a chance to re-stake its claim as a vital driver of innovation; a facilitator of deeper, more substantive, and "better" lives; and a home for the rich critical thinking and discourse needed to sustain and advance meaningful, inclusive, and participatory democracy.

ACKNOWLEDGMENTS

THE EDITORS have incurred many intellectual debts during our scholarly journeys, and we are especially beholden for those we have acquired while working on this volume. We thank Sylvia Gale for her confident vision in initiating the volume and inviting us to co-edit it. The Graduate School Press of Syracuse University has been unflagging in its commitment to seeing this volume to completion. Thanks to Stacey Lane Tice for garnering institutional support for the project at its conception. Glenn D. Wright has guided this project through the labyrinthine schedules and commitments of the editors and contributors in order to publish it as the book it became. We benefited from both wisdom and enthusiasm on the part of a stellar advisory board, and we would like to give special thanks to its members: Kevin Bott, Bruce Burgett, Jan Cohen-Cruz, Timothy K. Eatman, Sylvia Gale, Robin Goettel, Corinne Kratz, Julia Lupton, Louise Wetherbee Phelps, Kendall Phillips, George Sánchez, and Stacey Lane Tice. Chelsea Cramer was an early and valued member of the editorial team. We are grateful for the editorial support of Alecea Standlee, Shawn Loner, and Meg Marsh with the Syracuse University Graduate School. Time and again, we have appreciated contributing authors' scholarly rigor and ethical sensitivity, as well as their recognition of the urgency and importance of this project. Amanda Gilvin would like to thank Kevin Bott, Jan Cohen-Cruz, Sylvia Gale, Corinne Kratz, and Ali Colleen Neff for their incisive comments on earlier drafts of the introduction. Any remaining errors are hers alone. She also recognizes Cheryl Finley, Salah Hassan, Kaja MacGowan, and Cynthia Becker for their dedicated mentorship in all facets of her scholarly work. Georgia M. Roberts thanks Miriam Bartha, Bruce Burgett, Ron Krabill, and Kathleen Woodward for their institutional support, mentorship, and passionate dedication to graduate students and public scholarship.

COLLABORATIVE FUTURES

Introduction

Amanda Gilvin

IN HIS 1932 discussion of recent changes in higher education for African Americans, W. E. B. Du Bois complained of an increasingly commercial approach to learning on the part of students and the stubborn tendency of academics toward a pretense of scholarly objectivity. Such remarks may sound very familiar to those concerned with higher education reform in many parts of the world in the early twenty-first century. Du Bois argued,

> College teachers cannot follow the medieval tradition of detached withdrawal from the world. The professor of mathematics in a college has to be more than a counting machine, or a proctor of examinations; he must be a living man, acquainted with real human beings, and alive to the relation of his branch of knowledge to the technical problem of living and earning of living. (71)

With this volume, we have attempted to heed Du Bois's counsel by analyzing graduate education, fully accounting for graduate students as living people who interact with other real human beings, on their campuses and in many other places. The graduate students represented in this volume are those already "alive to the relation of … knowledge to the technical problem of living and earning a living."

With diverse scholarly and personal influences, the contributors in this volume identify their work by numerous labels. There are publicly active and publicly engaged graduate students, and their research projects may be community based, activist, radical, publicly driven and/or collaborative. Some projects found here relate to "service learning" in United States undergraduate education, but we address a much wider range of scholarship than what is included in these semester- or year-long programs that prioritize undergraduate student education. In the social sciences, and increasingly in the arts, scholars might call some of this work "applied," a term that conveys the transformation from theory into praxis. In this volume, praxis also creates theory. As editors, Georgia M. Roberts, Craig Martin, and I saw many commonalities within the aspirations, struggles, theory, methodology, and scholarship of those who contributed to this volume. Foremost among these was a shared, future-oriented commitment to increasing collaboration between graduate students and their partners inside and outside of academia, with respect for forms of knowledge often ignored in academic scholarship.

We identify the scholarship put forth and analyzed in this volume as publicly active because this descriptor, for us, best conveys the sense of having multiple publics and communities—inside, outside, and around academia. We acknowledge and defy the frequent insularity of academic practice by embracing the term *public*. Publicly active graduate education draws upon knowledge from outside of academia, and it contributes to discourses and change outside of colleges and universities in concerted ways. The word *active* is inclusive of the wide range of strategies described by the authors. Furthermore, the term *active* insists on the dynamism, contingency, and improvisation required by graduate students who do not wait until they have faculty positions to effect changes within their institutions and disciplines, but who innovate while still in training.[1] The graduate students in this volume intend for their education to contribute to transformative social change right now. Once highlighted, the boundaries that they challenge and transgress—between one discipline and another, between student and teacher, between expert and layperson, between the university and its locale—demonstrate this need for graduate student–initiated activity within an academic system that often suffers from administrative and scholarly inertia (hooks 1994).

This volume was initiated by one of our contributors, Sylvia Gale, as one of many projects she pursued while founding director of the Publicly Active Graduate Education (PAGE) program of the Imagining America: Artists and Scholars in Public Life consortium. Since its inception in 2004, PAGE has selected 116 fellows to attend the Imagining America annual conference, and the program quickly evolved to include at the conference a graduate student summit for PAGE Fellows to discuss their publicly active scholarship with one another. Several of the authors and editors have participated in PAGE summits, and the momentum begun with these energizing conversations and others like them deserves wider reach.[2] It is graduate students like ourselves, and like the inspiring colleagues we have met at PAGE summits, whom we see as our primary readership and co-contributors. Although we hope for a wide readership among faculty and graduate students' collaborators, this volume is addressed to the graduate student—or potential graduate student—who is passionate about scholarship that respects knowledge created outside of academia and that seeks progressive social change in various spheres, including but not exclusively academia.

It has been both heartening and educational to receive contributions from scholars at all stages of their academic careers. Enthusiastic authors demonstrated a broader commitment to the transformation of graduate education in the arts and humanities than we had anticipated. Senior scholars, graduate students, and junior faculty have worked together to write individual essays, and while all of the editors began as graduate students, we have benefited from the mentorship of our own faculty and from the observations of an advisory board of senior scholars. We were not the first to note the paucity of graduate students' perspectives in the ever-growing body of literature on the scholarship of engagement (and even in the larger discourse on doctoral education), but the essays bemoaning the absence of graduate students' voices appear in the very volumes that lack graduate student leadership and authorship.[3]

Current Discourses Around Publicly Active Graduate Education

The first discourse in which this volume intervenes highlights the contributions of Africana studies, gender and sexuality studies, postcolonial theory, and disability studies to publicly active graduate education. The ground-changing impact of African American and feminist activism and scholarship on all United States higher education in the 1960s and 1970s was in many ways foundational for the concerns charted in this volume (Aldridge and Young 2000; Collins 2000; Howe 2000; Rosen 2004). As pointed out by Timothy K. Eatman in this volume, much of the literature on publicly engaged scholarship has replicated structural inequities in higher education in its failure to acknowledge the institutional and scholarly innovations at historically Black colleges and universities (HBCUs) that predate many of the programs now often highlighted. The theoretical contributions of W. E. B. Du Bois and many other scholars often have been appropriated without sufficient or indeed any recognition. Faculty of color and women aspire to integrate their work for social change with their scholarship to a greater degree than their white, male, able-bodied, and/or socioeconomically privileged counterparts, and all of us working to promote publicly active scholarship are responsible for honoring and recognizing our debts to these intersecting scholarly interventions (Turner 2002). Africana studies, feminism, postcolonial theory, and queer theory are essential and fundamental components of contemporary publicly active graduate education.

Like all education, publicly active graduate education is inevitably and fundamentally shaped by dynamics of race, gender, and class. In

1990, Ernest Boyer's *Scholarship Reconsidered: Priorities of the Professoriate* suggested that the paucity of minority graduate students in American universities might be an indictment of American higher education. Institutions still have not adequately redressed these discrepancies. Boyer's indictment must now be confirmed, over 20 years after his comments, when American graduate programs still fail to reflect the racial and ethnic diversity of the population. Stephen Quaye (2005), an insightful voice of graduate student authorship in the published conversation about graduate students, insists that universities commit themselves to hiring more diverse faculty—which requires a more diverse undergraduate and graduate student body. We call for more investigations of the intersections of racial, gendered, and class discrimination in higher education, from the perspectives of potential students, undergraduate students, graduate students, and faculty. It is then incumbent upon universities, departments, and individuals to act on what they learn.

Meanwhile, the panicked descriptions of the "Crisis of the Humanities" have grown only more frantic since we began work on this volume, and the impact of the global economic crisis on college and university budgets has added urgency to a discourse on the purposes and utility of the humanities. With Evan Carton, Gale (2005) has noted elsewhere that this crisis is a chronic one, and we would be better served to reconfigure the humanities as something that we *do*, as a practice. By framing the humanities as dynamic and exploratory knowledge production instead of rigid disciplinary and disciplining traditions, we may disrupt the persistence of canons and open up space for publicly active forms of scholarship (Amor 2008). This perceived crisis may be chronic, but all graduate students in the United States' universities face challenges unique to this period of time in American higher education. The casualization of teaching labor, the corporatization of the university, and the consumerization of students all challenge our collaborative scholarly and personal aspirations.

Thomas Bender's contribution to *Envisioning the Future of Doctoral Education: Preparing Stewards of the Discipline* (2006) emphasizes the need for all historians to attain a kind of bilingualism that enables them to succeed in academia and to translate for other audiences. In the same volume, Catherine Stimpson declares that "the heroic and original humanist has been a solitary one.... Collaborative practices, common to the sciences, must now take hold in the humanities" (2006, 410). Many graduate students already practicing various kinds of bilingualism and collaboration subvert heroic narratives to imagine and become more human humanists. Seeking social change through the arts and the humanities is not ancillary or recreational—for many of us, it is precisely why we do our work within these fields. In response to well-positioned critics who exhort publicly engaged scholars in the humanities to *Save the World on Your Own Time* (Fish 2008), we insist that our scholarship *is* "our own time," and while we have no naive visions of a saved world, we do want a better one.

We wish to add our voices to the important conversation on graduate educational curriculum in the arts and humanities and its potential dissonance with graduate students' careers after graduate school. In order to address the perceived overproduction of Ph.D.'s and the often dim academic employment prospects for many graduates, the Woodrow Wilson Foundation began the Responsive Ph.D. initiative in 2000 to explore how schools could train doctoral students for a wider range of careers, especially those that would contribute to a perceived public good. The Responsive Ph.D. promoted publicly active graduate education, but only once such efforts were organized and institutionalized, and especially as a method of preparing students for nonacademic careers. For example, the Responsive Ph.D. lauded the University of Washington's Institute of the Public Humanities and the University of California at Irvine's Humanities Out There.[4]

The initiative portrayed graduate students as blank slates to be shaped and written upon by a strongly administrated graduate school. Scholars David Huyssen (2007) and Marc Bousquet (2002) have criticized the Responsive Ph.D. for failing to question university labor practices, while putting the onus on graduate students to either choose insecure, overworked academic jobs or corporate nonacademic employment. In a scathing critique of American doctoral education in which he defends graduate students' rights as workers, Bousquet characterized completed Ph.D.'s as the "waste matter" of higher education, for it is the cheap labor of graduate students that many universities seek to exploit; ironically, it is only upon graduation that many scholars find themselves unemployed.

Also responding to the ways that universities around the world are changing, the transnational Edufactory Collective has produced an important and fascinating body of work online (http://www.edu-factory.org/wp) and in meetings, based upon the understanding that institutions of higher education are crucial places of progressive activist and socially transformative organizing. According to the Edufactory Collective (2009), students and faculty must work together to recognize systemic injustices and insist on institutional change, rather than accommodating a system that might just be waiting to excrete its student-laborers.

Patricia Limerick (2008) acknowledges the constraints for young publicly active scholars, but regretfully gives her readers advice that is not acceptable for many of us and is not possible for the many graduate students who will never find tenure-track jobs, even if they write that "conventional dissertation":

> Here is the upshot: to become a university-based public scholar, a young person may well have to put that ambition into cold storage for a decade and a half. Go to graduate school, write a conventional dissertation, get a tenure-track job, publish in academic journals and in university presses, give papers at professional conferences to small groups of fellow specialists, comply with all the requirements of deference, conformity, and hoop jumping that narrow the road to tenure while also narrowing the travelers on that road, and *then* take up the applied work that appealed to you in the first place. You may need to write yourself a thorough and eloquent memo, early in this process and store it in an easily remembered and retrievable place, to remind yourself of the postponed and mothballed ambition to connect with the world that got you psyched for this career in the first place.
>
> I have my fingers crossed that I have this all wrong. (14)

She does. With this volume, and with the graduate scholarship analyzed within it, we are working to make sure that she is wrong.

In liminal positions with special advantages and vulnerabilities in the academic system, graduate students have unique perspectives to offer to an already lively conversation on publicly active scholarship. These include several volumes on engaged scholarship written from a social science perspective (Van de Ven 2007). *Engaging Contradictions: Theory, Politics, and Methods of Activist Scholarship*, edited by Charles Hale (2008), and *Higher Education for the Public Good*, edited by Adrianna J. Kezar, Tony C. Chambers, and John Burkhardt (2005), share many concerns and themes with our own, but neither focus on graduate education. The recently published *Handbook of Engaged Scholarship: Contemporary Landscapes, Future Directions* (Fitzgerald, Burack, and Seifer 2010) is concertedly didactic in nature, and analyses of graduate education pervade the many insightful essays, including several authored by graduate students. Amanda L. Voyel, Caroline Fichtenberg, and Mindi B. Levin observe that the focus on administration, faculty, and institutions has "marginalized students' past contributions to the movement" (2010, 370), and Diane M. Doberneck, Robert E. Brown, and Angela D. Allen commend the PAGE Fellows Program and the Emerging Engaged Scholars Program as "intentional, collaborative, and engaged leadership by graduate students" (2010,

401). Eric J. Fretz claims that "Graduate students are required to check their public imaginations at the door as they enter their graduate studies" (2010, 311). But those of us who snuck past the public imagination security are here, and we are part of the conversation on how to nurture a space for public imagination in graduate education. KerryAnn O'Meara's encouragement of all publicly engaged scholars to move beyond a pessimistic obsession with the challenges, risks, and problems of conducting publicly engaged scholarship resonates well with our forward-looking representation of publicly active graduate education (2010, 277).

Critical Reflections on Publicly Active Graduate Education in the Arts and Humanities

This volume is organized in a way that we hope will foster reflections on the reader's own work. In the first section, "Contextualizing Collaboration: Publicly Active Graduate Scholarship in United States Higher Education," authors provide both historical and contemporary contexts for what might be understood as movements to promote publicly active scholarship, and specifically, publicly active graduate scholarship. They also argue for directions in which we can work together to effect further change. Next, in "Programs of Action: Institutionalizing Publicly Active Graduate Education," authors address important efforts to create lasting change in graduate education by founding formal programs and initiatives. We conclude with graduate students' and former graduate students' reflections on their education, their work, and their lives in "A Balancing Act: Publicly Active Graduate Students' Reflections and Analyses."

In the first section, "Contextualizing Collaboration: Publicly Active Graduate Scholarship in United States Higher Education," we consider some of the major historical and contemporary discourses that have contributed to and continue to shape the experiences and choices of publicly active graduate students. Timothy K. Eatman introduces the important research that he has been conducting on publicly engaged scholarship, emphasizing the components that address graduate education. Drawing on this recent research, as well as his collaborations with Julie Ellison on Imagining America's important Tenure Team Initiative and the resulting publication, *Scholarship in Public: Knowledge Creation and Tenure Policy in the Engaged University*, Eatman demonstrates the rigorous scholarly potential of publicly engaged scholarship. His and Ellison's concept of a continuum of scholarship values diverse spheres of knowledge while simultaneously demanding excellence. Based on his research on higher education in the United States and on the histories, motivations, and self-definitions of publicly engaged scholars, Eatman offers concrete strategies for individuals, departments, and institutions to expand and improve their scholarship through public engagement.

Scholarship in Public sketches out possibilities in its "Pathways for Public Engagement at Five Career Stages," which is reprinted in Eatman's essay (p. 34). This work is absolutely essential if we are to see change in how publicly active scholarship is (or is not) recognized by disciplines, departments, and universities. We hope that universities continue to heed the report's recommendations, and that more evaluations for granting tenure take publicly active scholarship into account. Eatman's work answers the need for institutional analysis and advocacy by established scholars. By gathering the voices of publicly active scholars at various stages, this research also can orient students who feel isolated in their departments or institutions toward more supportive scholarly networks.

Faced with conflicting narratives about the land-grant institution where he studies, Timothy Shaffer looks at the history of United States land-grant universities to promote a graduate education that nurtures democracy and social justice. By examining different agendas from which land-grant institutions have emerged and developed over the past 150 years, Shaffer places graduate students and other scholars within diverse communities as civic actors, rather than "technocrats" and "experts," labels that evoke partial people whose research and knowledge isolates and insulates them from the aspects of their world that their research could be used to address. These are also the people Eatman tells us may shut down the "independent thinking mechanisms of the human brain." By creating space for multiple narratives about land-grant graduate education and its history, Shaffer recasts graduate students as participants in institutions constantly being renegotiated, thus refusing the image of burgeoning experts just waiting for that diploma so that they can start distributing their expertise through convoluted, but decidedly one-way, channels to the public.

As Eatman demonstrates, many publicly active graduate students participated in service learning as undergraduates, and Ivan Illich's speech delivered at the Conference on InterAmerican Student Projects in Cuernavaca, Mexico, in 1968 historicizes the contemporary vogue for undergraduate service learning in the Christian missionary and idealistic educational projects of the 1960s—and although now dated, its challenges to the paternalism inherent in many service-learning projects remain legitimate and important. Illich's contribution forces us to consider the differences between the publicly active scholarship to which we aspire and "service learning." Much undergraduate service learning in the United States remains lacking in critical thought, and the nature of students' schedules prevents long-term participation for most. We include it here to challenge our contributors and readers to envision and practice publicly active graduate education that attempts genuine collaboration and self-reflexivity.

In Illich's terms, we wish for graduate students the courage and integrity to work with people who can and might tell us to go to hell. In other words, although relatively powerless within the academy, graduate students enrolled in American graduate programs must reckon with their own power and privilege relative to those without the monetary, educational, or other resources to access what enrollment in universities afford us to varying degrees. For though even well-funded graduate students' stipends are not large by United States income standards and many more students rely on student loans, these American incomes still far surpass those of many of our collaborators, who may be in the United States or elsewhere. Travel, library cards, conferences, mentorship, funding sources: although the challenges and difficulties faced by graduate students are real and numerous, so too are the resources that many of us can access only in our roles as scholars enrolled in or hired by universities. In the words of Chris Dixon and Alexis Shotwell in this volume, we can and must leverage the resources of the university.

In an effort to recuperate the term *service learning* and improve the scholarly rigor associated with it, Susan Curtis, Shirley Rose, and Kristina Bross advocate for the implementation of service-learning projects on the graduate level. Answering the calls of the Kellogg Report for public land-grant universities to return to their founding aspirations to serve the American public, they designed a graduate-level service-learning course, and their discussions of its multiplying outcomes supports their argument that articles in academic journals and books published by university presses are not the only kinds of productive scholarship. The authors suggest that the Social Gospel movement that lasted from the 1890s through the 1920s offers lessons for implementing cultural and institutional change in American higher education that recognizes value in community-based scholarship. In addition to their central proposal that tenured faculty offer service-learning graduate courses, they advise others to publish widely in diverse outlets; to work with artists, labor unions, and activists; and not to wait for permission to conduct innovative teaching and scholarship. Curtis, Rose, and Bross demonstrate that widespread change to scholarship in the United States requires innovation on the part of individual students and professors—and advocacy and legitimization from institutions and organizations, such as the Kellogg Report and the Tenure Team Initiative.

As argued by Curtis, Rose, and Bross, as well as by Nicolas Behm and Duane Roen, the Kellogg Report has exerted great influence on American higher education, most forcefully upon the land-grant institutions about which and for which it was written. Although the excerpts from the report included in this volume address land-grant institutions, they provoke all of us to consider the influence of institutions on scholarship—and how those institutions might be improved. Addressing the perception that United States higher education institutions are unresponsive despite their research accomplishments and the unparalleled wide access they afford, the Kellogg Commission insists that land-grant universities, long known for their outreach, service, and extension programs, implement institutional plans for "engagement." Emphasizing reciprocal learning with partners, the report offers "a seven-part test" of engagement that provides useful benchmarks for any institution. Although firmly grounded in institutional portraits and recommendations, the Kellogg Report in many ways legitimated the work of publicly engaged scholars and administrators, and as noted by Curtis, Rose, and Bross, many scholars used it to promote their projects and to accomplish change within their universities.

Nicholas Behm and Duane Roen observe the changes that have occurred in American higher education since the publication of Ernest Boyer's essay, "The Scholarship of Engagement," and the Kellogg Report. They call for scholars to use documents published by the American Association of University Professors to advocate for and reflect upon their publicly engaged work. By drawing upon widely accepted guidelines for responsible scholarship established by the AAUP, graduate students can address the questions regarding the rigor of publicly active scholarship discussed by Curtis, Rose, and Bross. Yet most graduate students know little about the AAUP. Just as the Kellogg Report draws upon the historic purposes of land-grant institutions to encourage contemporary innovation, Behm and Roen look to the conventional guidelines established by the AAUP to give young scholars the authority and language to initiate dialogue with potentially resistant programs or institutions. Even for those graduate students who do not intend to become professors, these documents may be useful because they specifically address the roles and rights of graduate students within the university.

Ernest Boyer's essay, "The Scholarship of Engagement," was first presented as a presidential address at a Stated Meeting of the Carnegie Foundation for the Advancement of Teaching on October 11, 1995, and its subsequent circulation, along with Boyer's already influential and aforementioned book *Scholarship Reconsidered: Priorities of the*

Professoriate (1990), greatly impacted the Kellogg Report, Imagining America, and many other initiatives to encourage engaged scholarship. In *Scholarship Reconsidered,* Boyer had challenged United States higher education's increasing valuation of research and publication by proposing that the following kinds of scholarship be equally valued: the scholarship of discovery, the scholarship of integration, the scholarship of application, and the scholarship of teaching. He too emphasizes the history of land-grant universities, and he sounds the call the report of the Tenure Team Initiative has begun to answer by noting that engaged scholarship can endanger faculty careers. He insists that colleges and universities involve themselves more in K–12 schools in the United States, and doubtlessly would have commended programs such as UC Irvine's Humanities Out There and Syracuse University's course *Literacy, Community, Art,* both of which are discussed in this volume. In his historical reflections and prescriptions, Boyer presents a nationalist vision that belies the global scope of the engaged scholarship for which he had just coined a term, and his vision is also rooted in a nostalgia for land-grant universities with specific capitalist and nationalist ends.

I admire the optimism and hope in Boyer's work, for as Paulo Freire argues, "hope is an ontological need" (1994, 2). It is these attitudes in combination with a diplomatic clear-sightedness that have inspired so many in his audience, despite the relative vagueness of his observations and recommendations. He speaks of the "community" as a site where the university can "engage," and he takes heart in what was then a novel attempt by even large research universities to claim to be "communities" (Boyer 1990, 56). Many of us can attest to the difficulties in adjusting to these "communities," whether because of class, race, nationality, culture, sexuality, or disability. It is for these reasons that increasing diversity in higher education is so crucial, as argued by George Sánchez in this volume and by Stephen Quaye in *Higher Education for the Public Good: Emerging Voices from a National Movement.* Boyer and the Kellogg Report too easily romanticize the university as a "community" (Quaye 2005, 293–307). In analyzing why, despite its sheer meaningless, this term so ubiquitously reassures all actors despite their manifestly conflicting agendas, Miranda Joseph demonstrates how even the most well-intentioned invocations of "community" are frequently bound up in coercive, violent, and capitalist power.

As one of fiction writer Alice Munro's perspicacious characters observed of her neighbors bent on having a widow's unsightly house razed, the universities, colleges, and scholars who easily invoke "community" may be "the people who win, and they are good people; they want homes for their children and they help each other when there is trouble and they plan a community—saying that word as if they found a modern and well-proportioned magic in it, and no possibility anywhere of a mistake" (Munro 1968). Munro's character, Mary, concludes that "there is nothing you can do at present but put your hands in your pockets and keep a disaffected heart." Joseph demands instead that graduate students acknowledge the messily proportioned realities in which we work and recognize that a word like "community" can be wielded as a weapon perhaps more easily than it can inspire transformative education and personal growth.

In the second section, "Programs of Action: Institutionalizing Publicly Active Graduate Education," the authors profile work to institutionalize public scholarship in colleges and universities. While this section is not prescriptive, the essays detail how scholars have implemented different kinds of projects, which may aid readers in their own planning and assessment. Kristen Day, Victor Becerra, Vicki L. Ruiz, and Michael Powe demonstrate ways that scholars and institutions can heed Boyer's demand that they become more involved in K–12 schools. The Humanities Out There and Community Scholars programs at UC Irvine represent important innovations in graduate education that other schools might consider emulating.[5] Key to the success of such programs is the funding of graduate student labor. Importantly, these contributions explore the changing terrain of the career paths taken by graduate students who earn Ph.D.'s in the humanities. Not all of us will become professors. Not all of us want to become professors, and while we decry the casualization of teaching labor, our educational opportunities can and should enrich and prepare us for the spectrum of work that we may do. The authors offer another list of skills that can be constructively compared with the "Pathways for Public Engagement" compiled by Imagining America and included here in Eatman's essay, and they conclude with firm recommendations for institutional and cultural changes for graduate students in the humanities.

In "Getting Outside: Graduate Learning Through Art and Literacy Partnerships with City Schools," Judith Meighan profiles the publicly engaged undergraduate and graduate class that she has taught, while making the case for public engagement as a way to diversify the skills that graduate students develop. Her careful documentation of the steps that she took to implement and sustain her course demonstrate potential obstacles—and the persistent strategies she used to educate Syracuse University students while educating *with* them in the public schools of Syracuse, New York. The extensive quotations from students attest to the importance of faculty-led engagement projects, which can attract students who might not otherwise attempt publicly active scholarship.

In what was originally delivered as a Dewey Lecture at the University of Michigan's Ginsberg Center for Community Service and Learning, and later published in Imagining America's Forseeable Futures series, George Sánchez focuses on civic engagement and the urban university. He lauds programs that take undergraduate and graduate students into neighboring schools to provide arts education, but forcefully reminds scholars and teachers that "true service-learning" requires interrogation of the lack of arts education (and often, even basic quality instruction in other subjects) in many American public schools. The discrimination against K–12 students based on gender, race, and class affects access to university education later—and access to graduate school, faculty positions, and tenure after that. Sánchez emphasizes the importance of assembling a diverse group of students for public engagement projects. For him, this required an active recruitment of students for work in the Boyle Heights neighborhood of Los Angeles. To transgress literal and symbolic boundaries like Figueroa Avenue requires tenacity and strategy far beyond the crafting of an appealing class description. To advocate for principles of justice in Meighan's "outside" and Sánchez's other side of the street, universities and scholars must demonstrate those principles on campus too.

Linda S. Bergmann, Allen Brizee, and Jaclyn M. Wells support Sánchez's description of the increased attention, rigor, and evaluation needed to avoid the paternalism identified by Illich. Highlighting the professional skills that Brizee and Wells brought with them to graduate school, the authors also demonstrate that the work included training and practice in skills usually ignored in humanities graduate education. They advocate for empirical research in engagement projects so that the merits of those projects are measurable. Brizee also valorizes the personal relationships required with collaborators in order to create knowledge that will empower all participants.

As with traditional approaches to the humanities in United States higher education, graduate education in the arts has relied on exclusionary and insular narratives that discourage art intended to reach too far beyond the fences around academia and other parts of the mainstream art world. Like Meighan, Jan Cohen-Cruz outlasted the critics in her department, which should serve as further encouragement to ignore Limerick's advice, get our hands out of our pockets, and write entirely different memos to ourselves! Yet our hearts, disaffected or not, must be strong for the kinds of joint risk-taking and critical frameworks that Cohen-Cruz, like Sánchez, insists are essential for reciprocal, productive, community-based university education in the arts and humanities.

Marcy Schnitzer and Max Stephenson also take up reciprocity, arts programs, and nonprofit organizational capacity-building in an essay profiling the aims, methods, and partnerships of the Virginia Tech Institute for Policy and Governance. They advocate for strong institutional backing of what they term publicly driven engagement, while also supporting those programs initiated by faculty and students. They conclude with a list of elements essential to fostering publicly active graduate education: mentoring, institutional support, students supporting students, and community members as peers and co-learners. We know that all publicly active graduate students do not benefit from this assistance, but we second Schnitzer and Stephenson's call for the broad implementation of these components of graduate education.

Reiterating Curtis, Rose, and Bross's point that tenured faculty have significant responsibilities and powers in the transformation of publicly active graduate education, Ron Krabill sifts through the conventional advice that warns graduate students against publicly engaged scholarship. He offers a model for radically collaborative graduate mentoring, in which faculty advisors recognize the considerable knowledge and important perspectives that a graduate student brings to her scholarship. Likewise, in this model, both the mentor and student honor and value the knowledge of collaborators outside of the academic sphere. He also calls for institutional and systemic changes, and gives frank but encouraging advice to potential and current publicly active graduate students.

Austin Bunn founded the Patient Voice Project as a graduate student, and he too attests to the importance of institutional support, quipping that in this case, "a top-down ethos met a bottom-up idea." Reflecting on how the program was founded and continues to be sustained, Bunn frankly discusses both his perceived failures and his documented successes. He presents the Patient Voice Project as a transferable model, but others of his observations apply broadly to potential and current publicly active graduate projects. Like Bergmann, Brizee, and Wells, Bunn developed a well-researched pedagogy—despite founding the program before appreciating the need for one. Like Cohen-Cruz's faith in actors in prison, Bunn trusts that chronically ill writers have something to say, but seek the craft with which to do it. Bunn's experience represents the improvisatory nature of much publicly active graduate education, and demonstrates that the most important element is the passionate graduate student.

In the final section, "A Balancing Act: Publicly Active Graduate Students' Reflections and Analyses," graduate students affirm again and again our desires for graduate education to contribute to our growth as whole, living people, or for what bell hooks refers to as self-actualization (1994, 165). This demands a self-reflexive understanding of one's own professional motivations and aspirations, but also an idea about and a focus on, as Gale puts it, what we are *for* in all dimensions of our lives. The education required to emulate the vulnerable observer and the wounded healer in Ruth Behar's work (1996), or a transgressive teacher in the tradition of bell hooks, is infinitely more difficult (and rewarding) than Boyer's reassuringly clear categories of scholarship depict. To paraphrase Behar's comments on her commitment to the discipline of anthropology: it requires heartbreak, but that is the only kind of graduate education that is worth it to me.

Gale now feels that, in her promotion and education of graduate students under the auspices of Imagining America, she inadvertently ignored the most pressing priorities of PAGE summit participants—including her own. Her contribution to this volume offers a sensitive analysis of why, even within the supportive and innovative environment of Imagining America, systemic pressures shaped her views of her own goals, and those of the Imagining America PAGE program. Thus, while the inclusion in this volume of excerpts from *Scholarship in Public* and the document "Specifying the Scholarship of Engagement" responds to much the same pressures, Gale's contribution reveals the stakes: not just education and scholarship, but the futures of graduate students as living people engaged in public work with other real human beings. Gale's mapping exercise offers a challenging and dynamic way to visualize our careers, instead of (or perhaps in addition to) the linear arcs and trajectories of her title.

"Specifying the Scholarship of Engagement" is at once a daunting and an inspiring document. It is particularly useful in this section, in that graduate students can reflect on which skills they already possess, which their various projects may require, and which they should plan to acquire or refine. Imagining America seeks to validate the many sophisticated abilities on the list that are not frequently associated with conventional artistic work or humanities scholarship—and are certainly not explicitly included in graduate education in the arts and humanities. Many of these skills are ones that students learn *before* graduate school; others we cobble together as we need them, as Bunn, Gale, Dixon and Shotwell, and Neff all recount. The recognition of these various abilities as legitimate and important supports and guides those of us who might need to be both proficient weavers and critical theorists, who must hunker down in isolation long enough to write that "accessible prose," but also nurture the "purposeful relationships and networks" in our lives, along with the myriad other skills that

Imagining America proposes make up the scholarship of engagement.

Through concrete suggestions drawn from their own experiences, Dixon and Shotwell demonstrate the ability and the need of graduate students to seek transformative social change that, while acknowledging the unique challenges of our "apprenticeship" in academic life, draws on the resources and platforms that we can access only as graduate students. They offer particularly insightful comments on the need to critically question professionalization and individualism. While we may learn academic expectations of authorship and self-presentation that may be at odds with our priorities and understandings of self, a recognition of the class-based, racialized, and gendered power dynamics underpinning what we present *and* what we wear at conferences can improve the critical rigor we bring to our research.

Ali Colleen Neff agrees with Dixon and Shotwell that graduate students, uniquely positioned to innovate in their scholarship, are at the vanguard of publicly active graduate education. Historically this is a familiar location for them, as evidenced by the participation of graduate students in the anti-racist, anti-war, and feminist social and scholarly movements of the 1960s and 1970s. Through her ethnographic work on popular music in Mississippi and Senegal, Neff has taken inspiration from musical improvisation to innovate in her scholarly practices. Exploring ethnography as a method for social transformation, she explains that she has learned how to pursue multifaceted publicly engaged scholarship by listening to her collaborators' priorities and goals.

Damien Schnyder articulates the very personal motivations for his scholarly research. In this section, graduate students aver that an intellectual *and* emotional appreciation of our own desires, fears, and perspectives contributes to a far more rigorous scholarship than would a pretense of intellectual detachment. Schnyder's account also demonstrates the impact of sophisticated theoretical training in the graduate classroom on public work. It was the writing of Black theorists that he encountered at the University of Texas at Austin that equipped him to most fully engage with interlocutors like Malcolm Rapp and Hector Chavez, whose perspectives attest to the systemic globalized racism that Schnyder describes in exploring the connections between Mexican racial politics and those in Los Angeles.

Amanda Jane Graham, too, brings herself as a vulnerable observer to her scholarship that recognizes systemic and government-sanctioned injustices. Nadia Myre's collaborative artwork, *The Scar Project*, becomes a vehicle for Graham to experiment with a more collaborative and personal kind of scholarship than she encountered in her graduate seminars. Graham poses questions that resonate beyond art praxis and art criticism, challenging the paradigmatic single authorship of artworks and scholarly writing: "How can anyone say what she is still learning to feel?" Like the actors Cohen-Cruz meets in prison and the writers participating in Bunn's Patient Voice Project, Graham shows that graduate students, too, bring rich experience and knowledge, but seek craft to most fully express that experience and knowledge as part of their scholarly work. Graduate school is more readily characterized as a place for learning to think, but drawing upon feminist theory, Graham demonstrates that thinking and feeling are inherently intertwined, and that our emotions and personal motivations are fundamental aspects of our scholarship.

Although it brought additional pressures to my own balancing act in graduate education, working on this edited volume consistently has motivated me as I developed and pursued an unusual, multifaceted dissertation project. As graduate student and blogger Jonathan Senchyne explained in his response to a recent spate of columns advising against graduate education in the humanities (2011), for many of us—whether for reasons of class, gender, race, sexuality, or disability—graduate education provides life and career opportunities we likely would not have been able to obtain with any other form of preparation. Also, as the Edufactory Collective suggests, higher education is a key site of innovation, conflict, and change in our globalized, neoliberal world. Even the dwindling budgets of recession-era universities offer many resources we can leverage. Publicly active graduate education is messy, risky, and heartbreaking. We make ourselves vulnerable in all kinds of ways. Yet radical collaboration, scholarly rigor, and academic integrity may just require this vulnerability, especially if we are to achieve the greater critical thought and social justice to which all contributors to this volume aspire. Graduate education is not the only, or even the most important, site of political and social training, activism, and intervention, but it is a potentially significant one, as many collaborators and participants documented in this volume can attest—whether they are third-grade art students, medical patient writers, imprisoned actors, or graduate students. Following Curtis, Rose, and Bross's advice to public active scholars to publish in order to normalize and legitimize their work, we hope that this volume bolsters a broadly hopeful and critically sophisticated discourse on publicly active graduate education.

Notes

1. See Boyer in this volume, as well as Boyer 1990.

2. Other notable conferences and programs include the Emerging

Engagement Scholars Workshop (http://www.outreachscholarship.org/Initiatives/EmergingEngagementScholarsWorkshop.aspx) and the 2006 conference, "Civic Engagement and Graduate Education: Preparing the Next Generation of Engaged Scholars," organized by the Upper Midwest Campus Compact Consortium.

3. Damrosch, for example, asserts the importance of graduate student participation in the Carnegie Initiative on the Doctorate, but concedes that "only faculty—and senior faculty at that—have been commissioned to write essays for this collection [Golde and Walker 2006], one small sign of the pervasive updraft that silently reinforces our profession's built-in hierarchies" (2006, 41). George Walker makes similar comments in the same volume (419). Fretz and Longo (2010) also criticize volumes on engaged scholarship that do not adequately address or listen to graduate students.

4. Kristen Day, Victor Becerra, Vicki L. Ruiz, and Michael Powe analyze University of California at Irvine's Humanities Out There in this volume.

5. For more analysis of the impact of Humanities Out There, see Lupton 2008.

References

Aldridge, Delores P., and Carlene Young. 2000. *Out of the revolution: The development of Africana studies*. Lanham, MD: Lexington Books.

Amor, Monica. 2008. On the contingency of modernity and the persistence of canons. In *Antinomies of art and culture: Modernity, postmodernity, contemporaneity*, edited by Terry Smith, Okwui Enwezor, and Nancy Condee. Durham, NC: Duke University Press.

Behar, Ruth. 1996. *The vulnerable observer: Anthropology that breaks your heart*. Boston: Beacon Press.

Bender, Thomas. 2006. Expanding the domain of history. In *Envisioning the future of doctoral education: Preparing stewards of the discipline*, edited by Chris M. Golde and George E. Walker. San Francisco: Jossey-Bass.

Bousquet, Marc. 2002. The waste product of graduate education: Toward a dictatorship of the flexible. *Social Text* 70 (1): 81–104.

Boyer, Ernest L. 1990. *Scholarship reconsidered: Priorities of the professsoriate.* Princeton, NJ: Carnegie Foundation for the Advancement of Teaching.

Collins, Patricia Hill. 2000. *Black feminist thought: Knowledge, consciousness, and the politics of empowerment*. 2d ed. New York: Routledge.

Damrosch, David. 2006. Vectors of change. In *Envisioning the future of doctoral education: Preparing stewards of the discipline,* edited by Chris M. Golde and George E. Walker. San Francisco: Jossey-Bass.

Doberneck, Diane M., Robert E. Brown, and Angela D. Allen. 2010. Professional development for emerging engaged scholars. In *Handbook of engaged scholarship: Contemporary landscapes, future directions,* edited by Hiram E. Fitzgerald, Cathy Burack, and Sarena D. Seifer. Vol. 1, *Institutional change*. East Lansing: Michigan State University Press.

Du Bois, W. E. B. 1932. Education and work. *Journal of Negro Education* 1 (1): 60–74.

Edufactory Collective. 2009. *Toward a global autonomous university.* New York: Autonomedia.

Fish, Stanley Eugene. 2008. *Save the world on your own time.* Oxford: Oxford University Press.

Fitzgerald, Hiram E., Cathy Burack, and Sarena D. Seifer, eds. 2010. *Handbook of engaged scholarship: Contemporary landscapes, future directions.* 2 vols. East Lansing: Michigan State University Press.

Freire, Paulo. 1994. *Pedagogy of hope.* Translated by Robert R. Barr. New York: Continuum.

Fretz, Eric J. 2010. Student learning in the engaged academy. In *Handbook of engaged scholarship: Contemporary landscapes, future directions,* edited by Hiram E. Fitzgerald, Cathy Burack, and Sarena D. Seifer. Vol. 1, *Institutional change.* East Lansing: Michigan State University Press.

Fretz, Eric J., and Nicholas V. Longo. 2010. Students co-creating an engaged academy. In *Handbook of engaged scholarship: Contemporary landscapes, future directions,* edited by Hiram E. Fitzgerald, Cathy Burack, and Sarena D. Seifer. Vol. 1, *Institutional change.* East Lansing: Michigan State University Press.

Gale, Sylvia, and Evan Carton. 2005. Toward the practice of the humanities, *The Good Society* 14 (3): 38–44.

Golde, Chris M., and George E. Walker, eds. 2006. *Envisioning the future of doctoral education: Preparing stewards of the discipline.* San Francisco: Jossey-Bass.

Hale, Charles R., ed. 2008. *Engaging contradictions: Theory, politics, and methods of activist scholarship.* Berkeley and Los Angeles: University of California Press.

hooks, bell. 1994. *Teaching to transgress: Education as the practice of freedom.* New York: Routledge.

Howe, Florence. 2000. *The politics of women's studies: Testimony from thirty founding mothers*. New York: Feminist Press.

Huyssen, David. 2007. Response to the "Responsive PhD." *Academe* 93 (3): 49–51.

Kezar, Adrianna J., Tony C. Chambers, and John Burkhardt, eds. 2005. *Higher education for the public good: Emerging voices from a national movement*. San Francisco: Jossey-Bass.

Limerick, Patricia. 2008. Tales of Western adventure. In *Practicing public scholarship: Experiences and possibilities beyond the academy*, edited by Katharyne Mitchell. Oxford: Wiley-Blackwell.

Lupton, Julia Reinhard. 2008. Philadelphia dreaming: Discovering citizenship between the university and the schools. In *Practicing public scholarship: experiences and possibilities beyond the academy*, edited by Katharyne Mitchell. Malden, MA: Wiley-Blackwell.

Munro, Alice. 1968. The shining houses. In *Dance of the happy shades*. Toronto: McGraw-Hill Ryerson.

O'Meara, KerryAnn. 2010. Rewarding multiple forms of scholarship: Promotion and tenure. In *Handbook of engaged scholarship: Contemporary landscapes, future directions,* edited by Hiram E. Fitzgerald, Cathy Burack, and Sarena D. Seifer. Vol. 1, *Institutional change*. East Lansing: Michigan State University Press.

Quaye, Stephen Jon. 2005. Let us speak: Including students' voices in the public good of higher education. In *Higher education for the public good: Emerging voices from a national movement*, edited by Adrianna J. Kezar, Tony C. Chambers, and John C. Burkhardt. San Francisco: Jossey-Bass.

Rosen, Robyn L. 2004. *Women's studies in the academy: Origins and impact*. Upper Saddle River, NJ: Pearson Prentice Hall.

Senchyne, Jonathan. 2011. Working classes. *Bread yes, but also roses* (blog). July 28. http://jsench.wordpress.com/2011/07/28/working-classes/.

Stimpson, Catharine R. 2006. Words and responsibilities: Graduate education and the humanities. In *Envisioning the future of doctoral education: Preparing stewards of the discipline,* edited by Chris M. Golde and George E. Walker. San Francisco, CA: Jossey-Bass.

Turner, Caroline Sotello Viernes. 2002. Women of color in academe: Living with multiple marginality. *Journal of Higher Education* 73 (1): 74–93.

Van de Ven, Andrew H. 2007. *Engaged scholarship: A guide for organizational and social research*. Oxford: Oxford University Press.

Vogel, Amanda L., Caroline Fichtenberg, and Mindi B. Levin. 2010.

Students as change agents in the engagement movement. In *Handbook of engaged scholarship: Contemporary landscapes, future directions*, edited by Hiram E. Fitzgerald, Cathy Burack, and Sarena D. Seifer. Vol. 1, *Institutional change*. East Lansing: Michigan State University Press.

Part One

Contextualizing Collaboration

Publicly Active Graduate Scholarship in United States Higher Education

1

The Arc of the Academic Career Bends Toward Publicly Engaged Scholarship

Timothy K. Eatman

> A heterogeneous, fluid, tolerant academic culture ... a culture that celebrates the "prodigality" of knowledge—is a positive good."
>
> —Tenure Team Initiative, *Scholarship in Public*

WHILE I AM not much for television game shows, I do find myself intrigued by the quiz format, where the hosts asks adults basic trivia questions challenging them to recall information they learned in elementary school. The U.S. version, *Are You Smarter Than a 5th Grader?* which first aired in 2007, has gained increasing popularity.[1] For me the game show is more than an entertaining way to observe adults sweating over the potential embarrassment of not intellectually measuring up to the young children against whom they compete. In a subtle yet profound way, it also represents an opportunity to celebrate various dimensions of knowledge. While adult competitors have the valuable asset of experience with the application of knowledge, the students, having more recently engaged the material, may have freshness of perspective about its details, meaning, and potential uses. In any case, this arrangement allows us to catalyze knowledge in ways previously inaccessible. The mainstream of our knowledge economy would benefit from a more expansive posture. Indeed, the American education system writ large can be aptly characterized as a rigid, adult-centered sorting system and bureaucratic enterprise that effectively serves to reify dominant ways of thinking and approaches to knowledge creation (Campbell 1983; Grodsky 2007; Howard 2010; Kerckhoff 1976; Lee 2008; Milner 2010; Muscatine 2009; Nie, Junn, and Stehlik-Barry 1996; Payne 2008; Wolfe and Haveman 2001). This model is grossly ineffective for the majority of students who navigate public schooling in the United States. This is especially true for communities that are underrepresented in higher education and other places of privilege. And this reality is no less problematic in primary and secondary than in postsecondary contexts.

In a society where knowledge gatekeeping abounds (Bramble 2008; Garcia 2009; Swartz 2009), there is for me something powerful about valuing knowledge in expansive ways, about celebrating the generative nature of knowledge making and pushing back against normative frames and discourses that overlook or undertreat the reality that knowledge is socially generated. This is to say that that while the creation of knowledge and agreement in society hinges on the work of highly trained experts grounded in discipline and committed to the refinement of method, there is no less value in perspectives and knowledge embedded in quotidian, nonacademic practice. I am interested in how diverse sources of knowledge inside the academy and within the larger society can be appropriately valued, and the degree to which our knowledge economy can be sensitive to the range of ways of knowing, including experience-based knowledge. Constricting the rich diversity of knowledge supports the excessive veneration of privileged perspectives and limits our imaginative potential to meet pressing social issues and concerns. Why, for example, when we know so much about poverty, does poverty continue to worsen? Donald Stokes' *Pasteur's Quadrant* (1997) reminds us that there are alternatives to basic and applied knowledge/research and that most research is "use inspired"—that is, aimed at solving social issues. Economist Noreena Hertz, in her November 1, 2010, presentation in the online TEDTalks series, describes research demonstrating that the independent thinking mechanisms of the human brain tend to shut down when consulting "expert" advice. This should in no way be misconstrued as an attack against expert knowledge, but rather a caveat to the pervasive pressure to treat some sources of knowledge as above critique. Indeed, there is evidence that graduate students are taking the lead in changing norms of valuing and making knowledge in the academy of the twenty-first century.

Social psychologist Edmund Gordon urges members of the academic community to move beyond what he has identified as a prevalent excessive focus on knowledge production at the expense of pursuing understanding. Gordon calls for a level of sophistication among academicians that supports robust channels for accessing diverse knowledges, even going so far as to emphasize this approach as a *sine qua non* for so-called objective research. As Carol Camp Yeakey articulates Gordon's critique, "differing ways of knowing must not be regulated as a political or theoretical threat to the dominant paradigms, for conceptual pluralism must be assumed to be an essential feature for the advancement of all knowledge and especially of bodies of knowledge which claim to be objectively based" (Yeakey 2000, 296). How, for example, can we gain a sufficiently nuanced understanding of educational achievement in underserved elementary-school contexts if we rely exclusively on fundamental theoretical principles of cognitive learning and fail to triangulate that perspective with issues of social structure and community resources?

So what do a television game show and notions of diverse approaches to knowledge production have to do with the graduate school experience and publicly engaged scholarship (PES)? Using the model of the game show and asking, "Are you smarter than a graduate student?" I hope to explore the earliest segments of the academic career arc as domains of knowledge production. In addition, I will argue that there are equally valid and important modes of knowledge production manifest in nonacademic contexts, and that these are essential to maximizing the knowledge-making enterprise. I take this approach neither to disparage graduate students nor to impugn non–graduate students but rather to investigate the evidence that suggests PES is taking root as an important paradigm of scholarly inquiry. I do not want to suggest that conventional scholarly inquiry is being, will be, or should be replaced. As I told *The Chronicle of Higher Education* in a 2008 interview, excellent scholarship will always be just that, excellent (June 2008). However, true to the evolving and dynamic nature of knowledge creation, PES enriches and complicates the state of play in academe. In many ways, graduate students are demonstrating leadership in this regard which will be demonstrated as we turn later in the chapter to preliminary findings from a national study of the aspirations and decisions of graduate students and early-career scholars. I believe it is important to take the pulse of academe at this moment, as an important step in addressing the needs of that evolving group of knowledge producers who see themselves as publicly engaged scholars.

I seek to make three main points about PES in graduate education: 1) there is a growing core of individuals who conduct research and involve themselves in engaged community work both in the academy and in the larger society; 2) there is room within a continuum of scholarship for their work; 3) understanding their mindsets, needs, roles, and aspirations is an essential aspect of supporting the development of knowledge creators and nurturing the emerging citizenry of academe.

Knowledge Creation and a Continuum of Scholarship

In 2008 Imagining America (IA) published a report entitled *Scholarship in Public: Knowledge Creation and Tenure Policy in the Engaged University*, which I co-authored with Julie Ellison.[2] In the report we sought to develop a nuanced exploration and discussion of the increasing attention that publicly engaged scholarly work receives within higher education. This attention is evident in part through the growing number of institutions that have followed in the path of Portland State University, revising faculty promotion and tenure criteria to include PES principles and practices.[3] The report, inspired by publicly engaged scholars but geared toward providing useful information and analysis to policy makers in higher education, places special emphasis on the need to develop fuller understandings about the situation of graduate students. It draws on several years of research and consultation developed through IA's Tenure Team Initiative on Public Scholarship, co-chaired by Syracuse University President and Chancellor Nancy Cantor and Steven D. Levine, president of the California Institute of the Arts. The report locates publicly engaged academic work within a *continuum of scholarship* in four domains:

- a continuum of scholarship gives public engagement full and equal standing;
- a continuum of scholarly and creative artifacts includes those produced about, for, and with specific publics and communities;
- a continuum of professional choices for faculty enables them to map pathways to public creative and scholarly work; and
- a continuum of actions aimed at creating a more flexible framework for valuing and evaluating academic public engagement. (iv)

The notion of a *continuum of scholarship* resonates within the engaged scholarship community even as it requires more precise definition, explanation, and examples. We conceptualize this as a way to frame a space wherein knowledge producers can locate themselves and pursue the creation of knowledge in its sundry forms with dignity and respect:

> The term continuum ... does useful meaning-making work: it is *inclusive* of many sorts and conditions of knowledge. It resists embedded hierarchies by assigning *equal value* to inquiries of different kinds.... [W]ork on the continuum, however various, will be *judged by common principles,* standards to which all academic scholarly and creative work is held. (Ellison and Eatman 2008, ix–x)

This framing inspires a sense of agency that fuels some of the most substantial, well-developed, and impactful scholarly creative work and practice taking place today. It also facilitates a sophisticated discourse about knowledge creators, one that establishes "publicly engaged scholar" as more than just an academic identity demonstrating its eclectic potential.

Preliminary findings from IA research in progress, presented later in this chapter, suggest that it may be prudent to interrogate the prevailing ideology encoded in the notion of "the scholar" so as to provide for a more robust and inclusive definition, one fit to describe the range of thought leaders needed to address the complex, pressing issues of the day. This work indicates how it may be possible to value the intellectual orientations of emerging scholars who pursue knowledge creation in ways that have not been understood as "scholarly" in the traditional sense. It is important to note that in many cases this work emanates from project-based models and praxis or action research rather than basic research and traditional tech-transfer models.

Key Elements and Principles of Inquiry

This of course raises the question, "what is publicly engaged scholarship?" The definition that we offer is *Scholarship in Public* is as follows:

> Publicly engaged academic work is scholarly or creative activity integral to a faculty member's academic area. It encompasses different forms of making knowledge about, for, and with diverse publics and communities. Through a coherent, purposeful sequence of activities, it contributes to the public good and yields artifacts of public and intellectual value. (6)

Researchers have observed that the dearth of precise terminology in the field provokes confusion and disjuncture, especially between the work of administrators and faculty (Doberneck, Glass, and Schwietzer 2010; Kezar, Chambers, and Burkhardt 2005). The literature employs a variety of expressions to categorize publicly engaged scholars, with varying success. Terms like civic engagement have been challenged recently, based on the rationale that they are too amorphous to really be useful (Berger 2009). While it is beyond the scope of this chapter to take on these challenges, it is important to underscore the need for specificity. In this regard, I use the term *publicly engaged scholars* almost exclusively. I further propose that there are ten key elements of publicly engaged scholarship (PES). These specific and in some cases overlapping dimensions are described in Table 1.1.

These ten do not exhaustively delineate PES elements, however they do help provide a concrete sense of non-negotiable aspects of this work. Among the ten, five require special emphasis in this context: clear and adaptable definitions, democratic practice, public good impact, diverse scholarly products, and multiple career paths.

TABLE 1.1. Ten Key Elements of Publicly Engaged Scholarship (PES)

Key element	Brief description
Clear and adaptable definition	Providing sufficient specificity such that the core components are translatable across a range of disciplinary and methodological settings and transferable among institutional types or contexts
Well-articulated criteria	Demonstrating universal principles of sound research design, methodological rigor, and analytical depth, which are translatable to rewards systems
Peer review	Comprised of an identifiable group of recognized, experienced, and expert evaluators who may be located both inside and outside the academy
Democratic practice	Establishing the power, posture, and relationship dynamics as related to the establishment of research questions and work plan; reciprocity among campus and community-based partners is deeply embedded in PES work
Public good impact	Manifesting in clear and tangible artifact(s) or plan(s) with ameliorative potential
Location on continuum of scholarship	Ratifying the work as a serious knowledge-making endeavor by placing it along the continuum of scholarship.
Diverse scholarly products	Producing artifacts of scholarly work that take a variety of forms and that manifest at different points throughout the project
Multiple career paths	Facilitating career paths that hinge on research-based scholarly endeavor but may or may not include tenure-track faculty appointments

Interdisciplinary focus	Drawing on more than one academic discipline and acknowledging the essential contributions of each
Rewards	Expressing the value of the work through policy that provides both material and structural incentives

When thinking about the importance of *definitions,* I often recall being approached by a university provost after having given a keynote on PES at a conference of academic leaders a few years ago. He asked some challenging questions about my research and the continuum of scholarship. It was clear to me that he had serious doubts about how he might be able to stimulate a focused and sustained conversation on campus about public scholarship. However, he found the definition that I presented both compelling and useful as a starting place. Defining publicly engaged scholarship in a way that is solid but adaptable to various contexts is a key element of PES. It is useful not only for chief academic officers and dossier-preparing assistant professors, but for graduate students as they develop their engaged work and navigate some of the challenges associated with pursuing nontraditional knowledge creation work in traditional educational settings.

Democratic practice is perhaps one of the most distinguishing elements of PES because it runs counter to the learning models and approaches that are most commonly used throughout our educational system. As John Saltmarsh and his colleagues put it, "the dominant epistemology of the academy runs counter to the civic engagement agenda" (Saltmarsh, Hartley, and Clayton 2009). Especially at the graduate level, people are taught the primacy of the expert perspective and the idea that expertise somehow ensures objectivity when we study phenomena in the social realm. In the humanities, critical brilliance and nuanced contextualized critique garner the accolades. However, publicly engaged scholars take a different view. Public sociologist and Tenure Team member Craig Calhoun asserts in the report, "We have produced a system in which, instead of empowering students to do the things they think are important better, we teach them that something else valued by the discipline is what they should go after" (Ellison and Eatman 2008, 20). As we will see shortly from gleanings of preliminary findings from the PES study, publicly engaged scholars tend to be highly motivated in their work by issues of social justice and democratic practice. They are comfortable developing research inquiries and designing studies in nontraditional collaborative arrangements. It can be said that PES literally depends on democratic practice enabled by reciprocal exchanges between academic and community-based partners, each valued and respected for the experience and perspectives that they bring.

Stemming from its grounding in democratic practice, PES leads to work that manifests in some tangible *public good impact*. Public good in this sense means impact not reserved for groups or individuals based on social ascription or on ability to pay a fee or to leverage some esoteric network of privilege. Researchers have observed how true democratic practice in higher education can lead to positive public good impact (Boyte and Hollander 1999; Boyte 2004; Brown and Witte 1994; Butler 2000). In some cases arguably the most powerful impact is on the faculty and academic administrators who change their perspectives about what is possible in the world through engaged knowledge creation; this has the potential to percolate through their students and collaborators, elusive definitions of "public good" notwithstanding.

It is not difficult to imagine that *diverse products* would emerge from scholarly work generated by empowered knowledge producers who with agency and respect locate themselves along a continuum of scholarship depending on democratic practice. Regarding these products, *Scholarship in Public* calls for "expanding what counts":

> Community-based projects generate intellectual and creative artifacts that take many forms, including peer-reviewed individual or co-authored publications, but by no means limited to these. The continuum of artifacts through which knowledge is disseminated and by which the public good is served matches, in inclusiveness and variety, the continuum of scholarship. (Ellison and Eatman 2008, 11)

Other examples of diverse scholarly products include pieces written for nonacademic publications; presentations at a wide range of academic and nonacademic conferences, meetings, and participatory workshops; oral histories; performances, exhibitions, installations, murals, and festivals; new K–16 curricula; site designs or plans for "cultural corridors" and other place-making work; and policy reports.

There is also a great need for the development of *multiple viable career pathways* from which individuals can choose. Research from the Tenure Team Initiative led to the following observation about graduate students and their available career pathways:

> Graduate students are restless. Some are finding dissertation topics and peer mentoring networks that allow them to work out how to integrate engagement into their fields or disciplines.

> These groups emerge, for example, in the Public Engagement and Professional Development program at the University of Texas, the Black Humanities Collective at the University of Michigan, and the annual Public Humanities Institutes for graduate students at the University of Washington and the University of Iowa. Some students have found their way to degree programs designed to train publicly engaged artists and scholars, such as the Ph.D. program on Theatre for Youth at Arizona State. Others are taking charge of re-thinking the possibilities of graduate education itself through Imagining America's PAGE (Publicly Active Graduate Education) program.
>
> Their mentors may urge them to stop. The PAGE Fellow who remembered being advised to disengage from community commitments told an Imagining America audience, "I felt like someone was asking me to cut off my legs." She rejected this advice and took the risk. Especially for graduate students who have become accustomed to community service learning as undergraduates, perhaps writing a senior thesis that arose out of a community or public project, the transition to the civically disassociated world of a graduate program can be stressful. "There is tension in the system" between student-centered engagement, which is encouraged, and faculty-centered engagement, which is not.... (Ellison and Eatman 2008, 16–17)

Responding to the need for pathway models, the TTI report includes a hypothetical example of pathways for public engagement at five academic career stages (Ellison and Eatman 2008, 21). I reproduce it as Table 1.2 in this chapter in hopes that it may be useful in considering possible pathways within academic structures. It was not developed as a prescriptive device, but rather as a planning tool to empower publicly engaged scholars to envision engagement within a traditional faculty track. However, it is very important to note that there exist myriad pathways outside of academe that are viable and for which there is significant demand. These pathways should be developed by listening to the individuals who actually engage in nonacademic public work. This is one of the reasons that recommendations from *Scholarship in Public* led to the development of a national study of the aspirations and decisions of publicly engaged scholars. I turn to this data after considering the present context of engaged scholarship in higher education.

Historical Context and Development

We are in an era characterized by the burgeoning of a movement in the academy for civically engaged work. In *Dewey's Dream* (2007), their

TABLE 1.2. Pathways for Public Engagement at Five Career Stages: A Hypothetical Example

ACTIONS	Grad. Student	Asst. Prof. 1–3	Asst. Prof. 4–6	Assoc. Prof.	Full Prof.
I. DECIDING TO BE A PUBLIC SCHOLAR					
Establish "public good" focus area for teaching, scholarship, creative work	x	x	x		
II. BUILDING A KNOWLEDGE FOR PUBLIC SCHOLARSHIP					
Identify civic, public, community issues in your field and know who is working on them	x	x	x		
Map campus (people, programs, pathways)	x	x	x		
Map community (people, programs, issues)	x	x	x		
III. DEVELOP SKILLS: PRIORITIZE AND START TO ACQUIRE THEM					
Teaching, networking, presentation, writing and speaking accessibly	x	x	x		
Ethnography and oral history	x	x	x		
Documentation, evaluation, digital resources	x	x	x		
IV. MENTORING PUBLIC SCHOLARS					
Get mentoring	x	x	x		
Peer mentoring	x	x	x	x	x
Give mentoring				x	x
V. DOING PUBLIC SCHOLARSHIP					
Participate in Preparing Future Faculty programs (PFF)	x				
Teach community-based class		x	x	x	x
Join campus-community project team			x	x	x
Public presentation of knowledge		x	x	x	x
Supervise community-based undergraduate research			x	x	x
Get involved with national programs for engaged grad students and faculty	x	x	x		
Explore collaborative publication	x	x	x	x	x
VI. EXERCISING LEADERSHIP					
Coordinate project	x	x	x	x	x
Collaborate on course or curriculum development		x	x	x	x
Co-direct campus-community project	x	x	x	x	x
Write grant proposal		x	x	x	x
Speak for public scholarship and creative practice on key committees				x	x
Seek leadership role in national association				x	x
Launch publication project (journal, book series, position papers)				x	x
Serve as program or center director					x
Serve as chair or dean					x

Source: **Julie Ellison and Timothy K. Eatman, *Scholarship in Public: Knowledge Creation and Tenure Policy in the Engaged University* (Syracuse, NY : Imagining America, 2008), 21. Courtesy of the author.**

astute analysis of PES in the current era of American higher education and John Dewey's seminal impact, Benson, Harkavy, and Puckett (2007) argue that we are riding the early part of a third revolutionary wave within the academy. Benson and his colleagues reflect upon the first revolution, in the late nineteenth century, when American universities, beginning with Johns Hopkins, adopted the German model that privileged specialized research using approaches grounded in the natural sciences as the most valued form of scholarly activity. With the research university already essentially established, the mid-twentieth century ushered in a second revolution characterized by the cold war, the advent of entrepreneurial university, and the strong focus on science development and technology transfer ushered in a second revolution. The authors then describe a third revolution:

> The fall of the Berlin wall and the end of the cold war provided the necessary conditions for the 'revolutionary' emergence of the democratic, cosmopolitan, civic university—the radically new type of 'great university,' which William Rainey Harper had prophesized would advance democratic schooling and achieve practical realization of the democratic promise of America for all Americans. (78)

In the early 1990s Ernest Boyer offered an analysis of scholarship that distinguishes between—while attempting to equalize the value of—different intellectual functions and the social relations associated with them. Boyer and colleagues at the Carnegie Foundation set forth in *Scholarship Reconsidered* four types of scholarship that demonstrate knowledge creation in its most robust form:

1. The scholarship of discovery refers to the pursuit of inquiry and investigation in search of new knowledge.
2. The scholarship of integration consists of making connections across disciplines and advancing knowledge through synthesis.
3. The scholarship of application asks how knowledge can be applied to the social issues of the times in a dynamic process that generates and tests new theory and knowledge.
4. The scholarship of teaching includes not only transmitting knowledge, but also transforming and extending it.

In a 1996 essay, published posthumously and reprinted in this volume, Boyer urged the need for an epistemological shift framed by a fifth category, what he called the scholarship of engagement, "connecting the rich resources of the university to our most pressing social, civic, and ethical problems" (see p. 153 below).

Boyer viewed discovery and inquiry as governed by the normative model of scholarship and wrestled with ways to open it up. In particular, he was concerned with making the "assumptive world" of the research university more flexible and democratic, without sacrificing intellectual rigor (Rice 2006). Boyer's exasperation with the refusal of the system to grant scholarly legitimacy to crucial domains of knowledge making is both powerful and warranted.

With regard to the civic engagement movement of the last ten years, the present era in higher education can be characterized by a transition away from older, pedagogically centered models that stressed service learning, course-based work, and student placements to a model that is more integrative, that stresses the value of academic public work folding together research, scholarship, teaching, and community and public engagement in the broadest sense. This evolution has involved models of collaboration—citizenship rather than service—which stressed the desirability of deeper, richer, more sustained, and more transformative work in which community partners and academic partners effect change in both educational practices and public life. These in turn raise obvious and pressing questions about faculty rewards. Clearly associated but not as sharply focused are the issues surrounding graduate education that these shifts reveal.

This more ambitious approach introduced implicit and explicit challenges to many of the assumptions about academic life and disciplinary professionalism, including what counts as good scholarly productivity, which models of graduate education are strongest, how faculty scholarship should be assessed, what career pathways are viable for graduate students, and what kinds of professional trajectories are available for faculty. All of the most important issues that normatively shape the training of graduate students and faculty work tended to be disrupted by this new trend. The double fact of the growth of academic civic engagement on the one hand and increasingly explicit challenges to traditional models of academic life on the other puts these issues on the table.

The Wingspread Declaration on the Civic Responsibilities of Research Universities, issued in 1999, offers a powerful framework for PES, situating the call for public scholarship by faculty in the context of "a historic debate ... over the future of America's great public and research universities" (Boyte and Hollander 1999, 7). The Declaration stresses the significance of public scholarship as one of the most important ways in which faculty can forge "opportunities to work with community and civic partners in co-creating things of public value"; in particular, this touchstone document emphasizes the need for "diverse cross-disciplinary ... projects" (Boyte and Hollander 1999, 11). Effective campuses need faculty members in all fields who are public scholars, but such faculty members often are discouraged and put at risk by existing tenure and promotion policies. Even after many years of concerted efforts for change, public scholarship often goes unacknowledged within existing systems of evaluation. This is most problematic in graduate education because it has the effect of devaluing the posture and work that so many students see themselves as uniquely positioned to develop, and can promote a debilitating sense of dis-agency. This is particularly true in humanities, arts, and design fields that combine publicly engaged intellectual work with interpretive or expressive practices. We need to expand the reward system for tenure-track faculty and other publicly engaged scholars so that it does not constrain the flow of discovery.

I call to question the omission within the normative discourse on publicly engaged scholarship of the available and compelling examples that non-mainstream institutions like historically Black colleges and universities (HBCUs) and leaders within that community represent. Indeed, as Stephanie Evans points out, scholarship that emerges from PES fails to provide an adequate "focus on how African Americans have done so much to 'clean up' the dirty laundry of the United States and correct antidemocratic policies by contributing critical thought and constructive practices that demand and create social justice" (Evans et al. 2009, xii). Given the sordid history of segregation and the ways that higher education has been structured to manage the resulting disparities, this is not surprising (Calhoun 2006; Cantor 2009; *First Morrill Act* 1862; *Second Morrill Act* 1890; Trent and Eatman 2002). However it is now time to understand the implications of these structural decisions and effectuate change that leverage the entire system of higher education toward societal relevance and efficacy. Exploring the nexus of diversity, civic engagement, and student success is an area of opportunity in this regard.

Pitfalls, Challenges, and Agency

This history helps to contextualize our current mode. One major looming question is, can universities distinguish between public scholarship as civic engagement and public scholarship as activism without banishing either from academic legitimacy? I would say that there is much ground yet to cover in order to answer that question. Prior research makes apparent the challenges that publicly engaged scholars face in relation to traditional conceptions of knowledge making and how requirements that students often encounter during the course of a typical graduate program may impact their scholarly work.

For instance, many of the scholars who participated in the study of the aspirations and decisions of publicly engaged scholars to which we turn at the close of this chapter understand their work as essentially interconnected with a community-based enterprise and/or issue; they may themselves regard such work, a priori, as not scholarly by traditional standards, even though they are very much engaged in the development and critique of salient theoretical constructs and methodological approaches. This conception of their own endeavors appears self-defeating and even irrational in light of the origins of many recently legitimated disciplines.

Social movements can be bridges to knowledge. We see this in the history of African American Studies, Women's Studies, Disability Studies, and Gay and Lesbian Studies—academic fields that emerged through social movements and brought into the academy a characteristic mix of research, critique, policy-making, theorizing, public debate, the formation of new public spheres, and local organization building. (Ellison and Eatman 2008, 20). However, gaining greater clarity about the mindset of the publicly engaged scholar can help to mitigate this challenge.

The University of Michigan's excellent resource, *How to Mentor Graduate Students: A Guide for Faculty at a Diverse University,* was developed through an exemplary process of collaboration with graduate students and faculty members. It provides good advice and thoroughly convincing best practices. However, it presents graduate students almost exclusively as the recipients of wisdom, without attributing to them the capacity to exercise agency in electing research or creative projects informed by civic commitments and acquiring the skills needed to advance those projects. The language of mentoring often assumes lack, dependency, or neediness. Can we move toward a strength-based, or asset-based, model of mentoring?

Imagining America's PAGE program has shown us how networking and self-organizing by graduate students leads to growing agency. To date, over 300 graduate students in the humanities, arts, and design have applied for 60 PAGE conference fellowships. PAGE Fellows have established annual summits at the IA national meetings. These events are driven by a set of readings, collaboratively defined pertinent issues, and the deliberate shaping of a culture of peer mentoring, workshopping, and sustained collaborative writing collectives. The success of PAGE has implications beyond the cultural disciplines. It contains lessons for Preparing Future Faculty (PFF) programs nationwide. PFF programs, as valuable as they are, do not concretely address graduate students' futures as civic professionals or as future faculty in colleges and universities with a strong public mission. Integrating new modules on dimensions of engagement into PFF programs could clarify professional pathways for graduate students and early career faculty (Ellison and Eatman 2008, 20).

Profiles of Publicly Engaged Scholars in Graduate Education

How can we best understand the characteristics of publicly engaged scholars and the implications that their work holds for knowledge production in the academy? What challenges do publicly engaged scholars face in the knowledge economy and in the current climate within academe? Building on the TTI report, a national study developed by Imagining America to address these questions offers preliminary data that may be instructive (Eatman, Weber, Bush, Nastasi, and Higgins 2011). This study seeks to profile self-identified publicly engaged scholars to learn about their educational and career aspirations, including reflections on their identity development, professional evolution, and motivations. Additionally, we explore the degree to which mentoring and postsecondary experiences influence their interest in PES. A second section asks questions about the practice of PES as regards methodology and knowledge creation in the context of graduate school. A final section on aspirations probes what they see as viable career pathways.

The study employed focus groups to establish a mixed-methods survey instrument, which included some conventional measures from related studies. It was piloted nationally and used to develop interview protocols. The research in progress has analyzed 434 responses to a 54-item web-based survey and 54 structured telephone interviews with participants who self-identify as publicly engaged scholars. The survey respondent pool is overwhelmingly female (65%). The majority (65%) of survey participants identified themselves as White (non-Hispanic), 10% as Black or African American, and 5% as Asian or Pacific Islander. Taken together, the Latino group (Puerto Rican, Mexican American, and other Hispanic or Latino respondents) represents 6% of the sample. The full range of disciplines were represented among survey respondents, with the largest share (29%) in the humanities, followed closely by the social sciences (27%) and education (19%), with a much-smaller-than-expected 8% in the arts. Almost half of the respondents (48%) attended four-year public research institutions for their undergraduate education. Regarding the 54 qualitative structured phone interview participants, 58% were female. Seventy-five percent of telephone interviewees described themselves as White (non-Hispanic). The remainder identified as follows: 9% Asian, Asian American, or Pacific Islander; 6% other Hispanic or Latino; 6% "other"; and 4% Black or African American.

Summary of Survey Responses

The data reveal graduate students' and early-career publicly engaged scholars' perspectives on what motivates their scholarship, what kind of supports are necessary, and how publicly engaged scholars develop. A few key data points are worth considering here. For example, these data challenge the prevailing view that publicly engaged scholars are less concerned with the rigors of methodologically grounded, discipline-specific work. When asked what they hope to accomplish through engaged scholarship, the highest percentage (77%) indicate the desire to "expand knowledge, methods and/or scholarship in the discipline." The desire among respondents to achieve the same "in the public" registered a mere three percentage points lower (74%). This indicates the importance of breaking down the entrenched but seemingly false dichotomy of scholar and activist.

Another very compelling data point relates to the professional journey of publicly engaged scholars and what factors draw them to PES. Respondents were asked, "What experiences shaped your interest in publicly engaged scholarship in a significant way?" Graduate work (76.22%) was selected most frequently, followed by personal or professional mentors (63.11%), community service (60.89%), collegiate experiences (53.56%), and cultural involvements (53.33%). Work or internship experiences (45.78%) were cited more frequently than family members and friends (39.11%). This suggests that at least for this group of respondents, some combination of experiences associated with graduate school helped to facilitate interest in PES. Another important dimension that deserves attention here is collaboration. When asked, "Who do you consider the top three collaborators or partners in your publicly engaged scholarly work?" respondents listed community members (26.7%) first and faculty (24.55%) second, followed by non-profit organizations (17.19%) and fellow graduate students (14.29%).

These data provide a window into the mindset and professional identity of publicly engaged scholars. For example, consider that when respondents were asked how they define themselves within a PES context—given the opportunity to select all that apply from a range of items including "learner," "scholar," "researcher," and "teacher"—"learner" registered highest, with almost 75% choosing this identity as one that they embrace. At first glance this may not be surprising, given the preparatory nature of graduate education. Yet given the foregrounding of reciprocity within the larger PES context, these data require greater scrutiny. Coupled with evidence from the interview data (discussed below), "learner" here may very well speak to a posture or sense of respect that urges publicly engaged scholars to become situated within dynamic relationships in a way that is sensitive to the continuum of knowledge creation, especially as it extends beyond campus.

"Scholar" followed closely behind "learner" with 73.33%, slightly ahead of "researcher" (73.11%) and "teacher" (72.22%), the only other options to register within the 70% range. The next tier includes "interdisciplinarian" or one who crosses disciplinary boundaries, with a response frequency of 64%, which is also quite strong. Some might argue that this demonstrates a diminishing regard for disciplinarity; however, when considered alongside the earlier data point revealing respondents' great interest in expanding "knowledge, methods, and/or scholarship *in the discipline*," such a view does not seem tenable. Also quite worthy of note is the fact that almost a third (29.11%) of participants identify as artists, though only 8% claim the arts as their disciplinary domain. A finding like this stimulates greater interest in how participants define art and suggests that art constitutes a category of special relevance in the PES context.

Summary of Interview Responses

On average, interviews lasted between 20 and 30 minutes and followed a piloted protocol that asked participants to expound on their responses to the web-based survey. The interview protocol was comprised of questions about why participants value publicly engaged scholarship, supports that they have received or desired in relation to their PES work, and specific career aspirations. Six themes are emerging from the interview data:

- *Mentorship.* Interview participants detailed the importance of mentors who either introduced them to publicly engaged scholarship or supported them on a path of engaged scholarly work. Several participants referenced a single person who had a permanent effect on their scholarship and career trajectory.
- *Bridging worlds.* Interview respondents described the desire to bridge different aspects, values, and parts of their lives as a motivation for undertaking engaged scholarship.
- *Sphere of commitment.* This theme captures the importance of both engaging in the local community and the historical context and relationships between an institution and its local community, which may positively or negatively affect publicly engaged work.
- *Institutional recognition.* Publicly engaged scholars on the tenure track noted their institutional support. Many commented that for their university to fully commit to public

scholarship, schools and departments should recognize PES within the tenure process.

- *Creativity and flexibility.* Interviewees enjoyed practicing public scholarship and noted that it allowed for creativity and flexibility, both positive qualities.
- *Motivation.* While various extrinsic and intrinsic motivations inspired public scholars, recurring motivations included the benefits of using public scholarship as a form of pedagogy; personal and familial history; and a natural, innate, assumed desire to connect scholarship and service.

Analysis

While it is important to emphasize that these are preliminary findings, they are instructive and worthy of note. The research team has coordinated its analysis to draw from both the quantitative and qualitative data in developing a typology of publicly engaged scholars that comprises seven nascent profiles:

- *Cradle to Community*. This profile type describes scholars who become involved with their local communities because of personal values (e.g., religious, familial). Their involvement with the community may be what leads them to pursue graduate work.
- *Artist as Engaged Scholar*. This profile describes a local artist who uses the community as a "canvas." The artist as engaged scholar is grounded in both the academy and the arts.
- *Teacher to Engaged Scholar*. This profile is typified by the K–12 teacher who enters the academy for graduate work and teaching, but remains committed to the role of active researcher within secondary schools. College professors represented here may be looking for ways to improve teaching and learning and make connections with their students through publicly engaged work.
- *Program Coordinator to Engaged Administrator/Scholar.* This profile depicts an administrator in higher education who holds a leadership role in a center, an institute, or a consortium for campus-community partnership while also holding a faculty position.
- *Engaged Interdisciplinarian.* This profile depicts a scholar whose identification with one specific discipline is shallow, but who leverages every opportunity to drawn upon different domains of inquiry for the enhancement of community-

based work.

- *Activist to Scholar.* This profile captures the community activist who connects with the university and uses it as a platform to further pursue activism.
- *Engaged Pragmatist.* This public scholar "sees the writing on the wall" and recognizes that publicly engaged scholarship is becoming prevalent within the academy. For a scholar of this variety, motivation is grounded more in the perceived direction of higher education than in an abiding commitment to civic engagement.

Implications

Findings from this exploratory research are critical for developing new pedagogies, academic structures, and progressive answers to the myriad challenges that postsecondary education faces. We exist in a sociopolitical climate that demands solutions with a strong evidentiary base. Thought leaders must be able to frame and analyze challenges in rigorous, interdisciplinary, integrated, and robust ways. One core implication of the preliminary findings is that the next generation of scholars will exhibit multiple identities that suggest diverse ways of public engagement. Several correlates to this implication are worth highlighting.

- Identity formation does not necessarily predict the way that identity will be expressed through faculty roles of teaching, research, and service.
- Identity formation does not predict where scholars will find their institutional home, although it appears that they are carefully seeking supportive environments.
- Mentorship, even that of a sole mentor who is sensitive to PES work, can make an important difference in graduate school completion and career success.

Given the history of the civic engagement movement and especially the lack of attention placed upon graduate education in this evolving context, it is prudent to develop inquiries and systematic research programs that illuminate the aspirations and decisions of this new citizenry of academe.

Conclusion

The epigraph that opens this chapter urges academe to celebrate the "prodigality" of knowledge. While the term normally denotes wastefulness and excess, it is appropriate in this context because it appeals to our sense of expansiveness as a positive value in knowledge creation. Not unlike the question, "Are you smarter than a graduate student?" it provokes us to pay renewed attention to the normative discourses, practices, and rhythms of our knowledge economy. Through this kind of deep introspection—a process seldom seen at a systemic level within American higher education, as Calhoun (2006) admonishes—we can conceptualize and operationalize a continuum of scholarship along which scholars and practitioners both inside and outside of the academy can locate themselves with dignity and respect (Ellison and Eatman 2008). This should be a space where all forms of knowledge creation are both accorded value and subject to the conventional processes that interrogate the integrity of scholarly inquiry.

I join with other scholars in arguing that a new citizenry is emerging within the academy (Alperovitz, Dubb, and Howard 2008; Austin 2002; Beckman, Brandenberger, and Shappell 2009; Hale 2008; Herman 2000; O'Meara 2002; O'Meara and Rice 2005; Saltmarsh, Hartley, and Clayton 2009; Wendler et al. 2010). Key elements of publicly engaged scholarship, including but not limited to clear and adaptable definitions, democratic practice, public good impact, diverse scholarly products, and multiple career paths, seem to speak to the needs of many within this emerging generation of scholars. As addressed earlier in the chapter, it is important to note that "scholar" in this context indicates a participant in a "heterogeneous, fluid, tolerant academic culture" and more than just an academic identity.

Challenged by a fraught historical background, eclectic in some ways as it evolves yet still very much laden by social mores entrenching a culture of inequity and status hierarchy, American higher education as a system nonetheless moves forward in an arguably positive direction. The seminal work of the celebrated champions of engaged scholarship, John Dewey in the nineteenth century and Ernest Boyer in the twentieth, registers within higher education and the larger society a mechanism for realizing opportunities for pushing the boundaries of knowledge making. At the same time there are many thought leaders from communities within higher education, such as HBCUs, who have been rendered silent in the discourse of publicly engaged scholarship despite ameliorative and deeply engaged work; W. E. B. Du Bois and Septima Clark are two such examples (Evans et al. 2009). This reality bears out the need for a twenty-first-century Morrill-style consciousness that brings together and builds upon the 1862 and 1890 models in powerful ways that serve the present era.

Graduate students seek to pursue advanced degrees that prepare them intellectually as well as practically for the challenge of twenty-first-century leadership across the disciplines and in the world. Tools like the career pathways planning document for tenure-track faculty presented earlier may be useful to outline professional trajectories for engaged scholars. Profiles and models are being developed that demonstrate the aspirations and decisions of publicly engaged faculty (Doberneck Glass, and Schwietzer 2010; Peters, Alter, and Schwartzbach 2010). Similarly, models that serve the needs of graduate students, early-career academic professionals (contingent, tenure-track, and administrative) and engaged scholars connected to but working mostly outside of the academy are needed (Eatman et al. 2011). Such work will be useful for developing better graduate programs and attending to the arc of the publicly engaged career in ways that expand the continuum of scholarship.

Notes

1. At the other end of the generational spectrum, the show *Are You Fitter Than a Senior?* employs a similar dynamic with a focus on cardiovascular and aerobic health.

2. Notably, Professor Ellison is founding director emerita of the Imagining America consortium and progenitor of its Publicly Active Graduate Education (PAGE) program.

3. Others who have done so include Syracuse University, Providence College, the University of Minnesota, Missouri State University, the University of Memphis, the University of North Carolina at Greensboro, and Northern Kentucky University. Still others, like the University of Southern California, Tufts University, and Drew University, are considering such revisions.

References

Alperovitz, G., S. Dubb, and T. Howard. 2008. The next wave: Building university engagement for the 21st century. *The Good Society* 17 (2): 69–75.

Austin, A. E. 2002. Preparing the next generation of faculty: Graduate school as socialization to the academic career. *Journal of Higher Education* 73 (1): 94–122.

Beckman, M., J. W. Brandenberger, and A. S. Shappell. 2009. Graduate students and community-based learning. *Academic Exchange Quarterly* 13 (3): 45–50.

Benson, L., I. R. Harkavy, and J. L. Puckett. 2007. Dewey's dream: Universities and democracies in an age of education reform. Philadelphia: Temple University Press.

Berger, B. 2009. Political theory, political science and the end of civic engagement. *Perspectives on Politics* 7 (2): 335–50.

Boyer, E. L. 1996. The scholarship of engagement. *Journal of Public Service and Outreach* 1 (1): 11–20.

Boyte, H. C. 2004. *Going public: Academics and public life.* Occasional paper no. 10062. Dayton, OH: Kettering Foundation.

Boyte, H., and E. Hollander. 1999. *Wingspread declaration on renewing the civic mission of the American research university: The Wingspread conference.* Racine, WI: Campus Compact.

Bramble, N. 2008. Open access: Problems of collective action and promises of civic engagement. *SSRN eLibrary.* http://papers.ssrn.com/sol3/papers.cfm?abstract_id=1132870

Brown, D. W., and D. Witte, eds. 1994. *Higher education exchange.* Dayton, OH: Kettering Foundation.

Butler, J. E. 2000. Democracy, diversity, and civic engagement. *Academe* 86 (4): 52–55.

Calhoun, C. J. 2006. The university and the public good. *Thesis Eleven* 84 (1): 7–43.

Campbell, R. T. 1983. Status attainment research: End of the beginning or beginning of the end? *Sociology of Education* 56 (1): 47–62.

Cantor, N. 2009. A new Morrill Act: Higher education anchors the "remaking of America." *The Presidency* 12 (3): 16–22.

Doberneck, D. M., C. R. Glass, and J. Schwietzer. 2010. From rhetoric to reality: A typology of publicly engaged scholarship. *Journal of Higher Education Outreach and Engagement* 14 (4): 5–35.

Eatman, T. K., S. Weber, A. Bush, W. Nastasi, and R. Higgins. 2011. Study of publicly engaged scholars: Career aspirations and decisions of graduate students and early career professionals and practitioners. Unpublished research. Syracuse, NY: Imagining America.

Ellison, J., and T. K. Eatman. 2008. *Scholarship in public: Knowledge creation and tenure policy in the engaged university.* Syracuse, NY: Imagining America.

Evans, S. Y., C. M. Tayloy, M. R. Dunlap, and D. S. Miller, eds. 2009. *African Americans and community engagement in higher education: Community service, service-learning, and community-based research.* Albany: State University of New York Press.

First Morrill Act. 1862. 12 Stat. 503, 7 U.S.C. 301 et seq.

Garcia, A. 2009. *The gatekeeping behind meritocracy: Voices of NYC high school students.* Ph.D. diss., City University of New York.

Grodsky, E. 2007. Compensatory sponsorship in higher education. *American Journal of Sociology* 112 (6): 1662–1712.

Hale, C. R., ed. 2008. *Engaging contradictions: Theory, politics, and methods of activist scholarship*. Berkeley and Los Angeles: University of California Press.

Herman, P. C. 2000. *Day late, dollar short: The next generation and the new academy*. Albany: State University of New York Press.

Hertz, N. 2010. How to use experts—and when not to. TEDTalks. November. http://www.ted.com/talks/lang/en/noreena_hertz_how_to_use_experts_and_when_not_to.html

Howard, T. G. 2010. *Why race and culture matter in schools: Closing the achievement gap in America's classrooms*. New York: Teachers College Press.

June, A. W. 2008. Colleges should change policies to encourage scholarship devoted to the public good, report says. *Chronicle of Higher Education,* June 26. http://chronicle.com/article/Colleges-Should-Change/937/

Kerckhoff, A. C. 1976. The status attainment process: Socialization or allocation? *Social Forces* 55 (2): 368–81.

Kezar, A. J., T. C. Chambers, J. Burkhardt, and associates. 2005. *Higher education for the public good: Emerging voices from a national movement*. San Francisco: Jossey-Bass.

Lee, C. D. 2008. The centrality of culture to the scientific study of learning and development: How an ecological framework in education research facilitates civic responsibility. *Educational Researcher* 37 (5): 267–79.

Milner, H. R. 2010. *Start where you are but don't stay there: Understanding diversity, opportunity gaps, and teaching in today's classrooms*. Cambridge, MA: Harvard Education Press.

Muscatine, C. 2009. *Fixing college education: A new curriculum for the twenty-first century*. Charlottesville: University of Virginia Press.

Nie, N. H., J. Junn, and K. Stehlik-Barry. 1996. *Education and democratic citizenship in America*. Chicago: University of Chicago Press.

O'Meara, K. 2002. *Scholarship unbound: Assessing service as scholarship for promotion and tenure*. New York: RoutledgeFalmer.

O'Meara, K., and R. E. Rice. 2005. *Faculty priorities reconsidered: Rewarding multiple forms of scholarship*. San Francisco: Jossey-Bass.

Payne, C. M. 2008. *So much reform, so little change: The persistence of failure in urban schools*. Cambridge, MA: Harvard Education Press.

Peters, S. J., T. R. Alter, and N. Schwartzbach. 2010. *Democracy and higher education: Traditions and stories of civic engagement*. East Lansing: Michigan State University Press.

Rice, E. 2006. Rethinking scholarship and engagement: The struggle for new meanings. *College Compact Reader* 4 (1): 1–9.

Saltmarsh, J., M. Hartley, and P. H. Clayton. 2009. *Democratic engagement white paper*. Boston: New England Resource Center for Higher Education.

Second Morrill Act. 1890. Ch. 841, 26 Stat. 417, 7 U.S.C. 322 et seq.

Stokes, D. E. 1997. *Pasteur's quadrant: Basic science and technological innovation*. Washington, DC: Brookings Institution Press.

Swartz, E. 2009. Diversity: Gatekeeping knowledge and maintaining inequalities. *Review of Educational Research* 79 (2): 1044–83.

Trent, W. T., and T. K. Eatman. 2002. The tragedy of rejecting a viable solution for the development of successful collegiate academic incentive programs for African Americans. In *Equity and access in higher education: Changing the definition of educational opportunity*, edited by C. Teddlie and E. Kemper. Readings on Equal Education, no. 18. New York: AMS Press.

Wendler, C., B. Bridgeman, F. Cline, C. Millett, J. Rock, N. Bell, and P. McAllister. 2010. *The path forward: The future of graduate education in the United States*. Princeton, NJ: Educational Testing Service. http://eric.ed.gov/PDFS/ED509441.pdf

Wolfe, B., and R. Haveman, R. 2001. Accounting for the social and nonmarket benefits of education. In *The contribution of human and social capital to sustained economic growth and well-being*, edited by J. Helliwell. Vancouver: University of British Columbia Press.

Yeakey, C. C. 2000. Research, scholarship, and social responsibility: Social imperatives for a democratic society. In *Edmund W. Gordon: Producing knowledge, pursuing understanding*, edited by Yeakey. Advances in Education in Diverse Communities: Research, Policy, and Praxis, vol. 1. Stamford, CT: JAI Press.

2

The Land-Grant System and Graduate Education: Reclaiming a Narrative of Engagement

Timothy J. Shaffer

IN 2012 WE celebrate the sesquicentennial of the passage of the first Morrill Act. But for many Americans, "Morrill Act" has little meaning. Clarifying that this act, signed into law in 1862 by President Lincoln, created what became known as land-grant colleges and universities does little to help with this confusion. Let me tell a story to illustrate this.

Someone recently asked me about my research. I began to mention how I was interested in the civic mission and purposes of land-grant universities and cooperative extension as embodied in the work of academic professionals. There was a pause. The individual who asked me this question didn't know what I was talking about. He vaguely knew what extension was, but only thought that it had something to do with agriculture. "Land-grant," however, didn't mean anything.

I responded by mentioning that land-grant colleges and universities are in every state and several U.S. territories (109 institutions, to be exact).[1] These include Ohio State University, Pennsylvania State University, the University of Wisconsin, and Cornell University (my own institution). They were founded to be open and accessible to all people. They were the embodiment of a belief in education being a central element to democracy. With an explicit mission to educate students in practical disciplines such as agriculture, home economics (now human ecology), mechanic arts (now engineering), and the liberal arts, these institutions afforded citizens the opportunity to be part of what were called "democracy's colleges" (Ross 1942). These institutions offered students—both undergraduate and graduate—an opportunity to explore diverse disciplines of study while also belonging to a particular type of academic environment that had roots in serving an explicit public mission. The Kellogg Commission on the Future of State and Land-Grant Universities, tasked with identifying needed responses to structural change in public higher education, notes that a serious challenge we face is a disconnect between the land-grant's historical roots and its current manifestation (Kellogg Commission 2001). These institutions have tremendous resources and create new knowledge, but to what end? The authors of the Kellogg Report note that the public's complaints "add up to ... a perception that, despite the resources and expertise available on our campuses, our institutions are not well organized to bring them to bear on local problems in a coherent way" (Kellogg Commission 2001, 13). Land-grant universities may have missions to engage the public, but how that engagement occurs has not been clearly articulated.

Back to my conversation about my research: The response was not all that atypical for me when I speak about my work: "Well, that's interesting. We need to educate people and, I mean, I'm glad we have scientists figuring out how to fix our problems. This world's a mess."

I tell this story for two reasons. First, higher education's role in the mind of the American public isn't clear. For many, higher education is seen as an opportunity to improve one's economic status. It serves as a seemingly necessary step for social mobility and freedom to pursue interests of one's choosing. This attitude is increasingly moving beyond undergraduate education, as graduate degrees become necessary for many professions and positions. But connecting higher education to a notion of democracy is difficult, especially if "democracy" transcends categories that define it simply as a political structure rather than a way of life. David Mathews calls democracy "a way of living to maintain a good life in concert with others" (1999, 13) and Harry Boyte says a "democratic way of life" is "created through public, political work of the people" (2004, 93). For our purposes, I would suggest that we think of democracy as public relationships with other citizens. These relationships are challenging but necessary if we are to live in ways that go beyond isolated existence and what Michael Sandel calls "consumeristic" existence (2000, 80). Higher education's role is to help shape and inform citizenship through the development of students as well as through engagement work on the part of academic professionals.

Second, those within colleges and universities are often perceived as scientists or more broadly as "experts" who solve problems. They fix things. Their role is to provide information and resources for citizens and elected officials to make decisions. In many ways this is true. But what's absent from such a definition of academic professionals (and aspiring graduate students) is a view that situates land-grant institutions and those within them as civic actors.

We are more accustomed to thinking of academic professionals being detached from the world in some lab instead of viewing them as political actors engaged in communities. Such a narrative is pervasive and has been called the heroic metanarrative of land-grant universities

(Peters 2007). Yet there are counter-narratives to such a view. Restorying the narrative about land-grant institutions and the individuals within them helps academic professionals and graduate students take seriously the public nature of their work and the types of relationships that help to foster a more democratic society. We can learn a great deal about graduate education if we can look beyond the dominant narrative about what it means to be affiliated with land-grant institutions. This is a very important theoretical and practical issue because the culture of these institutions cultivates and/or challenges such narratives. As faculty members mentor and influence graduate students through the educational process, identifying the paradigms that shape how academic professionals view and engage in their work is of import. The dominant narrative of experts providing information shapes how many within and outside higher education see its role. Higher education, and the land-grant university specifically, is much more complicated than that.

This chapter is comprised of three parts. First, I will provide a very brief survey of the history of land-grant universities and the federal legislation that has supported the development of research and outreach programs, with an emphasis on graduate education. Because this is a survey, limitations of space mean that critically important issues and themes will not and cannot be addressed. I will sketch out some of the pivotal elements of the land-grant history, identifying the major milestones that shape these institutions. I also will note how the major elements of land-grant history have implications for publicly engaged graduate education.

Second, I raise questions related to what it means to be a graduate student at a land-grant institution and a contributor to the always-contested mission and public purpose(s) of these institutions. I take up what Scott Peters recognizes as the "main problems with the prevailing view of the historical nature and significance of the land-grant mission" (2008, 123). Peters' contention is that the history of the land-grant mission has been narrowly understood, raising questions not only about the historical accuracy of how we speak about and understand the land-grant system, but also about the ways in which land-grant institutions fulfill their public purpose of being the "people's universities" (123).

Third, I will identify some of the challenges and possibilities for contemporary graduate education at land-grant universities. In doing so, I will explore briefly how graduate education fits within this contested and conflictual view, understanding, and interpretation of the land-grant mission.

Land Grants and Democracy: The Morrill Act of 1862 and Its Impact

A common way to speak about the development and role of land-grant colleges and universities is to highlight some of the significant events that have helped to shape the identity of these institutions. I will follow in this tradition and then I will critique it, explaining why it is important in order to understand the complexity of these institutions, especially as we explore questions related to graduate education and the experience of graduate students.

In the early nineteenth century, the United States economy and culture were agricultural in focus, with 85% of the population (of European descent) living in rural communities along the East Coast (Eddy 1957, 1). It is fitting that these lines are found at the beginning of the first general account of the development of the land-grant movement, because the Morrill Act recognized agriculture as central to the development of the United States.

During the first half of the nineteenth century, there were two types of colleges and universities: publicly controlled and privately controlled. European universities where American professors had trained and taught previously greatly influenced these institutions. They were designed to serve a stratified society with limited democratic aspirations. College education was primarily reserved for "the leisure classes, the government leaders, and members of the professions" (Brunner 1962, 1). In many ways, this meant upper-class white men. Higher education institutions in the United States functioned in a similar fashion and maintained a classical curriculum, with only slight adaptations to the needs of a "pioneer people" (1).

In the United States, programs of graduate study first took root in three kinds of institutions: "new ones like Hopkins, Clark, and Chicago; strong private colleges like Harvard, Columbia, Yale, and Cornell; and such strong public institutions on the rise as California, Michigan, and Wisconsin" (Berelson 1960, 9). The modern public American research institution traces its roots to a handful of universities: the Universities of Georgia, North Carolina, Vermont, South Carolina, and Virginia. But the "real signal of public commitment" to university-based research came from the Morrill Act of 1862 (Rhoten and Powell 2011, 317).

Justin Morrill, a representative and then senator from Vermont, sponsored the Land Grant College Act, which was signed into law by President Lincoln.[2] Morrill had previously proposed similar legislation, eventually passed by Congress but vetoed by President Buchanan in 1859. Morrill, who had no formal education beyond secondary school, believed education could provide people access to a better way of life and make them better citizens. In a speech in 1888 about the Land Grant College Act, Morrill said that "the fundamental idea was to offer an opportunity in every state for a liberal and larger education to larger numbers, not merely to those destined to sedentary professions, but to those needing higher instruction for the world's business, for the industrial pursuits and professions of life" (Morrill 1888, 11).

The establishment of a national system of universities that blended liberal and practical education challenged the transplanted European approach to higher education. The Morrill Act gave each state 30,000 acres of federal land for each congressional representative from that state. These lands were federally owned and, if states did not have enough land, they were able to use property in other states, or to give land-grant funds to already-established agricultural or normal schools, which were then renamed. In all, nearly 17.5 million acres were distributed (Cohen and Kisker 2010, 115). That land was then sold to create endowments to support and maintain

> at least one college where the leading object shall be, without excluding other scientific and classical studies, and including military tactics, to teach such branches of learning as are related to agriculture and the mechanic arts ... in order to promote the liberal and practical education of the industrial classes in the several pursuits and professions in life. (Eddy 1957, 3)

Morrill recognized that American society (and its economy) needed both to address the changes taking place with increasing industrialization and to meet the agricultural demands of a booming population. It is important to note that the federal government did not have the ability to provide funds at this time. Thus, providing federally owned land was essential to establishing collegiate education, with the government functioning more as a real estate promoter than a funding source (Eddy 1957, 36). There was a need to educate new farmers in better agricultural practices as well as afford the opportunity to students for them to have both a practical and liberal education. These new colleges and universities did just that.

While states were charged with the task of creating new academic institutions, some had previously established colleges of agriculture. The precursor to Michigan State University often served as the example of what the land-grant colleges and universities might become (Clute 1891). These newly created public education institutions were designed to be "elite without being elitist, to provide access to knowledge and education to those previously denied such access" (Simon 2010, 100). Before this period, higher education was typically limited to white men from affluent backgrounds. These new institutions were to challenge that social norm and to expand educational opportunities for rural citizens as well as women and minority population.

Cornell University, home to New York State's land-grant colleges while also existing as a privately endowed university, was open to both men and women of all races and challenged many of the social conventions in the 1860s. Before World War I, the Cornell student body boasted "representatives from every quarter of the globe" and included many international students from Canada, Mexico, Cuba, China, and Japan, among many others. When graduate students were taken into account, "a still greater diversity and considerably larger total would be manifest (Von Engeln 1924). Told this way, Cornell appears to be welcoming of all peoples.

But in practice, women didn't come to Cornell's campus until 1870 and it was not until 1873 that the first woman graduated. In 1929, Ezra Cornell's founding ideal of "any person, any study" was put to the test in the person of Ruth Peyton, an African American undergraduate from Olean, New York. Peyton was denied residency in the women's dormitory because, as President Livingston Farrand wrote to Peyton's mother, "the placing of a colored student in one of the dormitories inevitably cause[s] more embarrassment than satisfaction for such a student.... [W]hile I have great sympathy for your feeling, I cannot order a change in the procedure of the Dean of Women, under whose jurisdiction the matter falls" (Farrand 1929). Students from around the world attended Cornell at the time, but some of those closest to home suffered discrimination because of their skin color. "Any person, any study" articulated a vision the university was not yet prepared to embrace in practice. In short, higher education offered an opportunity for women and minority populations, but institutions struggled to transcend cultural norms and practices of the middle-to-late nineteenth century well into the twentieth century. Rhetoric and reality sometimes remained quite distinct, as this quick look at Cornell's history reveals.

In many ways, the land-grant idea was a bold experiment. It "transformed higher education through the concept of service and direct links with industry and agriculture ... and expanded access to higher education" (Altbach 2011, 17). Many institutions were slow to embrace graduate education. Michigan Agricultural College (now Michigan State University) adopted a statute in 1861 that stated it could confer Master of Science degrees, and by 1881 was creating a more structured process for graduate education (Dressel 1987, 167). By the 1890s graduate education was flourishing, with one in ten students seeking a master's degree (Kuhn 1955, 236). But it was not until the 1920s that graduate studies (with doctoral programs for seven scientific disciplines) moved beyond its secondary status in the curriculum of the college behind undergraduate education (Widder 2005, 171). Ohio State

University, founded in 1870, did not begin accepting graduate students until the 1880s. This delay in implementing graduate education was common for land-grant colleges at the time. While institutions such as Cornell University were founded with graduate education as part of their mission, few graduate programs existed in the late nineteenth century. Increasingly, however, graduate education was becoming part of the educational experience of land-grant colleges and universities, initially in scientific and agricultural disciplines and then later in the humanities and the social sciences.

The first mention of graduate work by the Association of Land-Grant Colleges and Universities occurred in 1897, in the form of a resolution that stated graduate students should have access to and use of the Congressional Library, the Smithsonian Institution, the National Museum, and the scientific bureaus of the various departments of the government for the purpose of research and study (Rees 1962, 1). In many ways, land-grant colleges and universities began the development of science and technology in the United States (Carmichael 1961, 67). Within these institutions, the development of graduate education was founded on the central paradigm that one's worth was based on research.

One innovation of land-grant universities was the establishment from the late nineteenth century of agricultural experiment stations, which receive considerable federal, state, and private funding for research that informs educational work, both through teaching at the universities and in engagement work through cooperative extension. Experiment stations have been and continue to be deeply engaged with the teaching and training of graduate students whose work serves a public purpose, especially scholarship related to agricultural issues. Yet the way this public purpose is defined fits narrowly within the heroic metanarrative embodied by the service intellectual tradition. This tradition views one's work through the lens of creating knowledge for others to use (Peters 2010, 24–32). The service intellectual tradition also features characteristics of what is often assumed about the work of scholars: that social scientists (or other academics) must maintain a stance of disinterested and unbiased neutrality about their work. In this tradition, the proper function for the academic is the answering of scientific questions with scientific knowledge (Peters 2010, 26).

While these institutions were created to afford opportunities to citizens of lower classes who had previously been unable to attend college, to democratize higher education by opening its doors to those otherwise excluded, and to engage in research with a public purpose, many remained marginalized within these colleges and universities.

Some of the most striking examples of discrimination took place in the southern states. This led to the Second Morrill Act, 28 years after the original creation of the land-grant system.

The Second Morrill Act of 1890 and the Equity in Education Land-Grant Status Act of 1994

Northern members of Congress passed the First Morrill Act when members from southern states were absent because of the Civil War. After the Civil War and the reintegration of the Confederate states, there was a need to address the reality that southern states continued to have racial segregation. While some states used funds provided by the Morrill Act of 1862 for the education of African Americans at private institutions such as Virginia's Hampton Institute and South Carolina's Claflin University, as well as Mississippi's public Alcorn University, the majority of southern states took no action until they were "induced to do so under the terms of the Second Morrill Act of 1890" (Eddy 1957, 258).

The Second Morrill Act stipulated that "no appropriations would go to states that denied admission to the colleges on the basis of race unless they also set up separate but equal facilities" (Rudolph 1962, 254). This legislation provided funds and resources to historically Black colleges and universities creating educational opportunities for African Americans in southern states despite a prevailing climate of inequality (Spikes 1992). However, it should be noted that although most of these institutions were established following the Civil War and before 1900, their growth and development was restricted by lack of financial resources. This was true regarding general support for these institutions as well as for their explicit land-grant research well into the 1970s. Finally, in 1972, institutions that received funds subsequent to the 1890 legislation became part of the USDA's regular annual appropriation for agricultural research rather than receiving funds through a special grant renegotiated each year (Christy, Williamson, and Williamson 1992, xvii–xxi).[3]

B. D. Mayberry noted that the initial and most significant contribution of the 1890 institutions was to provide the mechanism for "4 million negroes (former slaves) to move into the mainstream of American society as citizens with all the rights and privileges embodied in citizenship through education" (Mayberry 1991, 36). Education was and continues to be a central factor in shaping human development. Thus, the creation of these institutions afforded African Americans opportunities that had previously been available only from private institutions.

The institutions funded under the Second Morrill Act remain

actively engaged in carrying out the tripartite land-grant mission of teaching, research, and service while maintaining commitments to those disadvantaged by racism and prejudice.[4] With slavery only recently abolished, the 1890 institutions had to address the low educational levels of African Americans by admitting students with only elementary or secondary levels of preparation (Humphries 1992, 4). This posed a severe challenge to what were in design and purpose tertiary institutions, but within a few decades graduate education also became a concern. Beginning with Prairie View A&M University and Virginia State University in 1937, and followed two years later by North Carolina A&T State, the 1890 institutions initiated graduate programs. In 1953, Florida A&M University established schools of law, pharmacy, liberal arts, agricultural education, home economics, and other disciplines, with master's-level education being the most popular (Humphries 1992, 6). Other institutions followed suit, though some, such as Alcorn State University and the University of Maryland Eastern Shore, did not create graduate programs until decades later—in 1975 and 1978, respectively (Christy, Williamson, and Williamson 1992, xx).

In a similar spirit, the Equity in Education Land-Grant Status Act of 1994 provided land-grant designation to 33 tribal colleges for Native Americans in Western and Plains states. This provided federal funding for teaching, research, and outreach, responding to the specific needs and interests of the Native American populations these institutions serve. Because many of these institutions and populations are geographically remote, the 1994 Act provided funds to increase extension work in areas such as agriculture; community resources and economic development; family development and resource management; 4-H and youth development; leadership and volunteer development; natural resources and environmental management; and nutrition, diet, and health.

What makes these institutions slightly different from their predecessors is the fact that these tribal colleges include community colleges, four-year institutions, and some institutions with graduate-level courses and programs. This group within the land-grant system continues to play an important role in increasing social and economic opportunities for Native Americans through affordable education as well as programs that respond to the particular needs of Native American communities.

While access and affordability have helped to define public higher education, the research and service dimensions of the land-grant mission are addressed through the work of campus faculty and the application of resulting knowledge via cooperative extension.

The Hatch Act of 1887, the Smith-Lever Act of 1914, and Earlier Engagement

The ability to realize the public mission of land-grant institutions relies, in part, on the Hatch and the Smith-Lever Acts. The Hatch Act established the agricultural station system in each of the colleges under the Morrill Act of 1862 to "aid in acquiring and diffusing among the people of the United States useful and practical information on subjects connected with agriculture, and to promote scientific investigation and experiment respecting the principles and applications of agricultural science" (Eddy 1957, 97). This act established and expanded experiment stations across the country on the campuses of land-grant colleges and universities.[5] Most faculty in land-grant colleges of agriculture have appointments that connect their research to experiment station work, and include "Hatch" research funds for original work on issues impacting the agricultural industry and rural life (Committee on the Future 1995, 8). Hatch funding has not been limited to commercial agriculture; the Rust2Green project in older at-risk industrial cities in New York State serves as an example of action research initiatives partially funded through Hatch grants.[6]

The Smith-Lever Act of 1914 established a system of cooperative extension service involving the United States Department of Agriculture, land-grant colleges and universities, and local communities, with the goal of educating and working with citizens through programmatic initiatives. Often cooperative extension shared information with citizens about current developments in agriculture, home economics, and other relevant subjects. But cooperative extension also engaged in work with citizens, seeking to address challenges facing individuals and communities that went beyond situations that only required technical expertise and knowledge. Cooperative extension's role goes beyond the application of research-based information to include important community work and leadership development.

Cooperative extension increased human and monetary capital for public work. But the idea of extension has roots deeper than the Smith-Lever Act. C. Hartley Grattan notes that "the first quarter-century of land-grant college history was one of toil and struggle, complicated by uncertainty of direction and unclear ideas about what and how to teach the students drawn to the colleges, and how to make the cumulating knowledge available to dirt farmers" (Grattan 1955, 201). Students who attended land-grant colleges went on to become faculty and administrators at these institutions, with Liberty Hyde Bailey being one of the most striking examples. Originally a farmer, Bailey became a student at Michigan Agricultural College and then went on to shape both academic life and the lives of many rural people and communities at the turn of the twentieth century as a faculty member and eventually dean of Cornell's College of Agriculture.

Bailey helps us to think critically about the history of land-grant institutions and cooperative extension because he saw agricultural education as a means to awaken in rural people a new view of life, rather than simply as a conduit of technical information (Peters 2006). He saw the colleges of agriculture and experiment stations having an important role in the "future welfare and peace of the people" to a degree that was then unforeseen (Bailey 1915, 98). For him, the role of these institutions was to help citizens to see the world differently and to act differently.

> The college may be the guiding force, but it should not remove responsibility from the people of the localities, or offer them a kind of co-operation that is only the privilege of partaking in the college enterprises. I fear that some of our so-called co-operation in public work of many kinds is little more than to allow the co-operator to approve what the official administration has done. (Bailey 1915, 100)

Bailey was suspect of much that his contemporaries identified as engagement with citizens. Land-grant universities had an important role to play and the faculty within them were important contributors to society, but the ways that university faculty and extension educators worked with citizens could vary widely. In some situations faculty expertise was utilized appropriately, while in others education was confused with the dispensing of facts. Peters quotes Bailey from a speech given on December 13, 1899, to the annual Farmers' Convention in Meriden, Connecticut:

> We know that we can point out a dozen things, and sometimes thirteen. But after all, it is not the particular application of science to the farm which is the big thing. The big thing is the point of view. The whole agricultural tone has been raised through these agencies. People are taking broader views of things and of life. Even if we did not have a single fact with which we could answer these people, it is a sufficient answer to say that every agricultural college and every agricultural experiment station, with all their faults, has been a strong factor in the general elevation of agriculture and the common good. The whole attitude has changed. It is the scientific habit of thought and no longer the mere extraneous application of science. (qtd. in Peters 2006, 212)

The role of the land-grant university (particularly the colleges of agriculture) and the experiment station was not just to provide information. It was also about working with citizens to help realize a different way of seeing the world. This is what Bailey called the "scientific spirit." Defining one's work in such a way challenges a dominant narrative about what land-grant universities were doing during this formative period around the turn of the twentieth century, when there was need of a "system capable of proving to farmers that 'book farming' was not a joke and that agricultural science, properly applied, would produce a better life for them and their families" (Scott 1970, x). There were competing agendas: some suggested that the technical skills of university scientists were alone sufficient to meet the need, while others adhered to the essential belief that citizens should apply their own knowledge in concert with new information from research.

In the early 1890s Pennsylvania State College, Cornell University, and the University of Illinois lent impetus to the extension concept by adapting techniques of adult education from the then-flourishing Chautauqua movement to engage farmers. By 1907, at least 39 land-grant colleges were "doing *something* in the way of extension" (Grattan 1955, 202; emphasis in original). The approaches to programming were diverse. They included lectures, short courses, summer schools, bulletin reports, circulars, cooperative experiments, exhibits at fairs, and demonstrations on farms.

Before and after the Smith-Lever Act, Seaman A. Knapp's demonstration method was foundational to the educational methods of land-grant colleges and cooperative extension. While Knapp placed much emphasis on economic gains, he was not solely focused on efficiency and technical expertise. Rather, his ultimate aim was "the development of a vibrant rural civic and cultural life" (Peters 1998, 133).

The language of the Smith-Lever Act reflects Knapp's demonstration model of education in its pronouncement that extension "shall consist of the giving of instruction and practical demonstrations in agriculture and home economics." This approach was employed in order to "aid in the diffusing among the people of the United States useful and practical information on subjects relating to agriculture and home economics" (Smith and Wilson 1930, 365). Importantly, the language of the Smith-Lever Act was not exclusively aimed at rural people. Rather, it was intended for all people within the United States. Today, much of cooperative extension's work takes place within urban and suburban settings addressing and responding to the needs of these communities.

In 1914, there was significant debate and disagreement over exactly "why a national system of agriculture was needed, what it was specifically supposed to accomplish, and how it ought to go about accomplishing it" (Peters 1998, 25). In short, there was never a unified mission or purpose for land-grant institutions or cooperative extension. Since their respective origins, how these institutions should fulfill their public mission has remained in question, despite the dominance of the heroic metanarrative and the false sense of univocality and directionality it imparts.

Recognizing this contested beginning for extension is imperative because the narrative often told about it is that of a single purpose—to transfer knowledge from experts at universities to people in communities. This becomes an important point, especially as we consider the role of graduate students and graduate education within this context. In short, the Hatch and the Smith-Lever Acts enabled land-grant institutions to fulfill their public mission by sharing knowledge with communities, while simultaneously creating opportunities for citizens to share their own knowledge—with other citizens but also with extension educators, through whom they help to inform future research within the universities and to cultivate active and engaged citizenship.

The Morrill Acts of 1862 and 1890 and the Equity in Education Land-Grant Status Act of 1994 have created a system of higher education in all 50 states and several U.S. territories rooted in the understanding that there *was* and *is* a need to have what many refer to as the "People's University" (Sherwood 2004, 2). Additionally, the Hatch Act of 1887 and the Smith-Lever Act of 1914 provided some of the mechanisms necessary to empower the vision of educators to create a system of higher education reaching well beyond the confines of a college campus into neighborhoods and communities across the United States. Higher education's role in American democracy goes well beyond the classroom, and extension has been one of the most important—if not most forgotten—forms of community-based education and development in this country.

To many, land-grant colleges and universities have been "the most celebrated and successful example of the articulation and fulfillment of the service ideal" (Crosson 1983, 22). The Smith-Lever Act institutionalized the public service mission, and the land-grant university continues to embody that ideal (McDowell 2001, 15–27). George McDowell writes that while there is some ambiguity about terms such as public service, outreach, extension, extended education, and engagement, the choice of wording depends more on one's audience and immediate discursive community than on significant semantic distinctions (2001, 15). Yet just this type of homogenizing statement contributes to confusion about what public engagement is and how it might be classified (Doberneck, Glass, and Schweitzer 2010). Such statements are problematic in that they frame the mission and purpose of land-grant institutions in particular ways. In order to speak to graduate education within the land-grant context, it is important to briefly explore the contested views of these universities and the individuals who comprise them.

Which Mission?

In quickly touching on the elements that have shaped land-grant institutions since their founding, we have made an implicit assumption. While we acknowledge the multiple avenues for academic professionals to contribute to public life, the differences are important. To create a new type of seed at the agricultural experiment station is one thing; engaging communities through the use of deliberative forums is another. Both are examples of engagement on the part of academic professionals within land-grant universities, but we would be remiss not to acknowledge considerable differences between the two. Our goal is not to judge between them, but to consider how we might broaden our conception of the mission and purpose of these institutions and the academic professionals and students within them.

With respect to graduate education, we can see these tensions play out today. While much support—both institutional and external funding sources—is given to those conducting research on issues of great importance, such as climate change and nanotechnology, work engaging citizens in participatory and democratic ways does not warrant the same support. A graduate student at Cornell who is working with New York City residents on community gardens faces different challenges than the graduate student who has received funding from a corporation developing nanotechnologies. The creation of new knowledge is central to the work of land-grant institutions as research institutions, but serious engagement with communities in the messy work of democracy also belongs. A challenge we face, as illustrated by the story I told at the beginning, is that land-grant institutions have been defined narrowly. The story is flat, misleading, and simply inaccurate. If we are only scientists saving the world, where do citizens and entire communities fit into this scheme?

Peters takes issue with the way in which the story of the land-grant system has been understood in the United States. He argues that "for more than a century, many scholars in land-grant colleges … have taken up such roles by becoming engaged in public work that addresses not only the technical, but also the social, political, and cultural aspects of agricultural and environmental problems" (Peter 2008, 121). Yet the official rhetoric of land-grant institutions has most often expressed their mission as being reactive, one-directional, instrumental, and apolitical. The identity and role of an academic, according to this view, is to have a "nonpolitical stance of unbiased and disinterested objectivity" (Peters 2010, 52). Vulnerable graduate students often adopt the same position. This issue transcends land-grant universities and is a serious concern for those invested in the civic role of higher education generally (Saltmarsh and Hartley 2011).

A nonpolitical role for academic professionals and graduate students supports their contributions to democracy, but only through the sharing of information and facts without regard for what those facts might mean or impact. This view of the academic professional fits in what Peters calls the service intellectual tradition, referred to above. It is not that these individuals do not care about their work; it is that they feel their role as an academic disqualifies them from being passionate and concerned citizens.

Noting how others have viewed their own work, Peters writes that some extension educators in the land-grant system have positioned themselves as both "responsive experts and proactive social critics and change agents" (Peters 2008, 129). That is, they have sought not only to provide technical advice, but to change the behaviors, attitudes, values, and ideals of their rural constituencies.

Liberty Hyde Bailey countered the dominant narrative of the land-grant mission and saw self-sustaining agriculture as having technical, scientific, moral, cultural, political, and even spiritual dimensions. Bailey argued in 1907 that land-grant colleges contribute to the public in a way that goes far beyond the "technique of agricultural trades" (Peters 2008, 130). In 1930, two scholars writing about the development and institutionalization of agricultural extension took note of the

> new leaven at work in rural America. It is stimulating to better endeavor in farming and home making, bringing rural people together in groups for social intercourse and study, solving community and neighborhood problems, fostering better relations and common endeavor between town and country … broadening the vision of rural men and women. (Smith and Wilson 1930, 1)

For Smith and Wilson, the "leaven" of land-grant institutions was to cultivate what was already within a community. Building on the expertise of scholars and extension agents, the land-grant mission was broadened when the knowledge-imparting expert was paired with the social critic who sought to create opportunities and support initiatives that foster a sense of community through engagement. These were individuals who were educators, not simply "experts" with facts.

Peters contends there are three stories in regard to the democratization of higher education: a dominant heroic metanarrative about technical and economic progress; a tragic counter-narrative about cultural, economic, political, and environmental oppression and destruction on the part of experts towards citizens; and a prophetic counter-narrative about the struggle for freedom and sustainability, with experts and citizens working collaboratively and relationally (Peters 2007, 6). While the metanarrative has dominated and the tragic counter-narrative has supplemented the history of land-grant institutions, the prophetic counter-narrative provides a voice for those seeking to develop a new rural civilization worthy of the best American ideals; land-grant colleges would catalyze this change rather than provide the answers. While many in higher education (not just land-grant institutions) are trying to more fully engage communities, there is a history that contrasts public work with service, two terms that are not synonymous with one another in this context. Public work is relational; it brings together individuals from different socioeconomic classes and draws on their strengths (Boyte 2004). Service, conversely, reinforces and encourages a demarcation between professionals and "ordinary" citizens. Looking to scholarship on the relationships within service learning can help our thinking about the importance of both language and practice (Clayton et al. 2010).

Thus, we must look back to the prophetic story of the land-grant mission in order to reclaim and reconstruct much of the work that has taken place in this system, especially after the Smith-Lever Act established cooperative extension. Peters argues that it is this narrative that "we most urgently need to learn and tell," especially as agribusiness and commercialization continue to dramatically change the landscape of rural America (2007, 22). The societal benefit of land-grant universities, their experiment stations, and their extension systems are "too often viewed as being only economic in nature" (Peters 2008, 145–46). A tremendous challenge that faculty and graduate students face is to think about the public's benefit from work that helps to build community in the Bronx through community gardens rather than only turning to economically profitable projects. Further, private investment in research also shapes what is and is not worthy of support. As higher education increasingly turns to private funds, the public mission of colleges and universities—especially land-grant universities—must be more than simply a vapid phrase on a website or in a brochure. Many institutions commit to engagement rhetorically, but fewer actually embody such claims.

This is not to say that many involved in the work of land-grant institutions do not see themselves as providers of expert knowledge for the general public. The metanarrative has attained that position for obvious reasons. However, there are other aspects foundational to the mission of the land-grant system that offer another way of seeing higher education's role in American democracy.

There are many who contribute to the prophetic narrative of land-grant institutions by working with citizens to address public problems rather than simply solving problems for them. Identified as civic professionals (Boyte and Fretz 2010; Peters 2003, 2004; Sullivan 2003, 2005), citizen professionals (Boyte 2008a), and/or democratic professionals (Dzur 2008), these public-spirited individuals acknowledge and embrace an approach to democratic life that situates them as co-creators of solutions in partnership with citizens, moving away from an inward orientation to one's institution or profession to one that is directed towards common goods (Peters 2010).

Many graduate students in courses I have taken at Cornell embody the desire to engage in public life through their professional work. At conferences sponsored by Imagining America and during the Emerging Engagement Scholars Workshop held at the National Outreach Scholarship Conference, I am encouraged by the many graduate students at other institutions who are committed to being engaged scholars. The challenge is to help foster and develop such public-spiritedness in graduate students while they complete course assignments, dissertations, and job applications.

Approaching one's work in this way shifts the academic professional's role from that of provider to that of catalyst; from offering solutions to "being partners, educators, and organizers of cooperative action" (Boyte 2008a, 15). For graduate students, this relational shift can be empowering to those who want to engage in scholarly work that "builds and sustains our basic public goods and resources … solves common problems and creates common things" (Boyte and Kari 1996, 16). This approach highlights the public dimensions of work, both individually and institutionally. It makes the distinction between "experts" and "citizens" problematic because *all* are citizens, with each bringing different skills, knowledge, and capabilities to the public work they do.

Today, as Boyte notes, "intellectuals inside and outside the academy have begun to challenge technocracy with citizen-centered politics"(Boyte 2008b, 87). The role of higher education in this context is to support a larger societal conversation about what is taking place within communities, drawing upon knowledge when needed rather than creating a division between academic experts and everyone else. Academics must be intellectuals as part of the world, not detached from it. But their work must be more than simply talk. It must include action. The broadest challenge of higher education is to advance democratic values and to join in movements that build citizen-centered democratic societies. It is only through this type of public work, Boyte argues, that higher education professionals—who often see themselves as outsiders with respect to civic life—can be brought back into a "common civic life" (Boyte 2008b, 102).

Still, the longstanding problem remains of dealing with the tension between expertise and democracy and how professionals have embraced or challenged this tension. At its core, this is a question about identity, for both individuals and institutions. William Sullivan writes, "Higher education seems to have lost an animating sense of mission. There is talk of reform, but mostly of an administrative and financial nature, with little attention to content and purpose" (Sullivan 2000, 21). Seeking to democratize relations between academics and others engaged in public work is not about returning to a golden era. Rather, it is about helping to usher in an ethic of lifelong learning that values and respects the diversity we find in our world today (Kellogg Commission 2001, 21–22).

As we think about the mission and purpose of land-grant universities (and higher education more broadly), we should take seriously the dominant narratives that shape the discourse about what institutions do, how they engage in their work, and where graduate students fit into this work. If we perpetuate the narrative that academic professionals are to contribute to democracy only through the creation and dissemination of knowledge, a more active and engaged approach to scholarship is unlikely to take hold. However, if we reclaim and reshape some of the narratives from early in the land-grant and extension history, we may reconceptualize what it means to be an engaged scholar. In short, we re-story the institution and the individuals within it. Concretely, such a re-storying helps to support those academics and graduate students who take seriously the public purpose of their work and the types of relationships that help to foster a more democratic society. These are not fads or completely new and untested ideas. They have long and rich histories, although somewhat lost.

We can challenge the dominant narrative about what it means to be a graduate student. This raises the possibility of developing new scholars who embody commitments to engagement through their scholarly work (Allen and Moore 2010). We now turn our attention explicitly to the role of graduate education in land-grant universities.

The Place of Graduate Education and Its Future Prospects

There are many dimensions we could explore in relationship to graduate education. I want to focus on how we *story* graduate education in land-grant institutions and what we might learn by not limiting that story to the familiar and expected. As was noted above, different narratives about the impact of academic professionals shape our experience of land-grant universities. We can view the institutions and those within them heroically, that is to say, as providers of knowledge and expertise. In this story, academic professionals and graduate students have answers the world needs and they contribute to the public good by providing those answers. In some contexts, this is completely appropriate and expected. In others, however, this approach is detrimental and destructive. We must learn how to respond to what is needed and/or wanted.

There are other ways we might think about the impact of academic professionals and graduates students, particularly as being in relationship with those they serve. Indeed, language such as "those they serve" begins to lose meaning in a context where we position academic professionals and graduate students in a collaborative role rather than as experts in a top-down paradigm. As more and more graduate students embrace scholarship that positions them in relationship with communities, listening to their own stories about such work can be critically important. Questions about what is appropriate for graduate research continue to function as hurdles for students who want to work with citizens in meaningful ways that position them as partners rather than traditional experts or researchers. One place where this challenge emerges is the graduate student's own relationships with his or her supervising faculty.

The development and mentoring of graduate students by faculty advisors and mentors has a profound effect on the academy. Because many academics position themselves and their work as part of the service intellectual tradition, many graduate students learn to function in similar ways—viewing their contributions to society through the creation of knowledge and sharing it through publications and presentations. Unless graduate students are afforded opportunities to take courses or conduct research that situates their work in and with communities, it will be difficult to broaden the ways that they think of themselves as civic actors or professionals. The academy is "far away from a cultural norm that evokes engagement as a normal outcome of scholarly practice" (McDowell 2001, 181). Because many graduate students view faculty as models for their own scholarly development, engagement's lack of value within the research-intensive environment of graduate training reinforces a position that privileges scholarship serving the public good only in the most narrow of terms. Graduate students mature into young scholars under the discipline of an "expert" model that tolerates *service to* society but discourages active *engagement with* civic life.

There have been various attempts to challenge this approach. The Kellogg Commission's report on the future of state and land-grant universities calls for a new kind of institution, one that commits to supporting such keys reforms as

- educational opportunity that is genuinely equal with respect to admissions;
- learning environments that meet the civic ends of public higher education;
- graduate education that is responsive to pressing public needs;
- using expertise and resources for social problems. (Kellogg Commission 2001, 34–35)

One of the challenges is to push back against the dominant of models of engagement that fit within the heroic metanarrative, especially with regard to funding and resources. Land-grant institutions have deep roots and traditions. These colleges and universities have engaged communities and have shaped higher education for 150 years. They have helped to address public problems by drawing on expertise as part of a democratic response. They have also widely embraced a model of education focused on a student's technical expertise to the detriment of civic orientations. There is need for a paradigm shift in how higher education positions itself as a political entity. What this means is that scholars and students must take seriously the complexity of the most pressing issues and the absence of easy or technical fixes. These problems are "wicked" (Rittel and Webber 1973), with few "right" and "wrong" answers and instead more questions that must be addressed within the context of relationships in communities. If graduate students want to do relevant work, they must take seriously the concerns, questions, and perspectives of communities (Stoecker 1999).

Because graduate programs are so demanding with respect to academic requirements and expectations, there is inevitably too much to do in a program and too little time to do it—unless engagement is embedded in one's program or research. An additional challenge is that many research (including land-grant) universities often see themselves as institutions focused on basic rather than applied research (Stanton and Wagner 2010, 413). The reliance on sponsored research has long shaped what is of value to scholars (Gumport 2011). For many graduate students, the idea that they might be "civic professionals" is not one that connects with the notion of being a scientist, academic, expert, or scholar. But if graduate students who are aspiring to become academic professionals are to respond to public issues, they must acknowledge that problems are difficult, multifaceted, and require more than technical knowledge. What is needed is not another technocrat, but someone who wants to function as a co-creator of solutions to problems.

The story of land-grant universities can easily be about solving the world's problems. The dominant narrative within the land-grant tradition has been that academic professionals have provided information for the public good. We have many examples of faculty members and graduate students contributing to the public in this way. They are doing important work. But if we only tell the story about discoveries in laboratories and not the graduate student working with community members in the Bronx, we are missing an important element of the land-grant story.

Notes

1. For a complete list of land-grant institutions and maps, visit http://www.csrees.usda.gov/qlinks/partners/state_partners.html#maps.

2. It should be noted, however, that Morrill was not the first to press this agenda. Jonathan Baldwin Turner suggested that federal land grants be given to states in order to establish industrial universities in the early 1850s. Turner championed the establishment of a state industrial university in Illinois (Nevins 1962).

3. For information about the history of research at 1890 institutions, see Mayberry 1976.

4.Tuskegee University is usually classed with the 16 official 1890 land-grant institutions. In 1881 an act of the Alabama legislature created what was then called the Tuskegee Institute, only to have the state establish and incorporate a board of trustees and name the school private. Nevertheless, it was granted 25,000 acres of land by the United States Congress in 1899 and is a cooperating partner with Auburn University and Alabama A&M University with respect to extension work. For these reasons, Tuskegee is generally included in lists of 1890 institutions.

5. In Connecticut and New York experiment stations are located off campus; elsewhere they are situated at land-grant institutions.

6. Visit http://www.rust2green.org for more information about this project.

References

Allen, A. D., and T. L. Moore. 2010. Developing emerging engagement scholars in higher education. In *Engaged scholarship: contemporary landscapes, future directions,* edited by H. E. Fitzgerald, C. Burack, and S. D. Seifer. Vol. 2, *Community-campus partnerships.* East Lansing: Michigan State University Press.

Altbach, P. G. 2011. Patterns of higher education development. In *American higher education in the twenty-first century: Social, political, and economic challenges,* edited by P. G. Altbach, P. J. Gumport, and R. O. Berdahl. 3d ed. Baltimore: Johns Hopkins University Press.

Bailey, L. H. 1915. *The holy earth.* New York: Scribner.

Berelson, B. 1960. *Graduate education in the United States.* New York: McGraw-Hill.

Boyte, H. C. 2004. *Everyday politics: Reconnecting citizens and public life.* Philadelphia: University of Pennsylvania Press.

Boyte, H. C. 2008a. *The citizen solution: How you can make a difference.* Saint Paul, MN, and Dayton, OH: Minnesota Historical Society Press in cooperation with Kettering Foundation Press.

Boyte, H. C. 2008b. Public work: Civic populism versus technocracy in higher education. In *Agent of democracy: Higher education and the HEX journey,* edited by D. W. Brown and D. Witte. Dayton, OH: Kettering Foundation Press.

Boyte, H. C., and E. Fretz. 2010. Civic professionalism. *Journal of Higher Education Outreach and Engagement* 14 (2): 67–90.

Boyte, H. C., and N. N. Kari. 1996. *Building America: The democratic promise of public work.* Philadelphia: Temple University Press.

Brunner, H. S. 1962. *Land-grant colleges and universities: 1862–1962.* Washington, DC: GPO.

Carmichael, O. C. 1961. *Graduate education: A critique and a program.* New York: Harper & Bros.

Christy, R. D., L. Williamson, and H. Williamson. 1992. Introduction: A century of service—The past, present, and future roles of 1890 land-grant colleges and institutions. In *A century of service: Land-grant colleges and universities, 1890–1990,* edited by Christy and L. Williamson. New Brunswick, NJ: Transaction Publishers.

Clayton, P. H., R. G. Bringle, B. Senor, J. Huq, and M. Morrison. 2010. Differentiating and assessing relationships in service-learning and civic engagement: Exploitative, transactional, or transformational. *Michigan Journal of Community Service Learning* 16 (2): 5–22.

Clute, O. 1891. The state agricultural college. *Bureau of Education Circular of Information.* No. 11, *History of higher education in Michigan,* edited by A. C. McLaughlin. Washington, DC: GPO.

Cohen, A. M., and C. B. Kisker. 2010. *The shaping of American higher education: Emergence and growth of the contemporary system.* 2d ed. San Francisco: Jossey-Bass.

Committee on the Future of the Colleges of Agriculture in the Land Grant System, National Research Council. 1995. *Colleges of agriculture at the land grant universities: A profile.* Washington, DC: National Academy Press.

Crosson, P. H. 1983. *Public service in higher education: Practices and priorities.* Vol. 7. Washington, DC: Association for the Study of Higher Education.

Doberneck, D. M., C. R. Glass, and J. Schweitzer. 2010. From rhetoric to reality: A typology of publically engaged scholarship. *Journal of Higher Education Outreach and Engagement* 14 (4): 5–35.

Dressel, P. L. 1987. *College to university: The Hannah years at Michigan State, 1935–1969.* East Lansing: Michigan State University.

Dzur, A. W. 2008. *Democratic professionalism: Citizen participation and the reconstruction of professional ethics, identity, and practice.* University Park: Pennsylvania State University Press.

Eddy, E. D. 1957. *Colleges for our land and time: The land-grant idea in American education.* New York: Harper.

Farrand, L. 1929. Letter to R. C. Peyton, July 22. Livingston Farrand Papers. Rare and Manuscript Collections, Cornell University Library.

Grattan, C. H. 1955. *In quest of knowledge: A historical perspective on adult education.* New York: Association Press.

Gumport, P. J. 2011. Graduate education and research: Interdependence and strain. In *American higher education in the twenty-first century: Social, political, and economic challenges,* edited by P. G. Altbach, P. J. Gumport, and R. O. Berdahl. 3d ed. Baltimore: Johns Hopkins University Press.

Humphries, F. 1992. Land-grant institutions: Their struggle for survival and equality. In *A century of service: Land-grant colleges and universities, 1890–1990,* edited by D. Christy and L. Williamson. New Brunswick, NJ: Transaction Publishers.

Kellogg Commission on the Future of State and Land-Grant Universities. 2001. *Returning to our roots: Executive summaries of the reports of the Kellogg Commission on the Future of State and Land-Grant Universities.* Washington, DC: National Association of State Universities and Land-Grant Colleges.

Kuhn, M. 1955. *Michigan State: The first hundred years, 1855–1955.* East Lansing: Michigan State University Press.

Mathews, F. D. 1999. *Politics for people: Finding a responsible public voice*. Urbana: University of Illinois Press.

Mayberry, B. D. 1991. *A century of agriculture in the 1890 land-grant institutions and Tuskegee University, 1890–1990*. New York: Vantage Press.

Mayberry, B. D., ed. 1976. *Development of research at historically Black land-grant institutions*. Tuskegee, AL: Bicentennial Committee of the Association of Research Directors.

McDowell, G. R. 2001. *Land-grant universities and extension into the twenty-first century: Renegotiating or abandoning a social contract*. Ames: Iowa State University Press.

Moreland, W. D., and E. H. Goldstein. 1985. *Pioneers in adult education*. Chicago: Nelson-Hall.

Morrill, J. S. 1888. *State aid to land grant colleges: An address*. Burlington, VT: Free Press Association.

Nevins, A. 1962. *The origins of the land-grant colleges and state universities*. Urbana: University of Illinois Press.

Peters, S. J. 1998. *Extension work as public work: Reconsidering cooperative extension's civic mission*. Minneapolis: University of Minnesota.

Peters, S. J. 2003. Reconstructing civic professionalism in academic life: A response to Mark Wood's paper, "From service to solidarity." *Journal of Higher Education Outreach and Engagement* 8 (2): 183–98.

Peters, S. J. 2004. Educating the civic professional: Reconfigurations and resistances. *Michigan Journal of Community Service-Learning* 11 (1): 47–58.

Peters, S. J. 2006. "Every farmer should be awakened": Liberty Hyde Bailey's vision of agricultural extension work. *Agricultural History* 80 (2): 190–219.

Peters, S. J. 2007. *Changing the story about higher education's public purposes and work: Land-grants, liberty, and the Little Country Theater*. Foreseeable Futures, no. 6. Ann Arbor, MI: Imagining America.

Peters, S. J. 2008. Reconstructing a democratic tradition of public scholarship in the land-grant system. In *Agent of democracy: Higher education and the HEX journey*, edited by D. W. Brown and D. Witte. Dayton, OH: Kettering Foundation Press.

Peters, S. J. 2010. *Democracy and higher education: Traditions and stories of civic engagement*. East Lansing: Michigan State University Press.

Rees, C. J. 1962. *Graduate education in the land-grant colleges and universities*. Baltimore: Division of Graduate Studies, Association of Land-Grant Colleges and Universities.

Rhoten, D. R., and W. W. Powell. 2011. Public research universities: From land grant to federal grant to patent grant instutions. In *Knowledge matters: The public mission of the research university,* edited by D. R. Rhoten and C. Calhoun. New York: Columbia University Press.

Rittel, H. W. J., and M. M. Webber. 1973. Dilemmas in a general theory of planning. *Policy Sciences* 4 (2): 155–69.

Ross, E. D. 1942. *Democracy's college: The land-grant movement in the formative stage.* Ames: Iowa State College Press.

Rudolph, F. 1962. *The American college and university: A history.* New York: Knopf.

Saltmarsh, J., and M. Hartley, eds. 2011. Introduction: "To serve a larger purpose." In *"To serve a larger purpose": Engagement for democracy and the transformation of higher education,* edited by Saltmarsh and Hartley. Philadelphia: Temple University Press.

Sandel, M. J. 2000. The politics of public identity. *Hedgehog Review* 2 (1): 72–88.

Scott, R. V. 1970. *The reluctant farmer: The rise of agricultural extension to 1914.* Urbana: University of Illinois Press.

Sherwood, J. E. 2004. The role of the land-grant institution in the twenty-first century. CSHE Research and Occasional Paper Series 6.04. http://escholarship.org/uc/item/1dp6w2cc.

Simon, L. A. K. 2010. Engaged scholarship in land-grant and research universities. In *Handbook of engaged scholarship: Contemporary landscapes, future directions,* edited by H. E. Fitzgerald, C. Burack, and S. D. Seifer. Vol. 1, *Institutional change.* East Lansing: Michigan State University Press.

Smith, C. B., and M. C. Wilson. 1930. *The agricultural extension system of the United States.* New York: John Wiley & Sons.

Spikes, D. R. 1992. Prefaceto *A century of service: Land-grant colleges and universities, 1890–1990,* edited by R. D. Christy and L. Williamson. London: Transaction.

Stanton, T. K., and J. Wagner. 2010. Educating for democratic citizenship: Antecedents, prospects, and models for renewing the civic mission of graduate education at research universities. In *Handbook of engaged scholarship: Contemporary landscapes, future directions,* edited by H. E. Fitzgerald, C. Burack, and S. D. Seifer. Vol. 1, *Institutional change.* East Lansing: Michigan State University Press.

Stoecker, R. 1999. Are academics irrelevant? Roles for scholars in participatory research. *American Behavioral Scientist* 42 (5): 840–54.

Sullivan, W. M. 2000. Institutional identity and social responsibility in higher education. In *Civic responsibility and higher education,* edited by T. Ehrlich. Westport, CT: American Council on Education/Oryx Press.

Sullivan, W. M. 2003. Engaging the civic option: A new academic professionalism? *Campus Compact Reader* (summer): 10–17.

Sullivan, W. M. 2005. *Work and integrity: The crisis and promise of professionalism in America.* San Francisco: Jossey-Bass.

Von Engeln, O. D. 1924. *Concerning Cornell.* 3d ed. Ithaca, NY: Cornell Co-operative Society.

Widder, K. R. 2005. *Michigan Agricultural College: The evolution of a land grant philosophy, 1855–1925.* East Lansing: Michigan State University Press.

3

To Hell with Good Intentions

*Ivan Illich**

IN THE CONVERSATIONS which I have had today, I was impressed by two things, and I want to state them before I launch into my prepared talk.

I was impressed by your insight that the motivation of U.S. volunteers overseas springs mostly from very alienated feelings and concepts. I was equally impressed, by what I interpret as a step forward among would-be volunteers like you: openness to the idea that the only thing you can legitimately volunteer for in Latin America might be voluntary powerlessness, voluntary presence as receivers, as such, as hopefully beloved or adopted ones without any way of returning the gift.

I was equally impressed by the hypocrisy of most of you: by the hypocrisy of the atmosphere prevailing here. I say this as a brother speaking to brothers and sisters. I say it against many resistances within me; but it must be said. Your very insight, your very openness to evaluations of past programs make you hypocrites because you—or at least most of you—have decided to spend this next summer in Mexico, and therefore, you are unwilling to go far enough in your reappraisal of your program. You close your eyes because you want to go ahead and could not do so if you looked at some facts.

It is quite possible that this hypocrisy is unconscious in most of you. Intellectually, you are ready to see that the motivations which could legitimate volunteer action overseas in 1963 cannot be invoked for the same action in 1968. "Mission-vacations" among poor Mexicans were "the thing" to do for well-off U.S. students earlier in this decade: sentimental concern for newly-discovered poverty south of the border

*Originally delivered as an address to the Conference on InterAmerican Student Projects (CIASP) in Cuernavaca, Mexico, on April 20, 1968. While written before the emergence of today's public scholarship movement, its withering indictment of paternalism speaks to one of that movement's animating concerns. The text printed here is based on a transcript available on the Swaraj Foundation website (http://www.swaraj.org/illich_hell.htm).

combined with total blindness to much worse poverty at home justified such benevolent excursions. Intellectual insight into the difficulties of fruitful volunteer action had not sobered the spirit of Peace Corps Papal-and-Self-Styled Volunteers.

Today, the existence of organizations like yours is offensive to Mexico. I wanted to make this statement in order to explain why I feel sick about it all and in order to make you aware that good intentions have not much to do with what we are discussing here. To hell with good intentions. This is a theological statement. You will not help anybody by your good intentions. There is an Irish saying that the road to hell is paved with good intentions; this sums up the same theological insight.

The very frustration which participation in CIASP [Conference on InterAmerican Student Projects] programs might mean for you, could lead you to new awareness: the awareness that even North Americans can receive the gift of hospitality without the slightest ability to pay for it; the awareness that for some gifts one cannot even say "thank you."

Now to my prepared statement.

Ladies and Gentlemen:

For the past six years I have become known for my increasing opposition to the presence of any and all North American "do-gooders" in Latin America. I am sure you know of my present efforts to obtain the voluntary withdrawal of all North American volunteer armies from Latin America—missionaries, Peace Corps members and groups like yours, a "division" organized for the benevolent invasion of Mexico. You were aware of these things when you invited me—of all people—to be the main speaker at your annual convention. This is amazing! I can only conclude that your invitation means one of at least three things:

Some among you might have reached the conclusion that CIASP should either dissolve altogether, or take the promotion of voluntary aid to the Mexican poor out of its institutional purpose. Therefore you might have invited me here to help others reach this same decision.

You might also have invited me because you want to learn how to deal with people who think the way I do—how to dispute them successfully. It has now become quite common to invite Black Power spokesmen to address Lions Clubs. A "dove" must always be included in a public dispute organized to increase U.S. belligerence.

And finally, you might have invited me here hoping that you would be able to agree with most of what I say, and then go ahead in good faith and work this summer in Mexican villages. This last possibility is only open to those who do not listen, or who cannot understand me.

I did not come here to argue. I am here to tell you, if possible to convince you, and hopefully, to stop you, from pretentiously imposing yourselves on Mexicans.

I do have deep faith in the enormous good will of the U.S. volunteer. However, his good faith can usually be explained only by an abysmal lack of intuitive delicacy. By definition, you cannot help being ultimately vacationing salesmen for the middle-class "American Way of Life," since that is really the only life you know. A group like this could not have developed unless a mood in the United States had supported it—the belief that any true American must share God's blessings with his poorer fellow men. The idea that every American has something to give, and at all times may, can and should give it, explains why it occurred to students that they could help Mexican peasants "develop" by spending a few months in their villages.

Of course, this surprising conviction was supported by members of a missionary order, who would have no reason to exist unless they had the same conviction—except a much stronger one. It is now high time to cure yourselves of this. You, like the values you carry, are the products of an American society of achievers and consumers, with its two-party system, its universal schooling, and its family-car affluence. You are ultimately—consciously or unconsciously—"salesmen" for a delusive ballet in the ideas of democracy, equal opportunity and free enterprise among people who haven't the possibility of profiting from these.

Next to money and guns, the third largest North American export is the U.S. idealist, who turns up in every theater of the world: the teacher, the volunteer, the missionary, the community organizer, the economic developer, and the vacationing do-gooders. Ideally, these people define their role as service. Actually, they frequently wind up alleviating the damage done by money and weapons, or "seducing" the "underdeveloped" to the benefits of the world of affluence and achievement. Perhaps this is the moment to instead bring home to the people of the U.S. the knowledge that the way of life they have chosen simply is not alive enough to be shared.

By now it should be evident to all America that the U.S. is engaged in a tremendous struggle to survive. The U.S. cannot survive if the rest of the world is not convinced that here we have Heaven-on-Earth. The survival of the U.S. depends on the acceptance by all so-called "free" men that the U.S. middle class has "made it." The U.S. way of life has become a religion which must be accepted by all those who do not want to die by the sword—or napalm. All over the globe the U.S. is fighting to protect and develop at least a minority who consume what the U.S.

majority can afford. Such is the purpose of the Alliance for Progress of the middle-classes which the U.S. signed with Latin America some years ago. But increasingly this commercial alliance must be protected by weapons which allow the minority who can "make it" to protect their acquisitions and achievements.

But weapons are not enough to permit minority rule. The marginal masses become rambunctious unless they are given a "Creed," or belief, which explains the status quo. This task is given to the U.S. volunteer—whether he be a member of CIASP or a worker in the so-called "Pacification Programs" in Vietnam.

The United States is currently engaged in a three-front struggle to affirm its ideals of acquisitive and achievement-oriented "Democracy." I say "three" fronts, because three great areas of the world are challenging the validity of a political and social system which makes the rich ever richer, and the poor increasingly marginal to that system.

In Asia, the U.S. is threatened by an established power—China. The U.S. opposes China with three weapons: the tiny Asian elites who could not have it any better than in an alliance with the United States; a huge war machine to stop the Chinese from "taking over" as it is usually put in this country; and forcible re-education of the so-called "Pacified" peoples. All three of these efforts seem to be failing.

In Chicago, poverty funds, the police force and preachers seem to be no more successful in their efforts to check the unwillingness of the black community to wait for graceful integration into the system.

And finally, in Latin America the Alliance for Progress has been quite successful in increasing the number of people who could not be better off—meaning the tiny, middle-class elites—and has created ideal conditions for military dictatorships. The dictators were formerly at the service of the plantation owners, but now they protect the new industrial complexes. And finally, you come to help the underdog accept his destiny within this process!

All you will do in a Mexican village is create disorder. At best, you can try to convince Mexican girls that they should marry a young man who is self-made, rich, a consumer, and as disrespectful of tradition as one of you. At worst, in your "community development" spirit you might create just enough problems to get someone shot after your vacation ends—and you rush back to your middle-class neighborhoods where your friends make jokes about "spics" and "wetbacks."

You start on your task without any training. Even the Peace Corps spends around $10,000 on each corps member to help him adapt to his new environment and to guard him against culture shock. How odd that nobody ever thought about spending money to educate poor Mexicans in order to prevent them from the culture shock of meeting you?

In fact, you cannot even meet the majority, which you pretend to serve in Latin America—even if you could speak their language, which most of you cannot. You can only dialogue with those like you—Latin American imitations of the North American middle class. There is no way for you to really meet with the underprivileged, since there is no common ground whatsoever for you to meet on.

Let me explain this statement, and also let me explain why most Latin Americans with whom you might be able to communicate would disagree with me.

Suppose you went to a U.S. ghetto this summer and tried to help the poor there "help themselves." Very soon you would be either spit upon or laughed at. People offended by your pretentiousness would hit or spit. People who understand that your own bad consciences push you to this gesture would laugh condescendingly. Soon you would be made aware of your irrelevance among the poor, of your status as middle-class college students on a summer assignment. You would be roundly rejected, no matter if your skin is white—as most of your faces here are—or brown or black, as a few exceptions who got in here somehow.

Your reports about your work in Mexico, which you so kindly sent me, exude self-complacency. Your reports on past summers prove that you are not even capable of understanding that your do-gooding in a Mexican village is even less relevant than it would be in a U.S. ghetto. Not only is there a gulf between what you have and what others have which is much greater than the one existing between you and the poor in your own country, but there is also a gulf between what you feel and what the Mexican people feel that is incomparably greater. This gulf is so great that in a Mexican village you, as White Americans (or cultural white Americans) can imagine yourselves exactly the way a white preacher saw himself when he offered his life preaching to the black slaves on a plantation in Alabama. The fact that you live in huts and eat tortillas for a few weeks renders your well-intentioned group only a bit more picturesque. The only people with whom you can hope to communicate are some members of the middle class. And here please remember that I said "some"—by which I mean a tiny elite in Latin America.

You come from a country which industrialized early and which succeeded in incorporating the great majority of its citizens into the middle classes. It is no social distinction in the U.S. to have graduated from the second year of college. Indeed, most Americans now do. Anybody in this country who did not finish high school is considered underprivileged.

In Latin America the situation is quite different: 75% of all people drop out of school before they reach the sixth grade. Thus, people who have finished high school are members of a tiny minority. Then, a minority of that minority goes on for university training. It is only among these people that you will find your educational equals.

At the same time, a middle class in the United States is the majority. In Mexico, it is a tiny elite. Seven years ago your country began and financed a so-called "Alliance for Progress." This was an "Alliance" for the "Progress" of the middle-class elites. Now, it is among the members of this middle class that you will find a few people who are willing to send their time with you—and they are overwhelmingly those "nice kids" who would also like to soothe their troubled consciences by "doing something nice for the promotion of the poor Indians." Of course, when you and your middle-class Mexican counterparts meet, you will be told that you are doing something valuable, that you are "sacrificing" to help others.

And it will be the foreign priest who will especially confirm your self-image for you. After all, his livelihood and sense of purpose depends on his firm belief in a year-round mission, which is of the same type as your summer vacation-mission.

There exists the argument that some returned volunteers have gained insight into the damage they have done to others—and thus become more mature people. Yet it is less frequently stated that most of them are ridiculously proud of their "summer sacrifices." Perhaps there is also something to the argument that young men should be promiscuous for a while in order to find out that sexual love is most beautiful in a monogamous relationship. Or that the best way to leave LSD alone is to try it for a while—or even that the best way of understanding that your help in the ghetto is neither needed nor wanted is to try, and fail. I do not agree with this argument. The damage which volunteers do willy-nilly is too high a price for the belated insight that they shouldn't have been volunteers in the first place.

If you have any sense of responsibility at all, stay with your riots here at home. Work for the coming elections: You will know what you are doing, why you are doing it, and how to communicate with those to whom you speak. And you will know when you fail. If you insist on working with the poor, if this is your vocation, then at least work among the poor who can tell you to go to hell. It is incredibly unfair for you to impose yourselves on a village where you are so linguistically deaf and dumb that you don't even understand what you are doing, or what people think of you. And it is profoundly damaging to yourselves when you define something that you want to do as "good," a "sacrifice" and "help."

I am here to suggest that you voluntarily renounce exercising the power which being an American gives you. I am here to entreat you to freely, consciously and humbly give up the legal right you have to impose your benevolence on Mexico. I am here to challenge you to recognize your inability, your powerlessness and your incapacity to do the "good" which you intended to do.

I am here to entreat you to use your money, your status and your education to travel in Latin America. Come to look, come to climb our mountains, to enjoy our flowers. Come to study. But do not come to help.

4

Publicly Engaged Graduate Research and the Transformation of the American Academy

Susan Curtis, Shirley Rose, and Kristina Bross

"TODAY, THE PROMISE of American public education must be made whole in a new era and a completely different world." With these words, the Kellogg Commission issued its sixth and final report to the National Association of State Universities and Land-Grant Colleges (NASULGC), urging a "renewal of the covenant" between public universities and the citizens that support them (2000, 9). The Commission had been assembled in order to study the state of land-grant education at a time when the calls for accountability at all levels of public education had begun to crescendo. The Commission released its report with a "sense of urgency and concern" about the future of public higher education in the twenty-first century, given growing skepticism on the part of many citizens that universities deserved continuing support. The final report urged universities to strive for superior classroom instruction, path-breaking discovery, and engagement with the wider community.

Universities that heeded this report recognized that it was asking the American academy to dramatically transform itself. The standard focus on research, teaching, and service had to shift toward "discovery," "learning," and "engagement," and such a shift involved far more than semantics. To embrace the latter trio of tasks was to insist that work in the university had to be relevant to the public and that retreat to the "ivory tower" was not an option. The last of these tasks—engagement—seemed the most revolutionary. While all of the present authors had in some small way brought our findings to non-university audiences through public lectures or talks to civic or social organizations, we had not conceived of it as a two-way street, nor had that work been particularly highly valued. In fact, in our departments—the Departments of English and of History—the mission was shaped by a commitment to both teaching and research, but the connection to civic involvement was seen as optional at best. University leaders like former Purdue University President Martin Jischke, who took up the challenge of the Kellogg Commission, spurred professors across all disciplines vigorously to explore ways of working collaboratively with community partners and to help make the university a real asset to the community and the state. The university provided monetary incentives to develop service-learning courses and to give public lectures and workshops across the state of Indiana. Both kinds of activities required attention to the manner of presentation to and interaction with community groups, a consideration of the "relevance" of our knowledge to social and economic challenges, and a willingness to create two-way partnerships with nonacademic people and entities who bring important knowledge to our collaborative endeavors.

The problem, which is the subject of this chapter, is how to make this renewal of the land-grant mission sustainable into the future. Institutional practices surrounding tenure and promotion, for example, have not always recognized the scholarship of engagement. The "default setting" for deciding tenure cases derives from the experience of senior professors; what was demanded of them should be demanded of assistant and associate professors.

We believe that one of the keys to transforming institutions of higher education is to develop graduate-level courses that are both community-based and rigorous, so as to develop a generation of university citizens who will be able to conduct, recognize, and evaluate the quality of engaged scholarship or teaching. In this chapter, we first explore our experience of developing a course at Purdue University that blended our traditional disciplinary skills with an innovative, collaborative seminar project. Second, we suggest that a model from the past—the emergence of the Christian Social Gospel movement at the turn of the twentieth century—might show universities a way to remake both institutional culture and practice. The first group of Social Gospel ministers developed a new message and praxis from the traditional seminary experience because the need for a more responsive ministry was palpable. They created a new learning environment in their institutions of learning, thus normalizing what had once been avant-garde.

In the final section of this chapter, we argue that engaged graduate research can help advance the legitimacy of engagement at the university in a similar way.

Archival Connections and an Opportunity to Engage

In many ways, we stumbled into this collaboration, and our relationship with one another and with the project evolved over the years. Curtis, a historian, first met Rose, a rhetoric professor, when she needed advice on what to do with a collection of 1930s and '40s books and political pamphlets donated to the American Studies program of which she was chair; a student had told her that Rose had offered a summer course on archives and might be able to offer assistance. They discussed relevant issues involved, and Rose gave Curtis the titles of books that might help her decide what to do with the collection. Collaboration, however, did not commence. Meanwhile, Bross, a literature scholar, introduced a section on archives in an undergraduate course on early American literature in order to help students understand where books came from. She had worked with the Tippecanoe County Historical Association (TCHA), where the students were permitted to look at some unprocessed original materials from which they were invited to derive some meaning. As a member of the American Studies program faculty, Bross told Curtis about the great experience her students had enjoyed at TCHA, and suggested the possibility of developing a graduate seminar. It was at this point that the idea of an archives initiative began to take shape.

Each of us came to this project from fairly pure disciplinary positions. Rose's interest in archives arose in large part from questions about the rhetoric of archival descriptions in institutional finding aids—how collections were named, organized, and described—and how that rhetoric affected how the materials were approached and read. Curtis had vast experience working in archives, but was intrigued by the process by which archival collections came into being. Bross brought the concerns of a literary scholar to the matter—who determines what is the "real thing," and how? Each of us could have pursued these questions along the tracks with which we were most familiar and continued working independently of one another. But our encounters occurred at about the same time that President Jischke was leading Purdue into the challenges of becoming more civically engaged. Importantly, Bross had experience with service learning at another institution, and she was a colleague to both Rose (English Department) and Curtis (American Studies). She organized meetings between the collections manager and executive director of TCHA and the three of us—both sides were eager for a partnership. It was the interdisciplinary American Studies program that gave us institutional space to work together. Purdue University's American Studies program had nearly a 40-year tradition of team-teaching that made a collaborative project imaginable.

In 2001, we began developing an interdisciplinary, community-based collaborative project, "Archival Theory and Practice." We secured external funding to develop a graduate service-learning seminar designed to improve future researchers' skills and to assist a local historical society, which was struggling to maintain a staff, in caring for its archival collection. Each of us scoured our fields for books that addressed archival issues, and we began assembling a small resource library. We also convened an archivist faculty interest group (AFIG), which drew faculty members from English, History, and Sociology, archivists and librarians on campus, and the staff of TCHA. AFIG formed a reading group and met regularly through one semester, discussing literature by historians, theorists, rhetoricians, and library scientists that addressed different aspects of the archives.[1] We spent nearly two years writing grants, studying the problem from both disciplinary and interdisciplinary perspectives, and negotiating with the director of TCHA the terms of our students' access to the unprocessed archives.

In 2004, thanks to a grant from the National Endowment for the Humanities, the American Studies Association Community Partnership Grant, and a Service-Learning Faculty Fellowship, the three of us offered the first version of the seminar to 21 graduate students in American Studies, History, Literature, Rhetoric, and Creative Writing. Our goal was twofold—to lead our students to original archival insights that would make them more effective, more thoughtful, and more creative researchers in their fields of study and to instill in them respect for engaged work, public scholarship, and the wider community that universities serve. Through regular reflections—in journals and in seminar discussions—students wrestled with the value of scholarship to the public and with academics' accountability to the men and women whose taxes help support the university. From the standpoint of the university-community partnership, the course succeeded; TCHA received the benefits of hundreds of hours of unpaid, highly skilled labor and of greater awareness of and access to its holdings. From the students' perspective, the course helped ground them as scholars and as citizens They processed collections that were used by others, and they relished having an outlet for a powerful impulse to serve in the community. Some students found dissertation and thesis projects, and some were inspired to see community-based projects as part of their future in the academy.

We have since offered versions of the seminar four times, working with local people and institutions and ending the semester with a student-run public program. In the most recent offering, 14 students worked with 11 collections, ranging from the papers and materials of a privately owned house designed and built by Frank Lloyd Wright, to the historical materials of a synagogue established in the nineteenth century, to a local restaurateur's sport history and memorabilia collection. The students also organized a day-long series of workshops designed to explore with attendees the importance of privately held archival materials to a better understanding of community history.

Participants shared parts of their collection and their knowledge of individual pieces. Students shared what they had learned about basic preservation and arrangement strategies as well as the centrality of documenting important family treasures for future generations. Indeed, new collaborations with people we have met at these public programs have moved our conceptualization of this project in new directions—toward memory and public memorials that we hope will deepen our engagement with the community.

Each of us was affected as well by our work with students, with each other, and with the community. Rose, for example, applied for and received a fellowship to study archival processing theory and practices with Purdue University Archivist Sammie Morris, which allowed her to develop a research agenda on the rhetoric of archival description. Bross organized a major conference entitled "Prophetstown Revisited," which took the occasion of the bicentennial of the pan-Indian movement led by Tecumseh and his brother, "The Prophet," in the vicinity of Purdue University, to bring together dozens of scholars and community members—both Native American and not—to explore the meaning of Native American experience then and now from a variety of perspectives. Collectively, attendees began developing protocols on the use of indigenous archives that spell out who can have access to them and under what conditions. It was a path-breaking effort to establish respect and reciprocity in the relationship between scholars of early America and the descendants of the native peoples they studied. Curtis's work as a researcher changed radically because of her involvement in the project. After preparing and teaching the course, she brought new theoretical concerns to archival research and experimented with a form of life-writing that was as much a reflection on archives and archival researchers as it was about her subject. Her career also moved increasingly toward civic engagement; she developed a college-wide program of linked service-learning courses, accepted a position on the board of a local nonprofit, and began developing projects in conventional courses that prodded students to think about their responsibilities to the wider community.

Promotion and tenure, however, did not depend upon this work. Curtis and Rose were full professors, and Bross had become a tenured associate professor on the basis of her national reputation as a scholar of early American literature. While engaged teaching and research have proved extremely rewarding, both personally and professionally, there have been some disheartening moments that reveal the tension between Purdue's mission as an engaged land-grant university and an institutional culture that nevertheless disparages engagement. Indeed, when we began developing the graduate course, Curtis contacted the

Graduate School to find out if there were any special steps needed to offer service learning at that level. She met resistance: the Graduate School did not want to approve a course that was "lightweight"; service learning was fine for undergraduates, but graduate seminars were supposed to be "rigorous." Colleagues, seeming to miss the point of the course, thought it was nice that we had "helped out" at the historical society but saw no other particular merit in the project. College-level administrators threatened to increase our teaching loads to "make up" for having team-taught the inaugural course, ignoring both the external funding that had come to the university from the NEH and the American Studies Association and the fact that high enrollment (relative to the single-digit enrollments typical of graduate seminars) more than justified our team-teaching. In 2009, Curtis collaborated with a colleague in Landscape Architecture to study the impact of service-learning grant programs on student learning, faculty career development, community partnerships, and university culture. A survey of department heads revealed that they generally placed less value on service learning and they assumed that those who excelled at service learning were not strong researchers. Faculty focus groups corroborated this sense that service-learning pedagogy is a waste of time, is discouraged, and is not rewarded. Finally, an examination of the vitae of faculty recipients of one or both of the service-learning grants sponsored by the university showed that engagement work is rendered nearly invisible by conventional ways of reporting achievement, which provide no clear method of documenting engagement activities or marginalize—literally—those efforts in end-of-report "service" sections.

These responses made us realize that some colleagues, both locally and in our professional organizations, do not embrace the ideals articulated by the Kellogg Commission; they are reluctant to take part in engagement activity themselves and are inclined to resist rewarding those who do. Moreover, a great deal of this resistance comes from the ranks of the most senior faculty and some department heads who hold the power to confer tenure and promotion and to determine merit-based salary increases. Seven years after the Kellogg Commission's report, a follow-up survey of college and university top administrators revealed that only 14% had taken any steps to revise tenure and promotion guidelines, and as most of us know, the power to interpret such guidelines is left in the hands of departmental committees made up of senior faculty, some of whom treat the promotion process as a kind of hazing ritual and reproduce past definitions and valuations of academic work (Byrne 2006). Most organizations in the business of ranking institutions of higher learning do not factor civic engagement into their systems of measurement. Productivity, as measured by the

National Research Council, the Faculty Scholarly Productivity Index, the Center for Measuring University Performance, and *Forbes* college rankings (which include the "Top Colleges for Getting Rich"), consists of the publication of books and articles; in addition to faculty productivity, institutional ranking regimes are invariably based on such criteria as faculty salaries, reputation, SAT and GRE scores, alumni giving and size of the endowment, average class size, and graduation and retention rates. In none of the formulas does one find reference to community-based engagement projects, promotion of democracy, service-learning courses, or indeed any indication of student learning. In other words, these entities are looking at quantifiable measures of existing resources and scholarly output without any regard for the impact they have on the world outside of the academy. One exception is the *Washington Monthly*, which bases its rankings on three criteria: the institution's performance as an "engine of social mobility (ideally helping the poor to get rich rather than the very rich to get very, very rich)"; the extent to which it fosters "scientific and humanistic research"; and its efficacy in promoting "an ethic of service to country" (*Washington Monthly* 2006).

So until institutions of higher learning fully embrace public scholarship and engagement, untenured faculty take risks embarking on such projects. As Patty Limerick recently has written,

> To become university-based public scholars, young people may well have to put their ambition into cold storage for a decade and a half. Go to graduate school, write a conventional dissertation, get a tenure-track job, publish in academic journals and in university presses, give papers at professional conferences to small groups of fellow specialists, and comply with all the requirements of deference, conformity, and hoop-jumping that narrow the road to tenure while also narrowing the travelers on that road. Then, once tenured, you can take up the applied work that appealed to you in the first place. (2008, C1)

Our experience shows that it is possible to develop graduate-level courses that introduce students to public scholarship and rigorous research practices. Interdisciplinary teaching in particular reinforces the collaborative spirit necessary to work effectively with community partners. The in-between nature of interdisciplinary work also helps loosen the hold of departmental culture on the participants. It is important to remember that faculty members who undertake a project like this after tenure are largely shielded from the judgment of promotion committees that are unsympathetic to the integrated scholarship of engagement, learning, and discovery. By using our privileged status to develop new pedagogies, our hope is that we are aiding students to conduct engaged research and to create lines on their vitae through the public presentations, conference papers, and dissertations that have so far emerged from the course. By doing so, we help our students make their commitment to public scholarship legible within their disciplinary fields. Still, one success story does not necessarily change institutional culture.

We know, however, that institutions can change, and in the next section we look to history to gain some insights into how transformation can occur. The conflicts that flare up over what constitutes tenurable and promotable scholarly activity can be understood in terms of cultural conflict and change.[2] Institutional culture embodies values and ideals; it defines the boundaries between acceptable and unacceptable belief and practice. Cultures do change, but not without groups of people pushing against the accepted boundaries and promoting an alternative set of imperatives that they encourage others to embrace. If we can shift the ground of the debate over engaged scholarship and teaching, we can better address the concerns of faculty on both sides of the issue.[3]

Lessons from Another New Era

The call for civic engagement in the 1990s came in the midst of growing concerns about the escalating costs of higher education and the seeming disconnect between the work of the academy and that of industries outside of it. At the same time, global networks of production and trade led, in some cases, to destabilization of familiar patterns of work, family, and community life, and an electronic technological revolution accelerated the pace of activity everywhere and demanded computer literacy of the workforce. Until the "dot-com" bubble burst at the end of the decade, societies at home and abroad witnessed widening gaps between the wealthiest and the poorest sectors. And while a college education seemed to be the ticket to future success, critics of higher education called into question the accountability of colleges and universities to prepare graduates for this brave new world and to focus their research expertise and financial resources on issues of broad social importance.

Although the Kellogg Commission was responding to these seemingly new difficulties in higher education, the language used by the Commission to make its case for engagement—"new era," "different world," and "renewal of the covenant"—calls to mind another period in American history when rapid social and economic transformation produced similar anxieties about the relationship between ordinary people and their public institutions, and about the responsibilities of professionals to the public good. The end of the nineteenth century, too often misremembered as the "Gay Nineties," was marked by social conflict and cultural anxiety. The nation was rocked by economic depression, class warfare, a farmer's revolt, violence and discrimination against racial and ethnic minorities, and a rapid increase in urbanization. Like our own day, when revolutions in technology and global interactions have altered the familiar world of our youth and produced a serious fracturing of the body politic and difficult economic times, the United States in the four decades after Reconstruction ended in 1877 struggled to adjust to the dislocations caused by national and international markets, social disparity, an "Immigrant Question," and the erosion of confidence in its national leaders.[4]

Americans also witnessed a flood of reform programs meant to restore harmony, order, and progress. The People's Party believed the country was divided between "tramps" and "millionaires," and they spelled out a political platform calling for greater accountability on the part of business and government leaders. Labor organizations from the Knights of Labor to the American Federation of Labor pushed for greater cooperation between employers and employees, collective bargaining, and a dramatic improvement in wages and working conditions. The academic field of sociology took shape as scholars sought new ways of understanding the structure and dynamics of society so they could figure out how to correct the imbalances they saw all around them. Many newly minted sociologists found allies and places of work in settlement houses, such as Jane Addams's famous Hull House in Chicago, whose residents strove to understand the lives of immigrant workers by living among them as neighbors. A host of new popular culture trends provide evidence of rebellion against the status quo. Ragtime music with its infectious rhythm, the "New Woman" with her demand for independence, and mass circulation magazines staffed by muckraking journalists and addressed to ordinary men and women—all vibrated with a desire to challenge the stale pieties of the privileged. Even Christian institutions got into the act with calls for new definitions of salvation, duties, and proper church programs. They established "institutional churches" that kept their doors open seven days a week and created programs meant to alleviate the suffering of individuals and families oppressed by low wages, long work days, and inadequate resources for hard times.[5]

While the resolution of these conflicts was neither smooth nor complete, it is apparent that by the early 1920s some of what had been considered outlandish in the 1890s represented the common sense of the day. Labor laws passed in the preceding two decades curbed the worst of the practices that had led to class conflict; programs to support farmers had calmed many fears in the agricultural heartland; the frightening "New Woman" of the 1890s appeared tame compared to the "Flapper," but neither New Women nor Flappers were quite ready to yield on their demand for greater opportunities and autonomy. Although race-based discrimination and extralegal violence and xenophobia continued apace (agricultural programs, for instance, had been directed to white farmers, leaving African American farmers to struggle), the very stereotypes upon which much of this abhorrent behavior was based fired the imagination of culture workers and performers in the mass culture that burgeoned in the "Roaring Twenties."[6]

Amid these social and cultural developments, the Social Gospel movement offers some interesting parallels with public engagement in the twenty-first century. Josiah Strong, one of the earliest adherents to the ideals of the Social Gospel, published his manifesto *The New Era* in 1893, a year when the United States was mired in economic depression and social conflict. The first calls for church-sponsored social reform and programs that went out in the 1870s were met with a mixture of scorn and skepticism. The concept of "social salvation," which insisted that individual piety without attending to the social needs of the world outside was insufficient for eternal salvation, dramatically altered long-held ideas about conversion and Christian living. Social Gospelers called into question the ethos of individual responsibility and urged individuals and congregations to attack the social sins that worked against the message of Jesus of Nazareth. In other words, Social Gospelers of the late nineteenth century responded to contemporary social and cultural crises by launching church-sponsored programs that presage, in fascinating ways, what is now university-sponsored "engagement." Social Gospel churches called for social service programs—day care for the children of working parents, industrial and domestic training for working-class teens, visiting nurses, inexpensive meals, wholesome entertainment, and employment services—and they reached out to the men and women hardest hit by industrial exploitation.[7]

Of course, there are as many differences as there are similarities between Social Gospel Protestants and engaged faculty members, or between religious denominations and universities. They shared a desire to be relevant to the communities in which they existed and they both saw their work as efforts to address and hopefully to solve serious social problems. But turn-of-the-century Protestants involved in social reform above all were determined to save souls; modern-day engaged scholars may or may not be so determined. "Community" was defined differently by the two groups as well—Social Gospelers focusing on their faith community as well as the neighborhoods surrounding their houses of worship, and the engaged scholar attending to neighborhoods, municipalities, regions, or particular partners without regard to religious identity, or even to geographic proximity, in some cases.

While a full-blown comparison between these two movements could be quite fascinating, that is not our purpose. What we would like to examine is the process by which Social Gospelers moved their ideas and practices from the margins of Protestantism to its center and how they embedded their ideas and values in seminaries as a way to ensure the reproduction of the next generation of socially aware clergy.

The Social Gospelers who pioneered in the introduction of social justice issues into the life of their congregations were educated in the same traditional ways as those who did not share their commitments. They had to take the same rigorous examinations in seminary and pass muster with congregational hiring committees. Like their seminary classmates, they confronted the challenge of Darwinian science to their faith in a supreme being, and they lived in a rapidly changing world. Social Gospelers noted the radical implications of technological change—namely, steam power and electricity—that brought the diverse people of the world into proximity with one another. But unlike their classmates who would later reject their beliefs, Social Gospelers felt a profound tension between the widespread suffering of men and women in industrial America and the message of the New Testament. Could hardworking people be blamed for their poverty, the product of social change rather than individual failure? Questions like this prompted them to blaze new theological trails and to introduce unconventional practices in their churches. And they were conscious of the lack of precedents for their work: Josiah Strong dubbed the period "The New Era," George Herron sought to define the "new redemption" (1893), Edward Scribner Ames articulated the "new orthodoxy" (1918), and Shailer Mathews entitled his autobiography *New Faith for Old* (1936). They found themselves facing problems in their congregations and in their communities for which the views on which they had been raised simply did not prepare them.

As the titles above suggest, one of their strategies to get traction for their ideas was to publish. They sought outlets for their work in both professional and popular presses. They doggedly introduced social terms into their sermons, church-sponsored programs, and publications. Some experimented with writing fiction, hoping to appeal to a wide readership and aiming to popularize the new ideas and practices of the movement.[8] They created regional and national networks of like-minded Christians—Walter Rauschenbusch's Brotherhood of the Kingdom exemplifies the impulse to join together to sustain one another even as they pushed one another to better, more rigorous analyses of the relationship between social conditions and religious faith. Social Gospelers also launched programs that caught the attention of large-circulation periodicals like *The Outlook, The Independent*, and *The Delineator*.

A breakthrough moment came in 1908, when Frank Mason North used an opportunity to address the newly founded Federal Council of Churches to present a paper entitled "The Church and Modern Industry," which outlined a set of principles for churches to endorse, embrace, and act upon in the name of social justice in those troubled times. The assembled representatives of more than 17 million American Protestants reportedly rose as one to approve the report. A review of the meeting published in the *Christian Advocate* claimed that North's presentation marked "the highest point of enthusiasm" at the conference and that "at its conclusion the applause was loud and long." One witness to the event called North's "the greatest paper on this subject that I have ever heard or read," and another called it "an epoch-making deliverance."[9] The council adopted part of "The Church and Modern Industry" as the "Social Creed of the Churches."

The Social Gospel by 1908 was no longer marginal. Many of those who leapt to their feet after North spoke had probably graduated from seminaries where these pioneers taught. Walter Rauschenbusch at the Rochester School of Theology had introduced courses on the social question in the 1890s—courses that he wished he had been able to take before he set out on his various reform campaigns. Books by other pioneers constituted a valuable resource library for seminarians interested in exploring Christian social responsibility. When they took positions in churches or schools of divinity, they expected to see such work as a legitimate part of the institution.

Social Gospelers challenged the accepted values associated with Victorian Christianity—individual responsibility, self-control, and hard work—because they no longer believed the truism that these virtues would bring success in life. They allied themselves with others seeking alternatives to the status quo: labor unions, progressive reformers, and lawmakers who sought to curb the excesses of industrialism. Defenders of liberal individualism occupied positions of power and clung tenaciously to the older system of values, but short of a resort to violence—and there certainly were instances of such violence—they could not maintain their power as a new historical bloc took shape.

The alternative ethic made headway in various culture industries—publishing houses, mass-circulation magazines, popular entertainment, and art. In the case of the Social Gospel, the "new faith" that people like Edward Scribner Ames professed was preached from the pulpit, was integrated into Sunday School literature, became the stuff of fiction, and found its way into the curriculum of seminaries and schools of divinity, where the next generation of clergy were being educated. By the early 1900s people in the pews likewise came to understand the world and the responsibilities of Christians in terms of social service. Moreover, connections between various forms of resistance linked reform to more general cultural change. Social Gospeler Charles Stelzle, for example, used ragtime music to attract working people to his noontime sermons in Chicago, and Elizabeth Stuart Phelps populated her reform novels with women seeking to break free of Victorian constraints. National organizations to which local institutions were linked—the Federal Council of Churches is a notable example—disseminated the new views and programs with increasing authority.

In these ways, working people, Protestant ministers, ragtime musicians, muckraking journalists, New Women, and political aspirants ushered in a new era and a different world. The older ideals did not disappear, but they no longer held sway as the legitimate organizing principles for the nation. The strategies pursued by Social Gospelers could prove useful to engaged scholars. Indeed, such efforts as working with artists, labor unions, and activists can be the stuff of engagement. Seeking new outlets for publication in the popular press or newly founded academic journals helps provide innovative work with both legitimacy and publicity. Social Gospelers did not wait for permission to insist that the advancement of social justice and democracy mattered and deserved to be at the center of their work; similarly, engaged scholars need not wait for permission to do work that addresses vital issues of the day. Finally, Social Gospelers created new allies and advocates by introducing their ideas into the curriculum and preparing the next generation of ministers and theologians, for whom a Christian commitment to social justice was simply common sense. This has been the most important lesson for us. For the graduate students who have taken Archival Theory and Practice, public scholarship and community engagement have become important aspects of their work in the university.

Public Engagement and Graduate Education

Land-grant universities were in their infancy at the moment when the social and economic crises of the late nineteenth century brought about the cultural shift discussed above. They were founded as a way to make higher education available to all people living in a democratic society and to work against the idea that learning was a privilege only of the elite. As they developed in the early years, these land-grant institutions played an important role in the communities and states where they were located, and many of the researchers who taught in them addressed issues of immediate concern. While Social Gospelers responded to concerns about immigration and the rise of the working poor with institutions and programs to address their spiritual needs, the land-grant universities addressed social and physical needs head on. At a time when immigration dramatically increased the size of the U.S. population, raising Malthusian fears of scarcity and famine, researchers at land-grant institutions attempted to introduce crops that would flourish in regions thought to be only marginally suited to agriculture (Jones 2004). While farmers struggled in the national and international markets, university extension agents recognized the pressures they faced and brought the latest findings of researchers to farmers across their states. Even as the middle class felt the ground giving way beneath them in the 1890s, worrying that the promise of upward social mobility for their children was slipping away, land-grant universities offered opportunities for their children to secure the education that would maintain their hold on prosperity.

When the Kellogg Commission invoked the need for "renewing the covenant," it was referring to this relationship between the people and their universities (Peters 2007). Although the specific nature of the dissatisfaction today is not the same as the upheavals of a century past, the objectives of "reformers" in both periods are remarkably similar. In the decade since the Commission issued its final report the scale of the challenges has increased. Those who believe that civic engagement is in fact a powerful way of reconnecting higher education and the wider public must continue to work toward legitimizing alternative pedagogies, professional practices, and institutional cultures.

The Imagining America consortium has begun that work. The recently completed work of the Tenure Team Initiative (Ellison and Eatman 2008), for example, is now circulating in institutions affiliated with the consortium. Their guidelines not only provide administrators and senior faculty members with standards by which to judge the quality of work by colleagues engaged in community-based projects, but also stoutly assert the importance of doing such work. Both Imagining America and the National Outreach Scholarship Conference provide opportunities for like-minded public scholars and engaged academics to learn from one another, to improve their practices by creating a body of scholarship within which to situate service and engagement projects, and to develop networks and connections among faculty and administrators to increase the impact of such work.

At the same time, as long as promotion and tenure policies and decisions at most universities continue to focus overwhelmingly on publication of basic research and to dismiss or ignore service learning and civic engagement as important elements of higher education, then each succeeding generation of newly minted Ph.D.'s and M.F.A.'s will be socialized into believing that research speaking exclusively to the professional association and the readers of leading disciplinary journals is all that matters. Some will be socialized into viewing the work of engagement as frivolous or lightweight. Others will experience conflict and dissonance as they seek to connect their professional endeavors with civic engagement, and that may compel them to give up on such projects.

Service learning at the undergraduate level offers students an invaluable opportunity to reflect on the meaning of citizenship and community membership. It encourages students to think in less self-centered terms. We believe the lessons of service learning are valuable to graduate students and essential to the transformation of higher education. Many of the people who enter graduate programs will be the future "citizens" of institutions of higher learning. They will either seek new policies or adhere to hidebound tradition. They will either sneer at service learning and public scholarship or embrace them as part of the responsibilities of the society's intellectual class. Unless we seek to produce the next generation of engaged scholars, the frustrations we face today will continue to get a new lease on life with each succeeding generation.

Our experience suggests that we need not perpetuate the either/or view of academic work and social responsibility. One of the goals of our Archival Theory and Practice seminar is to introduce graduate students to new ways of thinking about archives that will make them better researchers, conscious of what's missing from as well as what's been saved in archives, willing to explore unconventional archives, and cognizant of the experiences and voices of people who have too often occupied the margins of our scholarship. That work—conventional publishable research—also contributes to the new era and different world in which we live. At the same time, students learn firsthand how demanding and difficult, yet ultimately rewarding, community-based work is. They learn directly how dependent they are upon the people whose materials they preserve, arrange, describe, and study, and how theirs is not the only voice of authority. They see in us three faculty members who are striving to integrate holistically the three missions of the university—to advance knowledge through research, teaching, and engagement.

Notes

1. Jacques Derrida's *Archive Fever* (1996), Michel Foucault's *Archaeology of Knowledge* (1972), Carolyn Steedman's *Dust* (2002), Nicholson Baker's *Double* Fold (2001), Richard Cox's *Vandals in the Stacks?* (2002),

and Antoinette Burton's *Archive Stories* (2005) formed the nucleus of our reading; we subsequently assigned these books in the seminar along with other specialized studies of archives from anthropology, history, and literature.

2. For a good overview of the assumptions that undergird this analysis, with examples from multiple cultural transitions, see Lears 1985.

3. See Thornton and Jaeger 2008 for a slightly different examination of institutional culture.

4. The scholarship on this period is vast. For a valuable introduction to the turmoil of the era consult Painter 2009, Trachtenberg 1982, Lears 1981, Thelen 1972, and McGerr 1986.

5. Representative discussions include Goodwyn 1976, Bruce 1959, Salvatore 1982, Curtis 1994 and 2001, and Higham 1970.

6. On these developments consult Weinstein 1968, Gerstle 2001, Denning 1996, and Douglas 1995.

7. On the wide range of social programs introduced by the Social Gospel, see Hopkins 1943, Curtis 2001, and Gorrell 1988. For a summary of the opposition faced by Social Gospelers, see Rauschenbusch 1912, chap 1.

8. The most popular of these novels are Charles M. Sheldon, *In His Steps* (1897), and Elizabeth Stuart Phelps, *A Singular Life* (1894). As the daughter of one of the most orthodox Protestant theologians in the country, Austin Phelps, Elizabeth Stuart Phelps had shocked some of her father's colleagues with the 1868 publication of the novel *The Gates Ajar*, considered heretical by the Protestant establishment because it argued that a good, loving person who dies without having a conversion experience still will be welcomed by God in heaven.

9. For various accounts of North's speech, see Sanford 1916, Lacy 1967, Christian Advocate 1908, and Mathews 1936, 121.

References

Ames, Edward Scribner. 1918. *The new orthodoxy*. Chicago: University of Chicago Press.

Baker, Nicholson. 2001. *Double fold: Libraries and the assault on paper*. New York: Vintage Books.

Bruce, Robert V. 1959. *1877: Year of violence*. Indianapolis: Bobbs-Merrill.

Burton, Antoinette, ed. 2005. *Archive stories: Facts, fictions, and the writing of history*. Durham, NC: Duke University Press.

Byrne, John V. 2006. Public higher educational reform five years after the Kellogg Commission on the Future of State and Land-Grant

Universities. N.p.: NASULGC and the W. K. Kellogg Foundation. http://www.aplu.org/NetCommunity/Document.Doc?id=180.

Christian Advocate. 1908. Report of the church and modern industry. December 24.

Cox, Richard J. 2002. *Vandals in the stacks? A response to Nicholson Baker's assault on libraries.* Contributions in Librarianship and Information Science, no. 98. Westport, CT: Greenwood Press.

Curtis, Susan. 1994. *Dancing to a Black man's tune: A life of Scott Joplin.* Columbia: University of Missouri Press.

Curtis, Susan. 2001. *A consuming faith: The Social Gospel and modern American culture.* 2nd ed. Columbia: University of Missouri Press, 2001.

Denning, Michael. 1996. *The cultural front: The laboring of American culture in the twentieth century.* London: Verso.

Derrida, Jacques. 1996. *Archive fever: A Freudian impression.* Translated by Eric Prenowitz. Chicago: University of Chicago Press.

Douglas, Ann. 1995. *Terrible honesty: Mongrel Manhattan in the 1920s.* New York: Farrar, Straus and Giroux.

Ellison, Julie, and Timothy K. Eatman. 2008. *Scholarship in public: Knowledge creation and tenure policy in the engaged university.* Syracuse, NY: Imagining America.

Foucault, Michel. 1972. *The archaeology of knowledge.* Translated by A. M. Sheridan Smith. New York: Pantheon.

Gerstle, Gary. 2001. *The American crucible: Race and nation in the twentieth century.* Princeton, NJ: Princeton University Press.

Goodwyn, Lawrence. 1976. *Democratic promise: The Populist moment in America.* New York: Oxford University Press.

Gorrell, Donald K. 1988. *The age of social responsibility.* Macon, GA: Mercer University Press.

Herron, George. 1893. *The new redemption.* New York: Thomas Y. Crowell.

Higham, John. 1970. The reorientation of American culture in the 1890s. In *Writing American history: Essays on modern scholarship.* Bloomington: Indiana University Press.

Hopkins, Charles H. 1943. *The rise of the Social Gospel in American Protestantism, 1865–1915.* Cambridge, MA: Harvard University Press.

Jones, Jeffrey Jacob. 2004. 'The world was our garden': U.S. plant introduction, empire, and industrial agriculture, 1898–1948. Ph.D.

diss., Purdue University.

Kellogg Commission on the Future of State and Land-Grant Universities. 2000. *Renewing the covenant: Learning, discovery, and Engagement in a new age and different world.* Washington, DC: National Association of State Universities and Land-Grant Colleges. http://www.aplu.org/NetCommunity/Document.Doc?id=186

Lacy, Creighton. 1967. *Frank Mason North: His social and ecumenical mission.* Nashville, TN: Abingdon.

Lears, T. J. Jackson. 1981. *No place of grace: Antimodernism and the transformation of American culture, 1880–1920.* New York: Pantheon.

Lears, T. J. Jackson. 1985. The concept of cultural hegemony: Problems and possibilities. *American Historical Review* 90:567–93.

Limerick, Patricia Nelson. 2008. Tales of Western adventure. *Chronicle of Higher Education*, May 9.

Mathews, Shailer. 1936. *New faith for old.* New York: Macmillan.

McGerr, Michael. 1986. *The decline of popular politics: The American North, 1865–1928.* New York: Oxford University Press.

Painter, Nell Irvin. 2009. *Standing at Armageddon: The United States, 1877–1919.* New York: W. W. Norton.

Peters, Scott J. 2007. *Reconstructing a democratic tradition of public scholarship in the land-grant system.* Dayton, OH: Kettering Foundation Press.

Phelps, Elizabeth Stuart. 1868. *The gates ajar.* Boston: Fields, Osgood.

Phelps, Elizabeth Stuart. 1894. *A singular life.* Boston: Houghton Mifflin.

Rauschenbusch, Walter. 1912. *Christianizing the social order.* New York: Macmillan.

Salvatore, Nick. 1982. *Eugene V. Debs: Citizen and socialist.* Urbana: University of Illinois Press.

Sanford, Elias. 1916. *The origin and history of the Federal Council of Churches.* Hartford, CT: Scranton.

Sheldon, Charles M. 1897. *In His steps.* Chicago: Advance.

Steedman, Carolyn. 2002. *Dust: The archive and cultural history.* New Brunswick, NJ: Rutgers University Press.

Strong, Josiah. 1893. *The new era.* New York: Baker & Taylor.

Thelen, David P. 1972. *The new citizenship: The origins of Progressivism in Wisconsin, 1885–1900.* Columbia: University of Missouri Press.

Thornton, Courtney H., and Audrey J. Jaeger. 2008. The role of culture in institutional and individual approaches to civic responsibility at research universities. *Journal of Higher Education* 79 (2): 160–82.

Trachtenberg, Alan. 1982. *The incorporation of America.* New York: Hill & Wang.

Washington Monthly. 2006. The *Washington Monthly*'s annual college guide. http://www.washingtonmonthly.com/features/2006/0609.collegeguide.html

Weinstein, James. 1968. *The corporate ideal in the liberal state.* Boston: Beacon Press.

5

From *Returning to Our Roots: The Engaged Institution* Executive Summary with "Seven-Part Test"

*Kellogg Commission on the Future of State and Land-Grant Universities**

Executive Summary

We write both to celebrate the contributions our institutions have made to our society and to call on ourselves to do more, and to do it better.

Ours is a rich heritage of service to the nation. More than a century and a quarter after Justin Morrill and Abraham Lincoln brought the concept into being, the land-grant ideal of public university service to community and nation has spread across the United States and its territories. Our public institutions have provided access to higher education at a level unparalleled in the world. They have created a prodigious research engine. They have brought the benefit of new knowledge to millions of people.

Why, then, the need for change? Who says we need to do more? And what exactly is it that we need to do better?

Nature of the Challenges

One challenge we face is growing public frustration with what is seen to be our unresponsiveness. At the root of the criticism is a perception that we are out of touch and out of date. Another part of the issue is that although society has problems, our institutions have "disciplines." In the end, what these complaints add up to is a perception that, despite the resources and expertise available on our campuses, our institutions are not well organized to bring them to bear on local problems in a coherent way.

Meanwhile, a number of other issues present themselves. They

---

* Originally published in February 1999 by the National Association of State Universities and Land-Grant Colleges (now the Association of Public and Land-Grant Universities); see pp. 9–13.

include enrollment pressures in many Western and Southwestern states; long-term financial constraints and demands for affordability and cost containment; a growing emphasis on accountability and productivity from trustees, legislators, and donors; and urgent requests from policymakers for solutions to national and international problems of all kinds.

Against that backdrop, this Commission concludes that it is time to go beyond outreach and service to what the Kellogg Commission defines as "engagement." By engagement, we refer to institutions that have redesigned their teaching, research, and extension and service functions to become even more sympathetically and productively involved with their communities, however community may be defined.

Engagement goes well beyond extension, conventional outreach, and even most conceptions of public service. Inherited concepts emphasize a one-way process in which the university transfers its expertise to key constituents. Embedded in the engagement ideal is a commitment to sharing and reciprocity. By engagement the Commission envisions partnerships, two-way streets defined by mutual respect among the partners for what each brings to the table. An institution that responds to these imperatives can properly be called what the Kellogg Commission has come to think of as an "engaged institution."

We believe an engaged university can enrich the student experience and help change the campus culture. It can do so by enlarging opportunities for faculty and students to gain access to research and new knowledge and by broadening access to internships and various kinds of off-campus learning opportunities. The engaged institution must accomplish at least three things:

1. It must be organized to respond to the needs of today's students and tomorrow's, not yesterday's.
2. It must enrich students' experiences by bringing research and engagement into the curriculum and offering practical opportunities for students to prepare for the world they will enter.
3. It must put its critical resources (knowledge and expertise) to work on the problems the communities it serves face.

Students. The data are clear. Part-time students are the fastest growing population in higher education, and most of them seek a degree; white males will be a smaller and smaller proportion of the U.S. workforce; our student body is gradually becoming older; most master's degree candidates attend part time; and enrollment in independent study programs is increasing.

Preparation for Life. The Commission believes one of the best ways to prepare students for the challenges life will place before them lies in integrating the community with their academic experiences. Students are one of the principal engagement resources available to every university. Service learning opportunities undoubtedly help everyone involved—student, community, and institution. Nor should we overlook the opportunities to improve students' exposure to research in this service endeavor. There should be little distinction between the benefits of students participating in research and in public service.

Putting Knowledge to Work. Finally, the application of knowledge is a unique contribution our institutions can make to contemporary society. Because we perform the lion's share of the basic research in this country, new knowledge is one distinctive thing we can provide.

Here, the list of potential areas for engagement is endless. Hardly any of our institutions could commit themselves to the entire array.

The panoply of problems and opportunities incorporated in the phrase *education and the economy* requires attention. The traditional mainstays of extension on our campuses, *agriculture and food,* need to be renewed. In the most important way imaginable, our universities need to return to their roots in *rural America* with new energy for today's new problems. Despite the nation's massive investment in *health care,* an enormous agenda remains before us. It need hardly be said that we need a new emphasis on *urban revitalization and community renewal* comparable in its own way to our rural development efforts in the last century. We need to pay new attention to the challenges facing *children, youth, and families* in the United States. Finally, we need to redouble our efforts to improve and conserve our *environment and natural resources.*

The changing nature of the engagement agenda, in terms of our students, their preparation, and emerging problems, presents us with a daunting challenge. We are under no illusions about the difficulty of the task we have set ourselves. In addition, the new questions before us involve not only important issues requiring the application of hard data and science, but challenging, and frequently fuzzy, problems involving human behavior and motivation, complex social systems, and personal values that are controversial simply because they are important. This engagement agenda will require the best efforts of us all—and the courage, conviction, and commitment to see it through.

Institutional Portraits

Because no established body of research could be tapped to explore questions such as those, the Commission encouraged its member institutions to develop exploratory portraits of their engagement activities. Eleven institutions provided portraits: Arizona State University; Iowa State University; The Ohio State University; The Pennsylvania State University; Portland State University; Rutgers, The State University of

New Jersey; Salish Kootenai College; Tuskegee University; the University of California, Davis; the University of Illinois at Chicago; and the University of Vermont.

From these portraits, we conclude that seven guiding characteristics seem to define an engaged institution (see pp. 108–9). These characteristics—responsiveness, respect for partners, academic neutrality, accessibility, integrating engagement into institutional mission, coordination, and resource adequacy—almost represent a seven-part test of engagement.

In addition, several common themes or lessons emerged:

- *A clear commitment to the basic idea of engagement.* Our portraits reveal a set of institutions determined to breathe new life into their historic mission by going beyond extension to engagement.
- *Strong support for infusing engagement into curriculum and teaching mission.* These examples also portray institutions wrestling with broader concepts of outreach and service and struggling to infuse engagement into the life of the institution and its curriculum.
- *Remarkable diversity in approaches and efforts.* In the end, designing engagement is a local activity. It cannot be handed down from on high. But viewed from the ground level of the institution and its partners, the scope and diversity of efforts are impressive.
- *The importance of defining "community."* Each of these 11 institutions is working with several different communities in many different ways. Community has many different definitions extending from the neighborhood in which the campus is located to the world.
- *Leadership is critical.* Leadership to create an engagement agenda is crucial. Engagement will not develop by itself, and it will not be led by the faint of heart.
- *Funding is always an issue.* Despite the existence of a remarkable variety of funding approaches, the lack of stable funding for engagement remains a critical problem.
- *Accountability needs to be lodged in the right place.* Of all the challenges facing the engagement effort, none is more difficult than ensuring accountability for the effort. Practically every one of the 11 portraits cites the need to examine faculty promotion and tenure guidelines closely to make sure they recognize and reward faculty contributions toward engagement.

Recommendations

The engaged institution—one that is responsive, respectful of its partners' needs, accessible and relatively neutral, while successfully integrating institutional service into research and teaching and finding sufficient resources for the effort—does not create itself. Bringing it into being requires leadership and focus.

We believe that five key strategies need to be put in place to advance engagement. We recommend that:

- our institutions transform their thinking about service so that engagement becomes a priority on every campus, a central part of institutional mission;
- each institution develop an engagement plan measured against the seven-part template incorporated into this document;
- institutions encourage interdisciplinary scholarship and research, including interdisciplinary teaching and learning opportunities;
- institutional leaders develop incentives to encourage faculty involvement in the engagement effort; and
- academic leaders secure stable funding to support engagement, through reallocation of existing funds or the establishment of a new Federal-state local-private matching fund.

Among the significant problems facing society today are challenges of creating genuine learning communities, encouraging lifelong learning, finding effective ways to overcome barriers to change, and building greater social and human capital in our communities.

Engagement in the form of service learning, outreach, and university community partnerships can help address these problems. And it can also put the university to work on the practical problems of the day. In this endeavor everyone benefits, and students stand to gain the most. Close partnerships with the surrounding community help demonstrate that higher education is about important values such as informed citizenship and a sense of responsibility. The newer forms of public scholarship and community-based learning help produce civic-minded graduates who are as well prepared to take up the complex problems of our society as they are to succeed in their careers.

All of this is a lot to ask. But it is hardly a more ambitious vision for the twenty-first century than Justin Morrill's nineteenth-century vision of the land-grant university. Today, we are called on to re-shape Morrill's conception anew. If we succeed, historians of the future will continue to celebrate our contributions because we insisted that we could do more—and we could do it better.

A Seven-Part Test

Seven guiding characteristics seem to define an engaged institution. They constitute almost a seven-part test of engagement.

1. *Responsiveness.* We need to ask ourselves periodically if we are listening to the communities, regions, and states we serve. Are we asking the right questions? Do we offer our services in the right way at the right time? Are our communications clear? Do we provide space and, if need be, resources for preliminary community-university discussions of the public problem to be addressed. Above all, do we really understand that in reaching out, we are also obtaining valuable information for our own purposes?

2. *Respect for partners.* Throughout this report we have tried to emphasize that the purpose of engagement is not to provide the university's superior expertise to the community but to encourage joint academic-community definitions of problems, solutions, and definitions of success. Here we need to ask ourselves if our institutions genuinely respect the skills and capacities of our partners in collaborative projects. In a sense we are asking that we recognize fully that we have almost as much to learn in these efforts as we have to offer.

3. *Academic neutrality.* Of necessity, some of our engagement activities will involve contentious issues—whether they draw on our science and technology, social science expertise, or strengths in the visual and performing arts. Do pesticides contribute to fish kills? If so, how? How does access to high quality public schools relate to economic development in minority communities? Is student "guerrilla theater" justified in local landlord tenant disputes. These questions often have profound social, economic, and political consequences. The question we need to ask ourselves here is whether outreach maintains the university in the role of neutral facilitator and source of information when public policy issues, particularly contentious ones, are at stake.

4. *Accessibility.* Our institutions are confusing to outsiders. We need to find ways to help inexperienced potential partners negotiate this complex structure so that what we have to offer is more readily available. Do we properly publicize our activities and resources? Have we made a concentrated effort to increase community awareness of the resources and programs available from us that might be useful? Above all, can we honestly say that our expertise is equally accessible to all the constituencies of concern within our states and communities, including minority constituents?

5. *Integration.* Our institutions need to find way to integrate their service mission with their responsibilities for developing intellectual capital and trained intelligence. Engagement offers new opportunities for integrating institutional scholarship with the service and teaching missions of the university. Here we need to worry about whether the institutional climate fosters outreach, service, and engagement. A commitment to interdisciplinary work is probably indispensable to an integrated approach. In particular we need to examine what kinds of incentives are useful in encouraging faculty and student commitment to engagement. Will respected faculty and student leaders not only participate but also serve as advocates for the program?

6. *Coordination.* A corollary to integration, the coordination issue involves making sure the left hand knows what the right hand is doing. The task of coordinating service activities—whether through a senior advisor to the president, faculty councils, or thematic structures such as the Great Cities Project or "capstone" courses—clearly requires a lot of attention. Are academic units dealing with each other productively? Do the communications and government relations offices understand the engagement agenda? Do faculty, staff, and students need help in developing the skills of translating expert knowledge into something the public can appreciate.

7. *Resource partnerships.* The final test asks whether the resources committed to the task are sufficient. Engagement is not free; it costs. The most obvious costs are those associated with the time and effort of staff, faculty, and students. But they also include curriculum and program costs, and possible limitations on institutional choices. All of these have to be considered. Where will these funds be found? In special state allocations? Corporate sponsorship and investment? Alliances and strategic partnerships of various kinds with government and industry? Or from new fee structures for services delivered? The most successful engagement efforts appear to be those associated with strong and healthy relationships with partners in government, business, and the non-profit world.

6

Publicly Engaged Scholarship and Academic Freedom: Rights and Responsibilities

Nicholas Behm and Duane Roen

In 1996, amid growing criticism from media and citizens within the United States that higher education had abdicated its obligations and responsibilities to serve public interests and had become insignificant within and unresponsive to social and public spheres, the National Association of State Universities and Land-Grant Colleges received funding from the W. K. Kellogg Foundation to create a commission that would respond to these concerns and reconsider the role of higher education. Faced with this redoubtable task, the Kellogg Commission issued six reports that exhorted public and land-grant institutions to rethink, redefine, and revise their relationships with and commitments to communities. In its 1999 publication, *Returning to Our Roots: The Engaged Institution,* the Kellogg Commission described a pervasive public distrust of higher education, as colleges and universities were perceived as elitist, unresponsive, and antiquated (9). Moreover, the Commission noted that, because academic institutions are often perceived as collections of individual disciplines that practice territorial politics rather than engaged, interdependent partners, there is a lack of public confidence in the ability of academic institutions to competently and productively confront significant social challenges (9).

Against this backdrop, a cadre of colleges and universities, attempting to countervail the negative perceptions of higher education, has renewed and reaffirmed the historical commitments of public and land-grant institutions to serve local communities and the nation. These institutions have taken advantage of their significant financial resources and research facilities, their knowledgeable faculty, and their energized student bodies to construct and conduct myriad innovative efforts to address and solve significant problems that are impacting communities. For example, between 2000 and 2007, Campus Compact, a national coalition of colleges and universities that actively support civically engaged efforts, reported that its membership increased from 689 institutions to 1,144; in 2007 alone, the collective service efforts of these institutions had an estimated value of $7.1 billion (Campus Compact 2008, 1). Ernest Boyer's (1996) hope that academic institutions might transform from insular, irrelevant institutions to vibrant communities deeply involved in civic engagement may be coming to fruition. Boyer's writing has done much to promote the premise that a wide range of academic work, including public engagement, is scholarly. As result, more institutions are valuing a wider range of work, as evidenced by promotion and tenure documents that explicitly extol the virtues and mutual benefits of broadly defined scholarship.

Although literally hundreds of academic institutions are embracing the movement towards civic engagement and encouraging faculty and students to conduct publicly engaged scholarship, there may not be a concomitant movement to value and reward this scholarship. Inherently collaborative and not always amenable to traditional modes of academic production, publicly engaged scholarship is often incommensurate with what Boyer (1990, 1996) observed were the traditional paradigms of scholarship and priorities of the professoriate. Furthermore, some institutions, fearing the possibility of litigation, complaints from stakeholders, or unflattering press, may be reluctant to promote and reward publicly engaged scholarship because of its potential to incite controversy.

Publicly engaged scholarship can take a wide range of forms. For example, Duane Roen has worked with colleagues to develop a degree program that includes a track in writing about family history—the Project for Writing and Recording Family History. In concert with this program, Roen has worked with colleagues to establish a community outreach project in family history at Arizona State University. Among other things, the project offers public workshops in which community members write and share narratives about family. Postsecondary schools such as Arizona State University have developed diverse programs that advance the institution's mission and simultaneously serve the needs of the community. To ensure appropriate credit for their work and to minimize the possibility of conducting scholarship that makes their institutions and stakeholders vulnerable to negative consequences, scholars should consult several documents produced by the American Association of University Professors (AAUP), including the "1940 Statement of Principles on Academic Freedom and Tenure with 1970 Interpretive Comments," "Statement on Professional Ethics," and "Statement on Graduate Students." These documents emphasize that, although scholars are entitled to academic freedom, such freedom is concomitant with special duties and obligations that scholars must perform and recognize when pursuing publicly engaged scholarship.

In the remainder of this chapter, we discuss the AAUP documents and their importance, outline why the AAUP documents are imperative reading for any scholar conducting publicly engaged scholarship, and discuss how and why the AAUP documents should be required reading for graduate students.

A Brief History of the AAUP

The American Association of University Professors has a storied history. The association began in response to the dramatic changes in the American academic setting that occurred between 1883 and 1913. In those three decades, American higher education changed and expanded on many levels:

- there was a dramatic increase in the student body;
- the financial situation of many colleges and universities dramatically improved;
- the number and size of academic units increased;
- curriculum became more diversified;
- a cadre of new faculty was hired at colleges and universities across the nation;
- appointment and promotion for faculty became dependent upon publication, rather than teaching and service (Metzger 1965, 229–31).

These dramatic changes necessitated a professional organization that would lobby for the interests of faculty and ensure academic freedom. Furthermore, the AAUP was also formed in response to the high-profile dismissal of Edward Ross, a proponent of liberal economic theories, from Stanford University in 1901. Ross was fired amid suspicious circumstances, as his liberal economic views conflicted with those of a wealthy patron who may have exploited her economic and political leverage to have Ross dismissed.

A group of eight professors at Stanford, including Arthur O. Lovejoy, resigned to protest the firing of Ross. In 1913, recognizing the importance of establishing an ecumenical organization to advocate for the institutional and societal needs of academics, Lovejoy convinced 17 colleagues at Johns Hopkins University to distribute a letter to professors of equal rank at nine other leading universities, calling for the establishment of a national association of professors. The possibility of a national association was subsequently discussed in 1913 and 1914 at the respective annual meetings of the American Economic Association, the American Political Science Association, and the American Sociological Society.

In April of 1914, an organizing committee consisting of seven prominent academics, including John Dewey, met and motioned for the first annual meeting of a national association of professors. With 650 founding members of prominent academic rank, the AAUP first convened in 1915 for the purpose of advocating and safeguarding the various interests of professors. During the convention, President John Dewey established the 15-member Committee of Academic Freedom and Tenure (Committee A). Charged with drafting a document that articulated agreed-upon principles of academic freedom and procedures for ensuring it, the committee wrote the AAUP's first policy document on academic freedom and tenure: the "1915 Declaration of Principles on Academic Freedom and Academic Tenure." In its first year of existence, Committee A investigated several alleged violations of academic freedom, including cases at the University of Utah, the University of Pennsylvania, and Wesleyan University.

In the AAUP's 94-year existence, the organization's many policy statements and procedural guidelines have functioned prominently in institutions of higher education and in the professional lives of faculty, especially when due process rights have been infringed or when academic freedom has been contravened. The authority of the documents lies in their wide acceptance as authoritative by a multitude of institutions and academics within and across Carnegie classifications. Furthermore, the authority of the AAUP lies in its influence as an advocacy group in and around Capitol Hill and state legislatures: the AAUP tracks legislation, builds relationships with stakeholders and policymakers, and lobbies Congress and state legislatures when legislation concerning higher education is under consideration. The AAUP also files amicus briefs in legal cases that concern the infringement of academic freedom and tenure; the occurrence of sexual, gender, or racial discrimination; and other issues of import that reach state and federal appellate and supreme courts. Because of the AAUP's prominence and the general acceptance of its policies and statements, the organization's documents and guidelines are powerful resources to consult when planning and conducting publicly engaged scholarship, and when articulating how publicly engaged scholarship is academically rigorous and inherently responsive to the goals of an academic institution and the needs of a community.

Publicly Engaged Scholarship and the AAUP Documents

Since Boyer argued for the validation of the scholarship of engagement in 1996, academic institutions and academics have responded by designing innovative courses and programs, and by conducting intensive, cutting-edge scholarship that engages civic life in critical ways and that bridges the gaps between the academic, the social, and the political spheres. Many innovative programs within institutions are no longer "isolated islands" but, as Boyer hoped institutions of higher education would become, "staging grounds for action" (Boyer 1996, 32). Indeed, academic institutions across the nation have placed an emphasis on applying and making connections between what is learned and discussed in the classroom and what occurs outside the classroom in the public sphere on a local and national scale. For example, Arizona State University has long advocated for such connections, as evidenced by its ASU Community Connect initiative, whose website (http://community.asu.edu) lists hundreds of civic engagement projects. ASU Community Connect builds partnerships between students, the university, and various communities across Arizona to effect positive change. Other academic institutions have placed a high priority on publicly engaged scholarship as well, including the University of North Carolina at Chapel Hill and the University of California, Los Angeles. In 1999, the University of North Carolina at Chapel Hill established the Carolina Center for Public Service, an organization that promotes civic responsibility, engaged scholarship, and service that is responsive to the needs of communities across the state. To realize these goals, the center developed the Public Service Scholars program, in which undergraduate students participate in service-learning projects and nurture relationships between stakeholders situated within North Carolina. Similarly, UCLA has established the Center for Community Partnerships, which in 2002 launched its UCLA in LA initiative, co-ordinating collaborations between university and community partners in and around Los Angeles. Such collaborations have positively impacted the lives of many. For example, students in the UCLA School of Law's Critical Race Studies Program and the community organization A New Way of Life have worked to eliminate discrimination against those formerly incarcerated and to reduce the rate of recidivism in Los Angeles County (Benioff 2008).

At Arizona State University, graduate students become involved in publicly engaged scholarship. For example, in the previously mentioned Project for Writing and Recording Family History, graduate students conduct writing workshops for community members. An exemplar of community engagement is Xanthia Walker, who, as an M.F.A. student at Arizona State University, has helped young incarcerated women come to terms with socialization and body-image issues by staging a theatrical production featuring their writing (ASU 2010). Such engagement is not easily quantified, nor is its positive impact easily articulated in a traditional research-support article.

Part of the problem is that institutions of higher education have struggled to define and evaluate publicly engaged scholarship. Amy

Driscoll, a consultant for the Carnegie Foundation for the Advancement of Teaching, noted that many institutions, when applying for the foundation's voluntary classifications of levels of engagement, had trouble moving past "vague generalities" in articulating the success of their community and curricular engagement and the level of reciprocity between and among stakeholders (2008, 41). To obtain the community engagement classification, colleges and universities must provide documentation to fulfill Carnegie's two-part framework: Foundational Indicators and Categories of Engagement (2008, 39). For example, in fulfilling the Foundational Indicators section, institutions are encouraged to articulate how community engagement is embedded in their respective institutional missions and goals and to show how they provide resources to support such engagement. For the Categories of Engagement section, institutions should document examples of how faculty and students are already immersed in community engagement. Driscoll suggests that the inability of institutions to clearly describe and adequately assess engagement during this process may be the result of lingering perceptions of institutions of higher education as the "ivory tower," and points to a "need for new understanding, new skills, and even a different way of conceptualizing community" (41).

To negotiate these many significant challenges, scholars need to frame publicly engaged scholarship in terms that correlate with and emphasize the special duties and responsibilities outlined in the "1940 Statement of Principles on Academic Freedom and Tenure with 1970 Interpretive Comments" and the "Statement on Professional Ethics." These documents are fundamentally aligned with publicly engaged scholarship because they emphasize that land-grant and other public colleges and universities should be primarily concerned with serving the common good of local and national communities whose tax dollars are invested in such institutions. For example, at Arizona State University, Sonia Vega Lopez, assistant professor of nutrition, has the long-term research goal of designing interventions that help to prevent chronic diseases among Latino/a community members. Further, she involves graduate students in her research so that they too can work to enhance public health.

Additionally, the AAUP documents stress the importance of scholars' recognizing that their interests and endeavors outside of the academy should not supersede their myriad responsibilities within their respective institutions. The AAUP's "Statement on Professional Ethics" focuses more heavily on faculty members' responsibilities than some of the other documents do, urging professors to seriously consider their institutional responsibilities prior to engaging in work outside of their academic communities. Although professors possess the same "rights and obligations" as other citizens, they need to "measure the urgency of these obligations in the light of their responsibilities to their subject, to their students, to their profession, and to their institution" (AAUP 2006, 172). Publicly engaged scholarship thus emerges as both a right and an obligation of faculty members.

Of course, balancing institutional responsibilities with external interests and endeavors can cause tensions if institutional responsibilities are construed as focusing exclusively on teaching the institution's matriculated students, offering service to the institution's academic units, and conducting funded research. However, these tensions are eased when institutions encourage faculty to pursue publicly engaged scholarship. For state-funded institutions, publicly engaged scholarship should be commonplace because taxpayers and publicly elected policymakers rightfully expect diverse returns on their investments in higher education. The "1940 Statement of Principles on Academic Freedom and Tenure with 1970 Interpretive Comments" helps to clarify the public and social roles of postsecondary schools: "Institutions of higher education are conducted for the common good and not to further the interest of either the individual teacher or the institution as a whole" (AAUP 2006, 3).

Although these documents emphasize that professors are entitled to academic freedom in their scholarly and pedagogical endeavors in service to the common good, the "1940 Statement" notes that academic freedom carries with it concomitant duties and responsibilities. For example, it advises professors to judiciously broach controversial subjects in the classroom (AAUP 2006, 3). Rather, controversial subjects should be introduced only as related to the course material and the professors' scholarly expertise, and as pertinent to students' lives. Commenting on this element of the "1940 Statement," the "1970 Interpretive Comments" clarify that, although the original document seeks not to restrict or discourage productive discussion of controversial subjects, it "underscore[s] the need for teachers to avoid persistently intruding material which has no relation to their subject" (5).

The "1940 Statement" additionally counsels professors that their positions within a community as "members of a learned profession" and as "officers of an educational institution" require that they act with propriety and probity: Professors' "special position in a community," the "1940 Statement" relates, "imposes special obligations" (3). Among these is a recognition that, although professors are citizens and ought to avail themselves of the right to speak and write as citizens, they "should remember that the public may judge their profession and their institution by their utterances" (3). The "1940 Statement" acknowledges that, even when speaking or writing outside of the academy, professors cannot totally dissociate themselves from their roles as officers of an institution of higher education and as members of an academic community. To efficaciously negotiate the demands of these roles in their extramural pronouncements, the "1940 Statement" asserts that professors "should at all times be accurate, should exercise appropriate restraint, should show respect for the opinions of others, and should make every effort to indicate that they are not speaking for the institution" (4).

The "Statement on Professional Ethics" also notes that professors have special obligations when speaking and writing as citizens. Articulating similar admonitions as the "1940 Statement," the "Statement on Professional Ethics" advises professors to act judiciously when weighing their obligations as citizens and as professionals. The "Statement on Professional Ethics" specifically exhorts professors to refrain from implying that they represent the views and opinions of their respective institutions when speaking or writing as private persons (AAUP 2006, 172). A particularly interesting aspect of this document is its interest in promoting "public understanding of academic freedom" (172). With this recommendation, the document implies that professors' extramural utterances should not denigrate the profession or institution or call into question the validity of tenure and academic freedom. This is a particularly important caution given that publicly engaged scholarship often critically examines and vehemently decries health disparities, environmental and social injustices, poverty, homelessness, racial and sexual discrimination, and other significant social challenges facing communities and the nation. If not judicious with their extramural utterances and activities, professors may be dismissed as meddling intellectuals who have too little to do because of the security of tenure. On occasion, political pundits, social commentators, or political organizations may traduce tenure and the academy by decontextualizing and subsequently amplifying a professor's political and public activities and utterances, possibly compromising the professor's ability to effectively assume her various roles and responsibilities. One well known example of such traducement is Charles J. Sykes's *ProfScam: Professors and the Demise of Higher Education* (1988). Sykes indicts professors and institutions for abdicating their responsibilities to students and the general public, making such claims as "tenure is also the ultimate protection from accountability" and "tenure corrupts, enervates, and dulls higher education" (137, 258).

While affirming the special duties and obligations that are expressed in the "1940 Statement," the "Statement of Professional Ethics" offers several additional admonitions, corresponding to the roles that academic faculty assume. According to the "Statement of

Professional Ethics," professors' primary responsibilities, in terms of their scholarly expertise and discipline, are "to seek and to state the truth as they see it." Professors must apply "critical self-discipline" when developing scholarly competence, transmitting knowledge, and exercising intellectual honesty. In their roles as educators, professors bear the significant responsibilities of exemplifying "the best scholarly and ethical standards of their discipline," of acting as "intellectual guides and counselors" who encourage students along the path of free inquiry, of cultivating "honest academic conduct," and of protecting students' academic freedom (AAUP 2006, 171).

In their roles as colleagues, professors are to encourage "respect and defend the free inquiry of associates." Professors are obligated to demonstrate "respect for the opinions of others" while exchanging ideas and communicating criticism; to acknowledge "academic debt"; to refrain from malicious judgment of colleagues; and to assume responsibility for the shared "governance of their institution" (171). Moreover, as members of an institution of higher education, professors should be keenly aware of their role(s) within programs and institutions, and carefully consider and respect "their paramount responsibilities within their institution in determining the amount and character of work done outside it" (172).

However, in their current iterations, the AAUP documents seem to maintain distinctions between the myriad roles that faculty members assume. Contemporary publicly engaged scholarship, on the other hand, blurs traditionally delineated roles because it is not only interdisciplinary but "integrated across teaching, research, and service" (Sandmann 2006, 81). Or as framed by Barker, publicly engaged scholarship "consists of (1) research, teaching, integration and application types of scholarship that (2) incorporate reciprocal practices of civic engagement into the production of knowledge" (2004, 124). The publicly engaged scholar, then, could assume several or all roles—teacher, researcher, officer of an institution, member of a learned profession, citizen—simultaneously with no clear demarcation of where and when these roles end.

In other words, with publicly engaged scholarship the preservation of the private/public binary may be untenable, and extramural utterances and activities may be indistinguishable from intramural. When applying these documents to articulate, advocate, and develop publicly engaged scholarship, scholars need to strategically select elements of the documents to emphasize not only how their work satisfies the duties and responsibilities of the professoriate, but also how the scholarship realizes and affirms the institution's social commitments. As Sandmann has observed, publicly engaged scholarship is inherently messy (2006, 83). By framing publicly engaged scholarship in terms of the duties and responsibilities outlined in the AAUP documents, scholars can rely on the authoritative language of the documents to not only make sense of the inherent heterogeneity and messiness of the scholarship, but also to communicate its importance to potentially resistant academic and public audiences.

To more persuasively articulate how publicly engaged scholarship accomplishes all of this, scholars may additionally employ Boyer's five categories of scholarship. Boyer, in his groundbreaking work *Scholarship Reconsidered* (1990), challenged all stakeholders of academic institutions to revise traditional conceptions and paradigms of scholarship and academic work. He outlined four generative, interrelated, and recursive dimensions of scholarship and academic work: *the scholarship of discovery*, which emphasizes the processes of investigating, discovering, and constructing new knowledge; *the scholarship of integration*, which frames knowledge and scholarship within a larger and broader context by highlighting their interdisciplinarity; *the scholarship of application*, which focuses both on the ways in which knowledge can be employed to address prominent social issues and on how the process of application tests, revises, and constructs theory and knowledge; and the *scholarship of teaching*, which discusses the propagation, communication, and transformation of knowledge.

Realizing the importance of bridging academic and public lives and of utilizing the connections to construct new knowledge, Boyer later argued convincingly for the addition of the *scholarship of engagement*, which connects "the rich resources of the university to our most pressing social, civic, and ethical problems, to our children, to our schools, to our teachers, and to our cities" (1996, 32). The careful consideration of the AAUP documents and Boyer's conceptualization of scholarship will help faculty persuasively articulate how publicly engaged scholarship constitutes appropriate professional activity for the professoriate while furthering the social and civic functions of institutions of higher education.

AAUP Documents and Graduate Education

In *The Last Intellectuals: American Culture in the Age of Academe* (1987), Russell Jacoby noted that scholars have had a diminishing impact on the social sphere because they write in a specialized language accessible only to those familiar with the disciplinary discourse; structure their academic work in conformity with a system of rewards that discourages collaboration and interdisciplinarity; and dissociate themselves from political and social issues. Jacoby's stark observation prompted Boyer to challenge institutions of higher education to positively contribute to "intellectual and civic progress" in the United States, urging academic institutions to become a "more vigorous partner in the search for answers to our most pressing social, civic, economic, and moral problems" (Boyer 1996, 18).

However, many graduate programs may still reflect and subscribe to traditional conceptualizations of the academy, instructing graduate students to apprehend and reproduce valorized disciplinary discourses and paradigms and to conceptualize knowledge as individually created rather than collaboratively constructed, as disciplinary rather than interdisciplinary. Indeed, the narrow focus and hyper-specialization of graduate education too often leaves graduate students unprepared for the rigors and realities of the academy, as O'Meara and Jaeger have observed, while at the same time "the individualistic nature of graduate education is antithetical to the collaborative nature of engagement, although only the latter can address many societal changes" (2007, 12–13).

To become more vigorous partners in solving significant social challenges and to countervail the social and civic irrelevancy and intellectual paucity that Boyer and Jacoby depict, academics and the academy have to revise traditional notions of scholarship and what constitutes "legitimate" knowledge. This process, as Sandmann has written, ought to begin in graduate school with professional development programs and curricula that cultivate

- the recognition that one of the primary roles of institutions of higher education is to develop reciprocal relationships with communities, to the mutual benefit of all parties;
- the vision of "scholarship as the defining structure when beginning a collaborative project with the community";
- the ability to employ and frame scholarship in ways that emphasize interdisciplinarity;
- the development of the skills necessary for the co-construction of knowledge within a community, including "partnership, collaboration, and facilitation, as well as being a good listener, adaptab[ility], and patien[ce]" (2006, 83).

Investing in and committing to the development of these traits and skills in graduate programs today will have far-reaching benefits in the future, bringing "community engagement to the center of scholarly agendas, disciplines, departments, and institutions tomorrow" (O'Meara and Jaeger 2007, 21).

As part of their preparation for meaningful and scholarly social and civic engagement, graduate students should be provided the opportunity to peruse and discuss the AAUP documents. The documents possess gravitas because they are widely considered authoritative within and across academic communities, and offer graduate students a language with which they can persuasively advance publicly engaged scholarship to stakeholders, allowing graduate students to make evident how their publicly engaged activities affirm both institutional and social commitments and responsibilities. These documents help graduate students bridge the gap between academic and institutional cultures that lionize traditional notions of scholarship and knowledge and the complicated and interdependent elements of publicly engaged scholarship.

Becoming familiar with the AAUP documents, as well as with the American Association of University Professors, is important for several additional reasons. For instance, the AAUP can serve as a vigorous advocate for graduate students, promoting and defending their rights to academic freedom and fair treatment. Moreover, the documents produced by the AAUP, including the "Statement on Graduate Education," "Joint Statement on Rights and Freedoms of Students," and "Recommended Institutional Regulations on Academic Freedom and Tenure," can be employed to advance and defend the interests of graduate students. For example, the "Recommended Institutional Regulations on Academic Freedom and Tenure" stipulates, in Regulation 13, that graduate assistants must be afforded due process rights, including the opportunity to present a case and seek redress from a faculty grievance committee (AAUP 2006, 29). The "Statement on Graduate Students" also emphasizes that graduate assistants ought to have "access to a duly constituted hearing committee" to challenge a proposed dismissal and to present a grievance (AAUP 2006, 281).

Additionally, the "Statement on Graduate Students" puts forth nine other important considerations, including the following:

- Graduate students should be encouraged to openly express their opinions on course readings and topics.
- They are "entitled to the protection of their intellectual-property rights, including recognition of their participation in supervised research and their research with faculty."
- Graduate assistants ought to be provided with adequate training and supervision, as well as sufficient compensation and fringe benefits.
- Graduate students "should have the same freedom of action in the public political domain as faculty members" without being subjected to reprisals from the institution or department. (280–81)

Graduate students should also familiarize themselves with the

AAUP documents to apprehend the various roles and expectations associated with membership in a learned community. The "Statement on Professional Ethics" and the "1940 Statement of Principles on Academic Freedom and Tenure with 1970 Interpretive Comments," in particular, articulate the special duties, responsibilities, and expectations that are concomitant with membership in an academic community and discipline. Indeed, describing how professors ought to act as citizens, teachers, scholars, and officers of an institution, the AAUP documents and policy statements may be regarded as blueprints that outline how to professionally assume these various roles and fulfill the myriad responsibilities attached to them. For example, the "Statement on Professional Ethics" encourages professors to "practice intellectual honesty," to develop and improve "their scholarly competence," and to propagate the knowledge they have generated. As teachers, professors are enjoined to protect students' right to academic freedom, to urge students to vigorously dialogue about course readings and topics, to "foster academic conduct," and to "ensure that their evaluations of students reflect each student's true merit." The "Statement on Professional Ethics" further urges professors, in their collegial role, to "respect and defend the free inquiry of associates" and to exchange views on colleagues' ideas and scholarship in a mature, respectful manner. As officers of an academic institution, professors are exhorted to accept responsibility for shared governance and to abstain from acting in ways that may impede the assumption of the roles concomitant with their positions within the academy. As we have already seen, professors as citizens are asked to "promote conditions of free inquiry and to further public understanding of academic freedom" (AAUP 2006, 171–72).

Endorsed by a cadre of academic associations, councils, and societies, the "1940 Statement of Principles on Academic Freedom and Tenure with 1970 Interpretive Comments" similarly underscores the duties and responsibilities associated with the various roles professors assume, and explains the nature of academic freedom and the practices that ensure its propagation.

Reading and discussing the "Statement on Professional Ethics" and other AAUP documents in graduate school can be an effective professional development activity, particularly as one element of a comprehensive professional development program, such as Preparing Future Faculty, designed to prepare graduate students to successfully negotiate the rigors of the academy and the professoriate. To help graduate students meet the challenges of faculty life, universities need to do more than require that they complete coursework, comprehensive examinations, and dissertations. Universities also have a responsibility to help graduate students learn about a wide range of professional matters *before* entering the professoriate. Introducing graduate students to publicly engaged scholarship and its attendant issues is one effective way to do that.

Through initiatives that prepare graduate students for publicly engaged scholarship, that reward professors for conducting such scholarship, and that communicate the importance of publicly engaged scholarship to communities, academic stakeholders need to continue the invaluable work of galvanizing support for publicly engaged projects and scholarship. Such work can move institutions to what the American Association of State Colleges and Universities has defined as publicly engaged institutions. Such institutions are "fully committed to direct, two-way interaction with communities and other external constituencies through the development, exchange, and application of knowledge, information and expertise for mutual benefit" (2002, 7). The various AAUP documents can help advocates of publicly engaged scholarship articulate how such work fulfills the responsibilities of the professoriate and affirms the imperative that higher education serve "a larger purpose, a larger sense of mission, a larger clarity of direction in the nation's life" (Boyer 1996, 33). While such work benefits the community, it can also strengthen public trust in and support for higher education.

References

American Association of State Colleges and Universities. 2002. *Stepping forward as stewards of place.* Washington, DC: American Association of State Colleges and Universities.

American Association of University Professors [AAUP]. 1989. 75 Years: A retrospective on the occasion of the seventy-fifth annual meeting. *Academe* 75 (3): 1–33.

American Association of University Professors [AAUP]. 2006. *AAUP policy documents and reports.* 10th ed. Washington, DC: AAUP.

Arizona State University (ASU). 2010. Student artist reaches out to serve the community. *ASU News,* May 11. http://asunews.asu.edu/20100505_Walker.

Barge, J. K., J. E. Jones, M. Kensler, N. Polok, R. Rianoshek, J. L. Simpson, and P. Shockley-Zalabak. 2008. A practitioner view toward engaged scholarship. *Journal of Applied Communication Research* 36:245–50.

Barge, J. K., J. K. Simpson, and P. Schockley-Zalabak. 2008. Introduction: Towards purposeful and practical models of engaged scholarship. *Journal of Applied Communication Research* 36:243–44.

Barker, D. 2004. The scholarship of engagement: A taxonomy of five emerging practices. *Journal of Higher Education Outreach and Engagement* 9:123–37.

Benioff, R. 2008. Profiles of engagement: Tackling employment discrimination against former prisoners. University of California, Los Angeles Center for Community Partnerships. http://la.ucla.edu/profiles/new-way-of-life.shtml.

Boyer, E. 1990. *Scholarship reconsidered: Priorities of the professoriate.* Princeton, NJ: Carnegie Foundation for the Advancement of Teaching.

Boyer, E. 1996. The scholarship of engagement. *Bulletin of the American Academy of Arts and Sciences* 49 (7): 18–33.

Campus Compact. 2008. *2007 service statistics: Highlights and trends of Campus Compact's annual membership survey.* Providence, RI: Campus Compact.

Driscoll, A. 2008. Carnegie's community-engagement classification: Intentions and insights. *Change*, January–February, 38–41. http://www.carnegiefoundation.org/files/elibrary/Driscoll.pdf.

Jacoby, R. 1987. *The last intellectuals: American culture in the age of academe.* New York: Basic Books.

Kellogg Commission on the Future of State and Land-Grant Universities. 1999. *Returning to our roots: The engaged institution.* Washington, DC: National Association of State Universities and Land-Grant Colleges. https://www.aplu.org/NetCommunity/Document.Doc?id=183

Metzger, W. 1961. The first investigation. *Academe* 47 (3): 206–10.

Metzger, W. 1965. Origins of the association: An anniversary address. *Academe* 51 (3): 229–37.

O'Meara, K., and A. J. Jaeger. 2007. Preparing future faculty for community engagement: Barriers, facilitators, models, and recommendations. *Journal of Higher Education Outreach and Engagement* 11:3–26.

Pollitt, D. H., and J. E. Kurland. 1998. Entering the academic freedom arena running: The AAUP's first year. *Academe* 84 (4): 45–52.

Reynolds, P. 2006. Commentary and introduction: Service learning and community-engaged scholarship. *Journal of Physical Therapy Education* 20 (3): 3–7.

Sandmann, L. R. 2006. Scholarship as architecture: Framing and enhancing community engagement. *Journal of Physical Therapy Education* 20 (3): 80–84.

Simpson, J. L., and D. R. Seibold. 2008. Practical engagements and co-created research. *Journal of Applied Communication Research* 36:266–80.

Sykes, C. J. 1988. *ProfScam: Professors and the demise of higher education*. New York: St. Martin's Press.

INTERCHAPTER

Statements of the American Association of University Professors*

1940 STATEMENT OF PRINCIPLES ON ACADEMIC FREEDOM AND TENURE WITH 1970 INTERPRETIVE COMMENTS

In 1940, following a series of joint conferences begun in 1934, representatives of the American Association of University Professors and of the Association of American Colleges (now the Association of American Colleges and Universities) agreed upon a restatement of principles set forth in the 1925 Conference Statement on Academic Freedom and Tenure. *This restatement is known to the profession as the 1940* Statement of Principles on Academic Freedom and Tenure.

The 1940 Statement *is printed below, followed by Interpretive Comments as developed by representatives of the American Association of University Professors and the Association of American Colleges in 1969. The governing bodies of the two associations, meeting respectively in November 1989 and January 1990, adopted several changes in language in order to remove gender-specific references from the original text.*

The purpose of this statement is to promote public understanding and support of academic freedom and tenure and agreement upon procedures to ensure them in colleges and universities. Institutions of higher education are conducted for the common good and not to further the interest of either the individual teacher or the institution as a whole.[1] The common good depends upon the free search for truth and its free exposition.

Academic freedom is essential to these purposes and applies to both teaching and research. Freedom in research is fundamental to the advancement of truth. Academic freedom in its teaching aspect is fundamental for the protection of the rights of the teacher in teaching and

* Published in *AAUP Policy Documents and Reports*, 10th ed. (Washington, DC: AAUP, 2006), 3-7, 171-72, 280-82; available at http://www.aaup.org/AAUP/pubsres/policydocs/contents/

of the student to freedom in learning. It carries with it duties correlative with rights.**[1]**[2]

Tenure is a means to certain ends; specifically: (1) freedom of teaching and research and of extramural activities, and (2) a sufficient degree of economic security to make the profession attractive to men and women of ability. Freedom and economic security, hence, tenure, are indispensable to the success of an institution in fulfilling its obligations to its students and to society.

Academic Freedom

1. Teachers are entitled to full freedom in research and in the publication of the results, subject to the adequate performance of their other academic duties; but research for pecuniary return should be based upon an understanding with the authorities of the institution.
2. Teachers are entitled to freedom in the classroom in discussing their subject, but they should be careful not to introduce into their teaching controversial matter which has no relation to their subject.**[2]** Limitations of academic freedom because of religious or other aims of the institution should be clearly stated in writing at the time of the appointment.**[3]**
3. College and university teachers are citizens, members of a learned profession, and officers of an educational institution. When they speak or write as citizens, they should be free from institutional censorship or discipline, but their special position in the community imposes special obligations. As scholars and educational officers, they should remember that the public may judge their profession and their institution by their utterances. Hence they should at all times be accurate, should exercise appropriate restraint, should show respect for the opinions of others, and should make every effort to indicate that they are not speaking for the institution.**[4]**

Academic Tenure

After the expiration of a probationary period, teachers or investigators should have permanent or continuous tenure, and their service should be terminated only for adequate cause, except in the case of retirement for age, or under extraordinary circumstances because of financial exigencies.

In the interpretation of this principle it is understood that the following represents acceptable academic practice:

1. The precise terms and conditions of every appointment should be stated in writing and be in the possession of both institution and

teacher before the appointment is consummated.

2. Beginning with appointment to the rank of full-time instructor or a higher rank,[5] the probationary period should not exceed seven years, including within this period full-time service in all institutions of higher education; but subject to the proviso that when, after a term of probationary service of more than three years in one or more institutions, a teacher is called to another institution, it may be agreed in writing that the new appointment is for a probationary period of not more than four years, even though thereby the person's total probationary period in the academic profession is extended beyond the normal maximum of seven years.[6] Notice should be given at least one year prior to the expiration of the probationary period if the teacher is not to be continued in service after the expiration of that period.[7]
3. During the probationary period a teacher should have the academic freedom that all other members of the faculty have.[8]
4. Termination for cause of a continuous appointment, or the dismissal for cause of a teacher previous to the expiration of a term appointment, should, if possible, be considered by both a faculty committee and the governing board of the institution. In all cases where the facts are in dispute, the accused teacher should be informed before the hearing in writing of the charges and should have the opportunity to be heard in his or her own defense by all bodies that pass judgment upon the case. The teacher should be permitted to be accompanied by an advisor of his or her own choosing who may act as counsel. There should be a full stenographic record of the hearing available to the parties concerned. In the hearing of charges of incompetence the testimony should include that of teachers and other scholars, either from the teacher's own or from other institutions. Teachers on continuous appointment who are dismissed for reasons not involving moral turpitude should receive their salaries for at least a year from the date of notification of dismissal whether or not they are continued in their duties at the institution.[9]
5. Termination of a continuous appointment because of financial exigency should be demonstrably bona fide.

1940 Interpretations

At the conference of representatives of the American Association of University Professors and of the Association of American Colleges on November 7–8, 1940, the following interpretations of the 1940 *Statement of Principles on Academic Freedom and Tenure* were agreed upon:

1. That its operation should not be retroactive.
2. That all tenure claims of teachers appointed prior to the endorsement should be determined in accordance with the principles set forth in the 1925 *Conference Statement on Academic Freedom and Tenure.*
3. If the administration of a college or university feels that a teacher has not observed the admonitions of paragraph 3 of the section on Academic Freedom and believes that the extramural utterances of the teacher have been such as to raise grave doubts concerning the teacher's fitness for his or her position, it may proceed to file charges under paragraph 4 of the section on Academic Tenure. In pressing such charges, the administration should remember that teachers are citizens and should be accorded the freedom of citizens. In such cases the administration must assume full responsibility, and the American Association of University Professors and the Association of American Colleges are free to make an investigation.

1970 Interpretive Comments

> *Following extensive discussions on the 1940* Statement of Principles on Academic Freedom and Tenure *with leading educational associations and with individual faculty members and administrators, a joint committee of the AAUP and the Association of American Colleges met during 1969 to reevaluate this key policy statement. On the basis of the comments received, and the discussions that ensued, the joint committee felt the preferable approach was to formulate interpretations of the* Statement *in terms of the experience gained in implementing and applying the* Statement *for over thirty years and of adapting it to current needs.*
>
> *The committee submitted to the two associations for their consideration the following "Interpretive Comments." These interpretations were adopted by the Council of the American Association of University Professors in April 1970 and endorsed by the Fifty-sixth Annual Meeting as Association policy.*

In the thirty years since their promulgation, the principles of the 1940 *Statement of Principle on Academic Freedom and Tenure* have undergone a substantial amount of refinement. This has evolved through a variety of processes, including customary acceptance, understandings mutually arrived at between institutions and professors or their representatives, investigations and reports by the American Association of University Professors, and formulations of statements by that association either alone or in conjunction with the Association of

American Colleges. These comments represent the attempt of the two associations, as the original sponsors of the 1940 *Statement,* to formulate the most important of these refinements. Their incorporation here as Interpretive Comments is based upon the premise that the 1940 *Statement* is not a static code but a fundamental document designed to set a framework of norms to guide adaptations to changing times and circumstances.

Also, there have been relevant developments in the law itself reflecting a growing insistence by the courts on due process within the academic community which parallels the essential concepts of the 1940 *Statement;* particularly relevant is the identification by the Supreme Court of academic freedom as a right protected by the First Amendment. As the Supreme Court said in *Keyishian v. Board of Regents,* 385 U.S. 589 (1967), "Our Nation is deeply committed to safeguarding academic freedom, which is of transcendent value to all of us and not merely to the teachers concerned. That freedom is therefore a special concern of the First Amendment, which does not tolerate laws that cast a pall of orthodoxy over the classroom."

The numbers refer to the designated portion of the 1940 *Statement* on which interpretive comment is made.

1. The Association of American Colleges and the American Association of University Professors have long recognized that membership in the academic profession carries with it special responsibilities. Both associations either separately or jointly have consistently affirmed these responsibilities in major policy statements, providing guidance to professors in their utterances as citizens, in the exercise of their responsibilities to the institution and to students, and in their conduct when resigning from their institution or when undertaking government-sponsored research. Of particular relevance is the *Statement on Professional Ethics,* adopted in 1966 as Association policy. (A revision, adopted in 1987, may be found in AAUP 2006, 171–72.)
2. The intent of this statement is not to discourage what is "controversial." Controversy is at the heart of the free academic inquiry which the entire statement is designed to foster. The passage serves to underscore the need for teachers to avoid persistently intruding material which has no relation to their subject.
3. Most church-related institutions no longer need or desire the departure from the principle of academic freedom implied in the 1940 *Statement,* and we do not now endorse such a departure.
4. This paragraph is the subject of an interpretation adopted by the

sponsors of the 1940 *Statement* immediately following its endorsement which reads as follows:

> If the administration of a college or university feels that a teacher has not observed the admonitions of paragraph 3 of the section on Academic Freedom and believes that the extramural utterances of the teacher have been such as to raise grave doubts concerning the teacher's fitness for his or her position, it may proceed to file charges under paragraph 4 of the section on Academic Tenure. In pressing such charges, the administration should remember that teachers are citizens and should be accorded the freedom of citizens. In such cases the administration must assume full responsibility, and the American Association of University Professors and the Association of American Colleges are free to make an investigation.

Paragraph 3 of the section on Academic Freedom in the 1940 *Statement* should also be interpreted in keeping with the 1964 *Committee A Statement on Extramural Utterances*, which states inter alia: "The controlling principle is that a faculty member's expression of opinion as a citizen cannot constitute grounds for dismissal unless it clearly demonstrates the faculty member's unfitness for his or her position. Extramural utterances rarely bear upon the faculty member's fitness for the position. Moreover, a final decision should take into account the faculty member's entire record as a teacher and scholar."

Paragraph 5 of the *Statement on Professional Ethics* also deals with the nature of the "special obligations" of the teacher. The paragraph reads as follows:

> As members of their community, professors have the rights and obligations of other citizens. Professors measure the urgency of these obligations in the light of their responsibilities to their subject, to their students, to their profession, and to their institution. When they speak or act as private persons, they avoid creating the impression of speaking or acting for their college or university. As citizens engaged in a profession that depends upon freedom for its health and integrity, professors have a particular obligation to promote conditions of free inquiry and to further public understanding of academic freedom.

Both the protection of academic freedom and the requirements of academic responsibility apply not only to the full-time probationary and the tenured teacher, but also to all others, such as part-time faculty and teaching assistants, who exercise teaching responsibilities.

5. The concept of "rank of full-time instructor or a higher rank" is intended to include any person who teaches a full-time load regardless of the teacher's specific title.[3]
6. In calling for an agreement "in writing" on the amount of credit given for a faculty member's prior service at other institutions, the *Statement* furthers the general policy of full understanding by the professor of the terms and conditions of the appointment. It does not necessarily follow that a professor's tenure rights have been violated because of the absence of a written agreement on this matter. Nonetheless, especially because of the variation in permissible institutional practices, a written understanding concerning these matters at the time of appointment is particularly appropriate and advantageous to both the individual and the institution.[4]
7. The effect of this subparagraph is that a decision on tenure, favorable or unfavorable, must be made at least twelve months prior to the completion of the probationary period. If the decision is negative, the appointment for the following year becomes a terminal one. If the decision is affirmative, the provisions in the 1940 *Statement* with respect to the termination of service of teachers or investigators after the expiration of a probationary period should apply from the date when the favorable decision is made.

   The general principle of notice contained in this paragraph is developed with greater specificity in the *Standards for Notice of Nonreappointment,* endorsed by the Fiftieth Annual Meeting of the American Association of University Professors (1964). These standards are:

> Notice of nonreappointment, or of intention not to recommend reappointment to the governing board, should be given in writing in accordance with the following standards:
>
> 1. *Not later than March 1 of the first academic year of service,* if the appointment expires at the end of that year; or, if a one-year appointment terminates during an academic year, at least three months in advance of its termination.
> 2. *Not later than December 15 of the second academic year of service,* if the appointment expires at the end of that year; or, if an initial two-year appointment terminates during

an academic year, at least six months in advance of its termination.

3. At least twelve months before the expiration of an appointment after two or more years in the institution.

Other obligations, both of institutions and of individuals, are described in the *Statement on Recruitment and Resignation of Faculty Members,* as endorsed by the Association of American Colleges and the American Association of University Professors in 1961.

8. The freedom of probationary teachers is enhanced by the establishment of a regular procedure for the periodic evaluation and assessment of the teacher's academic performance during probationary status. Provision should be made for regularized procedures for the consideration of complaints by probationary teachers that their academic freedom has been violated. One suggested procedure to serve these purposes is contained in the *Recommended Institutional Regulations on Academic Freedom and Tenure,* prepared by the American Association of University Professors.

9. A further specification of the academic due process to which the teacher is entitled under this paragraph is contained in the *Statement on Procedural Standards in Faculty Dismissal Proceedings,* jointly approved by the American Association of University Professors and the Association of American Colleges in 1958. This interpretive document deals with the issue of suspension, about which the 1940 *Statement* is silent.

The 1958 *Statement* provides: "Suspension of the faculty member during the proceedings is justified only if immediate harm to the faculty member or others is threatened by the faculty member's continuance. Unless legal considerations forbid, any such suspension should be with pay." A suspension which is not followed by either reinstatement or the opportunity for a hearing is in effect a summary dismissal in violation of academic due process.

The concept of "moral turpitude" identifies the exceptional case in which the professor may be denied a year's teaching or pay in whole or in part. The statement applies to that kind of behavior which goes beyond simply warranting discharge and is so utterly blameworthy as to make it inappropriate to require the offering of a year's teaching or pay. The standard is not that the moral sensibilities of persons in the particular community have been affronted. The standard is behavior that would evoke condemnation by the academic community generally.

Notes

1. The word "teacher" as used in this document is understood to include the investigator who is attached to an academic institution without teaching duties.

2. Boldface numbers in brackets refer to Interpretive Comments that follow.

3. For a discussion of this question, see AAUP 2001 (88–91).

4. For a more detailed statement on this question, see "On Crediting Prior Service Elsewhere as Part of the Probationary Period," in AAUP 2006 (55–56).

References

American Association of University Professors [AAUP]. 2001. Report of the special committee on academic personnel ineligible for tenure. In *AAUP policy documents and reports,* 9th ed. Washington, DC: AAUP.

American Association of University Professors [AAUP]. 2006. *AAUP policy documents and reports*. 10th ed. Washington, DC: AAUP.

Statement on Professional Ethics

The statement that follows was originally adopted in 1966. Revisions were made and approved by the Association's Council in 1987 and 2009.

Introduction

From its inception, the American Association of University Professors has recognized that membership in the academic profession carries with it special responsibilities. The Association has consistently affirmed these responsibilities in major policy statements, providing guidance to professors in such matters as their utterances as citizens, the exercise of their responsibilities to students and colleagues, and their conduct when resigning from an institution or when undertaking sponsored research. The *Statement on Professional Ethics* that follows sets forth those general standards that serve as a reminder of the variety of responsibilities assumed by all members of the profession.

In the enforcement of ethical standards, the academic profession differs from those of law and medicine, whose associations act to ensure the integrity of members engaged in private practice. In the academic profession the individual institution of higher learning provides this assurance and so should normally handle questions concerning propriety of conduct within its own framework by reference to a faculty group. The Association supports such local action and stands ready, through the general secretary and the Committee on Professional Ethics, to counsel with members of the academic community concerning questions of professional ethics and to inquire into complaints when local consideration is impossible or inappropriate. If the alleged offense is deemed sufficiently serious to raise the possibility of adverse action, the procedures should be in accordance with the 1940 *Statement of Principles on Academic Freedom and Tenure,* the 1958 *Statement on Procedural Standards in Faculty Dismissal Proceedings,* or the applicable provisions of the Association's *Recommended Institutional Regulations on Academic Freedom and Tenure.*

The Statement

1. Professors, guided by a deep conviction of the worth and dignity of the advancement of knowledge, recognize the special responsibilities placed upon them. Their primary responsibility to their subject is to seek and to state the truth as they see it. To this end professors devote their energies to developing and improving their scholarly competence. They accept the obligation to exercise critical self-discipline and judgment in using, extending, and transmitting knowledge. They practice intellectual honesty. Although professors may follow subsidiary interests, these interests must never seriously hamper or compromise their freedom of inquiry.
2. As teachers, professors encourage the free pursuit of learning in their students. They hold before them the best scholarly and ethical standards of their discipline. Professors demonstrate respect for students as individuals and adhere to their proper roles as intellectual guides and counselors. Professors make every reasonable effort to foster honest academic conduct and to ensure that their evaluations of students reflect each student's true merit. They respect the confidential nature of the relationship between professor and student. They avoid any exploitation, harassment, or discriminatory treatment of students. They acknowledge significant academic or scholarly assistance from them. They protect their academic freedom.
3. As colleagues, professors have obligations that derive from common membership in the community of scholars. Professors do not

discriminate against or harass colleagues. They respect and defend the free inquiry of associates, even when it leads to findings and conclusions that differ from their own. Professors acknowledge academic debt and strive to be objective in their professional judgment of colleagues. Professors accept their share of faculty responsibilities for the governance of their institution.

4. As members of an academic institution, professors seek above all to be effective teachers and scholars. Although professors observe the stated regulations of the institution, provided the regulations do not contravene academic freedom, they maintain their right to criticize and seek revision. Professors give due regard to their paramount responsibilities within their institution in determining the amount and character of work done outside it. When considering the interruption or termination of their service, professors recognize the effect of their decision upon the program of the institution and give due notice of their intentions.
5. As members of their community, professors have the rights and obligations of other citizens. Professors measure the urgency of these obligations in the light of their responsibilities to their subject, to their students, to their profession, and to their institution. When they speak or act as private persons, they avoid creating the impression of speaking or acting for their college or university. As citizens engaged in a profession that depends upon freedom for its health and integrity, professors have a particular obligation to promote conditions of free inquiry and to further public understanding of academic freedom.

Statement on Graduate Students

The statement that follows was approved by the Association's Committee on Teaching, Research, and Publication in October 1999. It was adopted by the AAUP's Council in June 2000 and endorsed by the Eighty-sixth Annual Meeting.

Preamble

Graduate programs in universities exist for the discovery and transmission of knowledge, the education of students, the training of future faculty, and the general well-being of society. Free inquiry and free expression are indispensable to the attainment of these goals.

In 1967 the American Association of University Professors participated with the National Student Association, the Association of American Colleges, and others in the formulation of the *Joint Statement on Rights and Freedoms of Students.* The *Joint Statement* has twice been revised and updated, most recently in November 1992. The AAUP's Committee on Teaching, Research, and Publication, while supporting the Association's continuing commitment to the *Joint Statement,* believes that the distinctive circumstances of graduate students require a supplemental statement.

The statement that follows has been formulated to reflect the educational maturity and the distinguishing academic characteristics and responsibilities of graduate students. These students not only engage in more advanced studies than their undergraduate counterparts, but often they also hold teaching or research assistantships. As graduate assistants, they carry out many of the functions of faculty members and receive compensation for these duties. The statement below sets forth recommended standards that we believe will foster sound academic policies in universities with graduate programs. The responsibility to secure and respect general conditions conducive to a graduate student's freedom to learn and to teach is shared by all members of a university's graduate community. Each university should develop policies and procedures that safeguard this freedom. Such policies and procedures should be developed within the framework of those general standards that enable the university to fulfill its educational mission. These standards are offered not simply to protect the rights of affected individuals but also to ensure that graduate education fulfills its responsibilities to students, faculty, and society.[1]

Recommended Standards

1. Graduate students have the right to academic freedom. Like other students, they "should be free to take reasoned exception to the data or views offered in any course of study and to reserve judgment about matters of opinion, but they are responsible for learning the content of any course of study for which they are enrolled" (AAUP 2006a, 274). Moreover, because of their advanced education, graduate students should be encouraged by their professors to exercise their freedom of "discussion, inquiry, and expression" (274). Further, they should be able to express their opinions freely about matters of institutional policy, and they should have the same freedom of action in the public political domain as faculty members should have.
2. Graduate students' freedom of inquiry is necessarily qualified by their still being learners in the profession; nonetheless, their faculty

mentors should afford them latitude and respect as they decide how they will engage in teaching and research.

Graduate students have the right to be free from illegal or unconstitutional discrimination, or discrimination on a basis not demonstrably related to job function, including, but not limited to, age, sex, disability, race, religion, national origin, marital status, or sexual orientation, in admissions and throughout their education, employment, and placement (AAUP 2006b, 229).

Graduate students should be informed of the requirements of their degree programs. When feasible, they should be told about acceptance, application, and attrition rates in their fields, but it is also their responsibility to keep themselves informed of these matters. If degree requirements are altered, students admitted under previous rules should be able to continue under those rules.

Graduate students should be assisted in making timely progress toward their degrees by being provided with diligent advisers, relevant course offerings, adequate dissertation or thesis supervision, and periodic assessment of and clear communication on their progress. Students should understand that dissertation or thesis work may be constrained by the areas of interest and specialization of available faculty supervisors.

If a graduate student's dissertation or thesis adviser departs from the institution once the student's work is under way, the responsible academic officers should endeavor to provide the student with alternative supervision, external to the institution if necessary. If a degree program is to be discontinued, provisions must be made for students already in the program to complete their course of study.

3. Graduate students are entitled to the protection of their intellectual-property rights, including recognition of their participation in supervised research and their research with faculty, consistent with generally accepted standards of attribution and acknowledgment in collaborative settings. Written standards should be publicly available.
4. Graduate students should have a voice in institutional governance at the program, department, college, graduate school, and university levels.
5. Under the Association's *Recommended Institutional Regulations on Academic Freedom and Tenure*, graduate-student assistants are to be informed in writing of the terms and conditions of their appointment and, in the event of proposed dismissal, are to be afforded access to a duly constituted hearing committee.[2] They should be informed of all academic or other institutional regulations affecting

their roles as employees. Graduate-student employees with grievances, as individuals or as a group, should submit them in a timely fashion and should have access to an impartial faculty committee or, if provided under institutional policy, arbitration. Clear guidelines and timelines for grievance procedures should be distributed to all interested parties. Individual grievants or participants in a group grievance should not be subjected to reprisals. Graduate-student employees may choose a representative to speak for them or with them at all stages of a grievance.

6. Good practice should include appropriate training and supervision in teaching, adequate office space, and a safe working environment. Departments should endeavor to acquaint students with the norms and traditions of their academic discipline and to inform them of professional opportunities. Graduate students should be encouraged to seek departmental assistance in obtaining future academic and nonacademic employment. Departments are encouraged to provide support for the professional development of graduate students by such means as funding research expenses and conference travel.
7. Graduate students should have access to their files and placement dossiers. If access is denied, graduate students should be able to have a faculty member of their choice examine their files and, at the professor's discretion, provide the student with a redacted account. Graduate students should have the right to direct that items be added to or removed from their placement dossiers.
8. As the Association's Council affirmed in November 1998, graduate-student assistants, like other campus employees, should have the right to organize to bargain collectively. Where state legislation permits, administrations should honor a majority request for union representation. Graduate-student assistants must not suffer retaliation from professors or administrators because of their activity relating to collective bargaining.
9. In order to assist graduate students in making steady progress toward their degrees, the time they spend in teaching or research assistantships or other graduate employment at the institution should be limited in amount—a common maximum is twenty hours per week—and should afford sufficient compensation so as not to compel the student to obtain substantial additional employment elsewhere.
10. Graduate-student assistants, though they work only part time, should receive essential fringe benefits, and especially health benefits.

Notes

1. We recognize that the responsibilities of graduate students vary widely among individuals, courses of study, and institutions. Some provisions of this statement may not apply to students in professional schools who may have different types of responsibilities from those of students in other disciplines.

2. Regulation 13 in AAUP 2006c (29).

References

American Association of University Professors [AAUP]. 2006a. Joint statement on rights and freedoms of students. In *AAUP policy documents and reports,* 10th ed. Washington, DC: AAUP.

American Association of University Professors [AAUP]. 2006b. On discrimination. In *AAUP policy documents and reports,* 10th ed. Washington, DC: AAUP.

American Association of University Professors [AAUP]. 2006c. Recommended institutional regulations on academic freedom and tenure. In *AAUP policy documents and reports,* 10th ed. Washington, DC: AAUP.

7

The Scholarship of Engagement

*Ernest L. Boyer**

AMERICAN HIGHER education is, as Derek Bok once poetically described it, "a many-splendored creation." We have built in this country a truly remarkable network of research universities, regional campuses, liberal arts and community colleges, which have become, during the last half century, the envy of the world.

But it's also true that after years of explosive growth, America's colleges and universities are now suffering from a decline in public confidence and a nagging feeling that they are no longer at the vital center of the nation's work. Today, the campuses in this country are not being called upon to win a global war, or to build Quonset huts for returning GIs. They're not trying to beat the Soviets to the moon or to help implement the Great Society programs. It seems to me that for the first time in nearly half a century, institutions of higher learning are not collectively caught up in some urgent national endeavor.

Still, our outstanding universities and colleges remain, in my opinion, one of the greatest hopes for intellectual and civic progress in this country. I'm convinced that for this hope to be fulfilled, the academy must become a more vigorous partner in the search for answers to our most pressing social, civic, economic, and moral problems, and must reaffirm its historic commitment to what I call the scholarship of engagement.

The truth is that for more than 350 years, higher learning and the larger purposes of American society have been inextricably interlocked. The goal of the colonial college was to prepare civic and religious leaders, a vision succinctly captured by John Eliot, who wrote in 1636: "If we nourish not learning, both church and commonwealth will sink." Following the revolution, the great patriot Dr. Benjamin Rush declared in 1798 that the nation's colleges would be "nurseries of wise and good men, to adapt our modes of teaching to the peculiar form of our

*Originally published in the *Journal of Public Service & Outreach* (now the *Journal of Higher Education Outreach and Engagement*) 1.1 (1996): 11–20. Reprinted courtesy of the publisher.

government." In 1824, Rensselaer Polytechnic Institute was founded in Troy, New York, and RPI was, according to historian Frederick Rudolph, a constant reminder that America needed railroad builders, bridge builders, builders of all kinds. During the dark days of the Civil War, President Abraham Lincoln signed the historic Land Grant Act, which linked higher learning to the nation's agricultural, technological, and industrial revolutions. And when social critic Lincoln Steffens visited Madison in 1909, he observed, "In Wisconsin, the university is as close to the intelligent farmer as his pig-pen or his tool-house."

At the beginning of this century, David Starr Jordan, president of that brash new institution on the West Coast, Stanford, declared that the entire university movement in this country "is toward reality and practicality." Harvard's president, Charles Eliot, who was completing nearly 40 years of tenure, said America's universities are filled with the democratic spirit of "serviceableness." And in 1896, Woodrow Wilson, then a 40-year-old Princeton University professor, insisted that the spirit of service will give a college a place in the public annals of the nation. "We dare not," he said, "keep aloof and closet ourselves while a nation comes to its maturity."

Frankly, I find it quite remarkable that just one hundred years ago, the words "practicality" and "reality" and "serviceability" were used by the nation's most distinguished academic leaders to describe the mission of higher learning which was, to put it simply, the scholarship of engagement. During my own lifetime, Vannevar Bush of the MIT formally declared, while in Washington serving two presidents, that universities which helped win the war could also win the peace, a statement which led to the greatest federally funded research effort the world has ever known. I find it fascinating to recall that Bush cited radar and penicillin to illustrate how science could be of practical service to the nation. The goals in the creation of the National Science Foundation which led to the Department of Defense and the National Institutes of Health were not abstract. The goals were rooted in practical reality and aimed toward useful ends.

In the 1940s, the GI Bill brought eight million veterans back to campus, which sparked in this country a revolution of rising expectations. May I whisper that professors were not at the forefront urging the GI Bill. This initiative came from Congress. Many academics, in fact, questioned the wisdom of inviting GIs to campus. After all, these men hadn't passed the SAT, they'd simply gone off to war, and what did they know except survival? The story gets even grimmer. I read some years ago that the dean of admissions at one of the well-known institutions in the country opposed the GIs because, he argued, they would be married, many of them; they would bring baby carriages to campus, and even contaminate the young undergraduates with bad ideas at that pristine institution. I think he knew little about GIs, and even less about the undergraduates at his own college.

But, putting that resistance aside, the point is largely made that the universities joined in an absolutely spectacular experiment, in a cultural commitment to rising expectations, and what was for the GIs a privilege became, for their children and grandchildren, an absolute right. And there's no turning back.

Almost coincidentally, Secretary of State George C. Marshall, at a commencement exercise at Harvard in 1947, announced a plan for European recovery, and the Marshall Plan sent scholars all around the world to promote social and economic progress. Ten years later, when the Soviets sent Sputnik rocketing into orbit, the nation's colleges and universities were called upon once again, this time to design better curricula for the nation's schools and to offer summer institutes for teachers.

And one still stumbles onto the inspiration of that time. I remember, as commissioner, having a lunch in Washington. We thought we were talking privately about the federal program to help teachers under the Eisenhower administration, only to find we were being overheard at the next table, which you should always assume in Washington. And the man stopped by and said, "I just wanted to tell you that I was one of the NDA [National Defense Education Act] fellows at that time, and I've never had a better experience in my life." And the inspiration of the teachers who came back from the summer institutes touched teachers all across the country. The federal government and higher education had joined with schools toward the renewal of public education.

Then, in the 1960s, almost every college and university in this country launched affirmative-action programs to recruit historically bypassed students and to promote, belatedly, human justice.

I've just dashed through three and a half centuries, more or less. What I failed to mention were the times when universities challenged the established order, when they acted appropriately both as conscience and social critic, and that, too, was in service to the nation. And there were other times when campuses were on the fringes of larger national endeavors, standing on the sidelines, failing to take advantage of opportunities that emerged.

Still, I am left with two inescapable conclusions. First, it seems absolutely clear that this nation has throughout the years gained enormously from its vital network of higher learning institutions. And, at the same time, it's also quite apparent that the confidence of the nation's campuses themselves has grown during those times when academics were called upon to serve a larger purpose: to participate in the building of a more just society and to make the nation more civil and secure.

This leads me, then, to say a word about the partnership today. To what extent has higher learning in the nation continued this collaboration, this commitment to the common good?

I would suggest that in recent years, the work of individual scholars, as researchers, has continued to be highly prized, and that also, in recent years, teaching has increasingly become more highly regarded, which of course is great cause for celebration. But I believe it's also true that at far too many institutions of higher learning, the historic commitment to the "scholarship of engagement" has dramatically declined.

Almost every college catalog in this country still lists teaching, research, and service as the priorities of the professoriate; yet, at tenure and promotion time, the harsh truth is that service is hardly mentioned. And even more disturbing, faculty who do spend time on so-called applied projects frequently jeopardize their careers.

Russell Jacoby, in a fascinating book titled *The Last Intellectuals*, observes that the influence of American academics has declined precisely because being an intellectual has come to mean being in the university and holding a faculty appointment, preferably a tenured one, of writing in a certain style understood only by one's peers, of conforming to an academic rewards system that encourages disengagement and even penalizes professors whose work becomes useful to nonacademics—or popularized, as we like to say. Intellectual life, Jacoby said, has moved from the coffee shop to the cafeteria, with academics participating less vigorously in the broader public discourse.

But, what I find most disturbing—as almost the mirror image of that description—is a growing feeling in this country that higher education is, in fact, part of the problem rather than the solution. Going still further, that it's become a private benefit, not a public good. Increasingly, the campus is being viewed as a place where students get credentialed and faculty get tenured, while the overall work of the academy does not seem particularly relevant to the nation's most pressing civic, social, economic, and moral problems. Indeed, it follows that if the students are the beneficiaries and get credentialed, then let students pay the bill. And I've been almost startled to see that, when the gap increases in the budget, it's the student, and the student fees, that are turned to automatically—after all, it's a private benefit, and let the consumer, as we like to say, pay the bill.

Not that long ago, it was generally assumed that higher education was an investment in the future of the nation—that the intellect of the nation was something too valuable to lose, and that we needed to invest in the future through the knowledge industry.

I often think about the time when I moved, almost overnight, from an academic post in Albany, New York, to a government post in Washington, DC. These were two completely separate worlds. At the university, looking back, I recall rarely having serious dialogues with "outsiders"—artists, or "popular" authors, or other intellectuals beyond the campus. And yet, I was fascinated by Derek Bok's observation, on leaving his tenured post at Harvard, that the most consequential shifts in public policy in recent years have come not from academics, but from such works as Rachel Carson's *Silent Spring*, Ralph Nader's *Unsafe at Any Speed*, Michael Harrington's *The Other America*, and Betty Friedan's *The Feminine Mystique*—books which truly place the environmental, industrial, economic, and gender issues squarely in a social context.

I teach occasionally at the Woodrow Wilson School, in the public policy center, and I open the first class by asking, "How is public policy shaped in America? Where does it originate? How does the debate get going?" And almost always the undergraduates will start with the president, then Congress, or they might think of the state legislature. Then I ask them, has anyone ever heard of Rachel Carson, or Michael Harrington, and a kind of bewildered look appears. And yet the truth is that out of the seminal insights of such intellectuals public discourse begins, and very often Congress is the last, not the first, to act, trying to catch up with the shifting culture. So it is with the academy. One wonders why discourse between faculty and intellectuals working without campus affiliation can't take place within the academy itself.

But on the other hand, I left Albany and went to Washington, and I must say that I found government to be equally—or I'll go one step further—even more startlingly detached. In Washington, we did consult with lawyers and political pressure groups, driven usually by legislative mandates, and certainly by White House urges. But rarely were academics invited in to help put our policy decisions in historical, or social, or ethical perspective. And looking back, I recall literally hundreds of hours when we talked about the procedural aspects of our work and the legal implications, but I do not recall one occasion when someone asked, "Should we be doing this in the first place?," a question which I suspect could have been asked only by a detached participant with both courage and perspective.

Recently, I've become impressed by just how much this problem, which I would describe as impoverished cultural discourse, extends beyond government to mass communication where, with the exceptions of *MacNeil/Lehrer NewsHour* and *Bill Moyers Journal*, the nation's most pressing social, economic, and civic issues are endlessly discussed primarily by politicians and self-proclaimed pundits, while university scholars rarely are invited to join the conversation.

Abundant evidence shows that both the civic and academic health of any culture is vitally enriched as scholars and practitioners speak and listen carefully to each other. In a brilliant study of creative communities throughout history, Princeton University sociologist Carl Schorske, a man I greatly admire, describes the Basel, Switzerland, of the nineteenth century as a truly vibrant place where civic and university life were inseparably intertwined. Schorske states that the primary function of the university in Basel was to foster what he called "civic culture," while the city of Basel assumed that one of its basic obligations was the advancement of learning. The university was engaged in civic advancement, and the city was engaged in intellectual advancement, and the two were joined. And I read recently that one of the most influential commentators didn't achieve his fame from published articles, but from lectures he gave in the Basel open forum.

I recognize, of course, that "town" is not "gown." The university must vigorously protect its political and intellectual independence. Still, one does wonder what would happen if the university would extend itself more productively into the marketplace of ideas. I find it fascinating, for example, that the provocative PBS program *Washington Week in Review* invites us to consider current events from the perspective of four or five distinguished journalists, who, during the rest of the week, tend to talk only to themselves. And I've wondered occasionally what *The Week in Review* would sound like if a historian, an astronomer, an economist, an artist, a theologian, and perhaps a physician, for example, were asked to comment. Would we be listening and thinking about the same week, or would there be a different profile and perspective? How many different weeks were there that week? And who is interpreting them for America?

What are we to do about all of this? As a first step, coming back to the academy itself, I'm convinced that the university has an obligation to broaden the scope of scholarship. In a recent Carnegie Foundation report titled *Scholarship Reconsidered,* we propose a new paradigm of scholarship, one that assigns to the professoriate four essential, interlocking functions. We propose, first, the *scholarship of discovery,* insisting that universities, through research, simply must continue to push back the frontiers of human knowledge. No one, it seems to me, can even consider that issue contestable. And we argue, in our report, against shifting research inordinately to government institutes, or even to the laboratories of corporations that could directly or indirectly diminish the free flow of ideas.

But, while research is essential, we argue that it is not sufficient, and to avoid pedantry, we propose a second priority called the *scholarship of integration*. There is, we say, an urgent need to place discoveries in a larger context and create more interdisciplinary conversations in what Michael Polanyi of the University of Chicago has called the "overlapping [academic] neighborhoods," or in the new hyphenated disciplines, in which the energies of several different disciplines tend enthusiastically to converge. In fact, as Clifford Geertz of the Institute for Advanced Study has argued, we need a new formulation, a new paradigm of knowledge, since the new questions don't fit the old categories.

Speaking of bringing the disciplines together, several years ago, when physicist Victor Weisskopf was asked what gave him hope in troubled times, he replied, "Mozart and quantum mechanics." But where in our fragmented intellectual world do academics make connections such as these? We assume they live in separate worlds, yet they may be searching for the same interesting patterns and relationships, and finding solutions both intellectually compelling and aesthetic. I remember during the days of the lift-offs at Cape Kennedy, I was always fascinated when the rockets lifted successfully into orbit. The engineers wouldn't say: "Well, our formulas worked again." They would say, almost in unison, the word "beautiful." And I always found it fascinating that they chose an aesthetic term to describe a technological achievement. But where do the two begin and end?

Beyond the scholarship of discovering knowledge and integrating knowledge, we propose in our report a third priority, the *scholarship of sharing knowledge.* Scholarship, we say, is a communal act. You never get tenured for research alone. You get tenured for research and publication, which means you have to teach somebody what you've learned. And academics must continue to communicate not only with their peers but also with future scholars in the classroom in order to keep the flame of scholarship alive. And yet, the truth is that on many campuses it's much better to prepare a paper and present it to colleagues at the Hyatt in Chicago than to present it to the students on campus, who perhaps have more future prospects than one's peers.

Finally, in *Scholarship Reconsidered,* we call not only for the scholarship of discovering knowledge, the scholarship of integrating knowledge to avoid pedantry, and the sharing of knowledge to avoid discontinuity, but also for the *application of knowledge,* to avoid irrelevance. And we hurriedly add that when we speak of applying knowledge we do not mean "doing good," although that's important. Academics have their civic functions, which should be honored, but by scholarship of application we mean having professors become what Donald Schön of MIT has called "reflective practitioners," moving from theory to practice, and from practice back to theory, which in fact makes theory, then, more authentic—something we're learning in education and medicine, in law and architecture, and all the rest. And incidentally, by making knowledge useful, we mean everything from building better bridges to building better lives, which involves not only the professional schools but the arts and sciences as well.

Philosophy and religion also are engaged in the usefulness of knowledge, as insights become the interior of one's life. Recently, I reread Jacob Bronowski's moving essay on science and human values, which was written after his visit in 1945 to the devastation of Hiroshima. In this provocative document, he suggests that there are no sharp boundaries can be drawn between knowledge and its uses. And he insists that the convenient labels of pure and applied research simply do not describe the way that most scientists really work. To illustrate his point, Bronowski said that Sir Isaac Newton studied astronomy precisely because navigating the sea was the preoccupation of the society in which he was born. Newton was, to put it simply, an engaged scholar. And Michael Faraday, Bronowski said, sought to link electricity to magnetism because finding a new source of power was the preoccupation of his day. Faraday's scholarship was considered useful. The issue, then, Bronowski concludes, is not whether scholarship will be applied, but whether the work of scholars will be directed toward humane ends.

This reminder that the work of the academy ultimately must be directed toward larger, more humane ends brings me to this conclusion. I'm convinced that in the century ahead, higher education in this country has an urgent obligation to become more vigorously engaged in the issues of our day, just as the land-grant colleges helped farmers and technicians a century ago. And surely one of the most urgent issues we confront, perhaps the social crisis that is the most compelling, is the tragic plight of children.

In his inaugural address, President George Bush declared as the nation's first education goal that by the year 2000, all children in this country will come to school "ready to learn." Yet, we have more children in poverty today than we did five years ago. Today, a shocking percentage of the nation's 19 million preschoolers are malnourished and educationally impoverished. Several years ago, when we at The Carnegie Foundation surveyed several thousand kindergarten teachers, we learned that 35% of the children who enrolled in school the year before were, according to the teachers, linguistically, emotionally, or physically deficient. One wonders how this nation can live comfortably with the fact that so many of our children are so impoverished.

These statistics may seem irrelevant in the hallowed halls of the academy or in the greater world of higher learning, yet education is a seamless web. If children do not have a good beginning, if they do not receive the nurture and support they need during the first years of life, it will be difficult, if not impossible, to compensate fully for the failure later on. My wife, a certified midwife, has convinced me that the effort has to be made not only before school, but surely before birth itself, during the time when nutrition becomes inextricably linked to the potential later on.

To start, higher education must conduct more research in child development and health care and nutrition. I do not diminish this role at all. This, too, is in service to the nation. But I wonder if universities also might take the lead in creating children's councils in the communities that surround them. The role of the university would be to help coordinate the work of public and private agencies concerned with children, preparing annually, perhaps, what I've chosen to call a "ready-to-learn" report card—a kind of environmental impact statement on the physical, social, and emotional conditions affecting children—accompanied by a cooperative plan of action that would bring academics and practitioners together. James Agee, one of my favorite twentieth-century American authors, wrote that with every child born, regardless of circumstances, the potential of the human race is born again. And with such a remarkably rich array of intellectual resources, certainly the nation's universities, through research and the scholarship of engagement, can help make it possible for more children to be "ready to learn." Perhaps universities can even help create in this country a public love of children.

As a second challenge, I'm convinced colleges and universities also must become more actively engaged with the nation's schools. We hear a lot of talk these days about how the schools have failed, and surely education must improve, but the longer the debate continues, the more I become convinced that it's not the schools that have failed, it's the partnership that's failed. Today, our nation's schools are being called upon to do what homes and churches and communities have not been able to accomplish. And if they fail anywhere along the line, we condemn them for not meeting our high-minded expectations. Yet, I've concluded that it's simply impossible to have an island of excellence in a sea of community indifference. After going to schools from coast to coast, I've also begun to wonder whether most school critics could survive one week in the classrooms they condemn. While commissioner of education, I visited an urban school with a leaky roof, broken test tubes, Bunsen burners that wouldn't work, textbooks ten years old, falling plaster, armed guards at the door, and then we wonder why we're not world-class in math and science, or, for that matter, in anything.

Especially troublesome is our lack of support for teachers. In the United States today, teachers spend an average of four hundred dollars of their own money each year, according to our surveys, to buy essential school supplies. They're expected to teach 31 hours every week, with virtually no time for preparation. The average kindergarten class size in this country is 27, even though research reveals it should be 17. And, in one state, the average kindergarten size is 41. I've never taught kindergarten or first grade, but I do have several grandchildren, and when I take them to McDonald's or some other fast food spot, I come home a basket case just from keeping mustard off the floor and tracking all the orders that keep changing every 30 seconds. And I'm not even trying to cram them for the SATs. I'm just trying to keep body and soul together. Class size does matter, especially in the early years, and it correlates directly with effective learning.

About a dozen years ago, the late Bart Giamatti invited me to evaluate what was called the Yale–New Haven Teachers Institute. I was delighted to discover that some of Yale's most distinguished scholars directed summer seminars based on curricula teachers themselves had planned. And, incidentally, teachers in that program were called Yale Fellows. I was startled to discover that they were even given parking spaces on campus, which is about the highest status symbol a university can bestow. I'm suggesting that every college and university should view surrounding schools as partners, giving teaching scholarships to gifted high school students, just as we give athletic scholarships, and offering summer institutes for teachers, who are, I'm convinced, the unsung heroes of the nation.

During my Yale visit, I dropped in on a sixth-grade classroom in New Haven. Thirty children were crowded around the teacher's desk, and I thought it was a physical attack; I almost ran to the central office for help. But then I paused and discovered they weren't there out of anger, but intense enthusiasm. They had just finished reading Charles Dickens' *Oliver Twist*, and they were vigorously debating whether little Oliver could survive in their own neighborhood, speaking of relating the great books and intellectual inquiry to the realities of life. The children concluded that while Oliver had made it in far-off London, he'd never make it in New Haven, a much tougher city. I was watching an inspired teacher at work, relating serious literature to the lives of urban youth today.

This leads me to say a word about higher education in the nation's cities. It's obvious that the problems of urban life are enormously complex; there are no simple solutions. I'm almost embarrassed to mention it as a problem because it is so enormously complex, but we live in cities. They determine the future of this country. Our children live there, too. And I find it ironic that universities which focused with such energy on rural America a century ago have never focused with equal urgency on our cities. Many universities do have projects they sponsor in urban areas such as Detroit, Buffalo, New York, Philadelphia, and Baltimore, just to name a few. But, typically, these so-called model programs limp along, supported with soft money. Especially troublesome is the fact that academics who participate are not professionally rewarded.

Higher education cannot do it all, but Ira Harkavay of the University of Pennsylvania soberly warns that our great universities simply cannot afford to remain islands of affluence, self-importance, and horticultural beauty in seas of squalor, violence, and despair. With their schools of medicine, law, and education and their public policy programs, surely higher education can help put our cities and perhaps even our nation back together.

Here, then, is my conclusion. At one level, the scholarship of engagement means connecting the rich resources of the university to our most pressing social, civic, and ethical problems, to our children, to our schools, to our teachers, and to our cities, just to name the ones I am personally in touch with most frequently. You could name others. Campuses would be viewed by both students and professors not as isolated islands but as staging grounds for action.

But, at a deeper level, I have this growing conviction that what's also needed is not just more programs, but a larger purpose, a larger sense of mission, a larger clarity of direction in the nation's life as we move toward century twenty-one. Increasingly, I'm convinced that ultimately, the scholarship of engagement also means creating a special climate in which the academic and civic cultures communicate more continuously and more creatively with each other, helping to enlarge what anthropologist Clifford Geertz describes as the universe of human discourse and enriching the quality of life for all of us.

Many years ago, Oscar Handlin put the challenge this way: "[A] troubled universe can no longer afford the luxury of pursuits confined to an ivory tower.... [S]cholarship has to prove its worth not on its own terms, but by service to the nation and the world." This, in the end, is what the scholarship of engagement is all about.

8

Community

*Miranda Joseph**

IN THE CONTEMPORARY United States, the term "community" is used so pervasively it would appear to be nearly meaningless. And in fact the term is often deployed more for its performative effect of being "warmly persuasive" than for any descriptive work it accomplishes (R. Williams 1983, 76). Carrying only positive connotations—a sense of belonging, understanding, caring, cooperation, equality—"community" is deployed to mobilize support not only for a huge variety of causes but also for the speaker using the term. It functions in this way for Starbucks and McDonald's, both which display pamphlets in their stores proclaiming their commitment to community, as well as for the feminist scholar who seeks to legitimize her research by saying she works "in the community." It is deployed across the political spectrum to promote everything from identity-based movements (on behalf of women, gays and lesbians, African Americans, and others), to liberal and neoliberal visions of "civil society," to movements seeking to restore or reaffirm so-called "traditional" social values and hierarchies.

The relentless invocation of "community" is all the more remarkable given the persistent critique to which it has been subjected. Beginning in the late twentieth century, scholars have examined its use in the contexts of identity politics, liberalism, and nationalism, in each case pointing to its disciplining, exclusionary, racist, sexist, and often violent implications (Joseph 2002). Feminist activists and scholars have argued that the desire for communion, unity, and identity among women tended in practice to make the women's movement white, bourgeois, and U.S.-centric (Martin and Mohanty 1986). Feminist critics of liberalism have pointed out that the supposedly abstract political community constituted through the liberal state actually universalized exclusionary gendered and racial norms (W. Brown 1995). Critics of European and

---

* Originally published in *Keywords for American Cultural Studies*, edited by Bruce Burgett and Glenn Hendler (New York: NYU Press, 2007), 57–60. Reprinted courtesy of NYU Press.

postcolonial nationalisms have historicized the communal origin stories used to legitimate those nationalisms and emphasized the hierarchies and exclusions likewise legitimated by those narratives. Post-structuralist theories have underwritten many of these critiques, enabling scholars to argue that the presence, identity, purity, and communion connoted by "community" are impossible and even dystopic fantasies (I. Young 1990). In light of these critiques, many scholars have tried to reinvent community, to reconceptualize it as a space of difference and exposure to alterity (Mouffe 1992; Agamben 1993). Such stubborn efforts to build a better theory and practice of community only emphasize that the crucial question to pose about "community" as a keyword is this: Why is it so persistent and pervasive?

One answer to this question lies in the realization that particular deployments of the term can be understood as instances of a larger discourse that positions "community" as the defining other of capitalist "modernity." As Raymond Williams (1983) notes, "community" has been used since the nineteenth century to contrast immediate, direct local relationships among those with something in common to the more abstract relations connoted by "society." While community is often presumed to involve face-to-face relations, capital is taken to be global and faceless. Community concerns boundaries between us and them that are naturalized through reference to place or race or culture or identity; capital on the other hand, would seem to denature , crossing all borders, and making everything and everyone equivalent. The discourse of community includes a Romantic narrative that places it prior to "society," locating community in a long lost past for which we yearn nostalgically from our current fallen state of alienation, bureaucratization, and rationalization. This discourse also contrasts community with modern, capitalist society structurally; the foundation of community is supposed to be social values, while capitalist society is based only on economic value. At the same time, community is often understood to be a problematic remnant of the past, standing in the way of modernization and progress.

The narrative of community as destroyed by capitalism and modernity, as supplanted by society, can be found across a wide range of popular and academic texts; one might say that it is one of the structuring narratives of the field of sociology (Bender 1978). And it has taken on a fresh life in the works of contemporary communitarians such as Robert Bellah (1985), Robert Putnam (1993), Amitai Etzioni (1993), E.J. Dionne (1998), and others, all of which are aimed at least in part at nonacademic audiences. These words inevitably misread Alexis de Tocqueville's *Democracy in America* (1835) as describing a now lost form of local community that they believe would, if revived, promote democracy and economic prosperity and solve many contemporary problems, including drug use, crime, and poverty. In the post-Soviet era, "community," in the guise of nongovernmental organizations, has featured prominently in the promotion of "civil society" in both former communist countries and "developing" countries of the "Third World."

The discursive opposition of community and society provides a crucial clue to the former's pervasiveness in contemporary discourse; community is a creature of modernity and capitalism. Williams optimistically suggests that modernity positively constitutes communities of collective action. In *The Country and the City* (1973, 102, 104), he argues against the nostalgic idealization of pre-enclosure communities that he finds in late-eighteenth- and early-nineteenth-century British literature, pointing out that pre-enclosure villages supported "inequalities of condition" and that "community only became a reality when economic and political rights were fought for and partially gained." More pessimistically, Nikolas Rose (1999, 172, 174) reads the invocation of community as a central technology of power, arguing that in its contemporary deployments "community" is used to invoke "emotional relationships" that can then be instrumentalized. He suggests that the communities so invoked are required to take on responsibilities for "order, security, health and productivity" formerly carried by the state. And certainly there is substantial evidence for his argument in the proliferation of public-private partnerships, neighborhood watch programs, restorative justice initiatives, and the like, all of which mobilize familial and communal relations to promote subjection to law and order rather than to fight for economic or political rights (Lacey and Zedner 1995; Lacey 1996; Joseph 2006).

Community thus can be understood as a supplement to the circulation of state power and capital; it not only enables capital and power to flow, it also has the potential to displace those flows. Because the circulation of abstract capital depends on the embodiment of capital in particular subjects, the expansion and accumulation of capital requires that capitalists engage in an ongoing process of disrupting, transforming, galvanizing, and constituting new social formations, including communities. Community is performatively constituted in capitalism, in the processes of production and consumption, through discourses of pluralism, multiculturalism, and diversity, through niche marketing, nice production, and divisions of labor by race, gender, and nation.

This complex relation of community to capitalism is particularly evident in the promotion of nonprofit and nongovernmental organizations (NPOs and NGOs)—"civil society"—in the context of "development" in the United States and internationally. In the United States, nonprofit organizations are said to express community and often stand in for community metonymically. They are the institutional sites where people contribute labor or money to "the community." And they are posited as the form through which community might be reinvigorated as a complement to capitalism, providing those goods and services that capitalism does not. In the context of "development," NGOs have been explicitly promoted as a means for developing human and social capital and involving the poor in development projects—as, in other words, sites for constituting liberal capitalist subjects and subjectivities. At the same time, the necessity for such organizations suggests that subjects are not always already capitalist subjects. And in fact, the promotion of NPOs and NGOs has often been explicitly intended to stave off socialism or communism (Joseph 2002). The incorporation of subjects as community members at the site of the NGO can be understood as hegemonizing, wedding potentially resistant subjects (potentially or actually communist subjects) to capitalism.

The centrality of community to capitalism has been made even more explicit in the context of globalization. Politically diverse iterations of globalization discourse, both popular and academic, argue that capitalism now depends on communities, localities, cultures, and kinship to provide the social norms and trust that enable businesses to function, and that contemporary globalized capitalism is and should be more attuned to particular communities, localities, and cultures (Piore and Sabel 1984; Fukuyama 1995). While a number of scholars have portrayed the localization of culturalization of capitalism as a positive development, creating opportunities for local or communal resistance, others have emphasized the weakness, dependency, and vulnerability of the local. The claim that capitalism has just now discovered community is, however, problematic. It suggests that communities, and the economic inequalities between them, have not themselves been constituted by capitalism. To the contrary, the explicit deployment of community within globalization discourse tends to legitimate economic inequalities and exploitation as the expression of authentic cultural difference even as it articulates all communities and cultures as analogous sites for production and consumption (M.Wright 1999).

The project of examining "the seductions of community" remains a crucial one (Creed 2006). Exploring the ways in which community is constituted by or complicit with capital and power can reshape our understandings of the dimensions of our communities and the connections among them. Such exploration might enable us to recuperate and rearticulate the needs and desires for social change that are so often coopted by the uncritical deployment of the term.

References

Agamben, Giorgio. 1993. *The coming community.* Translated by Michael Hardt. Minneapolis: University of Minnesota Press, 1993.

Bellah, Robert, et al. 1985. *Habits of the heart: Individualism and commitment in American life.* New York: Harper and Row.

Bender, Thomas. 1978. *Community and social change in America.* Baltimore: Johns Hopkins University Press.

Brown, Wendy. 1995. *States of injury: Power and freedom in late modernity.* Princeton, NJ: Princeton University Press.

Creed, Gerald, ed. 2006. *The seductions of community.* Santa Fe, NM: SAR Press.

Dionne, E. J., Jr., ed. 1998. *Community works.* Washington, DC: Brookings Institution Press.

Etzioni, Amitai. 1993. *The spirit of community: Rights, responsibilities, and the communitarian agenda.* New York: Crown.

Fukuyama, Francis. 1995. *Trust: The social virtues and the creation of prosperity.* New York: The Free Press.

Joseph, Miranda. 2002. *Against the romance of community.* Minneapolis: University of Minnesota Press.

Joseph, Miranda. 2006. A debt to society. In *The seductions of community,* edited by Gerald Creed, Gerald. Santa Fe, NM: SAR Press.

Lacey, Nicola. 1996. Community in legal theory: Idea, ideal or ideology. *Studies in Law, Politics and Society* 15:105–46.

Lacey, Nicola, and Lucia Zedner. 1995. Discourses of community in criminal justice. *Journal of Law and Society* 22 (3): 301–25.

Martin, Biddy, and Chandra Mohanty. 1986. Feminist politics: What's home got to do with it? In *Feminist Studies, Critical Studies,* edited by Teresa de Lauretis. Bloomington: Indiana University Press.

Mouffe, Chantal. 1992. Democratic citizenship and the political community. In *Dimensions of radical democracy: Pluralism, citizenship and community,* edited by Chantal Mouffe. London: Verso.

Piore, Michael, and Charles F. Sabel. 1984. *The second industrial divide: Possibilities for prosperity.* New York: Basic Books.

Putnam, Robert D. 1993. The prosperous community. *American Prospect* 13:35–42.

Rose, Nikolas. 1999. *The powers of freedom.* Cambridge: Cambridge University Press.

Tocqueville, Alexis de. 1835. *Democracy in America.* Translated by Henry

Reeve. 2 vols. London: Saunders and Otley.

Williams, Raymond. 1973. *The country and the city.* New York: Oxford University Press.

Williams, Raymond. 1983. *Keywords: A vocabulary of culture and society.* 2d ed. London: Fontana.

Wright, Melissa W. 1999. The dialectics of still life: Murder, women and the maquiladoras. *Public Culture* 11:453–74.

Young, Iris Marion. 1990. *Justice and the politics of difference.* Princeton, NJ: Princeton University Press.

Part Two

Programs of Action

Institutionalizing Publicly Active Graduate Education

9

New Ways of Learning, Knowing, and Working: Diversifying Graduate Student Career Options Through Community Engagement

Kristen Day, Victor Becerra, Vicki L. Ruiz and Michael Powe

> We should expect holders of the highest academic degree not simply to know a great deal but to know what to do with what they know....
> —Woodrow Wilson Foundation, *The Responsive Ph.D.*

INCREASINGLY, graduate students in U.S. social sciences and humanities programs are gaining employment outside of traditional, tenure-track positions and indeed, outside of colleges and universities.[1] This shift reflects many factors, including an oversupply of candidates in many fields; decreased state and local funding to universities and subsequent institutional consolidation with fewer tenure-track positions; and a search for greater relevance among some students, including many students of color. The need to prepare graduate students for success in a broad array of nonacademic fields has captured the attention of authorities such as the Woodrow Wilson Foundation, with its Responsive Ph.D. program (Woodrow Wilson Foundation 2005; see also American Association of Universities 1998; Clement and Crider 2006; Nyquist and Wulff 2006). Many universities are reexamining graduate education on their campuses in light of changing career opportunities and the relevant skills and experiences these require.

For graduate students, community engagement can provide valuable professional skills and experiences that lead to nonacademic careers in business, government (including federal and state agencies), nonprofit organizations, and cultural institutions, and to non-faculty careers on campus in research organizations, outreach, and government relations. In this chapter, we examine how community engagement may help graduate students in the humanities and social sciences prepare for successful careers outside of academia. Preparing for nonacademic careers in humanities and social sciences presents special challenges compared to seeking nonacademic jobs in science and engineering, since the latter may be more prevalent and also more aligned with traditional graduate student preparation and focus on research.

Our analysis draws on two case studies from the University of California, Irvine: Humanities Out There (HOT) and the Community Scholars program. Together, the two programs provide graduate students from the humanities (especially English and history) and the social sciences (especially urban planning and public policy) with experience and training in areas such as curriculum development, K–12 classroom teaching, public speaking, grant proposal writing, applied research, report writing, and program evaluation. We examine these cases to highlight opportunities and challenges in linking graduate student engagement to nonacademic career preparation. Issues include the appropriate focus for graduate student activities, faculty support for nonacademic career paths and for graduate student engagement, the need for additional and distinct mentors for graduate students, and institutional funding support. We conclude with recommendations for employing engagement initiatives in ways that enhance graduate students' readiness for careers outside academia.

We define engagement as "the partnership of university knowledge and resources with those of the public and private sectors to enrich scholarship, research, and creative activity; enhance curriculum, teaching, and learning; prepare educated, engaged citizens; strengthen democratic values and civic responsibility; address critical societal issues; and contribute to the public good" (Civic Engagement Benchmarking Task Force 2005; in Bloomfield 2005, 3). Engagement involves activities such as service learning, community-based and applied research, and outreach.

Changing Career Opportunities for Graduate Students

Career opportunities for graduate students (especially doctoral students) are changing. At one time, doctoral education in most fields was regarded primarily as training for tenure-track faculty positions in colleges and universities. The likelihood that graduates will land such positions has decreased in recent decades (American Association of Universities 2001; Martin 2007). The percentage of full-time faculty positions that are tenure track has declined from 56% in 1993–94 to 49.6% in 2005–06 (IES, National Center for Educational Statistics, 2008; see also American Association of Universities 2001; Martin 2007). In the social sciences (including history), only 63.4% Ph.D. recipients were tenured or in tenure-track positions when surveyed five years after completing the Ph.D. (Nerad et al. 2007). Increasingly, tenure-track positions are replaced by contingent positions (part time, contract, or non-tenure-track). In 2003, fully 65% of all faculty positions were contingent (Martin 2007). Contingent positions are generally less desirable than tenure-track jobs, since contingent positions often offer lower rates of compensation, reduced job stability, and limited opportunities for participation in the full range of academic responsibilities (including research and service as well as teaching).

There are other signs of a changing job market for graduates of doctoral programs. A growing number of Ph.D. recipients are still seeking positions upon completion of their doctoral programs (American Association of Universities 1998). The number of doctoral graduates going into post-doc positions rather than permanent employment is also rising.

At the same time, the percentage of new Ph.D.'s working outside of academia is significant. In 2006, of those doctoral recipients who had firm commitments of employment upon graduation, only about half (54%) planned to work at educational institutions (Survey of Earned Doctorates 2009). A significant number of these Ph.D. recipients (18.2.%) were instead employed in business, government, or nonprofit organizations.

Doctoral students of color are even more likely to seek non-academic careers than are their non-minority peers (Golde and Dore 2001; in Woodrow Wilson Foundation 2005). In seeking nonacademic positions, students of color may be motivated by institutional barriers and by financial hardship and family commitments. Students of color often pursue higher education, in part, as a way to gain skills and knowledge that will benefit their communities. Thus, institutional culture that emphasizes "basic" research and that stigmatizes applied and community-based work may diminish the perception of universities as welcoming work environments for students of color. At the same time, the accumulation of significant debt while in graduate school often forces students of color to look for jobs outside the academy, where prospects may be more numerous, salaries more competitive, and opportunities for advancement greater. Additionally, family commitments can place limits on the geographic parameters for academic employment for some students of color (Latina Feminist Group 2001; Meyer 2008).[2]

There is a growing consensus among leaders in higher education that the graduate curriculum should equip students with the knowledge, skills, and experiences for a broad range of careers, including those outside of academia (American Association of Universities 1998; Nyquist and Wulff 2006). In social sciences and the humanities, non-academic careers include those in public history, technical writing, testing and assessment, training, market research, policy research, program evaluation, and nonprofit management, among others.

Skills Needed for Nonacademic Careers

Preparation for nonacademic careers is a lengthy process, akin to preparing for academic careers. A wide range of skills and experiences are required for success in nonacademic careers. These include the following:

Research/analytical skills

- Critical thinking skills
- Finding new information quickly
- Understanding complex contexts
- Thinking on one's feet
- Solving problems and identifying solutions
- Asking relevant research questions
- Conducting interdisciplinary research
- Using multiple research methods
- Interviewing skills
- Setting up databases
- Data analysis and interpretation skills and experience
- Designing research aimed at social change
- Experience in marketing research, program evaluation, assessment, Geographic Information Systems (GIS), survey research, etc.

Communication skills

- Conveying complex information and ideas to a non-expert audience
- Writing at all levels (websites, flyers, abstracts, reports, editorials, etc.)
- Speaking effectively before large groups and diverse audiences, including non-experts
- Basic skills in visual communications
- Editing

Entrepreneurial skills and experiences

- Writing effective grant proposals
- Computer and technical aptitude
- Imagination and creativity
- Track record of achievement
- Managing, motivating, evaluating others
- Experience in training, e-learning, curricular design and delivery
- Consulting, program development, venture/business planning, and project management

- Securing resources to support work
- Work experience in setting where seeking employment (nonprofit, government, etc.)

Effective personal skills

- Persuasion, social advocacy
- Leadership
- Listening skills
- Self-directed work habits (entrepreneurial spirit, ability to work independently)
- Flexibility, ability to change, willingness to learn
- Navigating complex bureaucratic environments, political savvy
- Performing under pressure and managing several projects simultaneously
- Delivering results quickly and keeping projects focused towards completion

Effective interpersonal skills

- Teamwork and collaboration
- Sharing power
- Negotiating competing agendas
- Social skills—ability to interact successfully with others
- Working effectively with diverse people
- Sense of ethics and responsiveness to community concerns, ability to empathize
- Capacity to develop trust, earn respect of communities[3]

Graduate students' success in the nonacademic job search is hindered by stereotypes about Ph.D.'s among potential employers. Stereotypically, Ph.D.'s are viewed as arrogant, lacking in common sense, and unable to communicate succinctly (Bryant 2005). Ph.D.'s are typecast as antisocial beings, unable to collaborate, uninterested in "real world" issues, and unable to function in office environments. Some employers fear that Ph.D.'s will leave nonacademic jobs when tempting faculty positions become available. A track record of involvement and of progressively increasing responsibility in engagement initiatives can provide evidence that counteracts these stereotypes and can allow doctoral students to develop desirable skills and traits.

Graduate Student Involvement in Community Engagement

Historically, community engagement has been largely tied to undergraduate education. Once students enter graduate programs, "far too often they shelve their civic interests, relegating them to the indulgences of a 'youthful past', to focus on the more 'serious' and mature challenge of professional training" (Stanton and Wagner 2006, 2). Barriers to engagement in graduate education, especially for doctoral students, are many. These barriers include mentors' limited knowledge about public scholarship, a lack of community engagement initiatives or conversations as part of graduate training, the requirement of a full-time commitment to academic studies, and emphasis on "basic" rather than "applied" research. Limited opportunities for financial support tied to engaged scholarship may also pose an obstacle.

A challenge for proponents of graduate engagement has been identifying the relevance of engagement for graduate education and professional development. KerryAnn O'Meara (2008) proposes that discussions of community engagement should be linked to early-career socialization processes for graduate students. She offers four assumptions for establishing community engagement in graduation education.

> One assumption is that there are concrete ways to connect graduate study to societal needs. A second is that doing so revitalizes graduate education while contributing significantly to society. A third assumption is that isolating doctoral programs from society limits the creativity, sense of responsibility, knowledge and skill development of future scholars. A fourth assumption is that the knowledge, skills, and values that graduate students acquire will also help them grow as professionals who find satisfaction in integrating different kinds of faculty work. (40)

In this context, community engagement can be seen as a vehicle for disrupting conventional ideas about and practices in graduate education while renewing thinking about "learning, knowing, and doing within disciplines" (O'Meara 2008, 40). The idea of engagement as creating new ways of learning, knowing, and doing also applies to the preparation of graduate students for nonacademic careers.

Doctoral training provides students with diverse skill sets, including the ability to analyze important problems, conduct independent research, write and present findings and recommendations, and teach others (Clement and Crider 2006). Engagement initiatives allow graduate students to employ skills they may already have from public, nonprofit, or educational work prior to entering graduate school. Graduate students' skills are an important source of tangible expertise that universities can bring to the table as they seek to partner with local communities. Moreover, through participation in engagement activities graduate students gain additional skills that may not be exercised in their dissertation research and teaching duties, such as overseeing budgets, planning and evaluating programs, political involvement, and working with diverse populations.

Further, engagement initiatives allow students to enhance personal and interpersonal skills. Through community engagement, graduate students meet professionals from outside the academy and thus expand their networks to include additional mentors with potential job leads. Community contacts challenge graduate students to learn (or relearn) how to communicate with individuals outside their disciplines and outside the university. Through engagement, graduate students demonstrate their commitment to public issues and their ability to work in teams and to function outside the academy. Engagement initiatives also offer graduate students concrete experiences in the kind of settings where they may seek future employment (e.g., nonprofits, local government). Such experiences are essential for future employability (Bryant 2005). In summary, community engagement enhances graduate students' career preparation by grounding their academic training, extending their experiences, and diversifying their personal and professional repertoire and approaches.

Incorporating community engagement into graduate education raises questions for universities and graduate departments, and requires new thinking about graduate training and development. The following case studies reveal some of the opportunities—and questions—tied to such involvement.

Case Studies of Graduate Engagement at the University of California, Irvine

The University of California, Irvine has been working to institutionalize civic and community engagement on its campus (see UCI Committee on Civic and Community Engagement 2009). As a research university, UCI has a special interest in engagement initiatives involving graduate programs and students. Two such initiatives are Humanities Out There (HOT) and the Community Scholars program. We present these cases as examples of how engagement programs can prepare graduate students for careers outside of academia. We also analyze these cases for the questions they raise about nonacademic career preparation.

Humanities Out There (HOT)

Humanities Out There is a flexible, creative partnership program between UC Irvine's School of Humanities and Orange County school districts that serves predominately low-income, Latino students.

Although the HOT model can be applied to any humanities classroom, HOT allows UCI's School of Humanities to reaffirm its commitment to underrepresented local students. HOT brings together public middle- and high-school teachers, graduate students, and undergraduate tutors in a shared enterprise of transforming recent scholarship into age-appropriate curricula calibrated to state standards in the form of lesson plans emphasizing critical thinking and writing skills. Thematic modules are presented in a series of classroom workshops, taught by teams of advanced graduate student leaders and undergraduate tutors working in collaboration with sponsoring teachers. The tutors themselves reflect the diversity of UCI's student body. During the course of the workshops, tutors become informal mentors who encourage aspirations to a college education (HOT 2009; UCI History Project 2009).

Founded in 1997, HOT has provided graduate students with opportunities to create lesson plans, shadow veteran teachers, mentor and manage undergraduate tutors, and implement assessment measures. Since 2001, 70 graduate student leaders, primarily from UCI's Departments of History and English, have worked with over 2,200 undergraduates in delivering curriculum to over 5,100 Santa Ana middle- and high-school students. Furthermore, 30 booklets in history and literature are in print, each containing multiple lesson plans.[4] Designed by the graduate leaders, the World and U.S. History units have had wide distribution through the California History–Social Science Project, a network of professional development seminars for teachers (Winters 2009). Humanities Out There does not have stable institutional funding, but cobbles together monies on a year-to-year basis to support graduate students with a 50% teaching assistantship, a level mandated by their union local in light of the work involved (this is discussed in more detail below).

For several HOT history workshop leaders, community engagement becomes a career path outside the academy. Three former HOT leaders are employed full time in UCI's California History–Social Science Project (CHSSP) and in the UCI Center for Educational Partnerships (CFEP), with one serving as CFEP's executive director. Five others, currently assistant professors at other campuses, apply the skills they learned in HOT in their new roles as historians involved in teacher education. HOT graduate students learn about pre- and post-test assessment and are involved in designing and implementing the tools for measuring learning outcomes for their Santa Ana pupils. Given the increased emphasis on accountability, as evidenced by the accreditation standards of the Western Association of Schools and Colleges' new assessment protocol (Western Association of Schools and

Colleges 2008), the familiarity of HOT leaders with creating and evaluating assessment measures will no doubt prove valuable to their future academic departments.

The most engaged HOT graduate leaders make a difference and measure it, too. Their ability to translate scholarship into accessible lesson plans, to work in partnership with others, to supervise a team of undergraduate tutors, and to create a classroom environment where learning is fun can be transferred to a variety of career settings outside the academy, including teacher education programs, private foundations, museums, and nonprofit community-based organizations (Winters 2009). As an innovative humanities partnership program, HOT reinforces the relevance of the humanities to building capacity and the public good. In the elegant words of founding UCI faculty member and celebrated poet James McMichael, "Capacity is both how much a thing holds and how much it can do" (McMichael 2006, 19). HOT demonstrates to UCI university faculty and administrators and to local school officials and teachers, how the humanities builds capacity in students at all levels.

COPC Community Scholars

UCI's Community Outreach Partnership Center (COPC) connects graduate students and faculty with community organizations to address local problems and concerns. Two COPC programs are particularly relevant in preparing graduate students for nonacademic careers: the Community Scholars program and a related set of COPC-sponsored, skill-based courses taught by professionals in urban planning and other fields.

The Community Scholars program connects masters and doctoral students in social science disciplines with community organizations to conduct applied research projects tied to pressing local needs. Each year, COPC issues a call for projects to advocacy and nonprofit organizations in the region. Submitting organizations describe their needs for specific research and/or technical assistance, and discuss how their proposed projects advance public impact, community building, and/or policy reform. Organizations also agree to serve as "clients" for projects they propose. All project proposals are reviewed by COPC staff before the list is disseminated to graduate students across campus.

Aiming to fulfill appropriate degree requirements, graduate students may elect to conduct a research or planning project from the list. (Most students use the Community Scholars program to complete the Professional Report requirement of the master's degree in Urban and Regional Planning or to conduct second-year Ph.D. research projects.) These students submit applications to become Community

Scholars. Accepted students receive a modest stipend and a small budget to cover project expenses. In return, Community Scholars are expected to consult regularly with their "client" organizations, conduct the requested research projects, and provide clients with professional-quality reports addressing the relevant community issues. In addition, Community Scholars attend a year-long training workshop that explores community-based research methods and ethics, and emphasizes the communication of research findings to diverse audiences (UCI Community Outreach Partnership Center 2009).

Many of the same "client" partner organizations participate every year. Clients include Orange County Communities Organized for Responsible Development (OCCORD), the United Way of Orange County, the Orange County Congregation Community Organization (OCCCO), and the Neighborhood Housing Services of Orange County (NHSOC), among others. In 2008–09, the program included nine Community Scholars and nine partner organizations. Past Community Scholars are now employed in settings that include private planning consulting firms, city agencies, and nonprofit organizations such as the Orange County Family and Children's Commission and the Service Employees' International Union.

COPC also sponsors graduate classes taught by local professionals and leaders of community organizations. These courses focus on professional skill development, including labor organizing, neighborhood planning, and grant writing for nonprofit organizations. Most COPC-sponsored courses involve a public impact project. The courses are designed to enhance graduate students' skills and to tie UCI knowledge-production activities to pressing community concerns. COPC covers the cost of hiring adjunct faculty instructors and also supports course activities (e.g., guest speakers, site visits, presentations to project clients). COPC-sponsored courses are popular with graduate students from urban planning, sociology, anthropology, and criminology. Course instructors also benefit by focusing engaged projects on activities tied to the instructors' own professional responsibilities and interests. Course instructors further gain from the relationships they establish with the university and with COPC staff, which have led to collaborative grant writing and other joint projects. Funding for the Community Scholars and for COPC-sponsored courses derives from extramural grants and institutional support.

Through these programs, graduate students engage with complex social issues in local settings, where their work must be informed by the tacit knowledge of community members and where results are expected to improve the lives of local people. More generally, COPC programs demonstrate to graduate students the pressing need for applied research that assists in real-world problem solving. These programs fulfill degree requirements and, at the same time, give graduate students a broader view of the applicability of their knowledge and skills in nonacademic settings.

Issues to Consider in Graduate Student Engagement to Support Nonacademic Careers

These case studies uncover critical issues that universities and graduate programs must consider in expanding graduate student involvement in community engagement and in preparing graduate students for nonacademic careers.

Need to Reconcile Graduate Curricula with Enhanced Graduate Student Engagement

The demands of engagement activities must be reconciled with graduate program curricula and objectives. If we seek to promote graduate student engagement, we must think carefully about how this can occur, not as an "add-on," but rather as an integral part of student development. For example, the Community Scholars program has succeeded, in part, because it builds on the existing structure for the Professional Report requirement in UCI's master's program in Urban and Regional Planning. It has been more challenging to adapt the Community Scholars program to engage doctoral students in urban planning and elsewhere on campus. O'Meara (2008) suggests that engagement should be incorporated throughout the graduate student career with experiences that progress from, for example, learning about community-based research methods and serving as a teaching assistant in a service-learning course, to conducting applied research and overseeing other students in engaged projects.

Increasing engagement raises questions about the appropriate focus of activities for graduate students in the social sciences and humanities, and especially for doctoral students. Should doctoral students' time, for example, be spent writing community-oriented reports and developing K–12 curricula, or should energy be concentrated solely on producing scholarly publications? Should students confine their employment while in school to research and teaching assistantships, or would internships in business, government, or cultural institutions also be appropriate (Johnson 2009; Nyquist and Wulff 2006)? Is community-based research an acceptable methodology for dissertation projects? Recognizing that many doctoral students will seek nonacademic careers may help faculty and graduate programs to broaden their thinking about appropriate work for students.

Rather than lengthening the graduate program by adding new

expectations, increasing graduate engagement may help to address the "time-to-degree" problem. Indeed, the fields with the poorest prospects for tenure-track academic jobs (history, English) have the longest time-to-degree (Woodrow Wilson Foundation 2005). Students often are reluctant to leave the university without a position in hand. By equipping students with relevant skills and experiences to succeed in non-academic pursuits, we may help to smooth students' progress through the degree program and into meaningful employment.

This issue is part of a larger conversation on the status and value of the humanities in higher education and in public life. Civic engagement initiatives are one way for humanities programs to demonstrate that value to their students and to others. For example, history doctoral candidates at Drew University participate in public humanities internships as part of their graduate training. In the words of Drew historian Jonathan Rose, "We recognize that we must train ... students for something more than careers as college-level teachers. And we have to move those students briskly to graduation without exploiting them as cheap academic labor" (2009, 37). Diversifying career options is not a new response to the current economic crisis. In 1999, the Townsend Center for the Humanities at the University of California, Berkeley sponsored a benchmark conference on the future of doctoral education in the humanities (Sommer 1999). The debate on the size, scope, and nature of graduate education has intensified in recent years, however, as searches for tenure-track positions have been routinely cancelled, postponed, or suspended. As the dean of Arts and Sciences at New York University, Catherine Simpson, colorfully explains: "'This is the year of no jobs'.... Ph.D.s are stacked up ... like planes hovering over La Guardia" (Cohen 2009a).

Need to Increase Faculty Support for Nonacademic Career Options and for Graduate Student Engagement

Graduate students express a deep desire to connect their disciplines with public problems, and to use their knowledge to assist their communities (Bloomfield 2005). Social responsibility emerged as a top agenda item for doctoral students at the 2003 National Conference on Graduate Student Leadership (Woodrow Wilson Foundation 2005). More than half of all doctoral students reported that they would like to be involved in some form of community service, but less than one in five reported having the opportunity to do so. Graduate students further note that they feel unprepared for work that connects their scholarship with the needs of society (O'Meara 2008).

More faculty support is needed to accommodate graduate student engagement. Proponents of graduate student engagement must work with faculty to challenge the idea that students should emulate their mentors' careers (Woodrow Wilson Foundation 2005). We also need to continue to educate faculty about engagement and to reassure them that engagement is not just "service," but rather is central to the scholarship of the university.

Faculty attitudes can be shaped by the efforts of major disciplinary organizations, which can do more to encourage engaged professional behavior (Bloomfield 2005). This could include support for presenting engaged work at conferences and publishing engaged scholarship in disciplinary journals. Many disciplines already incorporate a focus on engagement in their work; for instance, anthropology, sociology, and history boast public scholarship programs (O'Meara 2007). Recognition of public scholarship by the disciplines will help to socialize and support engaged graduate students.

At UCI, recent activities evidence a growing support for engaged research and teaching/learning on campus. The university recently established a campus-wide committee to institutionalize engaged research, teaching/learning, and outreach. UCI created a new administrative position, the director of engagement, and approved a new minor in civic and community engagement. In 2010, UCI initiated a new award for engaged teaching. In addition, UCI has for two years hosted an annual, regional conference on campus-community engagement (organized by COPC). This growing support for engagement may encourage UCI graduate students to become involved in these activities.

Need to Involve Additional People in Graduate Education

More and different people must be involved in preparing graduate students for success in nonacademic careers. What is needed is an active partnership between professors and leaders in business, government, cultural institutions, schools, and community and nonprofit organizations (Nyquist and Wulff 2006; Woodrow Wilson Foundation 2005). Graduate schools and programs may also partner with their career centers and alumni offices to build a more complete picture of career options for their graduates.

Graduate education is typically regarded as the province of tenured or tenure-track faculty, especially those at research universities. If graduate students are to participate meaningfully in engagement, however, students will also need sustained opportunities to learn from other kinds of people. This is especially critical when faculty do not have experience or understanding of principles or practices of engagement. In UCI's Community Scholars program, for example, the program director struggled to secure faculty to offer graduate courses that develop professional skills relevant to community-based projects—the kind of skills and experiences, that is, sought by community partners and nonacademic employers. COPC eventually found success by hiring adjunct faculty who are professionals in other areas (neighborhood planning, grant writing, etc.) to teach these courses. These adjunct faculty—who teach courses after their day jobs as nonprofit and public sector leaders—offer students alternative models for creating social change.[5] Some regular faculty continue to see such courses as more relevant for master's rather than for doctoral students. Also, institutional barriers may restrict the use of non-tenure-stream faculty to teach graduate courses. With regard to HOT, colleagues in the history department acknowledge the valuable skill sets acquired through participation in the program and actively promote graduate student involvement. As HOT director Lynn Mally observed in personal communication, "the program makes graduate students consider how the highly specialized material that they are learning can be conveyed to a broader audience. It is an incredible training ground for graduate students going into teaching at any level, since they are in charge of the content and the methods to convey that content."

To succeed in nonacademic careers, graduate students also must network with others outside the university. Involvement in engagement can provide graduate students with valuable career connections. By participating in campus engagement workshops, lectures, and events, graduate students can meet other engaged faculty, professional staff, and graduate students on their campuses. These individuals can be mentors and may provide internships, employment opportunities, and future job references. For example, through his involvement in organizing the COPC regional engagement conference described earlier, Michael Powe, the graduate student co-author of this chapter, built relationships with faculty members outside of his home department. This led to summer employment as a research assistant for a faculty member in Asian American Studies, and also to participation in a campus committee to design a new service-learning, study-abroad course. By attending regional and national conferences on engaged scholarship (and especially by participating on panels or moderating sessions), graduate students can also connect to the broader community of engaged scholars in their disciplines and beyond.[6]

Need to Reconsider How Graduate Students Are Funded

We must visit the question of funding for graduate students to promote engagement and to prepare students for nonacademic careers. Graduate students are typically supported through research or teaching assistantships or through fellowships while they conduct their dissertation research. To be viable, engagement must satisfy course requirements and/or provide adequate financial support for graduate students, including the cost of tuition and health insurance as well as salaries. Supporting graduate students is prohibitively expensive for many of the sources that fund engaged work, such as foundations, local governments, or nonprofit organizations. Further, universities are not competitive in applying to conduct community-based projects (evaluations, assessments, technical assistance, etc.) if the full cost of employing graduate students is included as part of the budget.

As one example, HOT graduate student leaders receive compensation equal to that of a half-time teaching assistant—approximately $25,000 in stipends and fees per academic year, including health insurance. The School of Humanities and the Graduate Division each fund two graduate students and UCI's Center for Educational Partnerships (CFEP) has matched with support for an additional four. While the National Endowment for the Humanities and the Woodrow Wilson Foundation once provided significant awards that underwrote the creation and publication of lessons plans as well as contributed to the funding of several cohorts of HOT graduate leaders, these grants expired several years ago. With a few notable exceptions, such as Dr. Fariborz Maseeh, private local philanthropists show little interest in graduate education in the humanities, or they lack resources to endow a full graduate fellowship. Furthermore, school districts are not in a financial position to contribute monetarily to the program at this scale. The lack of sustained financial support for graduate students in the project impedes long-range planning and is a source of persistent anxiety for the dean of the School of Humanities, the HOT faculty director, and graduate students themselves. Of course, this predicament reflects the larger issue of where the humanities fit in contemporary public education. Some humanists emphasize the relevance of a liberal arts education—the instrumental abilities to think critically, write clearly, and to weigh interpretations—while others decry what they consider a "service" model as they underscore the intrinsic value in contemplating the human condition. The place of humanities in a large research university remains contested. Through engagement, graduate students and their mentors can contribute to the larger project of justifying the humanities (Cohen 2009b).[7]

Universities must identify new ways to support graduate student engagement, such as through fellowships for public scholarship, assistantships for engagement activities, and tuition remissions for students who are employed in internships and related projects off campus. For example, UCI recently created a new, campus-wide "Public Impact Fellowship Award" to recognize graduate students who are involved in engaged research. Proponents of public scholarship must also investigate ways to facilitate graduate student involvement through channels other than paid employment, such as by accommodating internships for course credit and by building engagement into other aspects of the curriculum.

Conclusions and Recommendations

Increased community engagement by graduate students will have many other benefits, in addition to preparing students for nonacademic careers. Engagement will help recruit and retain graduate students and faculty of color. Many students and faculty of color have a desire to engage with communities outside their campus and to use their scholarship to address critical issues in the local context (Woodrow Wilson Foundation 2005). This commitment begins with students' lived experiences, which instill in many a sense of community obligation. In addition, taking courses in ethnic studies and related areas enriches students' understanding of the historical roots of contemporary struggles within their communities. This combination of lived experience and educational expertise contributes to innovative approaches to community partnerships. According to historian George Sánchez,

> American Studies and Ethnic Studies programs and departments ... house scholars who focus on race and ethnicity across a wide range of minority groups in the United States and abroad. Collectively, these strengths give [them] a certain intellectual power to engage with diversified communities facing a host of difficult and complex social and cultural issues now and in the future. (2008, 6)

Through engagement, graduate students may form new ideas about what constitutes scholarship and about how knowledge is produced. They may ask new questions and seek different types of answers.

Those students who do pursue faculty careers will benefit from engagement in terms of their future teaching and research. Even if graduate students do not remain engaged in later years, this experience may enhance their ability to evaluate their colleagues' engaged scholarship—for example, during reviews for promotion, in peer review of articles submitted for publication, and in assessing grant applications (O'Meara 2008). Finally, graduate students represent an important resource and a source of expertise that universities can bring to the table as they seek to partner with local communities.

At this critical juncture in graduate education, we are better served to think of graduate students not as the next generation of teacher-scholars but, more broadly, as the next generation of intellectual leaders (Woodrow Wilson Foundation 2005). Community engagement represents a critical tool in preparing students for these roles.

Notes

1. The authors would like to thank Christine Kelly for her helpful comments and Peggie Winters, Rosie Humphreys, and Lynn Mally for their research support.

2. A recent edited volume by Mary Howard-Hamilton and colleagues (2009) sheds light on these and other issues faced by graduate students of color.

3. Sources include Bryant 2005; Johnson 2009; O'Meara 2007; O'Meara 2008; University of San Diego Career Services Center 2009; Woodrow Wilson Foundation 2005.

4. These booklets are available by request from Peggie Winters, Humanities Out There, School of Humanities, UC Irvine, Irvine, CA 92697.

5. The employment of adjunct faculty to teach professional skills courses also raises questions, since these adjunct faculty face some of the issues raised earlier, such as low salaries for teaching. At the same time, since these adjunct faculty are typically full-time professionals in other fields, some concerns regarding adjunct employment do not apply (e.g., lack of benefits). Also, as noted earlier, adjunct faculty who teach professional skills courses benefit from opportunities to build relationships with university faculty and staff, and from opportunities to develop student projects related to their own professional responsibilities.

6. Such conferences include the Continuum of Service Conference organized by Western Campus Compact offices, the annual meeting of the Coalition of Urban and Metropolitan Universities (CUMU), and the International Conference on Service Learning and Community Engagement Research, among others.

7. For an insightful overview of the relevance of humanities education, see Laurence (2009).

References

American Association of Universities. 1998. *AAU Committee on Graduate Education report and recommendations*. October. http://www.aau.edu/publications/reports.aspx?id=6900.

American Association of Universities. 2001. *AAU non-tenure-track faculty report.* April 10. http://www.aau.edu/publications/reports.

aspx?id=6900.

Bloomfield, V. 2005. Civic engagement and graduate education. *Communicator* 38 (3), 1–2, 6.

Bryant, R. A. 2005. "But I have no skills." *Chronicle of Higher Education*, August 18. http://chronicle.com/jobs/news/2005/08/2005081801c.htm.

Civic Engagement Benchmarking Task Force. 2005. Resource guide and recommendations for defining and benchmarking engagement. http://*www.scholarshipofengagement.org/benchmarking/FINAL.doc.*

Clement, T., and D. Crider. 2006. *Summary report on the National Conference on Graduate Student Leadership*. St. Louis, MO: Washington University.

Cohen, P. 2009a. Doctoral candidates anticipate hard times. *New York Times,* March 6. http://www.nytimes.com/2009/03/07/arts/07grad.html?scp=9&sq=Humanities&st=cse

Cohen, P. 2009b. In tough times, the humanities must justify their worth. *New York Times*, February 24. http://www.nytimes.com/2009/02/25/books/25human.html?_r=1&scp=2&sq=Humanities&st=cse

Golde, C. M., and T. M. Dore. 2001. *At cross purposes: What the experiences of doctoral students reveal about doctoral education.* Philadelphia, PA: A report prepared for The Pew Charitable Trusts. *www.phd-survey.org/report%20final.pdf.*

HOT. 2009. Humanities Out There. http://www.humanities.uci.edu/hot/.

Howard-Hamilton, M., C. L. Morelon-Quainoo, S. D. Johnson, R. Winkle-Wagner, and L. Santiague. 2009. *Standing on the outside looking in.* Sterling, VA: Stylus.

Institute of Educational Sciences [IES], National Center for Education Statistics. 2008. *Digest of education statistics, 2007.* http://nces.ed.gov/pubsearch/pubsinfo.asp?pubid=2008022.

Johnson, M. 2009. Career FAQ's: Frequent questions about working beyond academe. http://www.ironstring.com/sellout/sellout_faqs/sellout_faqs.shtml.

Latina Feminist Group. 2001. *Telling to live: Latina feminist* testimonios. Durham, NC: Duke University Press.

Laurence, D. 2009. In progress: The idea of a humanities workforce. http://www.humanitiesindicators.org/essays/laurence.pdf.

Martin, S. 2007. The new academic job market: A reordering of the academic world has shifted opportunities for psychologists.

gradPSYCH 5 (1). http://www.apa.org/gradpsych/2007/01/cover-market.aspx

McMichael, J. 2006. *Capacity*. New York: Farrar, Straus and Giroux.

Meyer, L. D. 2008. 'Ongoing missionary labor': Building, maintaining, and expanding Chicana Studies/history; An interview with Vicki L. Ruiz. *Feminist Studies* 34(1–2):23–46.

Nerad, M., E. Rudd, E. Morrison, and J. Picciano. 2007. *Social Science PhDs – Five+ years out: A national survey of PhDs in six fields – Highlights report.* CIRGE Report 2007-01. Seattle, WA: Center for Research and Innovation in Graduate Education.

Nyquist, J., and D. H. Wulff. 2006. Re-envisioning the Ph.D.: Recommendations from National Studies on Doctoral Education. http://www.grad.washington.edu/envision/project_resources/

O'Meara, K. 2007. *Graduate education and civic engagement.* NERCHE Brief. http://www.eric.ed.gov/ERICWebPortal/contentdelivery/servlet/ERICServlet?accno=ED500538.

O'Meara, K. 2008. Graduate education and community engagement. *New Directions for Teaching and Learning,* no. 113: 27–42. doi:10.1002/tl.306.

Rose, J. 2009. Rethinking graduate education in history. *Perspectives on History* 47 (February). http://www.historians.org/Perspectives/issues/2009/0902/0902gra1.cfm

Sánchez, G. J. 2008. Challenging the borders of civic engagement: Ethnic Studies and the meaning of community democracy. Keynote address at the University of California, Irvine, February 7. http://www.ucicopc.org.

Sommer, J. 1999. Whither the humanities PhD? *Berkeleyan*, April 7. http://www.berkeley.edu/news/berkeleyan/1999/0407/phd.html

Stanton, T. K., and J. Wagner (2006). *Educating for democratic citizenship: Renewing the civic mission of graduate and professional education at research universities.* San Francisco: California Campus Compact.

Survey of Earned Doctorates. 2009. *Doctorate recipients from United States universities: Summary report 2006* (updated). Chicago: NORC at the University of Chicago. http://www.norc.org/projects/Survey+of+Earned+Doctorates.htm.

UCI Committee on Civic and Community Engagement. 2009. *Institutionalizing community engagement at UCI.* Unpublished report. Available from the Division of Undergraduate Education; University of California, Irvine; Irvine, CA 92697.

UCI Community Outreach Partnership Center. 2009. http://ucicopc.org/CA_COPC_Scholars.asp.

UCI History Project. 2009. The History Project. http://www.humanities.uci.edu/history/ucihp/.

University of San Diego Career Services Center. 2009. Prepare for the non-academic job market. http://careerucsd.edu/sa/GPrepareforNonAcademicJobMarket.sh.

Western Association of Schools and Colleges. 2008. *Handbook of accreditation*. http://www.wascsenior.org/findit/files/forms/Handbook_of_Accreditation___July_2008.pdf.

Winters, P. 2009. *2009 Humanities Out There Report*. Unpublished report. Available from the School of Humanities; University of California, Irvine; Irvine, CA 92697.

Woodrow Wilson Foundation. 2005. *The responsive Ph.D.: Innovations in U.S. doctoral education*. Princeton, NJ: Woodrow Wilson National Fellowship Foundation.

10

Getting Outside: Graduate Learning Through Art and Literacy Partnerships with City Schools

Judith E. Meighan

IN ELEMENTARY SCHOOL, we often fidget and fuss because we can't wait to get outside for recess or after-school play. Reading graduate student comments for this essay, it struck me that life is not so different in graduate school, though the "outside" we are eager to experience may be more complex than running around a playground for 20 minutes. The traditional model of graduate education tends toward confinement and, frequently, insularity. Lisa Pye, a doctoral candidate in Syracuse University's Cultural Foundations of Education program and a student in my publicly engaged course, *Literacy, Community, Art,* in 2008, remarked on just this quality in her written reflections on the course: "As a graduate student my life consists of classes, library research, and writing at my computer. There is very little opportunity to think outside of my reading, research and class discussions." Twenty graduate students and thirty-four undergraduates have completed *Literacy, Community, Art,* which I have taught five times, usually with a co-teacher. Ms. Pye noted that the course took her outside her traditional academic community in several ways. First of all, it was cross-disciplinary, bringing together art photography, art history, writing, education, museum studies, and community activism. This point recurred in remarks from other graduate students. "It is a terrific opportunity to incorporate multiple disciplines in a cohesive whole, breaking down traditional barriers of segmented disciplines," wrote Abigail Scaduto (M.F.A. in Museum Studies, 2009) the same year. "One learns more about each [discipline] and has a more comprehensive education."

The class not only enrolled both graduates and undergraduates, but was in fact built around multigenerational learning; participants ranged from professors with decades of experience to school-age children. Both spatially and intellectually, the course widened the circle of graduate experience beyond the campus to the surrounding neighborhoods and schools. "Finally," Ms. Pye explained, "I was part of a team, led by the expertise of professors who already engage in public scholarship [and] work with local community partners.... [I was] engaged in a project with high school students that created a tangible, experiential course for all involved. ... It also became a springboard for my dissertation research."

Ultimately for Ms. Pye, getting outside through publicly engaged learning augmented her scholarship, and she adapted the photography-literacy projects that were a hallmark of the course for her own work with students in Madagascar. These projects brought about, in her phrase, a "co-production of knowledge," with researcher and studied population working together as partners to produce data as well as interpretations. Like Ms. Pye, almost all of the graduate students from *Literacy, Community, Art* brought aspects of the course into the next stage of their careers. Some adapted the actual projects to a new venue. Others brought a commitment to community outreach and education to their work.

Given these devilishly recessionary times, this may be the bottom line that makes or breaks publicly engaged learning: Can it help in getting a job? The results from the students' own reports so far are good. However, before introducing the students and the paths engaged learning has taken in their professional lives, I want to address what went into making the course in the first place.

The training and experience for the course began well before I became a professional academic, which accounts for an approach that doesn't always fit into a university structure. Also, as is evident in Ms. Pye's comments, this particular type of public engagement involved many partnerships, which shifted into different constellations in each version of the course. Looking at these partnerships throughout the history and development of *Literacy, Community, Art* will help to sketch the complexity in building such a course, which sets goals for both the university students and the community partners. Then I will describe the course with a certain amount of detail to show the types of learning involved, including the co-production of knowledge identified and emulated by Ms. Pye. Finally, I will survey the thoughts and experiences of the graduate students who, like Ms. Pye, have completed the course and incorporated what they gained into the next step in their careers.

Beginnings

The *Literacy, Community, Art* course grew from my own zeal for active learning, which was not fostered in graduate school but in the museums of New York City. I had chafed at constraints when I was in graduate school studying the history of art. Often I tell people that my real graduate education came after graduate school when I worked for nearly ten years in museum education. Most of my experience came at The Museum of Modern Art in New York City, where I was responsible for all high school programs and lecturers, school programs workshops, teacher workshops, and advanced classes at the Lincoln Center Institute. I also worked in various capacities with the Solomon R. Guggenheim Museum (1984–85), the Metropolitan Museum of Art (1988–89), and the Museum Education Consortium Interactive Video Project (1988–90). At the museums, of course, I found superb art collections and many knowledgeable and sophisticated colleagues. Yet it was engaging the viewing public that stretched my own understanding of art and its history far beyond what I had done to achieve the Ph.D.

During my time in museums, the role of the educator shifted dramatically from giving information to facilitating connections. All viewers—whether preschoolers or senior citizens, native New Yorkers or non-English speakers from all over the globe—were approached as partners in discovering and exploring the works of art. Throughout the 1980s and 1990s, the education departments at many American museums expanded by adding new positions, enlarging facilities, securing dedicated donors, and increasing programming. During this period museums recognized the importance of outreach for sustaining their institutions. First of all, museum surveys showed the visitor population was aging and not being replenished by young people. Education programs for young adults and schoolchildren seemed ideal for cultivating new generations of viewers and members. Secondly, funders increasingly asked for statistics demonstrating diversity in visitors, and education department projects with New York City schools supplied the kind of diverse profile funders admired. With increased support and visibility, museum education acted as a hub for experimentation, research, and innovation. As museums promoted visual thinking and visual literacy as essential to modern education, I benefited from working with leading education researchers such as Abigail Housen and Howard Gardner and from in-house studies on the efficacy of facilitated learning.

The museum-outreach experience made me a firm believer in both learning through doing and educating through community-engaged activities. As I moved to the academy I brought with me a commitment to active learning.

When I arrived at Syracuse University in the Fall of 1993, neither innovation nor community-involved education was on the radar of my college or my colleagues. Full of youthful enthusiasm, I proposed to my department and to the larger art school faculty several educational models that adapted the community educational programs from the museum to the classrooms of the university. Not a soul was interested. The dean at the time told me flat-out that this was considered service and service did not count for tenure. The atmosphere could not have been more hostile. On my own, I started working with the teachers who taught my two children at the local public elementary school.

In 2004, after a year teaching at the Syracuse University study-abroad campus in Florence, Italy, I returned to a discussion on the city schools with Susan Peck, administrator in the Academic Affairs office of my academic unit, the College of Visual and Performing Arts. My college now had a more sympathetic dean, and the university had just hired a new chancellor who spoke positively about the arts. We decided to begin the research, development, and fundraising for a college-wide schools partnering program that would bring SU graduate and undergraduate students into the city public schools as mentors and bring city public-school students onto the campus. The vision we developed for this endeavor, initially called the Orange Partnering Project, is encapsulated in the prospectus reproduced on page 187. The document not only summarizes my approach to engaging city schools but also reveals my idealistic aspirations for what was, perhaps, an overly ambitious project.

From a Vision to the First Course, Spring 2006

In the academic year 2005–06, our fledgling Orange Partnering Project joined with several like-minded people pursuing closely related projects. This vociferous, energetic group was known for its three Marys—Mary Lynn Mahan, an exceptional art teacher at Edward Smith Elementary School; Mary Lee Hodgens, a dedicated program manager at Light Work photography center in Syracuse; and Mary Lou Marien, an activist art history professor and specialist in photography—as well as Doug Dubois, an accomplished art photography professor; Elaine Garrett, a skilled graduate assistant for the Orange Partnering Project; and myself. Combining many resources, including a Syracuse University Vision Fund grant awarded to the Orange Partnering Project, the group developed a course inspired by the work of photographer Wendy Ewald, a MacArthur Fellow and associate at the Center for Documentary Studies at Duke University. Ewald came to SU as a speaker in the "Beyond Borders" Symposium and also spoke with us. Light Work then sponsored a workshop led by a trainer from Duke University's Literacy Through Photography program (developed by Ewald); we all attended along with interested schoolteachers.

With this background, Doug Dubois and I designed and team-taught the pilot course, *Literacy, Community, Photography,* in the Spring

The Orange Partnering Project

Vision: The Orange Partnering Project builds long-term, sustainable collaborations between Syracuse University and Syracuse City public schools to establish academic excellence and cultural exchange in elementary, secondary, and university education. In the College of Visual and Performing Arts, we intend to create a sustainable model for embedding the arts in core school subjects, and, in the process, erase the artificial boundaries between public and private education.

Purpose: In the College for Visual and Performing Arts, the Orange Partnering Project brings together the faculty, students, and resources of the college with faculty and students of the Syracuse City School District. Through collaboration, teams of SU faculty, SU students, and city school teachers work together on curricula that can integrate the arts into required subjects such as math, science, and English Language Arts. The Orange Partnering Project strives to create a mutually beneficial, long-term partnership between Syracuse University and the Syracuse City School District that can give city school teachers and students access to the intellectual and financial resources of the Syracuse University arts community. In the university, faculty, staff, and students will further not only their academic, advisory, and scholarly experiences, but also their engagement as citizens committed to public education and community involvement.

For the city public schools, in addition to collaborative support in the classroom, resources will include

- teacher workshops
- grant-writing assistance
- in-class partnerships for curriculum development and assessment
- field trips linked to curriculum for students and parents
- artist-in-residence programs (from the community, the college, and outside the university)
- fundraising for materials and supplies
- in-service support for professional faculty development

For Syracuse University faculty and students, in addition to collaborative learning with the city school teachers, the educational experience will include

- workshops in arts integration and community art projects
- artist-in-residence opportunities
- courses in history and studio practices of social and community-based art
- support and training in grant writing
- fellowship support for graduate students

of 2006, with Mary Lynn Mahan as our in-school partner. Nineteen SU students enrolled—fourteen at the undergraduate (300-) level and five at the graduate (500-) level. Over a six-week period, the SU students worked as mentors to three fifth-grade classes and one fourth-grade class at Ed Smith Elementary. Prior to working with SU, Mary Lynn Mahan had piloted the Ewald-based photography project on her own with the collaboration of art photographer Stephen Mahan. Knowledgeable, dedicated, and organized, Ms. Mahan recruited enthusiastic classroom teachers, built support with the principal and the school, and expertly guided the SU mentors when they worked in the school. The SU students also put in extra effort to mount an exhibition of the fourth- and fifth-graders' photography and text. The brochure written and designed by the SU students (Figure 10.1) illustrates some of the photography, describes the project, and thanks all the many supporters. The students were so proud of the project and their contributions that the professors, Doug Dubois and I, are not even mentioned. I take this as a positive sign of ownership.

From this beginning, the College of Visual and Performing Arts has developed several courses that work within the city public schools. Beginning in August 2005, Chancellor Nancy Cantor established the Partnership for Better Education to support a university-wide engagement with the city schools.[1] Within this supportive environment, I continued with an adaptation of the pilot course, now titled *Literacy, Community, Art: Projects with Students at William Nottingham High School*.

Projects with Students at William Nottingham High School

I sought to expand the program to middle- and high-school students because this age group in Syracuse needs stronger connections with the university and these children are sadly underserved in arts education.[2] In June 2009, a study from the U.S. Department of Education drew attention to the lackluster achievement of eighth-grade students nationwide in the art and music fields. According to *The New York Times*, the results also allowed "federal officials to conclude that in music and art, white and Asian students scored higher, on average, than African-American and Hispanic students, girls outscored boys, and private schools outperformed public ones" (Dillon 2009).

Working with middle- and high-school students always has one big drawback: students change classes. There is no longer a teacher in charge of a single group of students for a full school day as in elementary school. Scheduling visits and field trips consumes many hours and a lot of energy. The Syracuse City School District added to the scheduling challenge by using a four-day system for high schools, meaning that a class can meet Monday, Wednesday, Friday one week and Tuesday

This spring, a Syracuse University art photography class and 4th and 5th grade art classes at Ed Smith Elementary School met together to explore, photograph, and write about themes of childhood identity and the school experience. our classes learned how photography uses art-making and visual language creatively to represent thoughts and ideas.

Our inspiration for this class is the work of Wendy Ewald, MacArthur Fellow and associate at the Center for Documentary Studies at Duke University. Ewald was a featured lecturer at this year's Syracuse Symposium, "Beyond Borders". Her decades-long involvement with community photography and visual literacy education has taken her to schools and towns all over the world. Ewald's curriculum and methods from Literacy through Photography, a program that stems from a "need we all feel to articulate and communicate something relevant about our personal and communal lives".

Acknowledgements

This project and exhibition were made possible through:

The Orange Partnering Project of the College of Visual and Performing Arts/Vision Grant from the Center for Support of Teaching and Learning

Light Work/Community Darkrooms

Department of Fine Arts, College of Arts and Sciences

Syracuse City School District

Edward Smith Elementary School

U Encounter Program

Division of Student Affairs Soling Program

The Syracuse Symposium

Special thanks to Mary Lynn Mahan, Mary Lee Hodgens, John Mannion, and Mary Lou Marien.

This class began in an effort to support Chancellor Nancy Cantor's Partnership for Better Education. It is a program established between Syracuse University and the Syracuse City School District to focus on four areas crucial to Syracuse's future: the arts, science and math, and educational inclusion and literacy.

From projects such as Learning through the Lens, Syracuse University and City schoolteachers will foster life-long commitment to continual learning, community pride and personal expression.

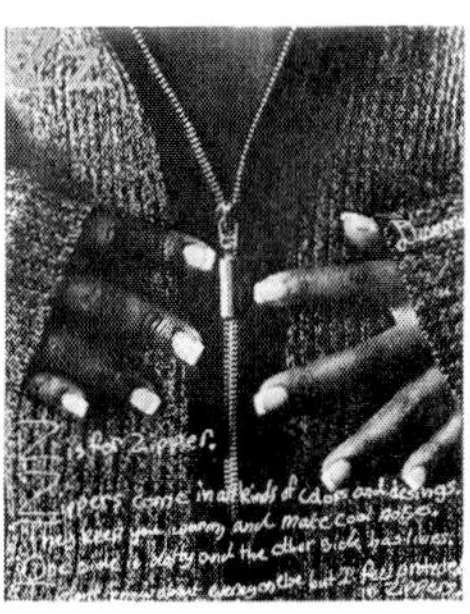

Learning through the Lens:
Collaborations with Children at Ed Smith Elementary School

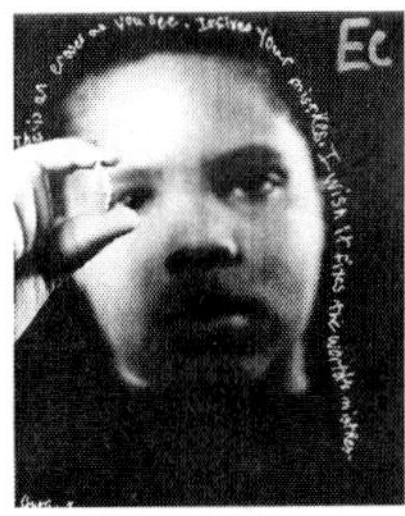

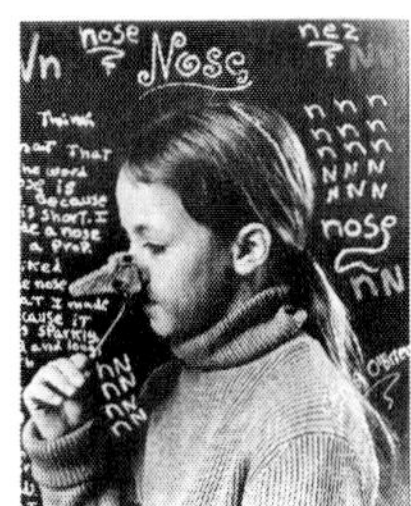

Mary Lynn Mahan, art teacher at Ed Smith Elementary, last year piloted a Literacy through Photography model with one class. It generated so much interest at Ed Smith that faculty and staff were eager to support this latest initiative.

Edward Smith Elementary School is a "Community of Caring", a philosophy defined by "creating strong support systems for students…by helping them to build sound decision making skills [and] open[ing] a continuing dialogue among family, peers, teachers, administrators, and the community at large."

Ed Smith is dedicated to inclusive learning by promoting diversity, openness, multiple abilities among classmates, and flexible problem-solving. Learning through the Lens underscored these ideals by providing the 4th and 5th grade art students an accessible medium by which to express their individuality.

P is for Perfect
With the guidance of the Syracuse University studentsand art teacher Mary Lynn Mahan, the 4th and 5th grade students approached their projects through one of 4 different themes (based on the Literacy through Photography model):

The Alphabet
Students of Mark Hammernik's 4th grade class were each assigned a letter, and asked to express this letter through a studio portrait. Each student illustrated the letter via an object or concept, and wrote text that creatively explained his or her visual choice.

The Best Part of Me
Diane Berman's 5th grade class was asked to identify a feature or ability that each student liked about him/her. The students then found a way to show this "best part" in one studio image. From noses to singing, the best parts found recognition in the class's images and words.

Family and Community
The 5th grade students of Valerie Brennan took 35 mm cameras to their school, homes and neighborhoods to show what family and community means to each student. A brief essay detailed how the photograph captured this concept.

Dreams
Mary Lou Balcolm's 5th grade students enacted their dreams through 35 mm photographs. Each student was responsible for identifying, staging, and capturing this concept in a singular image and poem.

In counterpoint to these projects, the Syracuse University students formed their own groups to produce images that would interact and "converse" with the Ed Smith student work. The themes the SU students worked with are:

The Students
Portraits of the 4th through 6th grade science fair and the 2nd grade's Judy Chicago dinner plate event captures the individuality of each of the subjects.

The Staff
Their work makes Ed Smith run smoothly. These portraits detail the staff in their environments and show how they contribute to the Ed Smith community.

The Teachers
What are the Ed Smith teachers REALLY like? This series of portraits offers clues to the personalities of some school faculty members.

The School
How do the objects of a school—the blackboards, chairs and more—tell of its people? These pictures examine the spaces in that exist before and after the bell rings.

FIGURE 10.1. Exhibition brochure for *Literacy, Community, Photography* pilot course, featuring work by Ed Smith Elementary students in Syracuse, NY. Courtesy of the author.

and Thursday the next week. Holidays, conference days, and snow days (a certainty in Syracuse) shift the schedule as well. The anonymous evaluations that SU students submitted consistently lauded the course and the professors, but lamented the difficulties with scheduling. In the 2008–09 academic year we would move *Literacy, Community, Art* to the fall semester to avoid snow days, the week-long holidays, and the standardized testing days that occurred in the spring.

Expanding the program to middle schools and high schools required identifying teachers who, like Mary Lynn Mahan, would not only embrace the SU partnership but also participate fully. This is not an easy task and it has become more difficult as schools demand more time to prepare students for standardized testing and as schools and teachers become weary of "special" programs that disappear after a year or two.

After an extended effort to begin a partnership with a middle school foundered on the shoals of restructuring, the *Literacy, Community,* Art course began work in Nottingham High School with technology teacher Randy Weatherby teaching photography. Nottingham High School, one of the four main city high schools, serves the city's eastside population as well as those city students who choose the school for its drama, arts, math, science, and English as a Second Language programs. Though the local news media generally identify the school as "inner city," the 1970s buildings, the extensive and well-maintained grounds, the new playing fields, and the Olympic-size pool give it the appearance of a suburban school campus. In 2009–10, the New York State School Report Card characterized the racial/ethnic profile of the 1,314 students as 60% African American, 22% White, 7% Latino, 10% Asian/Pacific Islander, and less than 1% American Indian. The report also indicated that 56% of the students were eligible for free lunches and 19% had limited proficiency in English.3 Of course, these bureaucratic statistics diminish the vibrancy of the school, which has a diversity that would be the envy of any rainbow coalition. The student body also reflects the large refugee and foreign-born populations of the city; students come from Africa, Eastern Europe, Asia, and Latin America.

Academically, the high school registered on the *Newsweek* list of Top Public High Schools for 2009 (968th), due to the number of students completing Advanced Placement courses and earning college credit from the SUNY College of Environmental Science and Forestry and from Syracuse University. Each year a dozen or so graduating students go to top-level colleges, including those in the Ivy League, and each year 30–40% of the incoming ninth-grade students drop out of school and do not graduate at all.[4] This last statistic, common to all of the high schools in Syracuse, is an obvious cause for great concern and intervention.

About 25 Nottingham High School students usually sign up for the afternoon beginning-level photography class; several, however, switch to other courses during the year. About half the students choose photography based on some genuine interest; others find leaving class with a camera to roam the halls and grounds very attractive. Every student knows and appreciates the class's reputation as an easy course. In the Fall of 2008 the class comprised 14 African Americans, 9 Whites (including a Serbian refugee), 1 Latino, and 1 South Asian American. Eight were boys and seventeen were girls. All four high-school grades were represented: two in ninth, seven in tenth, nine in eleventh, and seven in twelfth. In previous years, the class had a similar makeup and always three or four students who spoke a language other than English at home.

For some of the SU mentors, the students and dynamics at Nottingham High School seem familiar; for others, the density and the energy come as a surprise. For all who come from the University, the course affords an opportunity to crumble assumptions about city public schools and the bureaucratic jargon of "underserved populations" and "at-risk" students.

The photography-literacy projects that link SU student-mentors with the Nottingham High School students model the creative processes that are part of the art school education: brainstorming, mapping or sketching ideas, experimenting with a variety of images and words, editing and refining the images and words, executing the final work with care, and presenting it publicly. As it is short, our first workshop, nicknamed The Polaroid Workshop,[5] can serve as an example. Usually confined to one class period, it represents our way of working. There are three stages to this workshop: brainstorming using both images and writing, creating a nontraditional portrait, and experiencing how that portrait image communicates to others. The goal, to borrow from Julie Ellison, is to "find ways to challenge university students and [public-school students] to recognize and resist ... cliché" (2008, 467).

Handed a camera, most young people reflexively make a photographic portrait that resembles something familiar, like the pictures in a family photo album or on Facebook, or the poses on America's Next Top Model. To counter this reflex, the workshop begins with an exercise in extended focus where the students close their eyes, sit still in the manner of meditation, and make an inventory of themselves from head to toe. The next step is to create a map or diagram of that head-to-toe inventory and write about each part that represents what they like best. As with all the projects, the SU mentors first go through the workshop themselves and keep a record in their teaching journals. Figure 10.2, from the teaching journal of SU mentor Katie Schuering, shows her head-to-toe map with notations on her best parts.

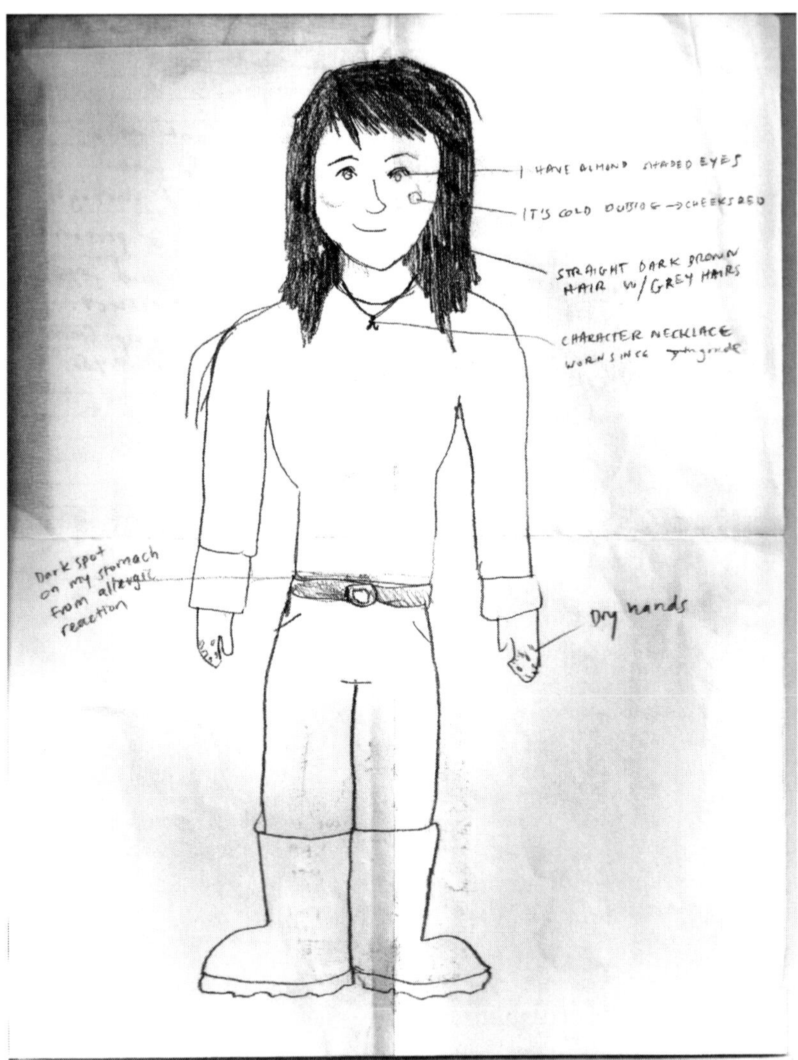

FIGURE 10.2. Head-to-toe "map" with notations, from the teaching journal of *Literacy, Community, Art* student Katie Schuering. Courtesy of the artist.

This diagram becomes the source for the two Polaroid photos each student will make. In Figure 10.3, Ms. Schuering explains why she selected the Polaroid of her hands as the image to represent herself.

FIGURE 10.3. Polaroid photos with explanations, from Katie Schuering's teaching journal. Courtesy of the artist.

In the final step, which further connects visual and word-based communication, every student chooses one Polaroid to pass along to someone who has not yet seen it. Each student takes a good look at the received Polaroid and then writes as if she or he were the person in the image. Figure 10.4, from the journal of SU student Abigail Scaduto, is an example of the completed exercise. Ms. Scaduto chose an image in which her arms are raised and passed it on to another SU student, who wrote, "I am a daughter. I am as full and grand as a tree...." The Nottingham High School students used the wood shop and school halls for staging their photographs. Often in these images a part stands for the whole—a visual analogue of the figure of speech known as synecdoche, which the students learn about in their English classes. To end the workshop, a few writers share the image and what they wrote with the class. The fun—and illuminating—part of the workshop comes when the image-maker hears the text written by the image-observer. More often than not, the image-maker acknowledges that the writer did capture something essential in the image.

FIGURE 10.4. Polaroid Workshop self-portrait by *Literacy, Community, Art* student Abigail Scaduto. Courtesy of the artist.

Before going into the school, there is planning, more planning, and still more planning. The SU mentors work with the course professors to translate the workshop into a lesson plan that the mentors can actually use for their first visit in the high school classroom. As a class we spend a lot of time crafting how to present a project that emphasizes creativity rather than putting students in the position of trying to guess what the teacher wants. We also talk about word choice, ways to be a facilitator, and how not to sound intimidating. From experience, I know that asking students to draw a picture brings out fears of not drawing well.

Instead, we introduce the idea of making a map of your body or a diagram of yourself from head to toe; stick figures are just fine. The goal of this exercise is to develop a way to record your thoughts; these thoughts can then inspire the photographs you make. A Polaroid/Best Part of Me lesson plan, created by the eight graduate students and one undergraduate in the Fall 2008 class, is excerpted on p. 196.

After the introductory Polaroid workshop, the SU mentors begin a series of visits that incorporate facilitated discussions of art photographs, work with a journal-sketchbook, word-sketching, and making both digital and analog photographs. In all, during the Fall of 2008, the SU mentors made 16 visits to the high-school classroom, plus two field trips. One trip was to see *Don't Look Back: Stories from the Salt City*, a play in which seven real-life residents of Syracuse tell their stories.[6] The second field trip, an essential part of the program, brings the high-school students to Light Work and Community Darkrooms on the SU campus. Here the students spend half a day making large-scale black-and-white analog prints in state-of-the-art darkroom facilities that they can access on their own as members of the community. The full sequence of the school visits and field trips for Fall 2008 is outlined in the appendix that accompanies this chapter (pp. 206–10). The final event is a public exhibition of the photographs and texts made by the high school students, which is held in public gallery spaces on the SU campus and has an opening reception for students, families, and school staff.

Perspectives from Graduate Students

In what ways does a publicly engaged course such as *Literacy, Community, Art* serve graduate students? On the pragmatic side, the students acquire skills and experiences that transfer to jobs in fields related to education and museums. More broadly, the course promotes activism and enriches their more conventional graduate work. By means of conversations, emails, and questionnaires, I asked the graduate students to comment on how the course connected to their field and their careers. I also reviewed their teaching journals, which included final written reflections and thoughts on lessons learned. Some of the comments from these sources are discussed below.[7]

The course certainly functions as shared territory for students training for related but different fields, and who usually would not cross paths. The graduate students have come from four different program areas, each with its own career objectives: Museum Studies, Art History, Transmedia Arts, and Cultural Foundations of Education.[8] All came to the class with some background in the visual arts and varying degrees of interest in community education. Some were experienced art

POLAROID PROJECT – THE BEST PART OF ME

Goal: Students will explore making self-portraits with Polaroid film and learn how they are perceived in the words of others.

Objectives:

- Introduce Polaroid cameras/film
- Introduce self-reflection, "mapping" of identity
- Introduce how to convey ideas with an image

Class Time: 12:50–2:10 P.M.

Materials: One Polaroid camera per four students, Polaroid film loaded into the cameras, paper, pen/pencils, tape or similar adhesive

Going to Nottingham: Abigail, Kimberly, Kelli

Schedule

12:50 Begin by settling the group down. Mr. Weatherby takes attendance.

1:00 Introduction of SU mentors to class and brief statement on today's project: "We will be doing a project *together* with Polaroid cameras."

1:05 KELLI leads: "First, sit, relax, close your eyes for a minute or two to think about yourself from the top of your head to your toes. Take an inventory. From head to toe, what do you really like about yourself; think about what is good about each part of you. What are the *best parts of you*?"

[Note: writing a script like the above helps embed the plan in your head.]

1:10 "OK. Open your eyes. We'll pass out some paper and pencils, if you don't have any."

- Have students make a map of themselves from top to bottom, using the whole page. Do not say draw. The process should be quick and easy. Make an example sketch on the board. "Don't be afraid to use the whole sheet of paper. Make a simple shape." Ask students to mark every place on their diagram with those *best parts* you thought about.
- Then add notes to say how that part tells something about you. If you think of something new, put it in.
- Have students circle the most interesting part of their body. What is the most special?

1:20 KIMBERLY leads: Introduce Polaroid camera.

- Show the basics of how it works: the shutter button, the flash, the focal length, and parallax. Explain simply while holding the camera. You may want to pass one around for the students to look through as you talk. Take one photograph as an example.
- Ask the students to form groups of four people. Each student works with a partner to come up with two photos telling about that *best part of you*. Give each group one Polaroid camera. One person directs and the other takes the photograph. Each person gets two shots. Split time between pairs; two shoot while the other two think about what they want to do. Seven minutes per pair.
- Go off with partners. "Be back at ______ with two photos of yourself." (about 15 minutes)

photographers; others had only the experience of taking snapshots. Some had done considerable work in community outreach; others, like Jennifer Wilkey (M.F.A., Transmedia, 2009), did not even consider public engagement an interest before coming to graduate school.

Once she was in graduate school in the College of Visual and Performing Arts, where community-engaged projects were already underway, Ms. Wilkey, who has a background in both anthropology and visual arts, was quick to recognize the possibilities of taking her photographic expertise into the community. Hearing about local opportunities in the public schools of Syracuse, she competed for and won Art$tart support to be the teaching artist for several classes at Salem Hyde Elementary School in Syracuse.[9] After teaching "three classes of sixth-grade students about art, photography, and personal expression," she enrolled in the *Literacy, Community, Art* course to deepen her experience and have a cohort of fellow practitioners for support and problem-solving. Publicly active graduate work, she wrote, encourages "thinking on your feet and being self-motivated." Josh Brilliant (M.F.A., Museum Studies, 2009) made a similar point: "Literally, every time I entered the classroom, both daycare and high school, something was different than what I had planned for.... I learned always to have plan B and think on my feet." To me, this is a fundamental life lesson that, to date, has not surfaced in the student commentary from my lecture-based classes. In *Literacy, Community, Art*, the SU students were in charge of all aspects of the projects with the community. The training, the practice, the critiques, and the discussions all occurred in the seminar room at SU. But out in the schools the SU students were the responsible parties; they came into the classroom, made the introductions, set the stage, and guided the project from beginning to end.

Furthermore, Ms. Wilkey found that *Literacy, Community, Art,* with its emphasis on collaboration and on encouraging another's voice, nourished and supported her goal to be a teaching artist engaged with students with disabilities. After graduation, she spent part of the summer working on art with a 13-year-old girl with autism. Ms. Wilkey's own photography, video, and installation art grows from collaborations with her mother and her brother, both of whom face serious health challenges. The long-term art projects with her brother James, who is epileptic and has some developmental disabilities, and her record of his day-to-day activities have been recognized with a 2010 Lucie Foundation Scholarship Professional Grant.[10]

Artistic collaboration that features two intertwining voices is also fundamental in the work of LaToya Ruby Frazier (M.F.A., Art Photography, 2007), who completed the original 2006 version of the course.

Her initial graduate school goals were to document issues of poverty and to introduce other young people to the power of media arts. While in graduate school, she expanded her vision and explored both public engagement in the schools and outreach through exhibittions, lectures, and art therapy. Her current photographic and video work, a continuing collaboration with her family, extends beyond classic documentary photography into the intimate and mutual explorations of family connections. On her website (http://www.latoyarubyfrazier.com), where one can view her still photography, she describes her work with her mother as follows: "Mom is co-author, artist, photographer and subject. Our relationship primarily exists through a process of making images together. I see beauty in all her imperfections and abuse. Her drug addiction is secondary to our psychological connection. When we are photographing each other we meditate on our difference and sameness." In addition to experiencing collaborative art while in the 2006 course, Ms. Frazier spent long hours designing the professional brochure that accompanied the "Learning Through the Lens" exhibition that was the culmination of the partner-ship. We rushed in with printed copies just as guests were arriving—a result of the exacting timetable in a very full and tightly scheduled single semester. Today, she is well versed in university exhibitions and the time demands of academic scheduling in her positions as associate curator at the Civic Square Art Gallery of Rutgers University and as part-time lecturer in the Visual Arts Department of the Mason Gross School of the Arts. In 2010, *Literacy, Community, Art* alum Josh Brilliant joined Ms. Frazier at Rutgers, where he is pursuing an M.F.A. in art photography and continuing his interest in activist art.

Art as a means for actuating ideals has a long history and has had its peaks and troughs on campuses in the late twentieth and early twenty-first centuries. Though far from a trend, there is currently a growing interest in activist art. Steve Belarovich (M.F.A., Computer Art, 2010) described himself as a budding activist targeting, in his words, "Globalization, War, Consumerism, and Oppression of the Government." He found the attention we gave to our student partners a positive strategy that reinforced ideas he admired in the writings of Brazilian educator Paulo Freire, author of *Pedagogy of the Oppressed* (1968). The *Literacy, Community, Art* course, he wrote, helped instill "the practice of being selfless." For him, the most significant experiences from this course included

- teaching high school students photographic composition and shooting practice
- facilitating classroom discussions about historical and current photographs

- exemplifying the role of teacher-facilitator in the classroom
- understanding how to connect with high-school students
- figuring out which grade level I feel the most comfortable teaching
- gaining experience in working with the community and with other artists/teachers.

While enrolled in *Literacy, Community, Art,* Mr. Belarovich used aspects of the class as he prepared an undergraduate course, Culture Jamming, that he taught in the Fall 2009 semester.

Kelly Pennington (M.F.A., Transmedia, 2010), also recognized that her work in *Literacy, Community, Art* informed her teaching in other classes. As a graduate student, she taught introductory photography and from our class discussions recognized "different learner types."[11] She notes, "Teaching each type of learner helps me to access my knowledge and organize it in a different way.... Unbeknownst to my students they are taking part in a big conversation with each other through me." Ms. Pennington, like Ms. Wilkey, saw herself prior to her graduate education as being involved in her "previous community as an artist only." Her experience in public engagement enlarged her view of herself and what she can do after completing her program. She reports feeling "better prepared for the path that I would like to set for myself after graduation. I hope to start a community environment that involves a school/summer camp and artist colony." Ms. Pennington also had the unique experience of being both a student and, in the following semester, a co-teacher of the *Literacy, Community, Art* course. As a course co-teacher she developed and revised budgets, which helped her in writing grant proposals and earning the residency at the Saltonstall Fellowship for the Arts. She drafted grants to support teaching, learned assessment techniques, exhibited resourcefulness in and soliciting in-kind donations, and gracefully negotiated unexpected disruptions to well-made plans.

The *Literacy, Community, Art* course opened a completely unexpected career path for Meaghan Ezen, who took the graduate-level course as a senior History of Art major. Shortly after her 2006 graduation, she was excited to find a program that extended the interests she developed in *Literacy, Community, Art:* the New Hampshire Reads Program, sponsored by Americorps. After a semester working in the Hopkinton School District, Ms. Ezen relayed to me the joy she found in rediscovering children's literature with her young students and developing creative projects:

> Being re-introduced to the world of children's literature as an adult has been quite an experience ... in some ways I believe that

> I enjoy the books more now. The best part of the job, besides the kids, is that I have total creative freedom. Each week I get to choose the books and make up the projects we'll be working with.

Ms. Ezen has continued teaching as an instructional assistant at Harold Martin Elementary School in Hopkinton, New Hampshire, and also works one-on-one with several special-needs students. She writes: "I've enjoyed the environment so much I am now positive I want to become an art teacher."

For Museum Studies graduate students, the *Literacy, Community, Art* course knit together theory with much-appreciated practice in the field. Elaine Garrett (M.F.A., Museum Studies, 2006) describes how well the course connected to museum practices: "This type of public engagement absolutely underscores the tenets of museum education—a discipline that focuses on building fun, rewarding, age-appropriate, interconnected patterns of thinking and problem solving that illuminate a particular historical, artistic, or scientific idea."

Ms. Garrett, as noted earlier, worked on The Orange Partnering Project and helped write the proposals for the initial grants that funded *Literacy, Community, Art.* She became particularly well grounded in our research on removing town-gown barriers and devising programs that incorporate college education into high schools. Having studied photography as an undergraduate at Ithaca College, she joined the 2006 version of the course with strong backgrounds in art photography and museum studies practices. In the course, she directly trained novice elementary-school students in darkroom techniques and guided them through the enlarger work, chemical baths, and finishing steps to produce their own professional-level analog prints. With others in the course, Ms. Garrett then mounted an exhibition with professional labels, wall text, brochures, publicity, invitations, and opening reception. She brought all this experience to her post-graduation job as a college admissions counselor, which included creating publications and marketing materials for higher education. Currently, she is an admissions officer at Southern Vermont College, connecting high-school students with college, an Orange Partnering goal.

Kimberly Griffiths (M.F.A., Museum Studies, 2009) made a point of praising the practical benefits of the course, such as learning about grant writing and working with a budget. "Going through all the steps ... of publicly engaging with a school will provide me with the set of tools ... to do similar work in the future." Ms. Griffiths came to the course already employed full-time as the Associate Curator of Education and Public Programs at Everson Museum of Art, a position she still holds. She enrolled in *Literacy, Community, Art* to explore ways to increase community connections at the museum, which serves the widely diverse communities and schools of central New York State. The course, she discovered, provided a "totally different way" to engage with the community. In Fall 2008, when Ms. Griffiths took the course, we had the luxury of spending ten weeks working directly with the high-school students in their classroom and on two field trips. At best, most museum programs only visit a classroom once or twice in conjunction with the students' trip to the museum. Longer school partnerships open the way for shifting the teacher-student dynamic, as Susan Cahan explained in Contemporary Art and Multicultural Education (1996), one of our readings that impressed Ms. Griffiths.

> Cahan [writes that] … the student should be encouraged to bring their personal experiences and knowledge to the table. She recognizes the importance of the student as an active participant in her education. This method can better prepare the students for adulthood. Our class kept this as a central goal … we were asking them to talk about, write about and photograph their identities. We were asking them to think about their place in the world and their identities.

The identity theme lends itself to adaptation, and one of the aims of the course is to give the SU students the tools to replicate the projects in new circumstances. Emily Marino (M.F.A., Museum Studies, 2010), wrote that she is leading a literacy-photography workshop at 171 Cedar Arts Center in Corning, New York: "I am using the journal that we put together while working with Nottingham [High School] and SU childcare [the SU Early Education and Child Care Center]. It should be very interesting and I am excited to get started!" Ms. Marino's journal, a requirement of the course, was an exquisitely organized three-inch binder that contained all the lesson plans, the photographs she made and the ones she collected for examples, photographs made with and by her student partners, her reflections on teaching, her responses to course readings, diagrams of the cameras used, and much more. She came away from the course with not only a semester of community partnership work but a thorough document to help her lead a workshop on her own. Her excitement reflects the enthusiasm and confidence many students find in having successfully worked with the community. Her workshop for ages 8–12 and 12–15 is an after-hours addition to her job as grants manager for The Arts Council of the Southern Finger Lakes, a position she accepted just two months after graduation.

The transfer of practical skills ripples outward. Nora Mattern (M.F.A., Museum Studies, 2009) shared the following story about the facilitated looking method known as Visual Thinking Strategies (VTS) that is part of the training I give the students in the course.

> The Visual Thinking Strategies was an aspect of the course that was particularly valuable for me. Since learning VTS, I shared the method with my mother, who is an elementary art educator and adjunct faculty at Penn State. She uses it on a very regular basis in the elementary classroom. She also taught a continuing education course for K–12 teachers at King's College in Wilkes-Barre on integrating art into the classroom. She asked me to come into the course to share VTS with her class of teachers. I gave a brief presentation, demonstrated how it is done, and then invited the teachers to use the method. It went really well and I think helped them to recognize that they are capable of sharing art with their students, even if they themselves do not have a strong background in it.

Ms. Mattern says her mother's students "are thrilled when they see her bring out the projector because they have responded so well to VTS." As with my own experience, Ms. Mattern relayed that VTS is a very valuable tool for the inclusive classroom. Students with special needs respond positively to being guided to tell about what they see is going on in a picture. Ms. Mattern, in addition to working in the classroom, spent a year with the Williams College–Mystic Seaport program. She has begun the Ph.D. program in Library and Information Science (with a focus in archival science) at the University of Pittsburgh.

Finally, in this discussion of how the course served the students, I want to return to Lisa Pye, whose comments opened this essay. After taking the course in the Spring 2007 semester, Ms. Pye adapted the photography-literacy projects for her dissertation research work in Madagascar. As a doctoral candidate in Cultural Foundations of Education, an interdisciplinary graduate program "created to support fundamental inquiry into the nature of education,"[12] she studies teenage students in Madagascar who are in transition as they move from their ethnically distinct home regions to attend a French-speaking university in a heterogeneous city of three million. Ms. Pye recognized that having these students make their own photographs and then speak and write about them opened up avenues of understanding unavailable to a conventional outside observer: "Instead of me taking the photos, my participants ... create their own photographs for themselves and their community. The knowledge—and knowledge production—is shared." These photographs and texts then become ambassadors to the wider world: the local voice, so to speak, articulating the successes and challenges of the present-day culture.

Ms. Pye brought some of the Malagasy photographs to the 2009 *Literacy, Community, Art* class. Given the opportunity to record themselves with a camera, many of the Malagasy young people showed themselves studying on their own at a desk. This made an interesting contrast to the first choice of the majority of Nottingham High School students, who preferred a Facebook-type shot featuring a group of friends grinning close to the camera. The Malagasy students also eloquently photographed doorways, yards, fences, and roadways, and spoke about the intimacy of the home interiors and the process of moving into the public realm as represented by the different kinds of exterior spaces. As Ms. Pye explained to our class, she would not have recognized the nuances of private-public relations symbolized by a yard, a fence, and an open road without the photographs and words of the Malagasy students themselves.

As is evident in these comments, public engagement opened the graduate students up to possibilities not imagined when they began graduate school and, for quite a few, brought them onto career paths where they are deeply involved with the community. In reviewing all the graduate student commentary, I also noticed the absence of passive voices. These students exhibited pride in accomplishments, commitment and passion, and a vision for their future. Checking in with students one, two, or three years removed from the course, I was surprised to find even more excitement about the value of the experience than in their original course reflections. Another testament to the course is that both Lisa Pye and Sasha Batorsky (B.F.A., History of Art, 2009) asked if they could come back to join the class on their own time as participant-assistants; they were great additions.

In my experience, there still exists an unresolved tension in the academy between traditional scholarship and activist work. During a recent departmental discussion precipitated by budget reductions, the *Literacy, Community, Art* course was characterized as an elective and marginal to any required curricula for art and design students. Once again, public engagement and community activism were seen as volunteer, do-good work and not valuable for building a career. Jennifer Wilkey argued, against this point of view, that courses such as *Literacy, Community, Art* should be a requirement for both graduates and undergraduates. Not only does this type of publicly engaged course give students skills and experiences for building the civic good, it also establishes a practice for the co-production of knowledge, something fundamental to a thriving community. From my perspective as a professor, the course offers a particular reward when the students recognize they now have pragmatic tools to put their idealism and visions for a better world into practice. The academy has shown them how to roll up their sleeves and get some much-needed work done beyond its boundaries. The students who have taken publicly engaged courses demonstrate in their post-graduation lives that they cherish the rewards of getting outside.

Notes

1. The complete history and program information is available at http://partnership.syr.edu/PARTNERSHIP.

2. On the importance of connecting high school students to the university, see Hoffman et al. 2007.

3. The report, issued February 5, 2011, is available online at https://www.nystart.gov/publicweb-rc/2010/2b/AOR-2010-421800010039.pdf .

4. For recent statistics, see the New York State School Report Card for 2009–10, online at https://www.nystart.gov/publicweb-rc/2010/2b/AOR-2010-421800010039.pdf.

5. This exercise with Polaroid cameras is adapted from the 2005 Literacy Through Photography workshop held at Light Work and from Wendy Ewald's "Best Part of Me" approach.

6. *Don't Look Back: Stories from the Salt City*, conceived and directed by Ping Chong, written and performed by Syracuse residents from Cambodia, Cuba, Macedonia, Mexico, the Onondaga Nation, Sudan, and the city itself.

7. All quotes from students are printed with their permission.

8. The M.F.A. students in Museum Studies follow a program that combines scholarship, exhibition design, and professional internships with the theory and practice of running a museum. Most become museum professionals as curators, registrars, educators, development specialists, managers, and directors. The majority of their professional research and scholarship is disseminated through exhibitions and museum publications. Students who complete the M.A. in Art History have learned to be scholars of art history skilled in original research, in crafting and presenting conference papers, and in writing for academic publication. Some take this degree in tandem with Museum Studies; others plan to go on for a Ph.D. in art history; still others find work in an art-related field. The M.F.A. is the terminal degree for students in Transmedia Arts (including art photography, art video, film, and computer arts), who train first and foremost to be practicing professional artists whose creative work is their research. Most do, however, apply for positions in art schools and colleges, which consider

the quality of their artwork, the promise of their exhibition history, and their teaching experience. The graduate program in Cultural Foundations of Education culminates in the Ph.D. and grooms interdisciplinary scholars and academicians.

9. Art$tart projects are made possible with public funds provided by the New York State Council on the Arts and are currently administered through the Cultural Resources Council of Syracuse (http://www.arts4ed.org).

10. Examples of this work are available online at http://www.jenniferwilkey.com/.

11. Ms. Pennington's reference to learner types comes from the class discussions of Gardner's *Frames of Mind*. Gardner identifies seven intelligences: linguistic, logical-mathematical, musical, bodily-kinesthetic, spatial, interpersonal, and intrapersonal. Each represents a different way to learn and process experiences and information.

12. See http://soeweb.syr.edu/academic/cultural_foundations_of_education/: "Graduate students draw on the disciplines of history, philosophy, and sociology to analyze issues related to inequality in education."

References

Dillon, Sam. 2009. Study finds instruction in art lags in 8th grade. *The New York Times*, June 16.

Ellison, Julie. 2008. The humanities and the public soul. *Antipode* 40 (3): 463–71. doi: 10.1111/j.1467-8330.2008.00615.x.

Gardner, Howard. 1983. *Frames of mind: The theory of multiple intelligences.* New York: Basic Books.

Hoffman, Nancy, Joel Vargas, Andrea Venezia, and Marc S. Miller, eds. 2007. *Minding the gap: Why integrating high school with college makes sense and how to do it*. Cambridge, MA: Harvard University Press,

Stokes, Suzanne. 2002. Visual literacy in teaching and learning: A literature perspective. *Electronic Journal for the Integration of Technology in Education* 1 (1): 10–18.

Appendix

Sample Schedules for *Literacy, Community, Art:* Projects with Students at Nottingham High School

Week	Readings, Assignments	Syracuse University: ART 300/500
1	1. Meighan, "Method for Looking" 2. Chapters 1-3 in Wendy Ewald's *I Wanna Take Me A Picture* (2001) 3. VUE website for material on Visual Thinking Strategies	Introductions; working out schedule for visits to Nottingham High School.
2	1. Alison Armstrong, "Visual Literacy: Humanities and the Fine Arts Curriculum" (2007) 2. Review Abigail Housen's Stages for Aesthetic Development. 3. Collect photos for your teaching journal: points of view, framing, "rule of thirds."	Art photographer Kelli Pennington introduces photo fundamentals; handout on "Basic Camera." Visit to Light Work exhibitions for Visual Thinking Strategies modeling & practice.
3	1. Chapters 4–6 in Wendy Ewald's *I Wanna Take Me A Picture.* 2. Consult Stephen Shore, *The Nature of Photographs* (1998/2007). 3. Read "Peter Pan in Kensington Gardens" chapters in J. M. Barrie, *The Little White Bird* (1902).	Basics of the camera & continuing with fundamentals such as depth of field; getting to know actual cameras and drawing a diagram of all parts for reference.
4	1. Literacy Through Photography website 2. "Community Arts 101" overview essays	Adult-adolescent collaborations in creating stories/artworks; Polaroid project.
5	1. Partners for Arts Education website 2. *Blueprint for Teaching and Learning in the Arts*	Guest speaker: Laura Reeder, founder of Partners for Arts Education

Week	Readings, Assignments	Nottingham HS: Visits with students	ART 300/500
6	1. Browse Kismaric, *American Children: Photographs from the Collection of the Museum of Modern Art* (1980) and other photo collections for art photos of children & teenagers. 2. Collect examples of photos for your journal.	Fri SU student-mentors' first visit to HS class. Polaroid "Best Part of Me" workshop.	Discussion of websites for Partners for Arts Education, the Steve Project, CAPE. Draft lesson plans on "The Many Sides of Me" for school visits.
7	1. Collect examples of Point of view (POV), framing for journal 2. Choose images for VTS discussion	Tues Concepts: POV and framing. Basic functions of digital camera; making camera diagram. Many Sides of Me project (examples: Me at School, Me Playing Sports, Me at Home, Me in my Neighborhood). Digital cameras go home. Thurs Slides & discussion: new POV & framing images; introduce editing & self-portrait. Editing workshop using photos on digital camera; choosing 10 photos & writing description, including talking about POV in photo.	Working with brainstorming & idea-producing techniques
8	1. Collect examples of narrative for your journal. 2. Write 2 pages on your identity in high school.	Tues Slides & discussion: narrative. Thumbnail Narrative Project: creating a narrative with five random student photos & writing a very short story.	SU students at Community Darkrooms; learning …

Week	Readings, Assignments	Nottingham HS: Visits with students	ART 300/500
9	1. Deborah Schwartz, "Dude, Where's My Museum? Inviting Teens to Transform Museums" (2005) 2. Collect examples of near-far, portraiture.	*Tues* Slides & discussion: near-far, self-portraiture Creating a narrative with your own photos *Thurs* Slides & discussion: spaces, self-portraiture. Writing activities: "I am a river ....," "I am like...," "I wish ...,"etc. poems. Brainstorming about space: Where am I? How do I show other people I am there? How do I relate to space? Present b&w analog cameras; diagram camera. b&w analog cameras go home.	Discussion of our own identities in high school. Review, critique & assess our work so far. Planning for upcoming school visits. Darkroom work: contact printing of SU students' photos
10	1. Collect examples of rule of thirds, symmetry, asymmetry, diagonals.	*Tues* Collect b&w analog cameras. In small groups, introduce rule of thirds, symmetry, asymmetry, use of diagonals. Examples for HS students to put in journals. Begin discussion of groups & the shaping of identity within the school. *Thurs* Slides & discussion of directing & dressing up as a character. Examples: Nikki Lee, Marcel Duchamp, Cindy Sherman, Saiman Li. Journal brainstorming: What is the opposite of you? Making sketches: planning to stage a photo. Digital cameras go home.	Planning for 2nd b&w camera workshops

Week	Readings, Assignments	Nottingham HS: Visits with students	ART 300/500
11	1. Ideas for assessment rubric	*Mon* Review & edit images from contact sheets. Catch up on projects & darkroom work. *Tues* FIELD TRIP: SU mentors & HS students see play *Don't Look Back.* *Wed* Review & edit images from contact sheets. Catch up on projects & darkroom work. *Fri* Help students choose best images. Collect journal folders for assessment.	Work in Community Darkrooms; SU students make their final b&w prints. Create assessment rubric to aid with 1st marking period for HS students.
12		*Wed* Negative selection & preparation for going to Community Darkrooms. *Fri* FIELD TRIP: HS students come to work at Community Darkrooms, 9 A.M. to noon; lunch on campus. HS students visit "Tracing Memory" photography exhibition at Light Work.	Nottingham High School students' field trip to COMMUNITY DARKROOMS. SU mentors, faculty assist high school students in creating good quality b&w prints.
13	1. Short presentations on community artists 2. Nato Thompson, *The Interventionists* (2006)		SU student presentations on established community artists Guest speaker: Sue Stonecash on writing grants for working in schools; Art$tart grants. Planning for exhibition & creating mockups.

Week	Readings, Assignments	Nottingham HS: Visits with students	ART 300/500
14		***Mon*** Computer work with digital images and layout.	BREAK
15	1. Susan Cahan & Zoya Kocur (eds.), *Contemporary Art and Multicultural Education* (1996)	*Mon* Prepare writing for images. Writing prompts. Sentences, description, poem, rap. *Wed* Final writing on both digital and b&w large-scale images. *Fri* EXHIBITION: Evening opening with refreshments at Warehouse Community Gallery, in downtown Syracuse, for students, parents, administrators, guests.	Continue SU student presentations on established community artists: Harold Fletcher, Mel Chin, Center for Tactical Magic, The Yes Men. Afternoon: Mounting exhibition at Warehouse Community Gallery; preparing for evening opening.
16		*Tues* Final visit: collect journal folders; pizza party.	SU students submit complete journal with reflection and commentary.

11

Crossing Figueroa: The Tangled Web of Diversity and Democracy

*George J. Sánchez**

Two Universities

I want to thank Lorraine Gutierrez and the Edward Ginsberg Center for Community Service and Learning for the opportunity to return to Ann Arbor and talk with you about my own ideas regarding the future of public scholarship and civic engagement in the twenty-first century. I am honored to present the fifth annual John Dewey Lecture, particularly given the stellar scholars who have presented this lecture before me. As a former faculty member at the University of Michigan, I have a deep fondness and respect for much of the commitments of individual faculty members, students, and the institution as a whole that have provided national leadership in the areas of public scholarship and community engagement.

Having served as the former director of the Program in American Culture here, I first need to acknowledge the enormous role that generations of scholars and teachers in that program have played and continue to play in engagement with the critical issues facing American society, from some of the early directors like Robert Berkhofer and David Hollinger, to the generation that I knew, including June Howard and Alan Wald, to the current generation of leadership of Phil Deloria and Kristen Hass. And over the past few years, I have gotten to know the wonderful work of Imagining America: Artists and Scholars in Public Life, headed by Julie Ellison, whose work in steering a national conversation about the role of the humanities in community service has been dramatic. In addition, the Arts of Citizenship Program, headed by David Scobey, has played a critical role in facilitating humanities and

*Originally delivered as the fifth annual Dewey Lecture, sponsored by the Ginsberg Center for Community Service and Learning at the University of Michigan, in October, 2004. The text as it appears here was published in Imagining America's Foreseeable Futures series, no. 4 (Ann Arbor, MI: Imagining America, 2005), 3–24. Reprinted courtesy of the author.

arts engagement with the local Michigan scene. But I have been most proud of the University of Michigan when I have watched the intellectual and political work of Pat Gurin and former Michigan faculty Sylvia Hurtado and Earl Lewis who, with friends and colleagues from around the nation, stood up to right-wing foundations and fought for the sanctity and sanity of affirmative action in front of the U.S. Supreme Court. This was community engagement of the highest order, combining the importance of diversity in what we see daily in our classrooms and scholarly communities with institutional support to take on those who would limit opportunity in this country. Of all those efforts, the University of Michigan can be very proud.

But I come also today to talk with you of my new institution, the University of Southern California, which is getting to be known for more than its number one football team, as one of a handful of urban universities with serious engagement in its local community. Unlike the history of land-grant universities, which in 1862 were mandated to combine "soil and seminar" in order to help rural communities in this nation to prosper, the mission of the urban universities, both public and private, has been more contentious, more susceptible to dramatic changes over time. This difference is particularly meaningful as the urban communities around them have been utterly transformed by migration, racial strife, industrialization, then de-industrialization, and increasingly by forces of globalism in which the basic infrastructures of jobs and economy are governed by entities as likely to exist outside as inside the nation. My journey home to Los Angeles, in other words, has taught me much about the interaction of the city and the urban university in matching each other's needs and wants, promoting visions of the future, and crafting strategies to improve the lot of its residents. And while I plan to talk a lot about USC and Los Angeles, I know that much of what I will say relates as well to the University of Pennsylvania, Yale, Columbia, Trinity College, the University of Chicago, and other colleges and universities that find themselves surrounded by the urban environment.

With over 31,000 students, USC has committed itself to an extensive program of service learning throughout the university's 18 separate schools. Currently service learning is a component in over 80 classes in over 25 departments. Each year, some 3000, or 18% of all undergraduate students participate in these courses, receiving academic credit for the community involvement and reflective work they do in the context of the course. USC has approximately 250 community partners, ranging from 20 K–12 public and parochial schools to an assortment of nonprofit organizations that serve as vehicles for improving the quality of life of residents of communities that surround both the main and the medical campuses. The newly adopted version of USC's strategic plan calls for delivery of a learner-centered education, and the expansion of service learning is a critical part of this new strategy for education in the twenty-first century. Unlike developments at other institutions like the University of Michigan and the University of Pennsylvania, which have adopted centralized approaches to the service-learning curriculum, USC maintains a decentralized approach. This system capitalizes on the independence of each of its professional schools and the 30-year history of the Joint Education Project (JEP) in the College of Letters, Arts, and Sciences.

Despite this widespread effort, service learning at USC sits at an important crossroads in its development, much like the programs at other urban universities. Indeed, what I want to concentrate my remarks on today is the seeming inconsistency of the widespread growth in service learning and community engagement at universities across the nation and the rapid decline in programs and commitments to make our own university communities more inclusive and diverse. I will argue that on the resolution of this inconsistency hangs the role of the university of the twenty-first century as a democratic institution, one that either is able to fulfill its rhetoric concerning civic responsibility, or one that is judged by the communities in which we reside to be full of empty promises and selfish motives.

I consider the growing commitment of universities to civic engagement as one of the most important changes in higher education at the end of the twentieth century and beginning of the twenty-first. Across the country, university presidents have taken up the 1994 call of Ernest Boyer for creating a new American college committed to improving the conditions of its own immediate surroundings. The Campus Compact, a group of university presidents committed to the growth of service-learning communities bringing students and community residents together, has grown from 13 members in 1985 to over 550 member institutions. The growth and importance of efforts on this campus, such as Imagining America and the Ginsberg Center, all speak to the central role that community engagement plays at Michigan in supporting and encouraging students and faculty to encompass in their education a commitment to improving the lives of other Michigan residents.

Other campuses, of course, have also developed extensive programs. One of the national leaders among urban campuses is the University of Pennsylvania, whose work in "enlightened self-interest" in West Philadelphia you heard about through Ira Harkavy, the first Dewey Lecturer for the Ginsberg Center, and the first director of Penn's Center for Community Partnership, created in 1992, a centralized vehicle to support efforts to engage the community throughout the campus. Penn, like USC, initiated these efforts because the university's reputation was suffering from its location in what most believed was a run-down ghetto neighborhood. At the University of Pennsylvania, the murder of a professor sparked serious recent efforts at community engagement; at USC, it was clearly the 1992 Los Angeles Riots, occurring right outside the doorstep to the university.

My own institution, the University of Southern California, won *Time* magazine's coveted College of the Year 2000 Award because of the many partnerships it has forged between the university and community groups in the area immediately surrounding the university. Its neighborhood outreach programs have reversed a trend dating from the Watts Riots of 1965 to close itself off from the surrounding neighborhood. Currently more than 60% of our students volunteer at some point in their undergraduate careers in university-sponsored programs with our neighbors. One meaning of the title for this talk, "Crossing Figueroa," celebrates the active encouragement at USC for literally and figuratively crossing one of the four streets surrounding the main university campus, Figueroa Avenue, to engage in this sort of volunteer activity.

USC students offer free Web design services to area nonprofits, act as coaches in USC-sponsored sports programming, serve as teachers in after-school science and math enrichment programs, and engage in multiple activities to improve the lives of those living around the campus. The campus has adopted the five public schools closest to the South Central Los Angeles campus, and regularly sends students to act as tutors at those schools. In an early example of direct community engagement, school parents, worried about crime in the neighborhood and their own children's safety walking home from school, asked USC to help organize them into watch patrols. This program has been successfully duplicated throughout southern California. My history department, along with the campus library, has digitized the archives of one of the oldest African American churches in Los Angeles, thereby preserving the important primary materials, and is involved in helping the church design small exhibits in its own sanctuary. Clearly USC, like so many other colleges and universities, has taken community engagement seriously and is working on many levels in the diverse neighborhoods surrounding the campus.

Civic Engagement and the Retreat from Inclusiveness

Yet at the very same time, I strongly believe that we are currently witnessing the rapid decline of institutional support for programs built since the civil rights movement to open predominantly white institutions of higher learning to a diverse community of scholars, students, and teachers. Despite the heroic efforts of Michigan faculty and administrators, as well as a host of other educational leaders, who participated in support of affirmative action programs in front of last year's U.S. Supreme Court decision, and despite the fact that most legal scholars hailed the 5-4 decision as a victory for affirmative action, the past year has seen the most rapid erosion of support for programs of access and support for minority students in recent history. According to an article in last month's *Chicago Tribune*, "throughout the country, schools ... are opening up minority scholarships, fellowships, academic support programs and summer enrichment classes to students of any race," and "colleges are interpreting the ruling to mean they can no longer offer race-exclusive programs designed specifically to help minority students." The article goes on to cite evidence from many of the same universities and cities that have led efforts at community engagement: Northwestern University in Chicago; Yale University in New Haven, Connecticut; the University of Illinois at Urbana-Champaign; and the University of Michigan in Ann Arbor (Cohen 2004).

While campuses have largely made these changes quietly over the summer of 2004, the world of major foundations that support higher education provoked a noisier reception when it, too, cut back and changed criteria. Foundations have been less able to make these changes quietly because they regularly interact with minority scholars who have received their funding in the past. Two years ago, on Halloween 2002, the James Irvine Foundation in California, the largest foundation in the state, eliminated their Campus Diversity Initiative, which had funded 28 private colleges and universities for diversity work. The Irvine Foundation eliminated its entire Higher Education Division one fateful day *before* the U.S. Supreme Court decision. This year, both the Mellon and Ford Foundations have "broadened" their eligibility requirements for undergraduate, graduate, and postdoctoral fellowships that had previously been available only to "members of selected racial and ethnic minority groups whose under-representation in the faculties of American colleges and universities was deemed severe and longstanding." In short, both programs are now open to non-minority scholars who support "diversity," and both programs have been renamed: "The Mellon-Mays Fellowship Program" and "The Ford Foundation Diversity Fellowships." Neither public announcement made clear another rationale for the change: the letters sent to about 100 colleges and foundations in 2003 by the Center for Equal Opportunity in Virginia, a conservative advocacy group whose general counsel is the familiar Roger Clegg, "threatening to file complaints with the U.S.

Department of Education's Office of Civil Rights if their race-exclusive programs weren't changed" (Cohen 2004).

If, as John Dewey wrote so long ago, "education is not preparation for life, education is life itself," then what life lessons have been learned by current minority scholars witnessing this retreat on the frontlines of higher education? This summer, I attended the first Mellon-Mays Retreat where undergraduate, graduate, and faculty scholars expressed heartfelt feelings of abandonment, resentment, and anger towards the Mellon Foundation for caving in so readily. In August, I read the words of minority Ford scholars from around the country that showed that similar sentiments were widespread, based both on their reaction to the Foundation's policy shift and on intimate knowledge of the lack of faculty diversity on their own campuses. From a scholar in Puerto Rico: "I do not think, sincerely, that we have achieved a significant representation in many research institutions, and we are going to see our presence even more diminished with measures like this." Another scholar in Connecticut noted that "writing from these parts ... where I am a visiting prof, the Terrain looks pretty lily white WITH affirmative action—I tremble to think of what it would look like without." Another scholar, from a research-extensive university in Missouri that "values diversity," reported similar on-the-ground situation: "Only 3 African Americans have made it from assistant to full professor [since 1969, and] over 75% of the departments have no African American faculty whatsoever."

Others discussed more readily feelings of losing voice during the unfolding process. A scholar in California noted: "I do think that we could have been afforded the opportunity to give our voice and experience on how the fellowship has opened avenues for us." "I was saddened," said another senior scholar from Missouri. She went on to relate that her own program had faced similar pressures to rewrite the parameters for awards and that university counsel had made it very clear that changes must be made because of "repeated, litigious attacks on such programs by They Who Must Not Be Named." Another scholar from Michigan wrote that she wasn't sure white scholars would ever feel the same sort of responsibility towards minority students: "I feel like I embody for my students of color, the possibilities that lay before them [and] I also feel a deep sense of responsibility to them." A more frustrated reaction from a senior scholar in California asked the question, "Why, oh why, must they [non-minority scholars] have every space? And why isn't the Foundation willing to fight more to make that case?" Another senior scholar from California summed up the general sentiment by stating: "The fact that the concept of 'institutionalized racism' has been replaced with the feel-good term of 'diversity' ... is, fundamentally, about white liberal institutions not wanting to share power in a truly authentic, democratic, and meaningful way."

Rather than raise these feelings of anger and abandonment to place blame or produce guilt, I hope I can put forward more general questions that all of us committed to civic engagement should be concerned about: How can our colleges and universities become symbols of civic democracy when our own faculty and students question our commitment to true democracy and civic commitment embodied in concepts of diversity? What happens when the rhetoric of civic engagement smacks into the realities of the current limitations of access and fundamental retreat from concepts of inclusiveness, whatever the root causes? I will return to the consequences of this policy shift in the closing moments of this talk.

I raise these issues in this forum because they mirror some of the critique of service learning that comes from practitioners of multicultural education, especially those who are trying to combine the two approaches. While service learning has been embraced by university presidents, as well as U.S. presidents of both parties, multicultural education and affirmative action have struggled since their inception, attacked by many as too radical or divisive. Critiquing white racism and a focus on eliminating racial oppression seems to have an explicit political and social change message, while there are some in the service-learning community that are more comfortable with "a thousand points of light" than with analyzing the forces at work producing societal inequities.

Changing Demographics and What They Mean for University Engagement

To highlight the centrality of these questions, I think it is critical to introduce the third leg of my analysis of our current tangled web of diversity and democracy: changing demographic trends for the twenty-first century. Nearly every demographer in this country will tell you that in this century the population of the United States will be dramatically altered by continued immigration and differential birth-rates. It is very likely, for example, that by the time the current incoming assistant professors are nearing retirement, the majority of the U.S. population will be of color. Already, almost one-third of the U.S. population is of color, with Latinos and African Americans both at about 13% of the U.S. population. In other words, the very "public" in the United States we will seek to engage in community partnerships will shift dramatically, and will look less and less like the faculty in our colleges and universities over the next 25 years.

Of course, this is already dramatically felt in the state of California, the most populous state in the Union, despite the warped public image of the state put forward by Governor Arnold Schwarzenegger and the entertainment industry. Since the year 2000, non-Hispanic whites have been a minority in the state, and currently over half of all babies born in the state and half of all children in California's K–12 public education system are Latino. Less than 5% of the students in L.A. Unified School District are non-Hispanic whites. In Los Angeles County, the most populous county in the nation, with a total population that is larger than 35 states, non-Hispanic whites make up less than 30% of the total population. This past week the U.S. Census Bureau reported that, for the first time, non-Hispanic whites were a minority of the population in neighboring Riverside and Orange Counties—yes, in the O.C., home of the currently hot television show featuring an all-white cast, racial minorities form the majority of the county (Rubin 2004).

At USC, "crossing Figueroa" means entering a world which, demographically, is starkly in contrast with the demographics of the current USC faculty. With only 35 African American faculty in a total faculty of 2,900 and only 40 Latino faculty, most USC faculty members exist in a world in which their peers are overwhelmingly white. Yet, "the community" which surrounds USC is decidedly made up of racialized minorities with nearly no residential whites (except for temporary student residents) for miles. Another way of putting this stark contrast is that the population that makes up no more than 15% of Los Angeles County's population—white men—are over 65 percent of the popuation in USC's faculty. USC, of course, is no different in these figures than most Research I universities who find themselves in urban communities in the United States. But in all these settings, the stark difference between the racial backgrounds of the faculty and that of the community is growing wider each year.

Of course, we know that the differences in background between our faculty and our communities are not just about race. A disturbing newspaper article this past week pointed towards the educational inequities that are currently embedded in most urban neighborhoods and that mark one critical difference between the fate of our faculty's children compared to the future facing most children in the community. This article, entitled "Just One Day to Make a Difference," discussed a rather noble effort by exclusive private school counselors to bring their wisdom and experience to hundreds of high school seniors from public schools interested in going to college. Public school students face a student-counselor ratio in Los Angeles County that can be higher than a thousand to one—indeed, at Banning High School there are 3,400 students and one counselor—while at Harvard-Westlake private school, 10 deans manage 90 students and only 30 seniors. As one frustrated counselor noted, "Our kids come from so much privilege. It's just two very different worlds" (qtd. in Chavez 2004).

Indeed, much of the student volunteerism that goes on at USC directly takes on the loss of services to inner city communities that has been created because of federal and local government cutbacks and embedded structures of inequality that affect surrounding communities. In California, for example, cutbacks in funding K–12 public schools forced school administrators to eliminate music from school budgets, particularly damaging in communities in which parents cannot afford private weekly music lessons. Jazz studies graduate students in USC's Thornton School of Music stepped in to direct public school music ensembles at the group that USC calls its Family of Schools, while undergraduates receive college credit for providing private and group music lessons. This coming fall, performance and music education majors will begin to offer keyboard and voice lessons as part of the schools' regular in-classroom curriculum.

But true service learning must go beyond the form of volunteerism—some have called it "charity" work—to analyze why these cutbacks have so crippled public education in our era of "No Child Left Behind." And how do these crippling inequities in schooling affect the way selective colleges and universities decide on who is meritorious in college admissions? Do we have obligations to admit and train those from schools that immediately surround us? And given the racial and economic disparities in Los Angeles that are reflected in the availability of music education and college counseling, how do we confront the possibility that our very acts of service delay the time when the larger society would have to confront the embedded inequalities in education and government services?

Paulo Freire, analyzing this form of charitable work towards the poor in Brazilian society, called these efforts "false generosity"—acts of service that simply perpetuate the status quo and thus preserve the need for service (Rosenberger 2000, 33). Let me clear: these acts are well-meaning and do immediate good, yet they also insidiously act to perpetuate a system of immense inequality and racial oppression. In 1970, Freire wrote:

> In order to have the continued opportunity to express their "generosity," the oppressors must perpetuate injustice as well. An unjust social order is the permanent fount of this "generosity".... True generosity consists precisely in fighting to destroy the causes which nourish false charity. False charity constrains the fearful and subdued, the "rejects of life," to extend their trembling hands. True generosity lies in striving so that

> these hands ... need be extended less and less in supplication, so that more and more they become human hands which ... transform the world. (2006, 44–45)

How can those of us who are committed to civic engagement in these communities operate effectively given the stark inequalities that mark the urban condition in the twenty-first century? Of course, it might be easy to see to step aside and believe that we should not engage with this enormous struggle because the gulfs between our universities and the communities they exist within are just too wide. And I suppose that many of us might be involved in civic engagement simply from a posture that to do nothing is to lose any semblance of individual power to effect change. I want to suggest that we must be strategic in our civic engagement in the twenty-first century in order to do good in our communities. Engagement must begin by making our own universities more open, more diverse, and more flexible. If we cannot change our own institutions towards these goals, it is highly unlikely that our efforts in surrounding communities will be taken seriously as movements for community empowerment and transformation.

The importance of diversity in our educational mission was one of the central themes of the research evidence that University of Michigan faculty put forward last year in front of the U.S. Supreme Court. To foster a true learning environment requires diversity of background and opinion among the student body in the classroom. Nowhere is that more evident, I believe, than in service-learning environments, where having a diverse group of students encounter, reflect, and learn from the community members they work with is critical for an expanded learning environment. Imagine a classroom where some students actually come from the communities they are studying, some from similar communities, others from quite different, much more privileged environments. Service-learning and community engagement may mean something quite different for each of these students, but having a diverse classroom to return to and discuss the implications of these differences is vital to understand oneself, one's peers, and the community members with whom we engage. As W. E. B. Du Bois wryly said over one hundred years ago about both studying "the Negro problem" and experiencing it, "being a problem is a strange experience" (2008, 5). Out of that "strangeness" can come profound observation and path-breaking theory.

The Boyle Heights Project

I learned that lesson during one of the first service-learning classrooms I organized as an assistant professor at UCLA. The class took place soon after the 1992 Los Angeles Riots and its purpose was to understand the history of multiracialism in urban communities by exploring Boyle Heights, a neighborhood just east of downtown L.A. that lies adjacent to the USC medical campus. Working with several community institutions and organizations, such as the International Institute, a social service provider in the neighborhood, Self-Help Graphics, a Chicano arts collective, and Roosevelt High School, the one public high school in the area, we collected names of individuals who had lived in Boyle Heights in the 1930s and 1940s, during its heyday as a multiracial community. The students learned about the work of these community organizations, and each picked an individual that they would extensively interview, placing this person's life in the context of the wider multiracial history of Boyle Heights. The histories that were produced by the students were then given back to each community member, as well as to the community institutions that we had interacted with.

But before the class began, I knew it would be critical to come into that community with a wide diversity of students, reflecting the diversity of 1992 in the classroom. I particularly focused on the three main ethnic groups in Boyle Heights—Mexicans, Jews, and Japanese—and recruited students into the classroom by working with UCLA's student organizations representing these groups. This was a time of enormous polarity and tension among UCLA students, exacerbated by the racial tensions of Los Angeles as a whole, and I was determined to make the classroom as multiracial as the Boyle Heights community of the 1940s was. Some students chose to interview members of racial groups that were similar to them, while others chose to interview across ethnic lines. The key was that we learned across those lines in our classroom, hearing about the individual stories from the interviewers, and asking collectively about how each individual influenced Boyle Heights, while shaped by their own racial, economic, and personal background.

Years later, after a sojourn in Michigan, I would have the opportunity to take that research back into Boyle Heights in a different forum as a faculty member at USC, working with another multiracial group of students. In collaboration with the Japanese American National Museum, another community institution in downtown Los Angeles, I organized a research team investigating this multiracial history that led directly to an exhibition at the museum that turned out to be the single most-attended exhibition in the 15-year history of the museum. At one of the many community forums which this project organized, I witnessed our USC undergraduate and graduate students leading discussion groups at the International Institute that brought together current residents of the community with former residents who had left Boyle Heights over 50 years ago. Sharing memories about the same location, these individuals bridged the racial, temporal, and geographic gap that prevents people in Los Angeles from connecting over common ground. When the exhibition opened months later, folks from all over southern California would come together again to share in these collective memories and think about what was in order to dream about what could be. The exhibition inspired others, from Roosevelt High School students to elementary teachers in Long Beach, to construct their own historical projects looking at multiracialism in the past as a way to understand our twenty-first-century future. In the end, this decade-long project produced a wide range of public scholarship from many of its practitioners: a major museum exhibition, a teacher's guide made free to all teachers, high school student radio projects, undergraduate and graduate research papers, and hopefully, within a year or so, my own next book.

Other USC faculty members are engaged currently in similar multifaceted experiences in community empowerment and social change. Two assistant professors in the American Studies program that I direct are political scientists who directly work on issues of immigrant empowerment. Ricardo Ramirez has joined forces with Janelle Wong and their community partners, NALEO, the National Association of Latino Elected Officials, and the Asian American/Pacific Islander Resource Center. Together, they study, support, and engage the process of citizenship formation and electoral voting with teams of graduate and undergraduate students working in multilingual Los Angeles neighborhoods. Other faculty, such as Terry Cooper of the School of Policy, Planning, and Development, are studying and working with newly formed neighborhood councils to broaden the level of public engagement in poor communities with local government. Each of these projects embodies a philosophy of citizenship and democracy that goes well beyond electoral politics.

Given Los Angeles' connection to a broader world community through immigration and culture, many projects have expanded well beyond immediate neighborhoods of the campus. Students in another course on Race and Ethnic Relations in a Global Society investigated the impact that immigration and sexuality had on the work of health care providers in Mexico. Their findings were used in a proposal to fund an AIDS education center and clinic on the U.S.–Mexico border. This past semester, business and engineering students worked with the African Millennium Foundation, a local nonprofit that raises money to fund women entrepreneurs in Africa. With a consulting group of 15 faculty who have conducted research in Africa for years, engineering students worked in teams to suggest how a principal of a school in the Congo could get electricity to her school, while business students served as "consultants" to women entrepreneurs in Burkina Faso to help them negotiate higher prices for their products. USC students serving as tutors to local eighth- and tenth-graders helped them sharpen their writing skills in preparation for the new handwritten SATs by creating a pen pal program between the L.A. youth and their counterparts in South Africa and the Democratic Republic of the Congo.

John Dewey and the Racialized World of Civic Engagement

I believe deeply that what I have been engaged with through the Boyle Heights project, and what other faculty and students have done through their engaged community work, is what John Dewey would recognize as "education for democracy." But key to this form of education is the fact that both community members and those from the institutions of higher education could dream of a multiracial democracy within their midst. For everyone in the Boyle Heights project could imagine a time and place where folks lived side-by-side in Boyle Heights and were forced to work out their problems, and we dreamed of a Los Angeles of the future where this could happen in our lifetimes. All of us, however, looked at ourselves and saw a team of researchers and students who were ethnically diverse. Consequently, we could imagine institutions of higher education as democratic institutions where access and knowledge would not be limited by one's race or economic circumstance.

As I gathered my thoughts for this talk, this contradiction in the world of John Dewey kept making its way back into my head. I am convinced by the voluminous writings of John Dewey that he was a major visionary who imagined a world where institutions of higher education would make substantial progress in advancing democracy and bringing true equity in the widest possible sphere. The Department of Pedagogy, which took him from Michigan to the University of Chicago in 1894, was intended to combine theory and practice in an innovative program of education research and training founded upon the new fields of psychology and philosophy. With the University Elementary School (later known as the Lab School) at its center, Dewey believed that education could forge a dynamic public sphere (Bachin 2004, 67–68). In *Democracy and Education*, Dewey wrote:

> A society which makes provision for participation in its good of all its members on equal terms and which secures flexible re-adjustment of its institutions through interaction of the different forms of associated life is in so far democratic. Such a society must have a type of education which gives individuals a

> personal interest in social relationships and control, and the habits of mind which secure social changes without introducing disorder. (2004, 95).

All students of American culture should recognize this intense American desire for "social changes without disorder." U.S. notions of democracy and individualism have long stressed that change happens through democratic processes and a general concern for the common good. In the early nineteenth century, Toqueville argued that social change in this nation arises from the exercise of civic responsibility on the part of educated and morally motivated individuals. Mitigating social tension has traditionally driven many volunteer programs to help the poor, from the Salvation Army to Jane Addams' Hull House. Many in the service-learning community trace its antecedents to the Civilian Conservation Corps (CCC) and the National Youth Administration (NYA) of the Depression era, government attempts to control the tensions arising from widespread joblessness.

Yet these communitarian impulses endemic in American reform, and so championed by John Dewey, rarely actively and persistently engaged the multiple sources of power that created inequality and persistent discrimination, and, indeed, the possibility that social disorder might be necessary to overturn structural inequality. They sought to ameliorate the results of social oppression, without fully intellectually engaging the actual sources of that oppression. Certain service-learning beliefs—for example, that people on the local level can solve their own problems—conveniently ignore the reality of the interdependent global village that we now live in, where the multitude of critical decision makers and economic producers are likely to live well outside our local neighborhoods. Indeed, some in the neighborhood are quick to point out that the university itself, through its employment or real estate practices, may be perpetuating systems of inequality while its students are engaged with the community.

There is a long history of these contradictions in the life of John Dewey himself. The same university that had recruited Dewey to lead its efforts also increasingly supported neighborhood organizations pushing for racial restrictions to fight back the growing African American presence in Chicago, beginning in 1894. The university's financial support of the Hyde Park Protective Association insured the value of the real estate around the campus and helped protect its borders from "undesirable elements" (Bachin 2004, 58–61). Indeed, when I hear some contemporary practitioners of service learning romanticize about the university before the corporatization of our institutions and the massive government funding of the military-industrial complex of the mid-twentieth century, I wince in remembering just how homogeneous the faculty and students actually were. These were institutions where W. E. B. Du Bois, the author of the magisterial *The Philadelphia Negro*, could not find employment due to the color of his skin.

Not too surprisingly, William Rainey Harper, the first president of the university and the person who had recruited Dewey to Chicago, would eventually lock horns with him over questions of academic centralization that conflicted with Dewey's notion of democratic social engagement through progressive education. Given the success of the Lab School, Harper sought to control and coordinate all facets of education in Chicago, professionalizing the teacher corps by requiring a college degree and encouraging disparity of pay between male career professionals and female teachers. The Harper Plan was opposed by the Chicago Teachers Federation in 1897, whose members wanted to preserve the connection between teachers and the communities they served. Dewey and several of his colleagues opposed the Harper Plan, but ultimately lost out when the Illinois State legislature outlawed union membership for teachers and sided with Harper. As Robin Bachin argues, in a wonderful recent book on the history of the University of Chicago in the South Side, "the more activist and democratic model of civic engagement promoted by Dewey became an auxiliary function of the university rather than a defining component of it" (2004, 72).

Moreover, the new model of civic engagement at the University of Chicago would spawn other intellectual efforts whose relationship with communities of color would continue to be wrapped in contradiction. In my own scholarly work on Los Angeles and urban culture in the early twentieth century, no institutional entity looms larger than the University of Chicago's Sociology Department. As the first school to commit the field of sociology in 1892, John Dewey would enter a university brimming with new fields poised to use urban communities as laboratories for the production of knowledge. Robert Ezra Park would take courses from Dewey and eventually emerge, as leader of the Chicago Sociology Department, to conceive of the major theoretical and spatial ways we think of race, ethnicity, and urban society. Dewey, Park, and almost all the major theorist in Chicago grew up in small rural towns—Park in the Midwest, Dewey in New England—which sparked their outsider imagination for viewing highly urbanized society, "a highly individuated, cosmopolitan arena where everyone was a stranger" (Yu 2001, 33).

Although Park and his budding cadre of sociologists were among the most sympathetic university professors of the 1920s and 1930s, a recent study by Henry Yu makes it clear that their civic engagement with the residents of Chicago and other urban areas produced research which was highly suspect for its unacknowledged positionality.

Yu argues that the outsider's perspective, cosmopolitan and interested in all cultures, was an illusion founded upon a denial of the one perspective that sat at the center of definitions of modernity. The deracinated, universal perspective removed from all points in space was imagined by elite white intellectuals as the embrace of all. In fact, this perspective fostered the "collection" of seemingly exotic nonwhite cultures, while it denied the relevance of the privilege and power of the collector. According to the sociologists, their studies reflected the point of view of knowledge itself (Yu 2001, 89).

Yu's work, however, does not stop at this critique of the sociologists in the University of Chicago. He goes on to analyze the careers and intellectual work of a small group of 20 graduate students of sociology recruited by Park and others from Japanese American and Chinese American communities. These scholars, originally recruited as translators and insiders to the larger professorial studies, often went on to do their own independent scholarly work, yet few could obtain permanent employment in academia due to discriminatory practices. For these fledging minority scholars, Yu argues, "objective detachment" was even more critical to their respect in the field than for white scholars (Yu 2001, 147, 169).

The "Third Culture" of Faculty Engagement: Between Academic Departments and Communities of Color

Two years ago, Julie Ellison wrote a thought-provoking paper for "The Research University as Local Citizen" conference at the University of California, San Diego, that confronted the "Two Cultures Problem" of liberal arts faculty in American research universities. In this address, she pointed to two professional cultures among faculty: the first was the dominant departmental culture and the second was what she called the "counterculture" of engagement, which involved the "pleasures of insurgency" and "growing, if still tenuous legitimacy" of those involved in service learning and community engagement (2002, esp. 3). Henry Yu's book, along with the thoughts of current Ford Fellows and others in ethnic studies, suggests a third faculty culture: one of professional ambivalence and bridge work between geographically close but socially distant communities of color; that is, the current culture for minority faculty at predominantly white universities.

In my experience at UCLA, Michigan, and USC, minority faculty, because of the scarcity of their numbers as well as continual challenges to their scholarly legitimacy in the academy, operate in this third culture, pulled between the commitments to communities of color almost all bring with them to the academy and the departmental culture which tells them either directly or mostly indirectly to abandon those ties or risk professional suicide. Many of the books mentioned by service-learning professionals—Robin Kelley's *Freedom Dreams* or Vicki Ruiz's *Unequal Sisters*—are incredibly successful and rare examples of negotiating this third cultural position. But too many other minority faculty are caught feeling their inability to negotiate the competing demands that they confront each day from colleagues on and off campus, students, friends, and families. In many ways, these faculty may be the most valued members of that counterculture of service learning, but they can only arrive there through the tortured processes we have developed in a departmental culture that is particularly alienating yet required.

But as the best practices in social change have shown, staying with departmental culture is not enough. In the post–affirmative action world that I believe we are quickly entering, there will need to be an academic rationale for the diversity we want in the classroom, in front of the classroom, and in the community through service learning. The new Ford Fellowship guidelines, for example, make awards based on maximizing the "educational benefits of diversity" and increasing "the number of professors who can and will use diversity as a resource for enriching the education of all students." Nowhere is that value more exemplified than in the realm of service learning and community engagement, where breaking down the boundaries between the academy and the community needs to be a critical goal of any successful program.

I worry that with a diminution of commitment to the further diversification of our faculty and research communities we may well return to the awkward social positioning of committed scholars of all colors that the works of intellectual history like Henry Yu's are uncovering. We need to promote an approach to scholarly engagement with communities that welcomes all to the intellectual table, and that is willing to examine all forms of community empowerment and dispossession. In order to promote a different world of scholarly engagement than that produced by John Dewey and his colleagues in the early twentieth century, we must first begin to acknowledge that our own institutions of higher learning are communities that must be nurtured to be truly democratic. Only then will we be able to sustain our own credibility among the urban neighborhoods and organizations that dominate the national landscape. This is my vision of a truly engaged university for the twenty-first century, in which both students and faculty regularly cross Figueroa and other border streets in both directions, enlarging dramatically our collective public sphere.

References

Bachin, Robin F. 2004. *Building the South Side: Urban space and civic culture in Chicago, 1890–1919.* Chicago: University of Chicago Press, 2004.

Chavez, Stephanie. 2004. Just one day to make a difference. *Los Angeles Times,* October 10.

Cohen, Jodi S. 2004. Minority programs eroding on campus: Supreme Court ruling has prompted colleges to rethink and revamp offerings that promote affirmative action. *Chicago Tribune,* September 29.

Dewey, John. 2004. *Democracy and education.* New York: Macmillan, 1916. Reprint, Mineola, NY: Dover.

Du Bois, W. E. B. 2008. *The souls of Black folk.* 1903. Reprint, Radford, VA; Wilder.

Ellison, Julie. 2002. The two cultures problem. Paper presented at conference, The Research University as Local Citizen, September, at the University of California, San Diego.

Freire, Paulo. 2006. *Pedagogy of the oppressed.* Translated by Myra Bergman Ramos. 1970. New York: Continuum.

Maurrasse, David J. 2001. *Beyond the campus: How colleges and universities form partnerships with their communities.* New York: Routledge.

O'Grady, Carolyn R., ed. 2000. *Integrating service learning and multicultural education in colleges and universities.* Mahwah, NJ: Lawrence Erlbaum Associates.

Rosenberger, Cynthia. 2000. Beyond empathy: Developing critical consciousness through service learning. In *Integrating service learning and multicultural education,* edited by Carolyn R. O'Grady. Mahwah, NJ: Lawrence Erlbaum Associates.

Rubin, Joel. 2004. O.C.'s whites a majority no longer. *Los Angeles Times,* September 30.

Yu, Henry. 2001. *Thinking Orientals: Migration, contact, and exoticism in modern America.* New York: Oxford University Press.

12

The Engaged Dissertation: Three Points of View

Linda S. Bergmann, Allen Brizee, and Jaclyn M. Wells

THIS CHAPTER examines a project at Purdue University and in Lafayette, Indiana, that addressed the issues involved with moving from service learning to more effective and sustainable *engagement with* the local community and potentially beyond it. It also considers the need for building research, collaboration, and sustainability into projects like the one examined here, the Community Writing and Education Station (CWEST).[1] Although all three authors reviewed and revised each other's parts, Linda Bergmann is primarily responsible for the introduction and overview, while Jaclyn Wells and Allen Brizee discuss their respective dissertation projects in later sections.

Introduction, Overview, and Context
Linda S. Bergmann

As a land grant university founded in 1869, Purdue has a long tradition of involvement with local communities and organizations, particularly through the extension services of the College of Agriculture and the College of Engineering's interactions with industry. In the strategic plan drawn up in the early years of the presidency of Dr. Martin Jischke (2000–2007), the fundamental work of the faculty was renamed: from teaching, research, and service, to learning, discovery, and *engagement*. This change reflects the influence of the Kellogg Commission, of which President Jischke was a member.[2] The Commission, founded in 1996 by the National Association of State Universities and Land-Grant Colleges (NASULGC), was charged with studying the work of land-grant and state universities and advocating directions for their future. The shift in Purdue's strategic plan was not merely cosmetic; it constituted a shift of focus from actions to assessable accomplishments, and it promised to counter the conventional relegation of "service" to the academic basement. The focus on engagement has continued past Jischke's presidency to the present, with various university- and college-level initiatives enacted to foster new projects that would more closely connect the university to its wider community. This includes the industries in Lafayette and elsewhere in the state, other educational institutions, and the agricultural constituencies served by its longstanding extension programs.

In the Purdue College of Liberal Arts, to which we all belonged at the time the project was undertaken, most community outreach consisted of service-learning projects in first-year composition, professional writing, and in some creative writing and literature courses. Service learning is particularly valuable in professional writing courses at both the undergraduate and graduate levels, because it teaches students what they need to learn in these practice-focused courses: how to write texts for real audiences who need to use them. Undergraduate professional writing courses, taken by juniors and seniors, require students to produce documents needed by nonprofit organizations and sometimes small businesses.

This kind of community service in courses has become prevalent at many colleges and universities over the past two decades. Service-learning projects in writing courses cover a range of experiences, from working with community organizations in small projects, helping people write community or family histories, or volunteering in social service agencies to producing documents needed by organizations and sometimes small businesses (Coogan 2005; Condon 2004). Since first-year writing students are expected to reflect upon and generalize from these experiences, much of the literature of service learning in composition testifies to its value for college students (Herzberg 1994; Heilker 1997). It can help students at all levels learn to address an audience, which can be particularly difficult because it requires that they progress from writing in conventional academic genres for teachers who usually know more about a topic than they do—the kind of writing most students do in high school—to writing for audiences that need to know and use what the writer has to say—the kind of writing one normally does in professional or civic work.

However, as proponents of service learning have observed, student writers are not always proficient enough to produce usable documents for their community partners (Cushman 2002). Moreover, colleagues who direct service learning classes or programs often informally tell us that setting up, directing, and assessing these projects is not the same as producing appropriate and effective discourse projects—although they seldom admit this problem in public. Many writing instructors who use service learning wonder whether this work diverts teachers' and students' time from other important work, particularly when the projects come and go without apparent effects on the partner. Moving from service learning to engagement, then, not only involves a change in wording, but also demands considerable critical scrutiny of the value of the work being done. CWEST is one of several projects undertaken by the College of Liberal Arts at Purdue to make its work more firmly rooted in engagement research and practice.

James M. Dubinsky, former director of the Center for Student Engagement and Community Partnerships (CSECP) at Virginia Tech and a longstanding proponent of applying service learning in composition and professional writing, summarizes and responds to even more fundamental criticisms of service learning (2002). Some faculty who are oriented toward the traditional humanities eschew the applied nature of technical or professional writing (and so see service learning as another feature of preparation for future work rather than the "learning for its own sake" that they value more highly as an aspect of liberal education); and some faculty in fields of writing studies are concerned that service learning follows a model that focuses on charity (which helps maintain the status quo) rather than on bringing about significant social change. Volunteer work can hide the actual cost of creating and maintaining necessary social services, and it can define essential social services and important artistic productions as private rather than public work. Dubinsky's model of re-envisioning service learning as a force for change has been a profound influence on the students who developed the CWEST project described in this chapter.[3]

Dubinsky's model also stresses a more collaborative approach than one-way service models (charity), where students volunteer their time (tutoring, for example) but do not complete writing projects *with* their partners. This collaborative model shapes the language students use during their projects, shifting from the term "client," which maintains a market-based approach, to "partner," which reinforces the idea of co-operation between students and civic organizations. Dubinsky's model includes methods of assessment and student reflection, to measure outcomes and to help students think and write about what they have accomplished in their service-learning projects.

While Dubinsky's model frames service learning as a way to help students gain practical knowledge about writing and working with civic partners, the methodology of engagement described by Brizee and Wells in this chapter envisions an even more participatory and empirical model. We argue that this participatory and empirical approach moves participants closer to long-term civic engagement and fosters closer relationships with community partners. Further, we assert that using more empirical methods of developing and assessing the relationships and deliverables emerging from such projects can help partners involved with civic engagement to establish and improve best practices and to analyze our experiences in empirical rather than just anecdotal terms. The CWEST project offers a model that faculty and students can use to draw closer to engagement scholarship, which is widely beneficial to community partners, students (both graduate and undergraduate), and the faculty who supervise such projects.

The engagement activities in the Purdue Writing Lab, where the on-campus parts of the CWEST project were located, have other, more local roots—institutional, intellectual, and material. The Writing Lab has been involved in a considerable number of projects with other disciplines and in the community since its inception in the 1970s. Some of these projects began as community engagement projects in courses in the Rhetoric and Composition and Professional Writing graduate programs, as students began to press beyond traditional concepts of service learning. Others emerged from involvement in Writing Across the Curriculum projects and other interdisciplinary work by faculty and students.

Since 1995, the Writing Lab has developed a widely known and used online resource, The Purdue OWL, which in 2009–2010 counted over 160 million visits in its annual report (Purdue University Writing Lab 2011).[4] The processes of building and periodically redesigning this widely respected tool have provided Writing Lab staff with ongoing interactions with Purdue faculty, other writing instructors, and eventually with teachers and writers around the world. The Writing Lab has for many years been involved with collaborations within the university community (students, faculty, and staff) in Writing Across the Curriculum and Writing in the Disciplines activities (Harris 1999; Bergmann and Conard-Salvo 2007). For example, the Writing Lab has worked on projects to improve writing with faculty and students in the College of Consumer and Family Sciences, the College of Agriculture, and the Departments of Civil and Mechanical Engineering. Writing consultants work with students from across the university to prepare résumés, cover letters, and personal statements in preparation for job fairs and graduate school applications. The body of practical knowledge gained from that work *inside* the university community has served as a basis for work *outside* the university (Bergmann 2010), such as judging writing competitions in local schools and working with engineers in the Indiana Department of Transportation to improve technical writing. The most important sources for engagement projects have been specific students' interest in and commitment to particular work with community projects and agencies, the impetus provided by university-wide engagement initiatives, and in College of Liberal Arts, the PLACE (Purdue Liberal Arts Community Engagement) Program begun in 2007, during which time the CWEST project was taking shape.[5]

Getting projects started at Purdue and other universities can seem relatively easy, given sufficient interest in reaching out across campuses and to communities. However, the issue of how to sustain projects beyond an initial burst of interest and a grant or two is more difficult to resolve (Grabill 2001), and this is one of the questions addressed by Brizee's and Wells's dissertations about the CWEST project. An important influence on the CWEST project was a talk at Purdue University in October 2007 by Rosemarie Hunter, Special Assistant to the President for Campus-Community Partnerships and Director of University Neighborhood Partners at the University of Utah.[6] She focused on the interface between engagement and research, stressing that to be successful and sustainable, engagement must benefit participants from both the community and the university. Community members must be involved, must have a strong, perhaps even a dominant role in shaping projects with the university, and must perceive some benefit from being involved. At the same time, to maintain sustained commitment by the university, projects must apply to their faculty's role as researchers—not just as teachers or volunteers (even though teaching may be part of these projects). Engagement projects may start from virtuous intentions, but to become successful and sustainable, these projects must also be central to the research concerns of all faculty and students who commit time and resources to them. Faculty sustain the institutional memory of the university; their publications record knowledge gained from long-term projects as they help build their careers. This direct, practical usefulness keeps faculty—many of them in the social sciences—involved over the long term because of a project's impact on their careers, and it helps programs recruit new participants.

The kinds of engagement encouraged by the first Kellogg Report and embodied in the programs Dr. Hunter described offer models from which Brizee and Wells started their work.[7] They used these ideas to build more empirical methodologies for assessing the learning process and its outcomes than the methodologies used by earlier service learning projects in writing.[8] The research-based engagement in their dissertation projects reflects their efforts to move from the idea of a one-way rhetoric of instruction aimed at an abstract audience to the idea of rhetoric as more democratic, multivocal, and ongoing interactions in real interpersonal situations—a conceptualization that allows space for continual assessment and adjustment of efforts.

Jaclyn Wells's and Allen Brizee's dissertations were based in the CWEST project, which involved preparing and supervising the development of adult basic education materials for a local adult literacy organization, the Lafayette Adult Resource Academy (LARA), and the state-wide employment organization WorkOne, which maintains an office at LARA. Wells and Brizee designed the CWEST project as a community engagement effort in a graduate course in public rhetorics and looked for ways to sustain the project beyond the limits of the course and of voluntarism. For their dissertation research, they tested new online instructional materials for usability and adapted them accordingly. They also investigated LARA's administrative and pedagogical characteristics in an effort to better align the online instructional materials to the program's strategies, needs, and goals.

Because working with community organizations can be complex, high-risk experiences that might sidetrack graduate students and lead to tension between colleges and communities, it is worth reviewing some of the previous experiences that contributed to Wells's and Brizee's qualifications and what these two graduate students brought to the CWEST project. Based on current engagement scholarship and best practices, Wells and Brizee decided to work with community organizations whose missions overlapped with their areas of expertise. Both were advanced students in Purdue's Rhetoric and Composition program, with experience teaching first-year composition and tutoring in the Writing Lab. Wells's coursework and previous experience with adult basic education made the Lafayette Adult Resource Academy a good match. When Wells learned that LARA needed online materials for preparing adult learners to take the written section of the General Educational Development (GED) test, she extensively studied the GED test and the study materials available to prepare for it. Brizee brought to the project a background in teaching and analyzing professional writing and in human-technology interaction through usability research on the Purdue OWL (Salvo et al. 2008). His expertise fit the need expressed by LARA, and particularly by WorkOne Express (the employment agency co-locating with LARA), for free, easily accessed online materials to assist people in composing job-search documents such as cover letters, résumés, and work applications. In addition, both graduate students had previous experience with service learning and project management, so developing and running a three-year engagement and research study, under the close supervision of their principal investigator (Bergmann) and two dissertation committees, was considered viable.

Wells's dissertation investigates whether and how easily and successfully CWEST instructional materials can be integrated into teaching at LARA, given the needs, goals, available resources, and teaching practices of LARA instructors. Its ultimate goal is to provide a model for university-community collaborations in the dynamic context of curriculum development for adult learners. Brizee's dissertation explores participatory strategies and empirical assessment in sustainable university-community partnerships, and ultimately seeks to develop an engagement methodology that can be used by writing centers and writing programs to replicate and aggregate data about the use and usability of such work. The collective goal was to develop methodologies to produce successful materials for adult education, to consider how success in teaching writing can be defined and measured, and to observe and record how those materials are actually used. As the following accounts show, the project involved careful, intensive investigations of the community organization and its clients, of the Writing Lab, and of the processes through which engagement projects are (and potentially can be) started and sustained.

At the time of this writing, both graduate students have defended their dissertations and have taken positions as faculty at other institutions. In the process of completing their research and writing and defending their dissertations, they learned to value and succeed in aspects of research that many Ph.D. students in English never face. They learned to negotiate between different groups, to have patience with the many things that can go wrong with schedules and meeting plans, and to deal with the material practices of sustaining engagement work, such as finding funding from various institutional sources (such as university research grants and scholarships, and funding as developers of instructional materials for the OWL). They also learned how to set budget priorities and work within the varying regulations and needs of both the university and the program they were assisting. Wells's and Brizee's accounts that follow argue for the value of the kinds of learning and knowledge that resulted from their work. In different ways, their accounts move from discussing what they did not know—that is, what they needed to learn—as students, to what they discovered as developing researchers.

In order to provide a clear picture of Wells's and Brizee's engagement and research project, a brief overview of the process follows. The CWEST project began in spring 2007, and the research, development, and revision of resources lasted for three years. This project was unique in that from its inception, it followed an iterative design process—in short, Wells and Brizee conducted research on deliverables that they were developing as the project progressed. Materials developed for the CWEST are stored on the Purdue OWL (http://owl.english.purdue.edu/engagement), and are available for continued free use by LARA, WorkOne, and any other interested agencies or individuals.[9] The research, development, and revision process of the CWEST project was organized into the stages below, guided by iterative design practices and research methods developed by Ehn (1992), Blythe (1998), Johnson (1998), and Simmons and Grabill (2007).[10] After Wells and Brizee submitted the formal project proposals to the Purdue Writing Lab and to LARA/WorkOne, along with the necessary IRB forms for Purdue University, they followed these iterative steps:

1. The GED phase (completed primarily by Wells)
    a. Met with LARA administrators and instructors to determine needs
    b. Developed paper prototype GED resources
    c. Met with LARA administrators and instructors to obtain feedback on paper prototypes
    d. Revised GED resources and posted them to the OWL
    e. Conducted classroom observations and interviews to study GED resources use and to obtain further feedback
    f. Revised final drafts of GED resources

2. The ESL skills resources phase (completed by Brizee and Cimasko)[11]
    a. Met with LARA administrators and instructors to determine needs
    b. Developed paper prototype ESL resources
    c. Met with LARA administrators and instructors to obtain feedback on paper prototypes
    d. Revised ESL resources and posted them to the OWL
    e. Conducted usability tests and interviews to study GED and ESL resources use and to obtain further feedback
    f. Conducted preliminary data analysis
    g. Revised GED and ESL resources and posted them to the OWL

3. The WorkOne workplace and life skills literacy phase (completed primarily by Brizee)
    a. Met with WorkOne administrators and instructors to determine needs
    b. Developed paper prototype WorkOne resources
    c. Met with WorkOne administrators and instructors to obtain feedback on paper prototypes
    d. Revised WorkOne resources and posted them to the OWL; developed PowerPoint presentations and hard-copy resources, as well as WorkOne marketing materials (brochure, flier, newspaper ad)
    e. Conducted usability tests and interviews to study WorkOne resources use and to obtain further feedback
    f. Conducted preliminary data analysis
    g. Collected student samples of cover letters and résumés
    h. Conducted independent rater evaluations of samples
    i. Analyzed all research study data in detail
    j. Revised WorkOne resources and posted them to the OWL.

After the proposal was accepted by all partners, Wells and Brizee developed, researched, and revised materials for three major areas:

GED preparation, ESL, and workplace literacy. To make the process smoother and best draw on each collaborator's expertise, Wells assumed primary responsibility for the GED preparation materials, a graduate student in ESL assumed primary responsibility for the ESL materials, and Brizee assumed primary responsible for the workplace literacy materials.

From Recognizing and Negotiating Difference to Applying Research
Jaclyn M. Wells

The Lafayette Adult Resource Academy (LARA) is located only a few miles from Purdue's campus, but the striking physical differences between the two make them seem a world apart. LARA's current location is actually a relatively new one: until just a couple of years ago, it was located in a similar neighborhood in downtown Lafayette, and LARA's original site was an abandoned jail. LARA is currently housed in a former school. The building's interior still resembles an elementary school, with classrooms painted light colors and hallways decorated with bulletin boards and posters. Rows of rundown houses surround three sides of the building, and the fourth side faces a local bar and a nonprofit thrift store. The site includes painted hopscotch boards in one corner of the parking lot, and playground equipment occupies the small yard that surrounds it. Discarded bottles and cans litter the yard, and a few small trees provide shade. During the day, cars crowd LARA's parking lot, and drivers often struggle to find parking spots. In the parking lot and right outside the building's entrance, people smoke, talk, and corral children. A busy street runs in front of LARA, with cars often speeding by en route to Lafayette's "main drag" a few blocks away.

In contrast, the Purdue Writing Lab resides in an academic building that also houses the English Department, a nationally recognized speech and hearing clinic, and classrooms and computer labs fully equipped with teaching and learning resources. The building faces the Purdue student union and neighbors three other academic buildings. Though a busy street runs near the building, a newly painted bicycle path and large pedestrian sidewalk contain the only traffic directly around the building. A few nearby parking spots provide short-term parking for security officers, but no more than a couple of parked cars can be seen from the front of the building at any time. A well-manicured lawn decorates the area between the academic buildings and student union, and provides pedestrians a bit of nature to look at while biking to class or walking to the union for more coffee. Numerous small trees shade the lawn and a large bronze "P" stands as a monument to the university. Signs on the building indicate the university's no-smoking policy, and signs around the building urge pedestrians to watch for bicycle traffic and to place recyclables in available receptacles.

I begin this narrative with a description of LARA's and the Purdue Writing Lab's location and appearance because the physical contrast between LARA and the Purdue Writing Lab came to symbolize for me many fundamental differences between the two institutions. These differences are significant for two reasons. The first is that differences between LARA and the Purdue Writing Lab can represent the more general distance between Lafayette and Purdue that initially motivated my involvement in the Community Writing and Education Station (CWEST) project. The second is that they have created challenges to the project that I did not (and could not) anticipate before becoming involved in it.

While fundamental institutional differences between LARA and the Writing Lab have presented challenges to creating and sustaining their partnership, recognizing these differences and thinking through how to negotiate them have provided significant lessons about community engagement. In this sense, the CWEST project added an experiential component to my graduate education in which I not only learned—as a student—about institutional differences between university and community groups, but also gained practice in addressing them. Perhaps the most significant lesson I learned from working on the CWEST project is evidence for why and how community engagement should involve empirical research. This lesson prompted my move from student to researcher, as the CWEST—and specifically the project's partnership between LARA and the Writing Lab—became the focus of my dissertation research.

The empirical study that is the focus of my dissertation investigates differences between LARA and the Writing Lab through research methods common in Rhetoric and Composition: case study, observation, focus groups, and interview. The study marked my shift from student to researcher, as I moved from recognizing and negotiating institutional differences to investigating them with empirical research methods conventional in this field. The shift from student to researcher involves the move from *absorbing* and *interacting* with knowledge (as I did during my work with the CWEST engagement project) to actually *creating* it (as I did in my empirical study of the project). The shift is also marked by how knowledge is used. As a graduate student my observations of institutional differences between LARA and the Writing Lab contributed to my own education, and my attempts to negotiate these differences must be measured by their contribution to the CWEST project. As a researcher, my investigation of these differences contributed to the CWEST, but hopefully will also increase knowledge in fields connected with Rhetoric and Composition about how writing programs can partner responsibly with adult basic literacy organizations.

In the early stages of my work on the CWEST project, I observed significant differences between the project's community and university partners. I return to my earlier description of LARA's location and appearance, because the physical contrast between LARA and the Purdue Writing Lab provides a tangible representation of their institutional differences. First, LARA's physical surroundings contrast greatly with those of the Writing Lab. The building that houses LARA is surrounded by homes and local businesses, whereas the building that houses the Writing Lab is surrounded by other academic buildings, libraries, and the student union. The Writing Lab's surroundings imply that it is part of Purdue's *academic* community, while LARA's surroundings imply that it is a part of a *residential* neighborhood in Lafayette (a neighborhood that is, significantly, low income). Second, there are important differences between other uses of the buildings that house LARA and the Writing Lab. The building that houses LARA is also home to a childcare program and WorkOne Express (a work preparation program), while the Writing Lab's building is home to classrooms, computer labs, and professors' and graduate assistants' offices, as well as to a prestigious audiology clinic. For LARA's adult students, education does not exist in isolation from the rest of their lives, but instead intersects with children and work; the shared space of the building implies this fact. Finally, LARA's location in a building that was previously intended for something different is significant, as is the fact that this location is a new one. Unlike Purdue's Writing Lab, which has had an established home of its own for over 30 years (although it has grown in the number of rooms allotted to it), LARA moves, and moreover, moves into places that are merely available, rather than built specifically for its use.

The first lesson presented by the CWEST project is that interaction between community and university participants is fundamental to sustained, thoughtful engagement. Ellen Cushman argues that public intellectuals must interact with the public outside of the university: "When public intellectuals not only reach outside the university, but actually interact with the public beyond its walls, they overcome the ivory tower isolation that marks so much current intellectual work" (1999, 330). After being introduced to Cushman's work in Professor Patricia Sullivan's Spring 2007 Public Rhetorics course, I decided to address Cushman's definition of the public intellectual through engagement with LARA. My own interest in community engagement in some ways complicates Cushman's definition of the public intellectual. Cushman follows the somewhat conventional move of defining the community as public, which by extension defines the university as nonpublic. What I witnessed as a resident of Lafayette—particularly the disconnect between the Lafayette and Purdue communities—sparked my interest in developing a university-community partnership. Thus, it was my role as a member of the public, a role I was invited to consider fully during the Public Rhetorics course, that spurred my interest in Cushman's call for public intellectualism, even as Cushman's definition of the public intellectual in some ways denied my own role as a member of the public. That the partnership between LARA and the Writing Lab grew out of this course reveals an interesting connection between the traditional learning in graduate classes and the practical knowledge gained by performing engagement.

I began the partnership between LARA and the Writing Lab by reviewing the adult basic education (ABE) literature. Some of the ABE "classics"—the work of Malcolm Shepherd Knowles (1970, 1984) and Alan B. Knox (1986), for example—helped me understand the theory behind teaching adults, but they did not reflect the realities of a community-based adult literacy organization like LARA. It became clear that establishing a partnership between LARA and the Writing Lab would require Brizee and me to get outside the classroom and away from our books. When we did, we began to understand the realities of LARA's circumstances. For example, we learned during our first meeting with LARA's assistant director that instruction at LARA occurs on a highly individual basis, with each student working individually with instructors to create a plan of study. This knowledge helped us understand how ABE theory about creating individual learning goals differs from setting goals in traditional educational institutions like high schools and colleges, which operate in semester-based, classroom contexts. Learning about LARA's highly individualized pedagogy helped me adapt ABE instructional materials housed on the Purdue Online Writing Lab (OWL) to LARA's emphasis on individualized learning. Without direct interaction with LARA administrators and teachers, this thinking process would have been less complex, and the partnership would likely have suffered.

The CWEST project also showed that different approaches to community engagement may be more or less appropriate given the university's and community's circumstances and goals. Nicole Amare and Teresa Grettano (2007) argue that community engagement should be tailored to the unique circumstances of both partners, as well as to the particular goals of the engagement work. They also argue that course-based service learning is not always the best option for community engagement: "To work toward community engagement and reap some of the benefits of traditional service-learning initiatives, [writing program administrators] at certain institutions need to devise alternative programs that work within their institutions' frameworks" (58). My work on the CWEST project pushed me to consider how writing program administrators can support community engagement projects that are appropriate to the university and community context (see Wells 2008 and 2010) in the way that Amare and Grettano discuss. This thinking added an engaged element to my graduate education in writing program administration that has supported my success as a faculty writing program administer interested in community engagement. Amare and Grettano describe Writing Outreach, a community engagement approach they work with, as "a type of service-learning program that may work well in a department interested in connecting or 'engaging' with community members for a number of legitimate reasons while unable to implement a traditional course-based program" (59). They argue that the benefits of Writing Outreach include the expertise that the university partners bring to the project and the project's potential for sustainability.

Prior to the CWEST project, my community engagement experience in Lafayette was limited to course-based service learning. Early in the Public Rhetorics course, I considered the possibility of a course-based service learning project to create instructional materials for LARA. However, because of the issues Amare and Grettano identify—specifically, the expertise of university participants and the potential for the project's sustainability—a partnership between LARA and the Writing Lab seemed more appropriate than a course-based service-learning project. In course-based service learning, undergraduate students are typically responsible for doing the work, which may raise problems when the students lack sufficient expertise to complete it well. In Writing Outreach, faculty members perform the work, and can apply their expertise to the project. Similarly, in the LARA-Writing Lab partnership, graduate students—experienced instructors of undergraduate writing courses—performed the work as we pursued our research on it. This is important because the instructional resources we created with LARA required more expertise to develop than most undergraduates have and more time than is available in a single semester.

A final lesson presented by the CWEST project is the importance of empirical research to community engagement. Jeffrey T. Grabill and Lynée Lewis Gaillet argue that "community-based work requires research" (2002, 64), further asserting that "a fundamental inquiry question attached to all such projects ... should be 'who is the community with whom we are working?'.... In order for a writing program to organize sustained community-based work, its partnership with 'the community' must be under constant scrutiny" (65–66). Designing a partnership between LARA and the Writing Lab convinced me that formal inquiry of engagement is a necessary part of useful, responsible community projects.

In coursework on empirical research, I studied how to conduct community-based research, but I fully understood its importance only when we began the CWEST project, and particularly when I began drafting the GED materials with LARA. Even though I had reviewed numerous existing GED instructional materials and studied how the test works, my first drafts of the GED resources for the CWEST were rough. To improve the materials, I had to draw on the expertise of LARA instructors, who could provide firsthand information about how adult students learn and the types of materials they respond to. Hence, instead of seeing research as a necessary stopover on the way to completing a course or writing a thesis or dissertation, I saw how research can and must inform work with community organizations. Rather than create GED instructional materials, post them on the Purdue OWL, and be finished with the project, Brizee and I intended to investigate our product and our partnership to improve both. In short, working on the GED preparation materials made research real for me.

Generally, my dissertation research investigated the sort of questions that Grabill and Gaillet urge scholars to raise about partnerships between community and university participants. Using case studies (including interviews and teaching observations) of four LARA instructors, my study focused on three major questions about how LARA instructors respond to the GED instructional materials:

- What are the needs, goals, available resources, and teaching practices of LARA instructors?
- How do LARA instructors respond to and use the CWEST?
- How do LARA *instructors'* needs, goals, available resources, and teaching practices influence how they respond to and use the CWEST? (Brizee's research, while investigating instructors' and adult learners' needs and expectations, focused more on the usability of online resources.)

The study had both immediate and far-reaching goals. The immediate goal of the research was to understand the instructors' response to the materials so that the latter could be improved. Improving the materials relates in part to the CWEST project's potential for improving relations between Lafayette and Purdue, which, as I mentioned earlier, motivated my involvement in the project. Whereas many community engagement projects do not produce a tangible, useful "product" for the community participant, formal research about the CWEST worked toward the creation of instructional materials that LARA can actually use and that similar agencies might adapt. Community engagement projects that carefully work toward such a product have the potential to improve university-community relations, as such work has clearer benefits for community partners than community engagement projects that do not result in a distinct product. Moreover, such formal research demonstrates that the university participants take seriously the community members' perspectives. This is particularly the case with a study like this one, in which the research clearly focused on studying the community participants' perspectives through interviews and their work through observations.

The broader goal of my study of the CWEST project was to investigate how university writing centers can partner with adult basic literacy programs. As part of this investigation, I raised questions about how LARA instructors responded to the CWEST project and how they believed the LARA–Purdue Writing Lab partnership could better address their needs as teachers of adult basic education. I also drew on the instructors' significant expertise in adult basic education to investigate how the partnership addressed the needs of LARA students and how it could more effectively do so. I return to my earlier point here about the move from student to researcher, from someone who *takes in* and *interacts* with knowledge to someone who *creates* it. The immediate goal of this research relates to my student role: research about LARA instructors' response to the CWEST provides another (more formal) method of thinking through how to negotiate the institutional differences between LARA and the Writing Lab that I observed, and therefore improve their partnership. The broader goal of my research, however, relates to my researcher role: my investigation of LARA instructors' response to the CWEST will contribute to Rhetoric and Composition's knowledge of community engagement, and more specifically, partnerships between community adult basic literacy organizations and university writing labs. The CWEST community engagement project was a valuable learning experience for me, and I expect my dissertation research about the CWEST will provide a basis for further research in a field that is currently questioning its public role.

Navigating and Connecting Institutions: Rhetorical Theory and Empirical Research in College-Community Partnerships

Allen Brizee

As a Ph.D. student in the Purdue Rhetoric and Composition program, focusing on professional writing and public rhetorics, I took coursework in the history and theories of rhetoric, as well as in empirical research methods. Two particular aspects of rhetorical theory assisted me in navigating and connecting Purdue and our community partners LARA/WorkOne: audience analysis (specifically, audience analysis borrowed from contemporary professional writing pedagogy) and discursive theories of rhetoric. These two rhetorical approaches provided a theoretical base for the participatory empirical research that guided our work during the CWEST university-community engagement project that grew into our dissertation work. Moreover, audience analysis and discursive rhetoric helped us develop and nurture a respectful collaborative relationship with our community partners, which was essential to the success and longevity of the CWEST project, a three-year research and engagement effort. Like Wells, my experiences with these rhetorical theories and research methodologies shifted dramatically as I matured from a student who was *absorbing* ideas in a classroom to an activist-scholar *applying* ideas in practice, with the intention of contributing to the knowledge of engagement scholarship in the writing disciplines.

Rhetoric and Engagement: Audience Analysis and Discourse Theory

Audience analysis and discourse theory are two closely aligned rhetorical methodologies that assist authors in producing communication, and in some cases in developing projects that satisfy readers' needs and expectations. A careful audience analysis can help authors better understand their readers by providing answers to heuristic questions of inquiry, while a discursive approach to writing aligns author and reader so that hierarchical relationships between parties are leveled to some extent. Audience analysis helps the author begin her inquiry into possible readers, and in our case collaborators, so that efforts (research, writing, etc.) better satisfy audiences' needs and expectations. Once this analysis is underway (it should never stop completely), a closer working relationship can flourish through a discursive approach to communication that forms a more participatory collaboration.

Audience analysis

My coursework in rhetoric and professional writing helped me develop skills in audience analysis, which in turn helped me better understand and connect with LARA/WorkOne during our engagement project. These audiences included institutions within Purdue University, such as the Writing Lab, the Office of Engagement, the Purdue Liberal Arts Community Engagement program, and the Institutional Review Board. Audiences outside our university institution included our community partners—LARA and WorkOne, as well as the learners who visit these organizations to continue their education and find jobs. In order to better understand these audiences and project partners, we drew upon methods of audience analysis from professional writing theory. Rhetorically based professional writing theory holds that authors should, as much as possible, understand audiences so that we can better address their needs and expectations when we work and write with them. This rhetorically based theory differs from a writing model, where authors work in perceived isolation to produce texts without trying to study or work with potential readers.

A common way of organizing audiences is to divide them into five categories: 1) gatekeepers (coworkers, boss); 2) primary audience (partners); 3) secondary audience (people within your client's organization); 4) stakeholders (customers, partners, etc.); and 5) shadow readers (*anyone* who might read the document) (Johnson-Sheehan 2005, 44–55; Anderson 2007, 73–88). In order to garner as much information as possible about this complex audience, professional writers have developed questions and research heuristics. For example, they might ask

- Who are my readers? What do they need? When, where, and how will they be reading (Johnson-Sheehan 2005, 45)?
- What are my readers' needs, values, and attitudes?
- In what physical, economic, political, and ethical context(s) will my readers *use* the communication (Johnson-Sheehan 2005, 47, 50, 54)?

Using rhetorically based audience analysis allowed Wells and me to better understand our potential audiences within Purdue and LARA/WorkOne and enabled me to more effectively engage in genuinely participatory collaboration and empirical research for the CWEST project. These questions are conventionally used to learn more about readers, but they can also be used to learn more about the people with whom we need to work. Moreover, these heuristics helped Wells and me compose documents necessary to launch the CWEST project, such as project and grant proposals, which were essential to fund the project and which were directed at distinctly different audiences:

- The *CWEST project proposal for LARA* had to be concise because LARA administrators have very busy schedules, and it had to explain clearly the purposes, goals, costs, and benefits of the project.
- The *CWEST project proposal for the Writing Lab* was much longer than its counterpart for LARA and included scholarly information and a detailed explanation of research methods and theory driving the project.

- The *proposal for the Purdue Student Engagement Grant* was based on a template that allowed it to fulfill institutional requirements.
- The *proposal for the Purdue Liberal Arts Community Engagement (PLACE) program* also was based on a (different) template that allowed it to fulfill institutional requirements.

Applying audience analysis helped me investigate the cultures, values, and goals of institutional structures within the Purdue system—the Office of Engagement, the Purdue Liberal Arts Community Engagement program, and the Institutional Review Board that evaluates research with human participants—so that we could satisfy the needs and requirements of these different organizations. By studying LARA's and WorkOne's culture, values, and goals, we were able to better understand their needs and develop effective communication strategies. Lastly, our careful audience analysis allowed us to develop research methodologies (interviews and observations) that would help us determine the needs and expectations of our community partners, and to assess the effectiveness of the resources we developed with LARA and WorkOne, such as usability tests and independent rater evaluations that measured the success of documents revised based on our online literacy resources.

Discourse theory

My coursework in classical rhetoric and professional writing theory also helped me move from student to researcher by introducing ideas of rhetoric that are less confrontational and combative than commonly studied strategies of persuasion, which operate in terms of "winning" an argument with an opponent. In classical rhetoric, scholars refer to the latter approach as eristic rhetoric. This zero-sum approach assumes that the only way of using rhetoric to prove a point is by disproving an opponent's point, an oppositional process that establishes a fallacious, damaging hierarchy between sides that can undermine cooperation and effective communication when members of different organizations try to work together. When stakeholders are trying to *build* cooperation, an eristic approach to rhetoric can contradict, or at least complicate, efforts to collaborate. Discursive rhetoric, not limited to a series of strategies for trapping and defeating opponents, encourages understanding and communication between parties, thus taking a more egalitarian approach to communication and fostering a more democratic discourse between stakeholders.[12]

Using discourse theory for our engagement project helped us identify and focus on the common ground that LARA/WorkOne shares with Purdue University and its Writing Lab. Since we had carefully researched our audiences, we could highlight the benefits of working collaboratively to develop literacy resources to be housed on the Purdue OWL, and we could use discursive rhetoric to explain how the CWEST works as a natural extension of both organizations' cultures, values, and goals (including missions and strategic plans). We conducted detailed audience analyses to learn as much as we could about the institutions we were trying to bring together, and we then followed a discursive model of rhetoric to communicate how all the institutions could better serve their own interests by joining together to work on the CWEST.

Put another way, discursive rhetoric, with its more egalitarian philosophical base, helped us form a more equal working relationship with LARA/WorkOne staff and students in which we used our expertise in rhetoric, writing, and technology but did *not* assume that we knew more than the members of LARA/WorkOne about what *they* do on a daily basis. By genuinely sharing expertise with LARA, I believe we helped them empower themselves in the creation process. Michele Simmons and Jeffrey Grabill (2007) describe taking this different path to engagement: "Citizens ... must have an art that is powerfully inventive and performative.... [T]hese performances are enabled by inquiry practices that allow citizens to understand the particular institutional systems (rhetorical situations) in which they find themselves.... [T]hey must be able to invent valued knowledge" (422).

During the CWEST project, I learned that the two rhetorical ideas discussed above—audience analysis and discursive rhetoric—form an effective method of navigating and connecting institutions. I also learned that audience analysis and discursive rhetoric can help scholars engage with communities and resist hierarchies in order to shift work into more equal collaborative spaces. Moreover, these methods form an effective platform to better understand our community partners' needs, record and measure feedback and results, and generate scholarship.

Empirical Research and Engagement

A natural extension of the theories driving the CWEST project—audience analysis and discursive rhetoric—are the empirical research methods we used to record feedback from our community partner and to measure the outcomes of our labor. As noted earlier in this chapter, empirical research has recently received a new impetus in Rhetoric and Composition studies; in the words of Richard Haswell (2005), it is identified as a replicable, aggregable, data-driven method of generating information, a kind of research that the field had drifted away from in favor of more text-based or anecdotal studies. Wells and I learned the value of this empirical process during the CWEST project, as we interviewed LARA and WorkOne instructors and students and conducted usability tests on the literacy resources. We also measured outcomes of CWEST use by enlisting local business people to rate the effectiveness of professional documents developed by WorkOne users. These steps helped in the iterative design process used to develop material that would meet LARA/WorkOne instructors' and students' expectations.

Empirical research is particularly important in civic engagement projects because it is difficult to ascertain how effective our college-community programs are when the information we have about them is anecdotal, as it often has been in projects undertaken by writing programs and other programs in the humanities. For example, we should be able to address these types of questions:

1. Did the project fulfill the needs of the community partner? How do we know?
2. Did the project fulfill the needs of our students (adult learners) and the requirements of our department and larger institution? How do we know?
3. What impact did the project have on all the stakeholders (community partner, adult students, institution)? How do we know the extent of the impact?

These questions are especially important for projects funded by universities or state and federal money because assessment is a key part of the funding process. Assessment also shows activists how to adjust efforts to better address the needs and expectations of community partners, students, and institutions. As Simmons and Grabill (2007) point out, the connection between rhetorical theory, outreach, and research is crucial to help citizens empower themselves: "Such a rhetoric must concern itself with the day-to-day rhetorical practices of 'everyday people'.... [I]t must concern itself with understanding how people create civic cultures, how they define themselves within recognizable public spheres.... [S]uch a rhetoric, in other words, must be empirical" (2007, 439).

Determining Needs and Expectations

Determining the needs and expectations of community partners can be part of audience analysis, but it is also an important part of empirical research in an engagement project like the CWEST. During initial interviews, LARA/WorkOne instructors identified three areas of need:

1. resources for helping students prepare for the writing section of the GED

2. resources for ESL learners
3. resources for job searches (résumés, covers letters, etc.).

We shaped the CWEST area on the OWL to fit these three areas. Specific expectations LARA/WorkOne instructors established were

1. ease of use (thus the usability tests)
2. online, print, and CD-ROM capabilities to address technology limitations at different LARA and WorkOne sites (LARA holds classes at the local jail; WorkOne is a statewide employment program)
3. limited text content and page length, and
4. an effective mix of text and graphics.

These needs and expectations, recorded through empirical research, allowed us to listen to our audience and develop resources *with* them, as well as to assess the effectiveness of our efforts—a process known as iterative design. Our research methods included a critical approach to mixed methods (Sullivan and Porter 1997). The study setting consisted of "real" (the LARA, WorkOne, and Purdue Writing Lab spaces) and virtual environments (the Purdue OWL and CD-ROM electronic spaces), addressing the research needs Locke, Silverman, and Spirduso (2004) call for when they argue for mixed-methods research: "When … the nature of the research problem makes it necessary to use both qualitative and quantitative data in developing a more thorough answer" (167).

Our quantitative methods included usability tests with LARA/WorkOne instructors and learners we conducted on the CWEST materials and the OWL Web area hosting the resources. Quantitative methods also included document evaluations from independent raters (the local employers who reviewed the cover letters and résumés) of WorkOne participants who used CWEST materials. Independent raters assessed participants' documents produced before and after participants used the CWEST. Qualitative methods included interviews with LARA/WorkOne administrators and instructors, open-ended questions on the usability test questionnaire, and classroom observations.

I used the empirical data that we generated to make resource development decisions as well as OWL/CWEST design decisions throughout the project. Particularly important to the technology decisions related to the project were the computer limitations at LARA/WorkOne. Staff at LARA/WorkOne stated that even through their lab contained computers with Internet access, some teachers and adult students did not feel comfortable using these technologies to learn and write, and so we developed print CWEST materials as well as online resources.

We built into the design process a series of usability tests, which integrated research methods developed during the four generations of OWL usability testing begun in 2006 (Driscoll et al. 2008; Salvo et al. 2009). As the online literacy resources were posted on the OWL in the CWEST area, we conducted usability tests that improved the navigation of the site by reducing the number of visible links in the navigation bar. For example, based on participant feedback, we implemented a drop-down navigation bar that displays links by sections rather than displaying all the resources available in that given section. When users select sections, the bar expands to display links to all the literacy resources. The first screenshot (Figure 12.1) illustrates the first CWEST page design. The second screenshot (Figure 12.2) shows the revision based on usability data.

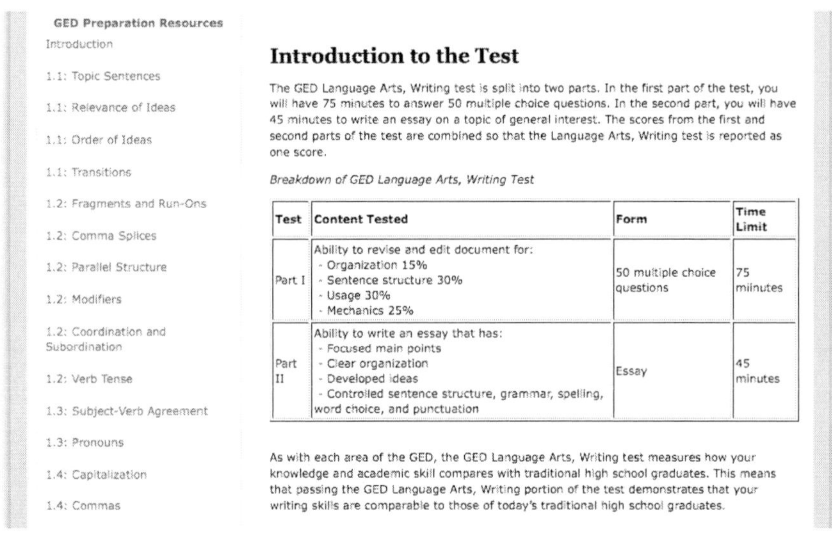

GED Preparation Resources

Introduction

1.1: Topic Sentences

1.1: Relevance of Ideas

1.1: Order of Ideas

1.1: Transitions

1.2: Fragments and Run-Ons

1.2: Comma Splices

1.2: Parallel Structure

1.2: Modifiers

1.2: Coordination and Subordination

1.2: Verb Tense

1.3: Subject-Verb Agreement

1.3: Pronouns

1.4: Capitalization

1.4: Commas

Introduction to the Test

The GED Language Arts, Writing test is split into two parts. In the first part of the test, you will have 75 minutes to answer 50 multiple choice questions. In the second part, you will have 45 minutes to write an essay on a topic of general interest. The scores from the first and second parts of the test are combined so that the Language Arts, Writing test is reported as one score.

Breakdown of GED Language Arts, Writing Test

Test	Content Tested	Form	Time Limit
Part I	Ability to revise and edit document for: - Organization 15% - Sentence structure 30% - Usage 30% - Mechanics 25%	50 multiple choice questions	75 miinutes
Part II	Ability to write an essay that has: - Focused main points - Clear organization - Developed ideas - Controlled sentence structure, grammar, spelling, word choice, and punctuation	Essay	45 minutes

As with each area of the GED, the GED Language Arts, Writing test measures how your knowledge and academic skill compares with traditional high school graduates. This means that passing the GED Language Arts, Writing portion of the test demonstrates that your writing skills are comparable to those of today's traditional high school graduates.

FIGURE 12.1. First-generation CWEST webpage design. Courtesy of the authors.

The drop-down menu is one example of the revisions we made to the navigation and the content of the CWEST area based on our empirical research. Other improvements included moving the search box from the upper right side of the pages into the navigation bar on the left side of the pages and adding more visuals to make grammar rules (such as prepositions) clearer.

However, it is important to remember that while theory-driven, empirically supported, and technology-based engagement can form *connections* between college and community, they cannot be the *only* methods of interaction. We worked very closely, on site, with LARA/ WorkOne administrators, instructors, and learners over a three-year period to develop the literacy materials collaboratively, adapting the rhetorical theories, methods of empirical research, and technology outlined in this chapter. Developing and maintaining these kinds of sustainable relationships is a vital part of moving from traditional short-term outreach efforts to long-term engagement scholarship informed by rhetorical theory and empirical research.

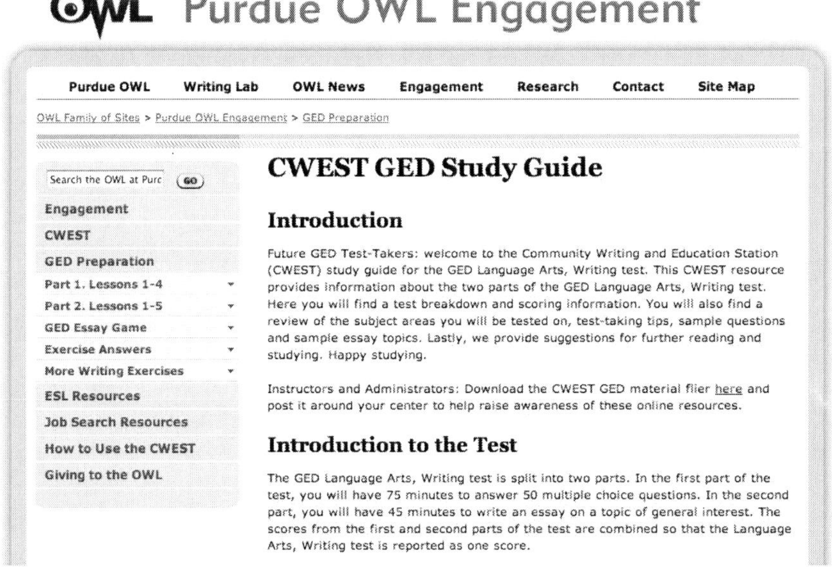

FIGURE 12.2. Second-generation CWEST webpage design. Courtesy of the authors.

Conclusion

Still inspired by the Kellogg Commission on the Future of State and Land-Grant Universities and its recommendations for public institutions of higher education in America, I conclude by pointing out how our graduate work in engagement connects with a number of their recommendations and goals and to show how engaged scholarship helps graduate students grow from learners into practitioners. In order to achieve the Kellogg Commission goals, the Kellogg Report provides universities with a seven-part test, reprinted in full on pp. 108–9 and outlined here:

- Responsiveness
- Respect for partners
- Academic neutrality
- Accessibility

- Integration
- Coordination
- Resource partnerships

During the CWEST project, I learned that rhetorical theories, empirical research, and technologies can work together to help university engagement projects work toward achieving these goals. Careful audience analysis, discursive rhetoric, empirical methods, and participatory technology design can make activist-scholars (as defined in Cushman 1996) more responsive to their communities and more respectful of the expertise of their engagement partners.

I also learned that when graduate students and their advisors imbed engagement in their work, they can address the commission's seven-part test. Especially important to writing across the curriculum and writing program administrators is how this work might address the commission's fifth test, integration. Fostering cooperation between different university institutions and projects speaks to some of the most important requirements of the writing program administrator's position. This was one reason it was important for us to establish a distinct engagement area on the OWL (http://owl.english.purdue.edu/engagement) and to connect with other engagement efforts at Purdue rather than develop web site exclusively dedicated to the CWEST.[13]

In addition, by connecting with other parts of our institution—the Institutional Review Board, the English as a Second Language Program (a Ph.D. candidate in ESL helped us develop the CWEST ESL resources), the Department of Foreign Languages and Literatures (a graduate student in FLL translated important CWEST documents into Spanish)—we addressed the coordination and resource partnership elements of the commission's test. Coordination raises awareness of engagement work and can, in turn, foster resource development from other parts of the institution. As a result, these partner organizations will be fulfilling *their* commitment to engagement by supporting our efforts and the efforts of our community partners.

The rhetorical theories I learned during coursework—audience analysis and discursive rhetoric—helped me move from student to researcher as we studied and navigated the institutions to which we belonged (Purdue University and its Writing Lab) and attempted to connect with community institutions Purdue serves (LARA and WorkOne). During this process, we integrated these rhetorical theories into methods of empirical research that also contributed to our ability to navigate and connect institutions that share similar goals, as noted in the LARA mission statement: "to teach academic and life skills to enable learners to make productive, ongoing changes in their personal lives, in society, and in public policy" (http://www.lsc.k12.in.us/

laraweb/mission/). I am convinced that our work with LARA/WorkOne could not have been completed without coursework in rhetorical theory and empirical research, but just as important as this classroom-based instruction is the practical experience Wells and I gained as we implemented these theories through the CWEST.

Notes

1. Additional information is available on the project website (http://owl.english.purdue.edu/engagement/1).

2. The third report of the Kellogg Commission, *Returning to Our Roots: The Engaged Institution* (1999), was a major influence on the development of the CWEST project discussed in this chapter. See the executive summary on pp. 103–7.

3. Dubinsky grounds his model in rhetorical theory, both classical and contemporary, and in so doing aligns with writing scholars who call for writing scholarship and pedagogy guided by theory.

4. The Purdue Writing Lab and its OWL are the achievement of Muriel Harris, who retired from her position as founding director in 2003.

5. The Purdue Liberal Arts Community Engagement (PLACE) was established in January 2007, but was suspended three years later due to budget cuts. Its website described the program as "a collaborative center for community engagement."

6. See http://www.partners.utah.edu for information about that well-established program.

7. Although the projects Hunter described were situated in the social sciences, her approach to them seems applicable to the fields of rhetoric and composition and professional writing. There has been an increasing call for more empirical research in writing and learning to write, and for a closer relationship of composition studies theory and practice to research in education, cognition, communication, and other social sciences (see, for example, Charney 1996). This call was widely circulated in Richard Haswell's 2005 argument for "replicable, aggregable, and data-driven" research in the field, and it has been facilitated by national and international projects such as the Research Exchange established in 2008 (http:/researchexchange.colostate.edu/).

8. These humanities-based methodologies typically relied on recording anecdotes and analyzing texts.

9. This ongoing accessibility is noteworthy given the sustainability shortcomings of many civic engagement projects highlighted by Grabill (2001). In addition, CWEST resources exist in print and digital form at

LARA/WorkOne and will be used by adult basic education and employment programs across Indiana, including programs within state correctional facilities.

10. The iterative and continual improvement theories outlined in the Kaizen and Six Sigma management and industrial manufacturing approaches also influenced the CWEST development process. The connections between the user-centered approach and the Kaizen continual improvement process are discussed in Brizee and Sousa (2006).

11. Tony Cimasko was an ESL specialist and Ph.D. candidate in ESL in the Purdue Department of English.

12. Robert Asen (2004) states that authors/activists should integrate discursive rhetoric into their notions of engagement and citizenship. Doing so, he argues, allows implementing two changes in traditional approaches of outreach: shifting the concept and definition of citizenship into a mode of public engagement (a sustained process of action) and expanding our notion of citizenship to include local, personal, and discursive acts, as well as national and public acts such as voting and demonstrating (191–92).

13. The OWL Engagement area now hosts six outreach projects other than the CWEST and has links to the Purdue Office of Engagement, Purdue Liberal Arts Community Engagement (PLACE), the Engineering Projects in Community Service (EPICS) program, and the webpage for service learning at Purdue.

References

Amare, Nicole, and Teresa Grettano. 2007. Writing outreach as community engagement. *WPA: Writing Program Administration* 30 (3): 57–74.

Anderson, Paul V. 2007. *Technical communication: A reader-centered approach*. 6th ed. Boston: Thomson/Wadsworth.

Asen, Robert. 2004. A discourse theory of citizenship. *Quarterly Journal of Speech* 90 (2): 189–211.

Bergmann, Linda S. 2010. The writing center as a site of engagement. In *Going public: The WPA as advocate for engagement*, edited by Shirley Rose and Irwin Weiser. Logan: Utah State University Press.

Bergmann, Linda S., and Tammy Conard-Salvo. 2007. Dialogue and collaboration: A writing lab applies tutoring techniques to relations with other writing programs. In *Marginal words, marginal work? Tutoring the academy to the work of the writing center*, edited by Bill Macauley and Nicholas Amauriello. Cresskill, NJ: Hampton Press.

Blythe, Stuart. 1998. Wiring a usable center: Usability research and writing center practice. In *Wiring the writing center,* edited by Eric Hobson. Logan: Utah State University Press.

Brizee, H. Allen, and Morgan Sousa. 2006. Kaizen in professional writing: Pedagogical possibilities. Unpublished paper.

Charney, Davida. 1996. Empiricism is not a four-letter word. *College Composition and Communication* 47 (4): 567–93.

Condon, Frankie. *2004.* The pen pal project. *Praxis: A Writing Center Journal* 2 (1). http://projects.uwc.utexas.edu/praxis/

Coogan, David. 2005. Counterpublics in public housing: Reframing the politics of service-learning. *College English* 67 (5): 461–82.

Cushman, Ellen. 1996. The rhetorician as an agent of social change. *College Composition and Communication* 47 (1): 7–28.

Cushman, Ellen. 1999. The public intellectual, service learning, and activist research. *College English* 61 (3): 328–36.

Cushman, Ellen. 2002. Sustainable service learning programs. *College Composition and Communication* 54 (1): 40–65.

Driscoll, Dana, H. Allen Brizee, Michael Salvo, and Morgan Sousa. 2008. Usability and user-centered theory for 21st century OWLs. Chap. 45 in *Handbook of research on virtual workplaces and the new nature of business practices,* edited by Pavel Zemliansky and Kirk St. Amant. Hershey, PA: Information Science Reference.

Dubinsky, James M. 2002. Service-learning as a path to virtue: The ideal orator in professional communication. *Michigan Journal of Community Service Learning* 8 (2): 61–74.

Ehn, Pelle. 1992. Scandinavian design: On participation and skill. In *Usability: Turning technologies into tools,* edited by P. S. Adler and T. A. Winograd. New York: Oxford University Press, 1992.

Grabill, Jeffrey T. 2001. *Community literacy programs and the politics of change.* Albany: SUNY Press.

Grabill, Jeffrey T., and Lynée Lewis Gaillet. 2002. Writing program design in the metropolitan university: Toward constructing community partnerships. *WPA: Writing Program Administration* 25 (3): 61–78.

Harris, Muriel. 1999. A writing center without a WAC program: The de facto WAC center/writing center. In *The Longman guide to writing center theory and practice,* edited by Robert W.Barnett and Jacob S. Blumner. Westport, CT: Greenwood Press.

Haswell, Richard. 2005. NCTE/CCCC's recent war on scholarship. *Written Communication* 22 (2): 198–223.

Heilker, Paul. 1997. "Rhetoric made real: Civic discourse and writing beyond the curriculum. In *Writing the community: Concepts and models for service-learning in composition,* edited by Linda Adler-Kassner, Robert Crooks, and Ann Watter. Washington, DC: American Association for Higher Education.

Herzberg, Bruce. 1994. Community service and critical teaching. *College Composition and Communication* 45 (3): 307–19.

Johnson, Robert R. 1998. *User-centered technology: A rhetorical theory for computers and other mundane artifacts.* Albany: SUNY Press.

Johnson-Sheehan, Richard. 2005. *Technical communication today.* New York: Pearson-Longman.

Kellogg Commission on the Future of State and Land-Grant Universities. 1999. *Returning to our roots: The engaged institution.* Washington, DC: National Association of State Universities and Land-Grant Colleges.

Knowles, Malcolm. 1970. *The modern practice of adult education: Andragogy versus pedagogy.* New York: Association Press.

Knowles, Malcolm. 1984. *Andragogy in action: Applying modern principles of adult learning.* San Fransisco: Jossey-Bass.

Knox, Alan B. 1986. *Helping adults learn.* San Francisco: Jossey-Bass.

Locke, Lawrence F., Stephen J. Silverman, and Waneen Wyrick Spirduso. 2004. *Reading and understanding research.* 2d ed. Thousand Oaks, CA: Sage.

Purdue University Writing Lab. 2011. *Purdue Writing Lab annual report for 2010–2011.* West Lafayette, IN: Purdue University.

Salvo, Michael, H. Allen Brizee, Dana Lynn Driscoll, and Morgan Sousa. 2008. *Purdue Online Writing Lab (OWL) usability report.* http://owl.english.purdue.edu/research/OWLreport.pdf

Salvo, Michael J., Jingfang Ren, H. Allen Brizee, and Tammy S. Conard-Salvo. 2009. Usability research in the writing lab: Sustaining discourse and pedagogy. *Computers and Composition* 26 (2): 107–21.

Simmons, Michele W., and Jeffrey T. Grabill. 2007. Toward a civic rhetoric for technologically and scientifically complex places: Invention, performance, and participation. *College Composition and Communication* 58 (3): 419–48.

Sullivan, Patricia A., and James E. Porter. 1997. *Opening spaces: Writing technologies and critical research practices.* Greenwich, CT: Ablex.

Wells, Jaclyn M. 2008. Collaboration, administration, and community engagement: One grad student's reflections. *Reflections: A Journal of Writing, Service-Learning, and Community Literacy* 7(3). http://

reflectionsjournal.net

Wells, Jaclyn M. 2010. Writing program administration and community engagement: A bibliographic essay. In *Going public: The WPA as advocate for engagement,* edited by Shirley Rose and Irwin Weiser. Logan: Utah State University Press.

13

When the Gown Goes to Town: The Reciprocal Rewards of Fieldwork for Artists

*Jan Cohen-Cruz**

> Our students need the city. They need to get right inside the life-force of the city and the community. They need not to be separate, because as long as they're separate, the only thing they can generate work about is themselves.
>
> —Carol Becker, "Our Students Need the City"

> Because you have imagined love, you have not loved; merely because you have imagined brotherhood, you have not made brotherhood.
>
> —Muriel Rukeyser, *The Life of Poetry*

AT THE AGE of twenty, as an actor in the NYC Street Theatre/Jonah Project, I co-facilitated a drama workshop at Trenton State Penitentiary, a maximum security prison. At its best, the workshop was a way for the men to shape energy hitherto expressed as rage into compelling statements about their personal lives, the criminal justice system, and society as they saw it. For my part, getting to know the participants through the deep language of art was nothing short of a revelation. The workshop initiated a profound shift in my perception of people in prison and, by extension, made me question other preconceptions I carried about groups of people I had never met. It made such an impact on my life that I came to regard the actor as a particular sort of anthropologist who could see through cultural stereotypes. I recognized a concomitant role for fieldwork in actor training, to expand actors' knowledge of people in diverse situations. How anthropologist Barbara Myerhoff described her own profession as attempting "to understand a different culture to the point of finding it to be intelligible, regardless of how strange it seems in comparison with one's own background," I imagined to be a worthy project for would-be actors (1978, 18).

---

*Originally published in *Theatre Topics* 11.1 (2001): 55–62. Reprinted courtesy of The Johns Hopkins University Press.

More than a decade later, in the late 1980s, the experience at the prison motivated me to create a community-based theatre course in the New York University Drama Department. As I had once done myself, the students came to confront their own stereotypes as they facilitated theatre workshops at venues such as psychiatric facilities and inner-city community centers. So meaningful was the fieldwork as a basis for learning in the Drama Department that the course was eventually adapted into the larger Tisch School of the Arts context. We now offer community-based internships in the arts to students from most of Tisch's eleven departments.

However, in the late 1980s community-based theatre was not yet recognized as a professional arts practice within either the academy or the theatrical mainstream. Our forays beyond the institutional walls were initially ignored, and then resisted. "Doesn't that belong in the School of Education?" an administrator demanded. "Do you think you belong in this department?" At issue here was our identity: Tisch offered conservatory training, while the School of Education taught arts of the "applied" variety. Tisch students were preparing to be artists, School of Education students, teachers. I insisted that a drama department of six hundred students (the number has since doubled) had an ethical responsibility to introduce a range of professions that someone with a love of theatre might pursue. But I stood warned.

What was really at issue? It is not unusual for professional artists to recognize the healing and educational capacities of art. However, art that is centered in efficacy—the difference Rukeyser articulates between imagining and doing the thing imagined—has a troubled reputation in Western thought. Some have traced this prejudice back to Aristotle, citing his idea that "the fine arts have no end beyond themselves" (Fergusson 1961, 32). Augusto Boal interprets Aristotle's emphasis on art's cathartic role in the same spirit: tragedy was intended to provoke the emotions of pity and fear in the spectators so they would not challenge the status quo when they left the theatre (1979, 36–37). Others, such as Suzi Gablik (1984), root resistance to socially active art in the tradition of modernism, which frees art from the necessity of relating to anything beyond its own borders. For many, it is precisely art's distance from everyday life that defines it as such and makes it identifiable as "high culture."

John Fiske has theorized the political implications of valorizing cultural distance. His ideas can be applied to an arts education that stays within the geographical boundaries of both theatre and the university as institutions. The distance maintained "between the art object and reader/spectator ... with claims to universality" downplays the necessity of engaging in the specifics of life out of which universals are discovered or indeed questioned. The distance "between the experience of the artwork and everyday life" eliminates living lessons as a source for art making and appreciating in favor of lessons that must be learned in specialized spaces. Fiske also examines the reasons for art's distance from economic necessity: "the separation of the aesthetic from the social is a practice of the elite who can afford to ignore the constraints of material necessity, and who thus construct an aesthetic which not only refuses to assign any value at all to material conditions, but validates only those art forms which transcend them" (1992, 154). Such a view allows art students to take their privileged positions for granted, while implicating other potential forms of employment as detracting from, rather than contributing to, their development as artists. Given this deep-seated ideology, it is no wonder my colleague was so resistant to the teaching of community-based theatre at Tisch.

Following these thinkers, I want to advocate for the transformative value of fieldwork in arts education by providing a practical overview of the evolution of our program at NYU. At the same time, with more than twelve years of concrete experience under my belt coordinating these fieldwork experiences, I want to note some challenges involved in forging partnerships between a university and various community organizations. This essay, then, is about both the abiding value and the ethical dilemmas of incorporating community-based workshops into the university education of young artists.

Expanding the Arts Paradigm

A fieldwork component in arts education works against a very old paradigm: the image of the artist as misunderstood loner, at odds with society. The creation of our community-based theatre course was catalyzed by a group of students who had taken my political theatre class and wanted hands-on experience with activist art. Most of these students found theatre overly narcissistic. Many shared the sentiments of Rukeyser: they were not satisfied performing plays about love or brotherhood; they wanted to do artistic work that put their ideals into action. With the Trenton State drama workshop as my north star, we created a course that met twice a week: one weekly meeting where we all met together, and one weekly meeting in which students facilitated or assisted a community-based arts workshop.

Over the years, an exciting range of projects has emerged from this course. One young woman, for example, built a documentary play about immigration with a class of third graders, based on interviews each child had done with a person born outside of the United States. A few other students worked with psychiatric patients on mythic scenes, under the direction of Emily Nash.[1] Another group of students facilitated a theatre workshop at a home for pregnant teenagers so they could quite simply play.

The work has been meaningful to students in a wide variety of ways. For many, the internships have provided them a chance to share their love of art with others. It has pointed to a new professional direction for others. Molly Gibeau, for example, became a social worker partially as a result of the class. As she later wrote me: "Helping the woman participate in that one theatre exercise in a locked [pyschiatric] ward at Mount Sinai Hospital felt more meaningful to me than acting in a play ever could" (Cohen-Cruz and Novak 1998, 87). Still others commented on the work's importance from a cultural perspective. Toya Lillard, an African American student, described her expanded understanding of her own identity as a result of workshoping with mostly African American, formerly incarcerated women: "We could truly enjoy and understand the value in sameness, and the importance of recognizing difference" (81). Lillard appreciated certain shared tastes and perceptions coming out of African American experience while recognizing differences from the women vis-à-vis class, age, education, and opportunities.

Not only did fieldwork enhance the students' education, but the classroom enhanced the students' fieldwork. The field can be highly disorienting. The prison workshop turned my world on its head: when I realized that criminality was often a response to desperate personal and social situations, my sense of a just world crumbled around me. I hoped that the classroom would provide students a place to contend with the emotional difficulties of the endeavor, reflect on their experiences, and recognize changes in perception as they were occurring. In our weekly meetings, I taught the students techniques to try out and ideas to orient them in the worlds they were entering. For example, we explored group-building exercises, improvisational structures, and closure games. We discussed how to deal with being the only white person in the room, feeling attracted to a student, or being scared of the neighborhood.

Despite initial institutional resistance to incorporating this fieldwork into an artist's education, I not only outlasted my inquisitor at NYU to become a tenured associate professor there but also helped to create a minor in applied theatre in the Drama Department in 1999. The courses in the minor introduce students to ways that theatrical practices extend beyond theatre as traditionally conceived into fields including education, medicine, therapy, political activism, community building, and social services.

In 1995 I was able to expand opportunities for artistic fieldwork beyond the Drama Department and into the larger context of Tisch.

Thanks to funding from AmeriCorps (President Clinton's national public service program), we engaged a cadre of Tisch students in an arts-for-violence-reduction initiative entitled Urban Ensemble. One graduate student and ten undergraduates specializing in photography, drama, and video trained for and facilitated arts workshops in community-based settings.[2] Our students studied conflict resolution, rudiments of teaching, and artistic techniques adapted to violence reduction, and led workshops with people from a halfway house for formerly incarcerated women, an East Harlem afterschool program, a community-building initiative focused on the creation and maintenance of several neighborhood gardens, and a program for adults who had dropped out of high school. In addition, up to sixty of us from these sites came together on a weekly basis for wildly unwieldy yet utterly appealing arts workshops.

The phrase "community service" does not accurately describe the nature of artistic fieldwork like Urban Ensemble. The term conjures up, after all, activities like serving meals in a soup kitchen with the soup server on one side of a counter, the soup receiver on the other. In Urban Ensemble, there is no counter: we are all in the soup together. With participants at our site-based projects, we have collaboratively produced plays, books of writing and photography, and videotapes. We have facilitated arts workshops combining participants from multiple backgrounds and locations. We have created Boal-based theatrical performances, songs, and poems. These are arts activities that necessitate joint risk taking. They are not soup kitchens.

After three years, NYU terminated its contract with AmeriCorps, largely because it was so expensive for the university (requiring hours of administrative support for endless reporting) and overly taxing for the students, many of whom also held jobs. Photography professor Lorie Novak and I resituated Urban Ensemble as an interdisciplinary arts course open to all Tisch students.[3] We expanded our partnerships to any not-for-profit organization that shared our interest in using the arts to meet any of a wide range of goals, in contrast to our AmeriCorps violence-reduction mandate.

The ongoing project relies on the principle of exchange. As young artists learn through contact outside the studio, community-based organizations are strengthened by skilled and energetic college students. Partly because we come from the outside, we hope to instigate what community artist Susan Ingalls (1996) calls "key positive" experiences, in which a positive experience outside the normal structures of family and school provides "significant psychological rewards and/or social recognition" that becomes "internalized as part of a child's emotional reservoir, instilling a sense of hope and resilience as s/he encounters challenges later in life." Though Ingalls is writing specifically about children, we have found that the value of key positive experiences holds true for adults as well, with the internships providing growth for teachers and students alike. A former student of ours, Jessica Ingram, drew on Ingalls to describe an example of this reciprocity in the following account from a photography workshop in a community center focusing on dreams:

> Nine-year-old Monique said she wanted to be with her mom in her dream and then the tears welled up in her eyes. We went to the side and she cried and told me how hard it is to talk to people and that she's lonely and just wants someone around to listen to her and understand. I understood because I feel the same way often. I remembered what Susan Ingalls said about being a sympathetic witness through the teaching we do. But I realized that Monique was also my sympathetic witness because she wanted to know how and why I understood, and I told her. Then we photographed her dream and in it, I played her mom. (Cohen-Cruz and Novak 1998, 27)

Urban Ensemble is the first course offered in Tisch's new Center for Art and Public Policy, founded on the belief that "young artists and scholars need an opportunity to incubate their ideas outside of the safe haven of the academy, in a dialectic with real-world problems."[4] The Center also offers courses that investigate the social, ethical, and political issues facing contemporary artists and scholars, and that examine public policy issues affecting artists' ability to make and distribute their work.

Raising Questions

Community-based programs like the ones I have described offer many benefits but also pose a variety of ethical challenges. While there is certainly enough community need for artists from both grassroots and university contexts, there is not always enough funding to support every artist with a project in mind. As large institutions with many resources to wield, universities often have fundraising professionals on their permanent staffs, as well as many employees more acculturated to grant language than most independent community-based artists. How will institutions of higher education contend with the competition factor inherent in fundraising, meaning that they may beat out the very individuals and organizations they wish to support? True, universities can initiate much community arts without fundraising largely because students are paid in credits rather than cash. But, in such cases, are universities taking jobs away from community artists by more easily offering for free a service that otherwise would be provided through a fee?[5] One solution to this problem is to work in three-way partnerships involving students, community-based organizations, and grassroots artists (whom the students assist).

As facilitators, we are often not of the communities in which we work. Given our students' limited time, how can they be present at their sites long enough to build trust? As Lucy Lippard states, "It is impossible to just drop into a community and make good activist art" (1984, 355). We need to find the means to contribute in meaningful ways despite each student's limited time commitment. This is a considerable challenge, given the amount of time community art takes. Will universities allow their students to spend sufficient time in fieldwork, in a participatory rather than the more conventional and concentrated classroom model? Whatever the case, the institutional commitment must be long-term, and, within this framework, each individual student should strive for a structured, rounded experience that has a beginning, middle, and end—not a recurring feature of all our participants' lives. Cultivating consistent, trusting relationships between community and university liaisons can go a long way toward building this framework.

Writing as outsiders about community arts raises other issues. Is such writing a form of cooptation? Will outsiders assess community arts according to only one standard—aesthetic, ideological, therapeutic? The language of university culture may be at odds with grassroots practice. How can critical writing avoid alienating the very people who are the subjects of and partners in the investigation? And underlying all these issues, how can we depolarize the insider/outsider construct in favor of different ways of looking at these experiences? Field experience challenges academics to rethink not just the expression but also the relationship between practice and theory. I struggle with the place of theory in my own writing, longing for the deeper inquiry that theory brings but wondering to what degree larger ideas need to grow directly out of the practices I am studying.

Then there is the question of training for the field. University students, even those most encumbered by financial difficulties, have the privilege of getting an education. It would be sadly ironic if the university became the only route to community-based arts jobs, thereby diminishing opportunity for those who cannot afford higher education. Is the university the only, or necessarily the best, venue for such preparation? I advocate for universities providing free workshops for community members involved in such partnerships.

Julia Ballerini points out other hazards in community arts. She counsels artists to watch that their attraction to sites like prisons and migrant camps not be a romance with "the untamed and uncivilized" that ignores cycles of poverty and despair, and to be vigilant that the art created there does not represent dire situations as picturesque or upbeat (1997, 162). A related issue arose in my own experience at Trenton State: the prisoners in the workshop refused the prison administration's request to make a video of our workshop. The participants feared that the administration would use the video to give the public the perception of the prison being a more humane place than the inmates believed it to be. Ballerini also counsels against "force feeding dominant aesthetics" to people with whom we work (179). Do we unconsciously perceive them as having no culture of their own? What motivates us? Are we insecure about our own art? Do our activities inadvertently "shift responsibility for those in need away from the government" (168)?

At their best, university/community arts collaborations offer reciprocal rewards. People in community settings frequently get as much, if not more, from participating in art making as from viewing it. Community artists gain from capable student interns who leave them freer to focus where they see fit. Student artists benefit from interaction with a range of human experience, no matter in which venues they ultimately work. Their consciousness is raised about who gets to make art and why. They learn that artists are not necessarily more talented than other people but rather have lived in circumstances that gave them the means for artistic development. They expand their sense of art's capacity, as well as their own artistic possibilities. In cultivating the expressive and communicative capacities of both students and community members, community-based work also develops more self-confident and giving human beings.

The profound art of people who lack craft but are overflowing with the need to express not only their own desires but also those of their communities challenges the dominant cultural paradigm that privileges individual over communal expression. My experiences in the field have spurred me to advocate for a broader conception of art that encompasses both extraordinary individual expression and extraordinary communal expression. Community-based fieldwork in the arts inevitably breaks out of a purely aesthetic frame into other subjective territories that long to be acted out—indeed, lived out—reminding us of art's ability to confront us with our deepest desires.

Notes

1. Nash's approach strengthens underutilized aspects of participants' personalities. A very fragile patient, for example, might portray a

fierce god in such an exercise. For more information, contact Nash at Creative Alternatives of New York, (212) 241-6636.

2. The students were guided by specialists and faculty mentors from three Tisch departments: Lorie Novak from Photography, Carlos de Jesus from Film and TV, and myself from Drama. See Cohen-Cruz 1997.

3. This was possible thanks to funding from the Gilman Foundation and the Kenan Institute of the Arts via the Liberal Education of the Arts consortium (LEA), of which Tisch is a member. Urban Ensemble is currently funded by the Deutsche Bank.

4. See the Office of Community Connections website (http://www.nyu.edu/tisch/community), again funded via LEA by Kenan and Gilman, as well as the Knight Foundation.

5. Some of these concerns were voiced at a recent gathering of nationally designated community arts trainers. For more information, see http://www.communityarts.net.

References

Ballerini, Julia. 1997. Photography as a charitable weapon: Poor kids and self-representation. *Radical History Review* 69:160–88.

Boal, Augusto. 1979. *Theatre of the oppressed.* Translated by Charles A. and Maria-Odilia Leal McBride. New York: Urizen Books.

Cohen-Cruz, Jan. 1997. Witnessing a drama of the soul. *High Performance* 75:15–19.

Cohen-Cruz, Jan, and Lorie Novak. 1998. *Urban ensemble: University/community collaborations in the arts.* New York: The authors.

Fergusson, Francis. 1961. Introduction to *Aristotle's Poetics.* New York: Hill and Wang.

Fiske, John. 1992. Cultural studies and the culture of everyday life. In *Cultural studies,* edited by Lawrence Grossberg, Cary Nelson, and Paula Treichler. New York: Routledge.

Gablik, Suzi. 1984. *Has modernism failed?* New York: Thames and Hudson.

Ingalls, Susan. 1996. Children and the Classics publicity materials. N.p.

Lippard, Lucy R. 1984. Trojan horses: Activist art and power. In *Art after modernism: Rethinking representation,* edited by Brian Wallis. Boston: D. R. Godine.

Myerhoff, Barbara. 1978. *Number our days.* New York: Simon and Schuster.

Rukeyser, Muriel. 1996. *The life of poetry.* Ashfield, MA: Paris Press.

14

Reimagining the Links Between Graduate Education and Community Engagement

Marcy Schnitzer and Max Stephenson Jr.

FEW QUESTIONS are more important for the vibrancy of our democratic institutions today than those concerning the warp and woof of the educational experience of students who will provide higher education to our future generations. This chapter argues that graduate social science, humanities, and arts programs should seek to develop rigorous and challenging public engagement research opportunities for their students. We focus on these fields due to our familiarity with their aims and content and do not mean to imply that other disciplines might not profit by considering ways to involve their advanced students in research in community. Graduate students in these curricula should be encouraged to connect with community concerns actively as they pursue their research and to develop reciprocal relationships with the individuals and communities in which they work. We contend graduate education can and must be more conducive to advancing the richness and depth of publicly driven engagement than is presently the case. We also argue that it should do so while recognizing and respecting the forms of knowledge and critical capacities of the members of the organizations and communities served.

To stimulate a broader dialogue and exchange of ideas on this important topic, we outline one model of graduate student civic engagement that we have self-consciously organized to be problem driven, research focused, and theoretically informed. Those characteristics define our approach to graduate student civic engagement in research and serve as means to help students attain more sophisticated analytical capabilities and highly developed empathetic imaginations. Appropriately framed civically engaged scholarship can provide graduate students particularly powerful learning opportunities not only to develop high-order reasoning and problem-framing skills, but also to develop a deep appreciation and appropriate humility concerning the heterogeneity of human experience and forms of meaning-making.

Our argument proceeds in five parts. We first sketch the recent national trend calling for broader university recognition of civically engaged scholarship. Next we point up the ways in which that call has so far been addressed and suggest means by which that base of understanding might be further refined. Third, we suggest that the growing demographic trend in favor of older graduate students, who return to school with already rich professional and life experiences, may favor civically engaged research models of learning. Fourth, we outline our own illustrative model of engaged graduate student scholarship and briefly provide five examples of ways that conception has thus far been operationalized. The research institute in which we work, the Virginia Tech Institute for Policy and Governance, serves all three missions of the land-grant university with which it is associated: discovery, learning, and engagement. Accordingly, we routinely enjoy opportunities to consider how theory, discovery, practice, and community may interrelate. Finally, we offer several observations on the forms and character of learning that engaged scholarship appears uniquely positioned to encourage in graduate students.

New Salience for Civic Scholarship and Pedagogy?

The distinction between *public engagement* and *publicly driven engagement* highlights the difference between services "done to," versus activities "undertaken with," communities. Full realization of publicly driven engagement in graduate education, expressed in the report *Calling the Question: Is Higher Education Ready to Commit to Engagement?* (Brukardt et al. 2004) rests in the extent to which graduate students are able to develop true partnerships with relevant publics, as well as the capacity of their institutions and programs to support such learning. As Brukardt and colleagues argue, "partnerships are learning environments. Too often the university arrives with the answers. True partnerships are spaces within which questions are created, there is genuine reciprocal deliberation and the work to find the answers is begun. It is within the partnerships that expertise both inside and outside the university is valued and honored" (9).

The Scholarship of Engagement "captures scholarship in the areas of teaching, research, and/or service. It engages faculty in academically relevant work that simultaneously meets campus mission and goals as well as community needs" (National Review Board for the Scholarship of Engagement 2002). Academic literature on college and university faculty scholarly engagement is well developed.[1] Undergraduate service-learning programs have been established at numerous colleges and universities across the United States and those too have spawned a vigorous literature (Stanton and Cruz 1999; Butin 2005). More than

1,100 institutions of higher education are members of Campus Compact, an organization dedicated to community service and service learning, but this number likely understates the total number of programs under way nationally. Moreover, with broad adoption of the Carnegie Foundation's new elective institutional classifications in 2006, engagement has now been recognized as a criterion in determining overall faculty performance at many colleges and universities. However, even the 2008 Carnegie framework was silent on the role of engagement in graduate education.

Service Learning as One Response to the Call for Student Community Engagement

The service-learning research community has long recognized the developmental benefits of undergraduate community service. Astin and Sax (1998), for example, have linked participation in a service-learning experience to "academic development, life skill development, and a sense of civic responsibility" (251). Eyler (2002) has argued that service learning enhances students' ability to understand complex social issues (517). Acknowledging the importance of progressively responsible service-related experiences, the Bonner Foundation has led the nation in developing a four-year student development model for its 27 Bonner Scholar campus programs (Bonner Foundation 2008).

In sum, many colleges and universities either have recently adopted some form of civic engagement as a component of undergraduate education and a criterion for evaluation of relevant faculty activities, or are in the process of doing so. What appears still to be lacking is a clear approach for recognizing and developing scholarly civic engagement among graduate students. We find this omission troubling, considering these individuals collectively constitute the future professoriate. Indeed, it might be argued they are already playing important professional roles: many shoulder undergraduate teaching responsibilities as they complete their advanced degrees.

There are, however, signs of hope that graduate student civic engagement is garnering more attention. Increasingly, graduate schools are developing mechanisms that encourage student scholarship in and with communities. Our own university, Virginia Tech, for example, has instituted a Citizen Scholar Experience as part of its Transformative Graduate Education program (Virginia Tech Graduate School 2010). Nevertheless, this program follows a basic service-learning model, in which graduate students are encouraged to select a project from a delimited list of available options, or to develop their own ventures to fulfill a service-related course requirement. They participate in an interdisciplinary seminar that addresses the role of engagement in the university's mission prior to pursuing their selected initiatives. But as useful as this sort of activity is, it lacks a robust theoretical conception of engaged scholarship as a critical component of the development of the research and teaching skills of the students involved in it. It does not encourage advanced graduate students to conceive of their scholarly roles as deeply enmeshed in and connected to community programs or community life, nor require that they employ theoretical ideas common in their work to help them make sense of the challenges and problems evidenced in the communities in which they are engaged. Nor, finally, does service learning demand that those so engaged grapple with the many alternate ways in which community members are conceiving of their life challenges and how those conceptions might relate to students' own research interests and purposes. For present purposes, a "community" may be local to a student's campus, in another state, or indeed in another nation. What is significant is that individuals develop habits of mind and analytical wherewithal to act sensitively, sensibly, and thoughtfully in the cultural contexts they confront. Students interested in international development may thus engage in community just as their colleagues who undertake local efforts might.

The "engagement gap" in graduate student development is related to the continued relatively marginal position of civic engagement as an aspiration of university mission—even in the more auspicious context of land-grant institutions, whose raison d'être includes such a goal. Given this reality, comparatively few professors are available who can model an integrated approach to their community-engaged research. But universities and colleges cannot wait on the inclinations of individual faculty members alone to secure a more civically engaged professsoriate. Instead, they must assume responsibility as institutions for assuring this result and encouraging faculty members with the requisite interest and capacity to pursue such purposes. Graduate students constitute a virtually untapped resource for exploring how such an integrated model of civic scholarship might be developed.

A "New" Sort of Graduate Student?

Among the critical overarching trends in higher education is the fact that the nation's collegiate student body is increasingly comprised of adult learners, defined as students above the age of 24 (Bash 2003, 44). This trend is less surprising, perhaps, for graduate programs. However, as Bash (2003) has suggested, individuals are now returning to graduate school later in their careers. Roughly 80% of adult learners are employed, earning incomes greater than $50,000 per year (Bash 2003, 46). *The Chronicle of Higher Education* (2009) has documented this graduate education trend, noting that in 2007 64% of full-time and 88%

of part-time graduate students are above the age of 24. Meanwhile, 18% of full-time and 47% of part-time graduate students are over age 34. Today's graduate students are more likely to have been employed in responsible positions and to bring with them a base of knowledge, skills, and experience that is qualitatively different from more traditional students. However, faculty accustomed to working with younger students may offer few opportunities for integrating this knowledge into a classroom setting.

At Virginia Tech, the Institute for Policy and Governance (VTIPG), the ASPECT (Alliance for Social, Political, Ethical and Cultural Thought), the Public Administration and Public Affairs (PAPA) and Planning, Governance and Globalization (PG and G) doctoral programs, and the Virginia Bioinformatics Institute have experienced such an influx of "older" graduate students in recent years.[2] Recognizing their special capabilities, VTIPG and its partners have provided closely integrated research and civic engagement opportunities that serve as outlets for these students' experience and creativity. Graduate assistants in these research entities and programs have been encouraged to utilize their professional background in service to communities even as they broaden and deepen their expert knowledge while pursuing their coursework and research responsibilities. For many of these students, a return to graduate study represents an important opportunity to obtain the concepts and analytic capacities that together allow them to make sense of the strategic and operating environments they have confronted (and often continue to confront) in their professional roles. In this important sense, graduate study informs in needful and compelling ways as it helps individuals understand and sort through their cumulative career experiences and challenges. For many of these students too, charged with leadership roles outside their graduate programs; advanced study allows them to exercise their responsibilities more effectively, as their organizations and staffs look to them to map possibilities for action and institutional positioning. The intellectual capacities obtained in advanced study offer the possibility of this set of capabilities. We next outline briefly the graduate education engagement model that VTIPG and its institutional partners have developed to assist these talented individuals.

An Integrated Graduate Student Civic Engagement Model

VTIPG and its institutional partners have developed a model of publicly driven graduate student engagement based in action research (Herr and Anderson 2005; McIntyre 2007; Stringer 2007). Doctoral students interested in civil society and community change and development processes learn from and with residents in the Central Appalachian region (where Virginia Tech's main campus is located) as they jointly seek to address compelling community problems. Students and regional residents collaboratively engage in capacity building by compiling data for adaptive community change, facilitating community-wide dialogue, and supporting implementation of community-driven actions. Through hands-on participation in community-based problem solving, students reflect actively on the extent and character of their engagement and their appropriate research roles in supporting sustainable community change that integrates social, economic, and environmental perspectives. VTIPG-affiliated graduate students work closely with a cadre of qualified faculty, other experienced doctoral students, and an array of community partners as they pursue their research in community.

This model has been developed on the basis of a combination of serendipitous doctoral enrollment trends and a willingness of the partnering programs to invest in and deepen graduate student knowledge and experience. The participating doctoral programs routinely enroll students returning to school following significant professional experience. Doctoral students recently have come to Virginia Tech with backgrounds such as nonprofit executive directors, development directors, executive staff of humanitarian relief organizations, returned Peace Corps volunteers, conservation field workers, and professional writers. These students came to graduate study with research agendas based in their professional experience and a strong desire to explore opportunities to extend their learning beyond the bounds of campus. What follows are descriptions of the types of community research and collaboration opportunities that recent doctoral students have had and in which they have played significant leadership roles. In each case, students have worked with community partners to identify issues (that is, their work is problem driven), have developed and shared possible ways and means by which those engaged could make sense of their perceived concerns (their work is theoretically informed), and have joined their own research interests to community claims and needs (their work is research focused).

Leadership Through the Arts

The Southside region of Virginia, including the communities of Danville, Martinsville, Chatham, South Boston, and surrounding areas, has been hard hit by recent changes in the social and economic landscape. Virginia Tech, as the largest nearby land-grant university, has engaged actively with the Southside region and its problems. Virginia Tech is serving the region by helping to catalyze the development of local leadership and by facilitating creation of forums that bring local residents together to confront challenges and visualize positive paths forward. Artists across the region have been identified as vital partners in this effort, since they are so often at the vanguard of social change. Art has the power to cause us to examine and challenge our assumptions and to consider new possibilities. Artists continuously create, organize, and produce, almost always within tight resource constraints. The potential for artists to serve as community leaders and facilitators of civic dialogue has been powerfully illustrated by the Animating Democracy project. Americans for the Arts launched the four-year Animating Democracy Initiative in tandem with the Ford Foundation to draw upon the arts to promote civic dialogue on important contemporary issues. The initial program provided grants to 32 cultural organizations to implement projects aimed at developing arts- and humanities-based civic dialogue. The original initiative has been continued under the aegis of Americans for the Arts, which has produced a series of books that highlight the lessons of the effort (for example, Korza, Bacon, and del Vecchio, 2008; Korza, Bacon, and Assaf 2005; Atlas and Korza 2005).[3]

Like Animating Democracy, the Leadership Through the Arts (LTA) program in Southside has sought to stimulate civic dialogue and public reflection through community-based arts initiatives. LTA began in 2005 with an exploratory "listening project" sponsored by VTIPG; faculty and graduate students, over the course of a year and a half, interviewed 70 area artists and arts supporters, building a database of the local artists and arts groups and studying how these relate to their communities. That initial phase led to dialogue between Southside artists and engaged university faculty and graduate students about the possibility of a collaborative effort designed to catalyze community dialogue about regional needs and challenges. A group of 12 local artists subsequently volunteered to serve as a steering committee for the project. This group has met on several occasions, working with Virginia Tech partners to translate a broadly shared vision into specific steps forward. A graduate student leader with significant community organizing experience has played a key role with faculty in facilitating the work of Leadership Through the Arts. The project not only has resulted in several community-driven grant proposals and programs, but has also generated three published peer-reviewed academic articles (Stephenson 2007, 2011; Stephenson and Lanham 2007) and two graduate capstone papers.

Nonprofit Capacity Building

VTIPG has longstanding relationships with local nonprofit organizations in the region near the Virginia Tech campus and across Virginia. For example, the Institute has been involved in a partnership with the Community Foundation of the New River Valley since before the Institute's formal creation nearly five years ago. Building on the expertise of its affiliated faculty and graduate students, VTIPG has, for the past three years, provided capacity-building services to the nonprofit community in the region. These have taken several forms: focused-topical workshops for groups of nonprofit executives and board members; regular, weekly discussion forums in which nonprofit leaders interact and share information and best practices; single-organization-focused governance interventions that build upon a comprehensive assessment of organizational challenges and prospects derived from interviews with staff, board members, donors, and clients; and special-focus consultation on needs identified by the organization's leadership. Whatever their specific forms, the primary goal of these various types of engagement is to provide continuous learning opportunities for the organizations with which VTIPG works. This approach allows the Institute and its partners to provide area nonprofits with the knowledge, capacities, and strategies necessary to lead their organizations more effectively and to improve their operations. The focus of the VTIPG capacity-building approach is unique among consultation processes because of its focus on continuous learning as opposed to "one-shot" workshops, as well as its emphasis on learning from and building upon the expertise of the organization and its constituencies.

VTIPG faculty and doctoral students have specifically engaged trustees and directors in the challenge of how to develop more effective governance practices. Rather than simply being exposed to "chalk talks" and expert lectures on how their organization should change, board members are engaged in active learning and deliberation aimed at identifying how they might address what they perceive to be their organization's key issues. In the process, directors become more instrumental in the life of the nonprofits they nominally lead. They contribute to the development of annual work plans with specific tasks and timetables for committees and members.

Graduate students and faculty members have been instrumental in convening, leading, and facilitating VTIPG topical workshops for nonprofit organizations, drawing on their own backgrounds in the field. Students also have brought their specific expertise to bear in studying how local nonprofits could collaborate more effectively to provide public health services for low-income residents. Other graduate students have provided capacity-building support to local nonprofit organizations on fundraising, time management, and arts-based economic revitalization. In all of these cases, doctoral students have assumed considerable responsibility in meeting with organizations and leaders, identifying and interviewing key stakeholders, scoping problems and challenges, and providing specific feedback and information. As in Southside, their work has been theoretically informed by the latest relevant scholarship—on capacity building, conceptions of governance, organizational learning, and stakeholder analysis, for example. These efforts have likewise been problem focused, and the problems addressed have been the product of dialogue rather than professional fiat. Finally, in each instance students and faculty have jointly determined a course of action with the organizations involved, while simultaneously considering how what is being learned may advance scholarly understanding of the concerns in play.

VTIPG-VBI Transdisciplinary Collaboration

VTIPG has entered into a unique partnership with the Virginia Bioinformatics Institute (VBI). VBI faculty members have considerable expertise in science and technology as these pertain to infectious diseases, including cutting-edge capabilities in computational biology and large-scale simulations of disease epidemics. Nonetheless, the organization's leaders have recognized the need to ally with VTIPG to affect health outcomes in the developing world. VTIPG and VBI faculty, leaders and affiliated doctoral students are working together to develop an intervention and partnership strategy that is both transdisciplinary in character and that draws on the expertise of faculty and doctoral students from each research institute. The institutes are designing a strategy to assist two sub-Saharan African nations (Ghana and Mali) with improving public health–related outcomes. VTIPG faculty and students bring a deep knowledge of development processes and governance dynamics in these nations, while VBI faculty bring their capacities in infectious disease and bioinformatics. The partnership has created opportunities for all involved to reflect on the vicissitudes and challenges of transdisciplinary research and engagement. Indeed, one VTIPG-affiliated doctoral student with a background in biological sciences is researching definitions and models of transdisciplinarity, using this project as a case study as part of his dissertation research. Other project faculty and graduate students are seeking to use their expertise to contribute to the project's larger vision. The project is theoretically informed by the latest scholarship on simulation modeling of large-scale epidemics (Barrett, Bisset, Leidig, et al. 2009; Barrett, Bisset, Chen, et al. 2009), on infectious diseases in sub-Saharan Africa, and on governance and development processes in this region. It has also sought to focus on a specific problem to which the transdisciplinary team could contribute consonant with its capacities and to do so with African partners such as the health ministries of Ghana and Mali and NIH-Mali in a context-specific way. In its start-up stages, the partnership already has spawned one doctoral dissertation, an academic conference paper, and a number of literature reviews likely to spur published work. The project also has fomented thinking about the theory of transdisciplinarity, even as project team members have sought to employ the construct to guide their engagement strategy. Theory building and reflection is occurring on at least two analytic scales.

Help Africa

Frequently, students are in a position to initiate their own engagement projects. PG and G doctoral student affiliated with VTIPG and formerly employed by World Vision, an international nongovernmental organization focusing on children's issues, now aids in overseeing an NGO he helped to found in his home nation of Togo. The student's contacts and the broad capacity-building focus of the NGO Help Africa have enabled a community-minded research project in Togo and neighboring Ghana. A group of faculty and doctoral students have together analyzed the region's development needs, political situation, and existing capacities to craft a vision for a regional development center to be collaboratively developed and located in Lomé. Work to date has been driven by careful analysis of the region's current needs and challenges (that is, it is problem- and research-focused) as well as how a collaboration might best be framed and organized (it is theoretically informed). Next steps will involve preliminary meetings with relevant government and civil society representatives.

Student Dissertation Research

In addition to their key roles in determining the type and scope of direct service provision to communities and community-based organizations, several VTIPG-affiliated graduate students have sought to use their professional experiences to inform their dissertation research. Several of these individuals enrolled in graduate school with a keen interest in community-based collaboration and interorganizational dynamics. They have selected dissertation research that focuses on community involvement in local environmental sustainability issues, local representation in the transnational public sphere, and investigation (through direct participation) of the process of developing a model of interdisciplinary collaboration. A student who had led a sustainable co-housing project focused her research on co-housing communities as sites in which to build social capital. Students with direct experience in humanitarian relief provision have employed their experiences as a foundation on which to build research to improve humanitarian accountability to service recipients, to facilitate corporate social responsibility in garnering medical supplies and donations, and to build leadership and capacity for organizational governance. In every case, students are utilizing relevant research and theory while seeking to address a specific problem of social significance. As noted above, their research often reflects not only their intellectual interests but also their aim to acquire capacities to make sense of their professional worlds and challenges.

Some Additional Dimensions and Implications of These Projects

Several key factors must be present to support this type of engaged research, absent which participating graduate (mostly doctoral) students would find it far more difficult to pursue such work. These include the capacities of the faculty involved, the missions and operating philosophies of the principal research center involved, the characteristics of the graduate students engaged, and the opportunities presented by civic participation itself.

Mentoring

Faculty affiliated with VTIPG recognize and value graduate student engagement in community and they are able to advise students on how to translate their academic and professional knowledge and experience into research practice and skills suited to the purpose. While graduate students are actively involved in projects in the arts, it is still relatively rare for faculty in the social sciences, fine arts, and the humanities to have the experience that can support them, and these faculty members understand that their responsibility in many ways mirrors that of students engaging members of the community: to work respectfully with partners while simultaneously offering them opportunities to consider new ideas and thereby to change and to grow. Thoughtful mentors also know when to counsel patience and forbearance, when to cheerlead if a partnership is going awry, and when simply to listen, as experiences are recounted and new narratives of meaning constructed.

Institutional Support

VTIPG is uniquely positioned at the intersection of research, teaching, and engagement. The Institute administers a graduate certificate in nonprofit management for the School of Public and International Affairs that is open to students in all disciplines across the university. Further, Institute faculty, staff, and affiliated students engage in research that addresses on-the-ground issues such as coordination of humanitarian aid, organizational governance, and the institutional impact of private philanthropy. VTIPG also collaborates with local organizations to sponsor international workshops for community foundations, supports networking and professional development opportunities for community-based organizations, and participates in and supports local nonprofit organization collaborative efforts. Its institutional base allows VTIPG-affiliated faculty and students to draw upon a common vision, in which service to communities is critically informed by the knowledge and perspectives of community members themselves. These views are communicated through relationship building, facilitated substantially by graduate students working with and in community and nonprofit organizations.

Students Supporting Students

For working professionals, the transition to graduate school can be disorienting and demoralizing. One may have been previously recognized for certain abilities and expertise that do not necessarily confer advantage in graduate education. Fellow students can be instrumental in affirming and reassuring mature graduate students that they can conduct research and produce scholarly work. More importantly, students can support each other in integrating the theoretical and experiential in their academic work. The "view from outside," from communities as well as from previous professional experience, can afford new insights into the development of relevant project theory, approach, and methods. Professionally experienced students can also work alongside their less experienced peers, for whom concepts of interviewing, community organizing, and professional writing represent new challenges.

Community Members as Peers and Co-learners

Graduate students attempting to "bridge the gap" between practitioner-based knowledge and academic knowledge are in a unique position to develop peer relationships with community leaders when involved in community-engaged research. Further, working in communities can decrease the alienation that professionals transitioning to graduate student life may feel in the academy, and simultaneously give them confidence that their experience can still be of service to others.

Placing graduate students in settings that can support engaged research affords them special opportunities to build their academic competencies in an environment that equally values the experience and priorities of those with whom they are interacting. Civically engaged graduate students are not simply processing abstract knowledge and offering it as technical assistance, but are applying, shaping, and contributing to the co-creation of knowledge that, at its best, has the advantage of reflecting community needs and aspirations.

Conclusions

Current thinking concerning graduate student engagement tends to ask students to understand the relevance of their discipline to public life without necessarily employing their knowledge in communities. We have offered an alternative approach in which graduate students, suitably mentored and supported, are assumed to possess capacities that can both be refined and brought to bear in civically engaged research. This is especially true, we have argued, for those increasing numbers of students returning to graduate study following several years of professional experience. These individuals bring the perspective born of practice, and typically also exhibit a thirst to learn and to see ideas come to fruition. As a group, these students are especially well positioned to engage with communities in research and to employ the ideas derived from their academic training to make sense of the everyday challenges they confront in the workplace.

We have argued that graduate social science, arts, and humanities student community engagement that is research driven, problem focused, and theoretically informed can enrich educational experience even as it provides significant value to the communities and organizations served. This is so, we have suggested, irrespective of whether such engagement is undertaken by preprofessional or experienced students. It doubtless does so by assisting participants with issues and concerns they believe significant. And it does so, too, by allowing the faculty and students involved to see how their ideas may matter in their social application. But, as important as these characteristics are, this form of graduate education has three still more important advantages. First, in its demand that students and faculty confront the heterogeneity of interests, norms, and values at play in even small communities and organizations, it requires these individuals to grapple with points of view and perspectives often quite different from their own or from those suggested by their professional education and acculturation. We think this reality healthy, as it demands that those engaged learn to respect alternate identities and discern ways of involving individuals in projects that ultimately seek to improve their lives in some way. Second, students and faculty members alike must wrestle with the fundamental problem of how to honor and ensure the dignity of all with whom they interact as a part of working in a society that aspires to be ever more fully democratic. Third, if the sort of civic engagement outlined here ultimately demands democratic humility, it requires also that students develop very high-order analytical and reasoning capacities. Dealing in interdisciplinary work groups and with disparate groups of individuals demands that those so engaged cultivate the ability to listen attentively, to reason by analogy, and to develop analytical frames rooted in the norms and values of those engaged so as to create new and shared metacognitive frames that permit common understanding of social problems.

Engaged scholarship allows, or better, requires, students and faculty to develop these abilities if they are to succeed. It requires both highly developed empathetic imagination so as to regard the diverse views of those in community with whom one is dealing with respect, and robust intellectual capacity so as to allow opportunities for shared cognitive frames to emerge that allow the potential for the emergence of common understanding and action. Our hope is that the principles that guided the engagement examples offered here may translate broadly to a range of graduate student disciplines and experiences. It might be argued that programs with a less obvious connection to community-based work pose a challenge for developing the next generation of engaged graduate student scholars. Nevertheless, the problem-focused and theoretically informed interdisciplinary research outlined here has successfully fostered partnerships among students and faculty members from a diverse array of disciplines, including some in the life sciences, civil engineering, forestry, and theater arts. These teams have organized themselves to engage with communities to address collaboratively framed challenges, giving hope that engaged research may provide unparalleled learning opportunities for students, faculties, and communities alike.

Notes

1. See, e.g., Bringle et al. 1990; Fairweather 1996; Glassick et al. 1997; Driscoll and Lynton 1999; Lynton 1999; Sandman et al. 2000.

2. The Virginia Tech Institute for Policy and Governance was founded in 2006 as a unique university-level research center whose broad mission was to span and integrate where possible the university's interest in learning, discovery, and engagement across its eight colleges. The graduate certificate program VTIPG oversees in nonprofit and nongovernmental organizations draws disproportionate numbers of in-career students and its projects and faculty routinely attract older and more professionally experienced doctoral students for work and study.

3. More information on Animating Democracy is available on the project's website: http://www.artsusa.org/animatingdemocracy.

References

Astin, A., and L. Sax. 1998. How undergraduates are affected by service participation. *Journal of College Student Development* 39 (3): 251–63.

Atlas, C., and P. Korza. 2005. *Critical perspectives: Writings on art and civic dialogue.* Washington, DC: Americans for the Arts.

Barrett, C., K. Bisset, J. Leidig, A. Marathe, and M. Marathe. 2009. Estimating the impact of public and private strategies for controlling an epidemic: A multi-agent approach. In *Proceedings of the Twenty-First Innovative Applications of Artificial Intelligence Conference,* edited by Karen Haigh and Nestor Rychtyckjy. Menlo Park, CA: AAAI Press.

Barrett, C., K. Bisset, J. Chen, S. Eubank, B. Lewis, V. S. A. Kumar, M. Marathe, and H. Mortveit. 2009. Interactions among human behavior, social networks, and societal infrastructures: A case study in computational epidemiology. In *Fundamental problems in computing: Essays in honor of Professor Daniel J. Rosenkrantz,* edited by S. Ravi and S. Shukla. Dordrecht, Netherlands: Springer.

Bash, L. 2003. *Adult learners in the academy.* Bolton, MA: Anker.

Bonner Foundation. 2008. Program description: Student development. http://www.bonner.org/campus/bsp/BSPdescription/studentdevel.htm.

Bringle, R. G., R. Games, and E. A. Malloy, eds. 1990. *Colleges and universities as citizens.* Needham Heights, MA: Allyn & Bacon.

Brukardt, M., B. Holland, S. Percy, and N. Zimpher. 2004. *Calling the question: Is higher education ready to commit to community engagement?* Milwaukee: Milwaukee Idea Office, University of Wisconsin–Milwaukee. http://www4.uwm.edu/milwaukeeidea.

Butin, D. W., ed. 2005. *Service learning in higher education: Critical issues and directions.* New York: Palgrave Macmillan.

Chronicle of Higher Education. 2009. College enrollment by age of students, Fall 2007. *Almanac of Higher Education,* August 24. http://chronicle.com/article/College-Enrollment-by-Age-of/48171/.

Driscoll, A., and E. A. Lynton. 1999. *Making outreach visible: A guide to documenting professional service and outreach.* Washington, DC: American Association for Higher Education.

Eyler, J. 2002. Reflection: Linking service and learning—linking students and communities. *Journal of Social Issues* 58 (3): 517–34.

Fairweather, S. 1996. *Faculty work and public trust.* Boston: Allyn & Bacon.

Glassick, C. E., H. M. Taylor, and G. I. Maeroff. 1997. *Scholarship assessed: Evaluation of the professoriate.* San Francisco: Jossey-Bass.

Herr, K., and G. Anderson. 2005. *The action research dissertation: A guide for students and faculty.* Thousand Oaks, CA: Sage.

Korza, P., B. Bacon, and A. Assaf. 2005. *Civic dialogue, arts and culture.* Washington, DC: Americans for the Arts.

Korza, P., B. Bacon, and M. del Vecchio. 2008. *The arts and civic engagement tool kit: Planning tools and resources for animating democracy in your community*. Washington, DC: Americans for the Arts.

Lynton, E. 1995. *Making the case for professional service.* Washington, DC: American Association for Higher Education.

McIntyre, A. 2007. *Participatory action research.* Thousand Oaks, CA: Sage.

National Review Board for the Scholarship of Engagement. 2002. Evaluation criteria for the Scholarship of Engagement. http://schoe.coe.uga.edu/evaluation/evaluation_criteria.html.

Sandmann, L. R., P. G. Foster-Fishman, J. Lloyd, W. Rauhe, and C. Rosaen. 2000. Managing critical tensions: How to strengthen the scholarship component of outreach. *Change* 32 (1): 44–52.

Stanton, T., and N. Cruz. 1999. *Service learning: A movement's pioneers reflect on its origins, practice and future.* San Francisco: Jossey-Bass.

Stephenson, M. 2007. Developing community leadership through the arts in Southside Virginia: Social networks, civic identity and civic change. *Community Development Journal* 42 (1): 79–96.

Stephenson, M. 2011. Conceiving land grant civic engagement as adaptive leadership. *Higher Education* 61 (1): 95–108.

Stephenson, M., and K. Lanham. 2007. Aesthetic imagination, civic imagination, and the role of the arts in community change and development. *International Journal of the Arts in Society* 1 (3): 83–92.

Stringer, E. T. 2007. *Action research.* 3d ed. Thousand Oaks, CA: Sage.

Virginia Tech Graduate School. 2010. Citizen Scholar Engagement: Program requirements. http://www.grads.vt.edu/graduate_school/tge/cse/requirements.html.

15

Graduate Mentoring Against Common Sense

Ron Krabill

Common Sense

If common sense is the detritus of accepted truth from past eras (Gramsci 1972), then graduate students who want to engage in public scholarship have layers of sediment to work their way through during graduate school. This common sense is institutional in character. It makes claims about how one should be professionalized and, in so doing, sets the boundaries of what actions can be included as part of the profession. Its reach extends far beyond any single university, discipline, or academic association, deeply coloring the ways in which faculty imagine themselves and how they should train the next generation of scholars. Thus graduate mentoring becomes a key location in which the common sense of academia—with all its contradicttions and inconsistencies—is used to discipline (in Foucault's expansive sense of the term) graduate students even as it is being passed on to them.

What are the key moments when the received knowledge of graduate training works to limit students' ability to engage in public scholarship? How might faculty mentor against the grain of this common sense? If the kind of work showcased in this volume is to flourish, what are the ways that faculty mentors can not only get out of the way of such work (which is sometimes necessary) but also help to encourage and facilitate this kind of research?

One place to start to deconstruct the common sense of graduate training is to look for the statements that we often hear repeated in the context of graduate mentoring—many of us may have repeated the phrases many times ourselves—that caution students against engaging in public scholarship. A variation of these statements can also be found after a student has begun a public scholarship project; in this instance, the caution is against the student going "too far." As Gramsci understood, common sense always holds internal contradictions, as well as seeds of accuracy, in tension with the layers of collective lived experiences over many years. In other words, what any social group understands as common sense cannot be simply dismissed as wrong because it reflects parts of the lived experiences of that group. Common sense is not inaccurate. It is just not accurate enough, because it fails to take into consideration the institutional and systemic forces that shape those experiences.

So our task here is to examine those moments when graduate mentoring reinforces academia's common sense that public scholarship is the wrong path for a graduate student to pursue. The fact that those moments may sometimes contain good advice for the individual student complicates our task, but it does not make it impossible. Indeed, common sense is arguably at its strongest when what is seen as good advice for the individual perpetuates the inertia of the institution.

Public scholarship is great, but wait until you have a tenure-track job to do it.

Along with its (arguably) more common variant directed at assistant professors—wait until you have tenure—this phrase perpetuates the belief that engagement in explicitly public, and especially political, projects can only be conducted after you have climbed the academic hierarchy to a certain sufficient point. For the graduate student, it says that you should just get through graduate school as quickly as possible, after which you can start the real work of the academy. The fact that acquiring a tenure-track job—possibly the narrowest choke-point in academic careers—is immediately followed by the call to wait a bit longer, until you have tenure, is indicative of the statement's danger. While a tenured position reduces the immediacy of the publish-or-perish imperative and protects positions from (some) political attacks, reaching that point takes a minimum of 10–15 years in many fields. To expect graduate students and junior faculty to spend that amount of time practicing more traditional research, then shift gears intellectually and methodologically into public scholarship, underestimates both the potential depth of public scholarship as a research practice and the power of repetition to ingrain more traditional practices and academic common sense. Meanwhile, the future of the traditional tenure-track job remains increasingly uncertain; graduate mentors should prepare their students for emerging academic markets that may look very different from today's university, much less the university of the twentieth century (Newfield 2008; Schuster and Finkelstein 2006).

Public scholarship takes too long and is too complicated to complete for your dissertation.

There is no doubt that one of the biggest practical obstacles to public scholarship is the time required to do it right. As the projects described in this volume attest, building relationships with partners outside of the university, building in sufficient feedback loops for the information you gather (whether you do that through performance, data, or deep hanging out), and allowing for the different timelines of various stakeholders all make public scholarship more complicated and time-consuming than a more traditional dissertation. The pressure on departments to confer graduate degrees within a certain period—a metric that often figures into national rankings—increases the demand to choose more streamlined paths to degree completion. And students' own justified desires to finish graduate school and move on to faculty or other positions drive this pressure as well, even as a weak economy and limited job opportunities cause some students to delay the actual date of completion. Graduate mentors thus need to help their students develop a realistic sense of the scope of their projects while simultaneously developing different kinds of support—financial, intellectual, and temporal—to focus on their research. Crucial in this formula is a mental shift that must occur among graduate mentors, departments, and funding agencies: a recognition that public scholarship is exactly that—scholarship—rather than an extension of service or teaching or extracurricular activity, even as it often incorporates these elements as well.

Public scholarship is fine, but you need to do it in addition to, rather than in place of, more traditional research.

This statement grows out of two related concerns with public scholarship: first, that it involves so many collaborators that it becomes difficult to claim as your own work when applying for jobs; and second, that it isn't recognized as "real" scholarship and therefore you need to have both types of research in your repertoire. Each of these claims again raises the question of public scholarship's legibility to broader audiences and common-sense assumptions about what counts in academic professions. Graduate mentors need to assist students to author papers and participate in professional conferences and workshops that lay claim to their scholarship *as scholarship,* while maintaining full integrity in their collaborations. Perhaps more essentially, mentors need to learn how to find outlets for their students' work that acknowledge public scholarship as a form of knowledge production equal in validity to the single-authored paper or presentation.

The second concern, that public scholars should have both modes of research in their repertoire, seems infinitely reasonable at first blush, and in fact publicly engaged scholars almost always operate within both modes at different moments in any given project. However, graduate mentors need to be vigilant that this does not become another form of academic speed-up, where junior scholars are expected to produce research in both modes at a far greater scale than either their mentors or their colleagues creating more traditional forms of research outputs. In other words, the solution to making public scholarship legible must not simply be to duplicate the public work in traditional forms. Such an approach runs the risk of nullifying the very strengths of public scholarship and burning out our best, most committed early-career scholars.

Public scholarship is great if you don't mind teaching at a school that isn't as good.

Leaving aside the obviously problematic formulation of "a good school"—which in this phrasing is assumed to be defined explicitly through its embrace of more traditional modes of knowledge production—this statement fails to acknowledge the degree to which public scholarship actually allows graduate students to stand out from the crowd in many applications. Due to the success of organizations like Imagining America and Campus Compact over the past decades, public scholarship and its fellow travelers, community-based and service learning, have become keywords in the mission statements and strategic plans of many universities across the higher educational spectrum. The logics of public scholarship may not have fully permeated faculty cultures at high-prestige schools (or most others, for that matter), and many of these changes in promotional language serve as thinly veiled tropes for business as usual. Nonetheless, public scholarship by graduate students can garner significant positive attention for both their institutions and their careers, further improving job opportunities. More importantly, if we truly believe that integrated public scholarship improves the insights garnered by our research, then public scholarship will also strengthen the more traditional lines of our academic work and strengthen job candidacies accordingly.

However, a second strand of academic common sense is at play in these assumptions around what makes a school good—namely, that the prestige of the school or the perceived quality of the faculty positions it offers is an objective measure of job satisfaction for those who would hope to land jobs at that institution. While the resources of high-prestige institutions often outstrip those of more modest reputation—an issue of significant import to faculty and graduate students alike—where those resources are directed also impacts the kind of work one can accomplish at various locations. Take my own position as an example. I am a professor at a "satellite" campus, Bothell, of the University of Washington (UW). Common metrics for academic jobs would see my position as a secondary one, lesser than that of my colleagues at the "flagship" campus in Seattle. We have slightly higher teaching loads and very different teaching structures, and certainly higher demands for institutional service. Yet for the type of work I do—collaborative, publicly engaged, interdisciplinary media and cultural studies—having a foot in both the R1 tri-campus university system of UW and the innovative community of scholars at UW Bothell has been the best of both worlds, both in terms of intellectual engagement and in terms of material resources.

For publicly engaged graduate students, determining which colleges and universities hold the promise of being a good school, or providing a good job, requires an additional layer of investigation to move beyond common-sense assumptions. Rather than viewing this as an additional burden, graduate students looking toward faculty positions can also redefine the kinds of institutions that might make for a good professional trajectory, opening up their career possibilities to places and programs that would otherwise seem too far off the beaten path to be viable. In other words, public scholarship can and should be understood to broaden a graduate student's future opportunities instead of being considered solely in terms of limiting and complicating the job market.

Public scholarship is great, but you need to write about it in a way that makes it legible to traditional academics.

This is perhaps the most pernicious advice passed on by graduate mentors, not because it is false, but because it so strongly illustrates the grounding of common sense in accurate but incomplete concerns. Of course public scholarship must be made legible to others, including those who may be hostile to the entire endeavor as well as those who may be sympathetic but uninformed. In this respect, public scholarship is no different than any other form of scholarship; one of the greatest challenges of academic life is to communicate complex, highly developed ideas in clear, concise ways for the benefit of others who have not focused the same energy on those ideas. Yet publicly engaged work should not carry this burden to any greater or lesser degree than more traditional modes.

The danger lies in an expectation that public scholarship win legitimacy by adapting itself to traditional forms of research. If the modes of producing knowledge differ in public scholarship, then the communication of that knowledge will necessitate, at least at times, a different format. Take, for instance, the newly arising field of digital scholarship (whether publicly engaged or not). The idea that knowledge generated through new forms of digital collaboration and engagement will best be expressed through a single-authored, peer-reviewed article in a printed journal with prestige from an earlier era seems unlikely, if not entirely implausible—not only because such an article will often be judged to be outside the scope of such a journal, but more essentially because the knowledge produced by such a project will be insufficiently captured by the journal's medium. Public scholarship thus needs to explore new modes of communicating the knowledge it produces, matching its means of production with its means of dissemination, consumption, and assessment (and often blurring the lines between these functions). While these new modes of expressing public scholarship may not be understood as quickly or as broadly as more traditional forms of scholarly publishing, they will sometimes be necessary to remain true to the work itself, the knowledge it produces, and the politics it embraces.

Challenging Common Sense

If these preceding statements of well-intentioned advice represent the half-truths of graduate mentoring common sense, what are the proactive efforts that faculty mentors can take in conjunction with and in support of their publicly engaged graduate students? I would like to propose three approaches to mentoring that offer a way forward: first, graduate mentors should rethink the mentoring process as radically collaborative; second, graduate mentors should embrace and foster multiple possible professional trajectories for the graduate students with whom they are working; and third, graduate mentors should become active agents of structural institutional changes that will better support students engaged in public scholarship. In offering these approaches I want to emphasize that I am not claiming to have mastered them, or even in some cases to have previously embraced them. Rather, they seem to hold the most promise in overcoming the limitations of our profession's common sense and forging new directions for public scholarship and the academy as a whole.

Radically Collaborative Graduate Mentoring

Much is made of the buzzword *collaboration* in today's academy; indeed, it is difficult to find a mission statement or strategic plan that does not invoke the term. We must therefore be clear what we mean by collaboration or, as I am arguing here, radical collaboration. The essence of radical collaboration is a displacing of the assumption that the graduate mentor holds greater knowledge or experience of the practices of public scholarship than his or her graduate students. While this may be the case, my experiences indicate that it often is not. Graduate students—particularly those who subsequently pursue publicly engaged scholarship—are often entering graduate school with previous knowledge and experiences of working with political issues, social movements, or community-based organizations, and as such they often bring to the table a deep political commitment to understanding those experiences with greater theoretical depth. Graduate students doing publicly engaged work often find themselves in a position of greater expertise than their mentors in crucial facets of their public scholarship, and this inversion of assumed expertise occurs much earlier in the student experience than with traditional models of graduate education. The radical collaboration of graduate mentorship is a bringing together of these experiences that sees great opportunity in such an inversion rather than attempting to subordinate the knowledge generated by engaged work outside of academic settings to the knowledge created by the academy. In this formulation, a graduate mentor becomes a guide through many of the opportunities and pitfalls of graduate school, but also remains open to learning of the opportunities and pitfalls of engaged work outside the academy, without reducing that work to a mere case study or test site for academic theory. To accomplish this, mentors often must rely on students at least as much or more than the reverse.

Such radical collaboration must also extend beyond the pairing of the faculty mentor and advisee. Graduate mentors should actively welcome the collaborators with whom publicly engaged students are working closely into the overall mentoring process. Integrating the community-based mentors of graduate students into their overall academic experience may blur the distinctions between a student's public-ness and their scholarship; such blurring, if welcomed by the student, may also serve to reduce the tension so many students experience balancing their academic and community-based commitments. Integrating community-based mentors can occur in a number of ways—they may attend academic presentations, serve some sort of evaluative role regarding the student's work, meet with the graduate mentor, and so forth—and could vary in terms of their formality or informality. For instance, one could imagine community-based mentors serving as outside readers for theses (as they sometimes do in the M.A. in Cultural Studies program I coordinate), or as part of a jury for arts-based exhibits or performances. But the integration I am arguing for is less dependent on its formality—for as we know, formalizing such relationships can often spell their doom—than on its flexibility in fully welcoming collaboration across multiple sectors often left out of the academic equation.

Radical collaboration does not mean that faculty mentors must subordinate themselves to the political or relational priorities that their students bring, becoming mere rubber stamps for students' projects. Faculty mentors do bring their own expertise, not only in the subject area within which they conduct their own research and teaching, but also within the academy as both social institution and intellectual project. Mentors need to help graduate students understand the limitations as well as the strengths of their publicly engaged work, how that work fits into existing literatures and academic fields, and how to make informed choices around the direction and extent of their public scholarship. Likewise, graduate students seeking to integrate public scholarship may not always like what they hear from their graduate mentors; they may receive feedback that seems to undercut their previous commitments and understandings of their own work, or pushes them in unforeseen directions. Radical collaboration calls for students and faculty alike to work through these moments with dedication and intellectual care, so that neither falls into the temptation of simply dismissing the other as naive or stubborn, or too far on one side of the (false) publicly engaged/scholarship divide.

Finally, radical collaboration can also mean getting out of the way. Paradoxically, sometimes the most supportive act a graduate mentor can take is to allow the graduate student to pursue publicly engaged scholarship the academic ends of which may not be immediately clear to the mentor. While mentors have a responsibility to express those concerns and frame the possible drawbacks to any given path a student may choose, they must also gauge the power they hold within the institution and adjust their "advice" accordingly, taking care not to overdetermine a student's trajectory. My experience has been that the political commitments of a student's publicly engaged work are often what sustain that student through graduate school; mentors therefore need to resist the temptation to purge such work from a student's repertoire in the name of academic expediency.

Fostering Multiple (Possible) Professional Trajectories

The path to a career in academia that faculty know best is, of course, the path that they themselves took. As mentioned earlier, these more traditional trajectories are becoming less and less available in the current climate of higher education. But rather than stopping our analysis of the academy at the point of bemoaning what has been lost from older models (though this remains crucial at times), graduate mentors should also work with their students to imagine new trajectories that can carve out spaces for publicly engaged work both within and outside of the academy. A number of fellowship programs cater expressly to doctoral candidates exploring nonacademic careers; these programs were pioneered by the Woodrow Wilson Foundation in the 1990s and, most recently, include the new ACLS Public Fellows program (http://www.acls.org/programs/publicfellows/). The wider scope of previous experiences with which many students now enter graduate school only increases the imperative for mentors to be informed regarding multiple possible career trajectories for their students.

For some students, this may mean future careers in organizations with more explicitly public or collaborative orientations than the academy: nongovernmental and community-based organizations, think tanks, arts and performance-based groups, K–12 education, and public policy groups, to name just a few. Although some disciplines have a longer tradition of directing graduates into these types of careers, faculty across disciplines tend to dismiss these trajectories as of less merit than the faculty positions that they themselves hold. However, these choices are not only Plan B for those who are unable to land academic jobs, as is often assumed by faculty, but the first choice for many new graduates and the aspirational choice of many current students. For one recent Ph.D. graduate of the UW, a job at a major international human rights organization matched her desire to apply the theoretical work of her dissertation to ongoing, direct advocacy on contemporary issues. Yet some of her graduate mentors described their disappointment that she did not choose to "hold out" for a "real" job; they presumed that a faculty position was both her preferred choice and the more prestigious option. Sometimes these more subtle assertions of prestige and preference do more to indicate a mentor's lack of respect for publicly engaged work than any explicit attack. As graduate mentors learn to respect the knowledge and experiences generated outside of our institutions, we need also to respect the choices of our graduates who pursue professional trajectories that take them away from our own networks and professional comfort zone without seeing that as a failure of the department or a personal disappointment.

At the same time, graduate mentors must begin to imagine and shape new opportunities for both graduate education and postgraduate employment within the academy that not only permit but encourage publicly engaged scholarship. Such efforts can range from supporting professional organizations that promote public scholarship to working with faculty and graduate students within their own universities to make more visible the publicly engaged work already taking place. Mentors who are familiar with the professional networks of faculty working in the field and who give graduate students access to those networks represent an invaluable resource for graduate students entering the academic job market.

Similarly, graduate mentoring must also take seriously the concerns of individual students who see their career pathways—academic or otherwise—obscured by their involvement in public scholarship, rather than sacrificing those students on the altar of institutional change, as discussed below. In this category I include students who have done substantial publicly engaged work and then decide they want to refocus their efforts along more traditional lines of knowledge production, as well as students who are engaged currently in community-based work but resist making that work visible within their own scholarship. As much as we may seek to develop stronger profiles for our institutions as publicly engaged, we also need to respect the integrity of those commitments and the individuals who enact them. Not everyone can or should do public scholarship; the point is not to shift the traditional academic track to a publicly engaged one, but rather to make room for both tracks to be acknowledged as legitimate modes of scholarship.

Becoming Agents of Institutional Change

Each of the two recommendations above requires primary implementation on the level of individual relationships between mentors and students, but each also hints at the need for a larger, systematic change on the level of institutions. For instance, if publicly engaged work is to be recognized as a legitimate form of scholarship, this requires not only that the individual mentor and student acknowledge it as such, but that other faculty and students (at both the home university and more broadly), institutional review boards, professional organizations, promotion and tenure processes, university and departmental ranking systems, and hiring committees also recognize it as such. While this is an undeniably tall order, it presents an immense opportunity to rethink higher education and its possibilities, particularly as these discussions are already taking place within the context of shrinking budgets, the privatization of public universities, and the commercialization and instrumentalization of education more generally.[1] Higher education is changing; public scholarship has the opportunity to shape that change.

Thus we return to the institutional nature of common sense and to Gramsci's conviction that no system of hegemony, including its common sense, is ever a closed circuit of power. There are always opportunities to subvert and challenge that common sense. If we are to contest common-sense assumptions around graduate mentoring in support of publicly engaged scholarship, then institutional space must be carved out for that work in order for the interpersonal mentoring relationship to thrive.

First and foremost, this means developing programs that encourage and recognize public scholarship as scholarship, both within specific colleges and universities and across the higher education sector.

Imagining America's Tenure Team Initiative (TTI) attempts to do exactly this for junior faculty on the tenure track. While the TTI focuses specifically on reworking promotion and tenure documents and processes, its impact has been felt throughout the university in the form of heightened recognition of public scholarship in graduate education as well as in faculty research. Likewise, the University of Washington's Graduate Certificate in Public Scholarship seeks to acknowledge graduate students engaged in this work by supporting them with coursework in public scholarship, mentoring, conference funding, and the conferring of a formal certification. Imagining America's Publicly Active Graduate Education (PAGE) program brings together engaged graduate students from across many universities at their annual conference and in ongoing projects, as well as connecting participants to senior scholars. Many other programs on the master's level, like UW Bothell's Cultural Studies and New York University's Arts and Public Policy programs, explicitly encourage publicly engaged graduate research as part of their curriculum.

Other necessary institutional changes include the prioritization of funding structures for publicly engaged work, the explicit naming of community-based work in academic job advertisements (even if it is only one among a number of possible areas of concentration), and finding ways to tell our story that resist the rankings of departments and schools according to metrics like job placement (wherein only academic jobs count) or time to completion of degree (which, while an important statistic, can disadvantage departments encouraging public scholarship). The more public scholarship begins to appear across multiple documents and infrastructural systems within and across universities, the more it will become visible as a viable route for graduate students and faculty alike.

One particularly challenging institutional structure to address is the Institutional Review Board (IRB). While many faculty have learned the habit (or common sense) of avoiding the IRB whenever possible, public scholarship provides a useful moment to reassert the importance of a substantive engagement with research ethics. One of the most useful steps a mentor can do to support publicly engaged graduate students is to further educate the IRB on the ways in which public scholarship is indeed research, needs to be understood as such, and engages with the field of research ethics in important and meaningful ways. A graduate student I was advising once panicked when her application for IRB approval was returned, declaring that her project was not, in fact, research. While being released from IRB oversight was a relief for the student and conducting her project was simplified as a result, the lack of recognition of the project as research carries with it deeper institutional implications surrounding the marginalization of public scholarship. Avoiding the IRB and its approval processes may at times be expeditious, but such declarations shape the broader contours of what is understood to count or not count as scholarship. Particularly given public scholarship's deep engagement with the ethics of research and knowledge production, educating the IRB becomes a crucial step in fostering institutional change.

Graduate student funding must also be refashioned to provide greater support for those involved in public scholarship. Funding for students is too often tied to labor—whether teaching, research, or administration—that pulls them *away* from their publicly engaged scholarship, rather than supporting them *within* that work. While this dynamic rings true for most graduate students regardless of their involvement with community-based work, the results are particularly egregious for those students tackling the more time-consuming and unpredictable requirements of public scholarship. We must take care not to praise (and use for our own public relations campaigns) the hard work of student public scholars while simultaneously refusing to fund that work itself. Finding funding sources to actively support publicly engaged scholarship remains at the top of the priority list for graduate mentoring, as does providing students with further training in grant writing and other fundraising skills that may prove crucial in sustaining their public scholarship over a career.

Finally, graduate mentoring needs to resist the temptation to encourage publicly active students to engage in the speed-up of the modern academy without lending a critical eye to that speed-up. This may be the most difficult institutional change of all, as well as the most difficult to negotiate in individual cases. In an economic and professional atmosphere where finding jobs—whether academic or otherwise—becomes more and more competitive, reward systems all encourage graduate students to place productivity above all else. As we develop programs to recognize public scholarship, we would do well to avoid formalizing those programs to the point where they become yet another qualification or professional hoop that students must jump through as they pursue academic success. In other words, our efforts to make public scholarship more visible should avoid making some projects (or types of projects) visible at the cost of rendering other projects even less visible. Within this context, mentors need to work on institutional expectations that recognize and value the scholarship resulting from long-term, committed public engagements over flashier but less substantive partnerships, while also helping graduate students navigate the increasingly intense demands of their profession in a manner that allows them to develop a solid record of scholarship in a sustainable, integrative way.

Ultimately, graduate mentoring for public scholarship must tackle the systemic project of changing institutional norms and expectations to better encourage and recognize public scholarship. Without working on this larger project of institutional change—a project in which senior faculty have immensely more power than their junior colleagues and graduate students—the common-sense advice to the individual student to avoid or limit their involvement in public scholarship will remain salient and difficult for individuals to overcome.

So, What's a Graduate Student to Do?

What seems, and perhaps once was, good advice for the individual may no longer be so. Part of what makes common sense so insidious is the way in which it blinds us to changing contexts, so that we continue to believe that enlightened self-interest remains on the side of common sense, failing to notice that the profession is making new space for the innovations of public scholarship. While the bulk of this essay has been aimed at ways for mentors to improve graduate mentoring, this conclusion briefly takes up the opportunities available to graduate students (and junior faculty) to improve the mentoring they receive. For if graduate students are in many ways more prepared for the rigors of public scholarship than their mentors, and mentoring does become a more radically collaborative process, then graduate students themselves will become central players both in transforming the one-on-one relationships of mentoring and in promoting the structural changes necessary to foster vibrant environments in which public scholarship can thrive.

First, seek the advice of all the potential mentors with whom you feel comfortable; do not limit yourself to a single mentor, or your formal program advisor. Be as entrepreneurial as you can in finding possible mentors who can address different parts of your overall interest in public scholarship. Contact supportive local and national organizations for suggestions. No one voice or perspective can grasp all the possible avenues for your own publicly engaged scholarship or career. And do not be surprised if the advice you receive from multiple mentors is contradictory; that most likely means that you are receiving a decent range of opinions.

Second, seek mentors outside of the academy who can help you keep perspective and stay grounded in your political commitments. Community-based mentors can be invaluable in helping you avoid taking yourself too seriously as an academic, while simultaneously reminding you of why you are engaged in the academy in the first place. Such mentors can also help keep your decision to work within academic institutions an active choice, rather than a default position based on your previous views of the world and your place within it.

Third, cultivate your relationships with mentors; continue to draw connections between your interests and projects. Suggest co-authoring a piece with mentors you feel have insights that would help flesh out work with which you are engaged. And keep the lines of communication open. Many mentors are working formally and informally with a large number of students; while you should respect their time, you should also be willing to assert yourself in order to stay on their radar. Keeping faculty invested in your projects and up to date on your progress will help them to be better mentors for you.

Fourth, insist on the radical collaboration for which I argue above. Pursue your public scholarship with commitment and confidence, and be willing to push back if necessary to carve out the space for the publicly engaged work that sustains you as a graduate student and as a person. Put the community-based mentors with whom you work in touch with your graduate mentors. Be willing to switch mentors if need be. And accept that sometimes the advice you receive from mentors within and outside the academy may be more accurate than you wish to admit.

Finally, and most importantly, do not wait until you reach some future stage of professional development to engage in the debates around public scholarship and its role within the university, whether they take place one-on-one with your mentors, within your cohort of graduate students, or within your department, your university, professional organizations, community partnerships, or amongst broader publics. These debates and the academic infrastructures they propose will shape the field—your field—for years to come. Take an active role in generating the insights that will challenge the assumptions of academic common sense and make our institutions more conducive to public scholarship in the future.

The notion that public scholarship is somehow less than fully realized scholarship, or that it distracts graduate students from the "real" work of research and getting "good" jobs, remains firmly ensconced in the common sense of academia. That common sense is not impenetrable, however, and effective graduate mentoring, when taking a radically collaborative form, can not only nurture a new generation of scholars but also educate existing faculties regarding the immense theoretical and empirical potential of public scholarship. It is to this task that we commit ourselves, together, as publicly engaged mentors and students.

Notes

1. See, for example, the work of Edufactory (http://www.edu-factory.org/wp).

References

Gramsci, Antonio. 1972. *Selections from the prison notebooks of Antonio Gramsci.* Edited and translated by Quintin Hoare and Geoffrey Nowell Smith. New York: International Publishers.

Newfield, Christopher. 2008. *Unmaking the public university: The forty-year assault on the middle class.* Cambridge, MA: Harvard University Press.

Schuster, Jack H., and Martin J. Finkelstein. 2006. *The American faculty: The restructuring of academic work and careers.* Baltimore: The Johns Hopkins University Press.

16

First and Lasts: Lessons from Launching the Patient Voice Project at the Iowa Writers' Workshop

Austin Bunn

IN NOVEMBER of 2004, in a dim conference room in the student center at the University of Iowa, I sat across from a sweet and disarming school librarian named Stephanie, with a spray of pages between us. Stephanie had a stage-four brain tumor that had been discovered two months before, and she wore a flashy, tropical scarf over her head to hide her hair wispy from chemotherapy. She'd driven up from Hills, a small town about 20 miles south of Iowa City, and even though she spent her days around books, sometimes she had trouble reading words on the page. I had decided, improbably, to light a candle, for the ceremony of it all, though I was nervous the flame would trigger the fire alarm and we'd end up drenched. A few weeks before, in my first days as a graduate student at the Iowa Writers' Workshop, I'd had this idea to start an expressive writing program for people struggling with chronic illness. Suddenly I was in a room, executing on my good intentions, and I realized I had no idea what I was doing.

Six years later, the Patient Voice Project has not only endured but come to thrive and expand—improbably, given that first night. This fall, we'll have classes starting in Ames (at Iowa State), Ann Arbor (the University of Michigan), and Iowa City. Looking back, I've come to see my experiences with the Patient Voice Project as one of my primary "educations" in graduate school.—None of it took place in an actual classroom and much of it, like that class with Stephanie, I bluffed my way through. So six years on, as a young academic now, I find myself wondering what the lessons were for me, in matching public engagement with passion, in squaring the creative process with discernable (and grant-able) outcomes. Besides the line item on the CV—a not insignificant benefit in a difficult job market—what did I take away it? For the purposes of this chapter, I want to study the biography of this idea—the conditions for the PVP's inception and reception to its current adolescence—in an effort to encourage other graduate students to harness their enthusiasm, but also to consider, realistically, the challenges that lie ahead.

In our impromptu workshop, I asked Stephanie to describe her childhood bedroom. For the next ten minutes, we would both simply write in silence. This is a typical Patient Voice exercise because the assignment has a big front door. In the six years since its inception, we have worked with people with all kinds of conditions and predicaments, but everybody had a childhood bedroom. And the memories of the place evoke immediate feelings and precise observations, with a whole range of responses—people spend a lot of time in their childhood bedrooms: staring at their pet rocks, posters, or in my case a space shuttle model hanging from a sewing thread. As a rule, I do my own assignments (when I'm not distracted, as a college professor, by attendance and prep!), and I think this is an important principle of civic-minded writing instruction: no prompt should be flung at students like homework. When teachers hand down assignments like edicts, it's easy to ignore your own vagaries or the subtle stumbling blocks. This assignment gets complicated by one constraint: the writers are not allowed to use "to be" as a verb. It's flat, it's easy, I told Stephanie, and it's a "state of being" verb and we're looking for vibrant life here. She would have to write without it.

I started writing and this assignment, for a reason I only half understand, entered me anew. I suppose the stakes seemed higher with Stephanie in the room, and her bravery and willingness—and trust in me—made me risk a new honesty. I found myself returning to the loft in my father's house, a spare bedroom built by my father and, oddly, branching off *another* guest bedroom. Inside, two twin beds tucked against the eaves, covered by my father's scratchy, thin army blankets. These beds served as the sleeping arrangement for my twin brother and me. An air conditioner hung in the window, where the cicadas wiggled in and scared the bejesus out of us. The beds folded up, but the mattresses seemed made of super springs, so on boring afternoons they turned into makeshift trampolines. This was not exactly my childhood bedroom. We occupied this bedroom on alternating weekends, as was the divorce agreement. Before long, my description of this room conjured up a specific memory in my mind, a single night in that room, when, at ten years old, I wept and whispered my last wishes into the ear of a stuffed animal, terrified of what would happen to me the next morning. As I wrote, the story spilled out: I had a surgery scheduled for 7 A.M., a time that seemed to me the very hour of doom. The hospital was an hour away, at the Children's Hospital of Philadelphia, and my father's house was closer than my mother's, hence this impromptu sleepover mid-week. My trip to CHoP (as it was known, terrifyingly) was for a minor surgery, but when you're ten, no surgery is minor. The question that typically and understandably follows is, *what for?* Answering that question, without awkwardness and shame, took me years and led, in no small way, to the Patient Voice, the program that, at that moment in the Iowa Memorial Union with Stephanie and the spell of our scribbling, I claimed to be launching.

The ten minutes were up. Stephanie and I shared our descriptions—to bring the assignment full circle—and when I read mine, I felt vulnerable and utterly at risk: the classic graduate student mistake of over-sharing. If anything, the Patient Voice has taught me that you cannot predict what chain of associations will elicit good writing. Stephanie smiled. Her husband, she said, had had the same surgery. Lesson number two: you can never predict just how much you share.

The Patient Voice Project, through the generosity of the University of Iowa and the commitment my fellow graduate students at the Writers' Workshop M.F.A. program, has taught over a hundred students in the Iowa City area, funded by an array of state and national grants. The premise: The Patient Voice Project offers free expressive writing classes for people struggling with chronic illness—cancer and mental illness, primarily—taught by Writers' Workshop graduate students. The program began with pilot funding in 2005, from the Provost's Office at the University, followed by Iowa Humanities Council grants, and has since won a national, competitive, multi-year grant from Johnson and Johnson/The Society for Arts in Healthcare to expand. The program has been profiled by several newspapers and radio outlets. For my work on it, I was included in the University's "Be Remarkable" advertising campaign and have spoken about our pedagogy at multiple conferences. Stephanie's tumor is in remission, she continues to run her library in Hills, and her daughter is beginning to discover Stephen King.

The Iowa Writers' Workshop, begun in the 1930s, is the oldest graduate program in creative writing in the country, and I couldn't begin to encapsulate the instruction I received there. My own writing feels like it has gone through boot camp, and certainly the Patient Voice benefits from the intense culture of younger poets and fiction writers there. But I know that the hours I spent with Stephanie, over the course of ten weeks that stretched for a year, taught me at least as much—about humility, resilience, the way stories make experience (not the other way around), and most important, how our personal narratives tell us equally about what will come next as what has come before.

Six years in, The Patient Voice Project has come to a critical stage in its growth and as I write this essay, from Michigan, where I'm at my first tenure-track job, the fate of the program is much on my mind. We could not have had an easier time getting this program off the ground, for reasons I'll detail in a moment. My fellow graduate students committed their time and enthusiasm to an untested program and brought it into the world in ways I never could have imagined. Hospital administrators and social workers had faith in us and opened doors in what looked to me like walls. But, as the creator, I believe the Patient Voice Project has come to a common point of transition for new service programs—expand or fade—and I wonder just how (and if) it will live up to its promise, much as I am convinced it can, and what steps remain for us to get there. Can this program outlive its founder?

The program benefited from a supportive home institution, and when other graduate students ask me about how the PVP managed to launch so easily, I answer that we were, foremost, lucky; a top-down ethos met a bottom-up idea. The president of the University of Iowa, David Skorton, had deemed 2005 "The Year of Public Engagement." The school wanted to distinguish itself. Fifteen projects, created by faculty, staff, and students, would receive between $5,000 and $10,000 from the university to start new initiatives: including a seminar on human-animal relationships (involving stints by students in an animal shelter), a "milk bank" for mothers, and free ESL instruction for migrant workers. The Patient Voice received a $10,000 "pilot" grant in mid-2005, as the Year of Public Engagement was ramping up.

But it helps to *have ideas*, since the origins of any given program, I suspect, are coincidental, as the Patient Voice Project was. At our first orientation, an administrator came to talk about the University's community arts program. Arts Share, a 501c3 division of the school, brought dancers, theatre artists, musicians, and writers into local schools for workshops. After her talk, I approached her to propose expressive writing instruction for the chronically ill. I had just come from a year as a hospice volunteer in New York City and wanted to continue that work but somehow tether it more securely to my graduate study. I also knew the University of Iowa had a medical school, two hospitals, and many smaller clinics and outpatient facilities. Good ideas respond to the communities they come from, obviously. Would they be interested in supporting it? The administrator was interested and said she would propose it to the provost that oversaw her program. Three weeks later, she called to say the University wanted to fund us for a single year. Suddenly, I needed to have a program, a pedagogy, and *students*. In retrospect, I have to admit that friendly university administrators—those willing to push for us—helped immeasurably.

The inertia of academe is familiar to all of us. It can be difficult enough to carve out time for our own research from our teaching responsibilities, and the idea of jump-starting an original project might seem an impossibility. My primary thought has to do with program design. Was there a way to serve two communities simultaneously: both the chronically ill *and* graduate students?

We conceived the Patient Voice Project with the lightest footprint and level of commitment possible. From the hospital and clinics, all we wanted was *permission* to promote the program; we didn't need any other resource—classes took place off site at the public library (or university buildings). Preparation mattered.[1] An outline of the medical benefits and aspects of the program doesn't belong here, but the specific references and research were essential when we made our case to medical professionals comfortable with hard data and not soft benefits like "self-expression." The Provost's Office's financial support—and imprimatur within the university setting—helped credentialize us, and networking helped us liaison with an internal medicine doctor on the faculty willing to serve as our "faculty advisor," another key step of legitimization. More important, we argued that we would work to bring the voices of those struggling with chronic pain into a broader conversation about contemporary care, with an anthology, a public reading series, broadsides, and media exposure.

I should admit here that when I say "we" I mean "I." I scheduled, attended, presented at every single one of those meetings. This "we" isn't false humility as much as it is another technique of persuasion: I needed my audiences to trust that I wasn't alone, just as I trusted that soon enough I would not be. And I wasn't truly alone; several doctors interested in patient narratives, the Workshop, or writing generally gave me excellent advice along the way. The "we" created strength in numbers when I was alone, at the other end of the cold call, representing a "program" that was, more accurately, an idea.

Meanwhile, I plotted the appeal to graduate students, our fellow teachers. As you can expect, graduate students want freedom and authority in their volunteering and service experiences, ones which demand little preparation and utilize and reward their existing knowledge base (and might even lead to a job after school). Finally, they want to be *paid*. The Patient Voice classes would be free to students, but we paid an honorarium to graduate students of $300 for ten weeks of classes. Thirty dollars for a one-hour class, with no prep? Understandably, we were a popular service opportunity. M.F.A. grad students face dim prospects in academe, so the PVP gave students teaching experience they would never get otherwise, with guidance and training but the freedom to design their classes as they saw fit. (At the same time, working with the sick required ethical attention; part of the training meant explaining to the instructors—and providing a script to deliver to their students—that we weren't social workers, had no medical training, and were there strictly as writing tutors, not doctors.) The academic market for creative writing positions, as with most fields, is exceptionally competitive, and the exposure to civic instruction has broadened our instructors' resumes in valuable ways. Some have even gone on to social work degrees.

With buy-in from the administration and eager grad students, the Patient Voice now faced its two most significant challenges: identifying a "student" population and developing a pedagogy. The former was perhaps the most trying, but the latter is what, I believe, will be the Patient Voice Project's lasting contribution to the field.

Any new social service program faces the problem of finding its own clients. Many new projects affiliate with specific institutions, which can save many hours of public information campaigning. We didn't have that option. Though we had the University of Iowa stamp of approval, the Patient Voice needed to discover how to reach patients on its own. Those ads on the public buses in Iowa City? An expensive failure. Even I couldn't read the website address, and the phone number was obscured. I had the idea to distribute nicely designed table tents in the hospital cafeteria, featuring poetry and essay excerpts, but they yielded no new patients. (Fortunately, the hospital's "Project Art" wing was willing to pay for them.) But that two-sentence mention in the daily hospital newsletter? A huge success. And more importantly, *free*. Of course, mentions in the media went a long way—interviews on the local talk show always brought a spike in calls to the Patient Voice phone number that Arts Share had set up. Ultimately, regular presentations at local support groups drummed up interest and word of mouth spread steadily. The Writers' Workshop casts a long shadow in Iowa City, and no doubt the mythology of the program had a certain appeal. But the Writers' Workshop was an example of town-gown divide: the program flew in literary luminaries for readings, but graduate students rarely (if at all) interacted with the community. So basic bridges needed to be built.

In retrospect, one of the smart decisions I didn't know we were making was to invest early in an attractive, adaptable brochure. We paid a designer to compose a full-color, three-fold brochure that could also, when opened, serve as a poster.[2] It created an impressive sense of authority and intention; we looked like we knew what we were doing. We've printed thousands of these and the brochures seem to travel—they're the first step in the localization efforts as the Patient Voice expands. I think new social service projects under-consider the ways in which their marketing communicates their message.

Now, to the pedagogy of our Patient Voice classes, taught by our grad student instructors. Community service—especially in one's field—is, no doubt, a privileged and rewarding experience. But I also believe that, if you're reading this volume, you're already convinced of this. In my experience, too much of the conversation seems occupied with warm self-congratulation and vague uplift. I feel there's a critical conversation that needs to happen among those passionate about public engagement, especially in the health care field, that concerns instructional method.

I believe, disappointingly, that far too many social service programs run by educators have a hit-or-miss, impromptu teaching method. Many expressive writing programs designed for wellness, in their current iteration, emphasize offloading instead of *ideas*, distraction instead of writerly development. I can't speak authoritatively for other community art programs, but the tradition of "art therapy" centers on "distractionary" techniques—music or painting—that happen *in situ* and are aimed at helping patients get their minds off their condition. These therapeutic models try to foster creative positive experiences and soften the clinical atmosphere. They are, by and large, one-offs; a guitarist visits a hospital for an afternoon or a visual artist teaches a watercolor class for a rotating and irregular audience of inpatients. Most often, these *in situ* offerings emphasize play and escape and socialization. I'm all for them. But they are not enough if the intention is to affect patients' lives after their hospital stay.

Similarly, many expressive writing classes operate on the principle that *any* writing is good writing. Writing itself—journaling, letter writing, intentional reflection of any sort—may be rare enough (both for the ill and the rest of us) that it is worth cultivating and celebrating. But I believe that patients are idea-poor. They may be eager to write but also to perceive anew. In my experience, the students in writing classes tailored for the ill want new techniques for experiencing their own condition. They have come as far as they can on their own. They are aware that their own stories seem elusive and shapeless. They see their listeners grow bored or lost, but the effort to repair that narrative wreckage exhausts them. So we have work to do, as writing teachers in this field, but we need to think about *outcomes* instead of soft objectives like "expressiveness."

We spent a lot of time thinking: what are we teaching exactly, and why? I think the PVP distinguishes itself on the intentions of its pedagogy. When I've presented on the PVP at conferences, our pedagogy is almost exclusively what audiences want to know about—what readings we use, how we use them. (For this reason, we produced not simply an anthology of PVP writings but a primer on the classes, including syllabi.) The Iowa Writers' Workshop emphasizes uncommon aspects of writing that have, not surprisingly, found their way into our teaching philosophy and practice. I don't have the space here to outline them in great detail, but as an overview, Patient Voice classes (one hour a week, for eight to ten weeks) are split into two distinct areas of emphasis: state of mind and narrative agency. The first asks students to consider how their mood and attitude influence what and how they perceive, how language reflects those attitudes, and how that process might be reversed: how language might influence perception itself. The second seeks to develop a stronger sense of *choice* in their life stories, to eradicate passivity and focus on moments of personal control and resilience. As these two ideas build on each other, we ask each class to build to something—a poem, a single essay, a lyric—that can act as the culmination of the class. This final project goes through one revision, in an attempt to teach the basic principle that all effective writing is in revision.

We want to give students in a Patient Voice class an opportunity to wrestle with the big issues of their care, but we also don't want them to remain over-focused on their identities *as patients*. To that end, we ask the participant to draw up what we call "the Two Benchmarks." This looks like two chronologies—one featuring their peak experiences in their life, in seven-year intervals, and one centered on their major experiences as a patient. With these two chronologies, the patient has thrown a lot of clay onto the table, metaphorically speaking, and gives the instructor material to work from. Together, they look for linkages, first times and last times, unexpected connections, patterns of response. That first "client" in the program, Stephanie, for example, wrote about getting lost at a firemen's fair when she was a girl and feeling abandoned. This connected to the experience of getting lost at the giant Houston hospital. From these two related experiences, Stephanie wrote a short piece about how she coped with being lost.

Of course, some exercises bomb—and, perhaps most annoyingly, exercises that unleash pages of good writing in one class can dud in another. And you run the risk of edging into difficult material unknowingly. I remember asking Stephanie to write her daughter a "letter" about an adventure she had in her life—I wanted her to write some action with a sense of discovery. She started and stopped cold. She couldn't do it. Writing the letter felt too much like something for her to read after her mother's death. So we dropped it.

In general, the Patient Voice emphasizes specificity, which is a basic lesson of any creative writing class. The specificity of sense information, of bright specific verbs, of snatches of speech that have stayed in your head. You'd be surprised at how generalizing most prompts are in the field of therapeutic or self-expressive writing. It's a common error when non-writers teach writing: the idea that you get to the universal through the general, the abstract, the "poetry" of broad categories: hope, love, fear. The opposite is true. Early in the program's development, I went to a conference on writing and wellness and the instructor asked us to write a five-line poem about our feelings of "otherness." I had no idea where to begin. It's entirely possible that this prompt worked as a trigger for others in the room. But I suspect that that level of abstraction is almost always a challenge for new writers—and leads to abstraction and generalities in the writing itself. I vowed that our program would aim for precision and the details of every unique life.

The frustrations of public-engaged teaching with the chronically ill are predictable. The Patient Voice works with, almost exclusively, outpatients, and they can make irregular students. Their health gets in the way, and uneven attendance makes any pedagogy almost pointless. They can be lonely and needy—a part of our training now includes strategies for getting participants to write instead of talk (which happens all too often) and preparing patients for termination of the class. We're not social workers and we have to make sure both student and teacher are well aware of that fact. At this point, we have standard language we teach our instructors to use in the first class that lets the participants know we're there strictly as writing tutors, and cannot give advice on anything beyond writing. It can be difficult at times to limit your empathy—writers try to cultivate their sensitivities—but boundaries are essential for effective teaching in this field. In one case, when an instructor attempted to create a "friendship" with a former patient, she found herself fielding late-night phone calls and constant invitations for coffee. This is the exception, but an important caution.

No doubt, new ethical dilemmas lurk every time we launch a new class. On one occasion a student in a community mental health clinic wrote, vividly, about his suicide attempts; on another, a woman in a group at the local Gilda's Club decided her pain was more important than others'. For now, we have a protocol: an instructor feeling overwhelmed or challenged contacts our medical advisor, copying the traditional protocols in an academic department with undergrads. It happens that instructors themselves feel that the material is intense or unsettling, and while I can't speak for all of them, most report that this is why they get involved in working with the chronically ill in the first place: the sense of genuine stakes and need to tell. Students in the PVP come to class with zero sense of entitlement, unlike many undergraduates. And their stories are necessary to them. In addition, many of our instructors, not surprisingly, come from families that have struggled with illness.

Perhaps most frustrating is the sense that the class only reaches those who are already converts to the benefits of writing. Without question, the vast majority of participants in the Patient Voice (it is voluntary, after all) are women. They journal, they like to read, and expressive writing makes sense to them. Men, in my experience, treat writing exercises as though they were chores to finish as quickly possible. They drop their pens noisily to the table when they are done, inevitably before everyone else, punctuating their work. This gender bias won't be overcome easily, if ever. And perhaps, like homeopathy, we need to admit to ourselves that only a certain portion of the population will be interested in expressive writing for wellness. But for programs like the Patient Voice Project to thrive, they need to identify continually new audiences and new communities of writers. This work is tiring and demands strong marketing sensibilities and more than part-time investment, vulnerabilities of small nonprofit programs.

I realize the Patient Voice Project may not be a model program for the very reason that the conditions of its creation were so unique and fortuitous that they are difficult to imitate: a university actively engaged in fostering new programs, a passionate grad student in a program that offered significant amounts of unstructured time, and a teaching-hospital community both small enough and innovative enough to endorse an experiment. But I also believe that the graduate students reading this book may see in our experience opportunities of their own, in ways that I could not predict. The PVP, after all, is poised for expansion; are you interested in starting up a branch in your city, at your school? I've tried to outline the steps in our origin story that seem to me adaptable and exportable, but I have come to believe that one of the PVP's enduring outcomes is the sense that programs like it are *possible*.

The problems of the body can seem unspeakable, as common as they might be. One third of all people will get treated for cancer at some point in their lifetimes. One percent of all boy babies are born with *cryptorchidism* ("missing flower"), or undescended testicles, as I was. Most are operated on within the first two years. I was diagnosed in the spring of fifth grade, at the threshold of puberty, when the risks for lifelong impact (infertility, testosterone imbalance, maturation delays) are highest. I missed school for a week for the surgery. I suspect that that would have been the sum total of the experience—some bruising, some shame, nothing exceptional for a pre-teen—except the first surgery failed, and the story of my illness took on greater proportions. I returned to the Children's Hospital a second time, more terrified than ever. Would I grow up? Would I become a man?

This time at the hospital, though, I looked around me. Kids with catheters, IV trees, sutures, and shaved heads passed me in the halls, on the elevator. I knew I had gotten off easy. I awoke in the post-op room in a welter of screaming with no nurses or parents present. I remember propping myself up on my elbows and calling out, "It's OK, we're OK, we're going to be fine." I thought that if we could just talk, maybe we'd be rescued. We could rescue each other. It would be an overreach to say this was the origin of the Patient Voice Project, but it would not be wrong either.

Oliver Sacks, in his terrific memoir of recuperation, *A Leg To Stand On*, quotes the eighteenth-century German writer Novalis: "Every disease is a musical problem, every cure a musical solution" (Sacks 1998, 110). For Sacks, this meant learning to walk again after knee surgery to the rhythmic phrasings in classical recordings. I might paraphrase and say every sickness is a problem of narrative, and every cure is partly a story. For me, the plot of my illness did not exist for me until the fall of 2004, when I found myself beginning a conscious effort to put it into form with Stephanie, in a conference room, our single, ridiculous candle winning against a cold November night.

Notes

1. I learned quickly that nurses were almost impossible to schedule meetings with; they're simply overworked. Doctors might meet for lunch hour, and appreciated the copies of research I brought. But most, I think, preferred my short PowerPoint presentation that outlined the program, the benefits, the costs, and discrete needs. Ultimately, though, doctors could not "recommend" the program, since we had no data on our specific health outcomes. However, doctors largely controlled the culture of the clinic, and they permitted our brochures in the waiting rooms and lobbies.

2. The brochure is available as a PDF file at our website, http://artshare.uiowa.edu/pvp/index.html

References

Sacks, Oliver. 1998. *A leg to stand on*. New York: Simon & Schuster.

Part Three

A Balancing Act

Publicly Active Graduate Students' Reflections and Analyses

17

Arcs, Checklists, and Charts: The Trajectory of a Public Scholar?

Sylvia Gale

FOR SEVERAL YEARS I have been involved in and have led conversations about what publicly active graduate education is, how graduate students move to and through it, and what it looks like for institutions of higher education to support engagement within and alongside graduate professional and disciplinary trajectories. Increasingly, though, I have come to think that the very idea of an engaged trajectory is misleading—at least in the sense that we understand professional trajectories in our disciplines and within the academy generally: as a series of stages with various attendant rights and responsibilities, each stage leading (though not necessarily gracefully or with any certainty) to another, with (more or less) clear benchmarks, timelines, and adjudicators.

The impulse to map the engaged graduate trajectory (or its softer cousins, the "arc" and "pathway") is understandable, and has been tremendously useful in opening conversations about how to advocate for, support, and incorporate engagement within new and established graduate programs. I remember distinctly the first time I heard the phrase "the arc of the public scholar"—from David Scobey, during an Imagining America board meeting in 2005—and how uplifting and legitimating it felt to me. Yes! This crazy-making muddle of projects, programs, and plans goes somewhere! It has a shape! The idea of an arc—solid, recognizable, structural—felt at once buttressing and expansive. I wanted to climb it, stand up on top, and slide down the other side.

I took the phrase right to the group of Publicly Active Graduate Education (PAGE) fellows assembled at the Imagining America conference that year, only the second year of the PAGE initiative. My notes from our conversation reflect the energy we found in the arc imagery. In response to the question, "What is your ideal outcome for your own career? Or, what do you want to be doing in five to ten years?" the Fellows and I generated an enthusiastic if generic list of hopes and desires: "Inhabit a variety of roles—teacher, administrator, community worker, activist, family member; know where I live—be fully a part of my place; be called to reflect, to study outcomes; be seen as a resource; be recognized as a leader; have multiple identities validated and acknowledged; have creative and innovative freedom."

When I read this list now, I am struck by the ways that our list reflects our desires for a *way* of being and living in many ways directly in tension with our current status as transient, generally underappreciated, and entirely overcommitted graduate students. At the time, though, I did not stop to explore or make meaning of the fact that these were the kinds of answers we gave most readily and urgently, though I remember feeling a little surprised, and maybe even uncomfortable, that our answers weren't more explicitly "professional." Never mind. The list was a launch pad for my real concern—the concern that the image of an arc made tangible and that shaped both the rest of our conversation that afternoon and most if not all of my subsequent efforts to foster and lead a national network of graduate students via PAGE. If we wanted to get *there* on the arc—to that just-over-the-curve outcome, that next place along the pathway, that idealized landing to which our trajectories led—then what did we want and need? What skills? What resources? What would it look like for our graduate institutions to support our passage?

Mapping the links between where, as graduate students with a spectrum of public and scholarly commitments, we believed ourselves to be going and what we needed from our institutions in order to get there more smoothly proved to be an effective framework for expanding the PAGE network and for growing its presence both within and outside Imagining America. Our lists of what our institutions could do to support us were always rich and multiply scaled. In 2005, for example, we urged universities to:

- offer research and/or writing courses that require us to translate our dissertation project to multiple audiences, including nonacademic genres;
- create innovative postdoctoral fellowships that integrate teaching and mentoring, community programming, research, and writing;
- offer internships and/or credit for a variety of work experience, or offer courses structured to encourage these connections;
- help us learn about raising money and introduce us to funding agencies and officers;
- give us access to the university's immense publicity

machine, which can help us design and copy flyers, send out press releases, etc.

Our conference conversations were always well attended by professors and administrators who wanted to hear "what graduate students want." I made a point of ending the final PAGE activity at every conference with an even more focused conversation about what new forms of support PAGE needed from Imagining America, and these lists—which Imagining America founding director Julie Ellison affectionately called "PAGE's yearly demands"—always produced concrete improvements and expansions to the PAGE program.

That desire to map and substantiate the arc of the public scholar, which so forcefully drove my leadership of PAGE, is an impulse evident in IA's effort to specify the skills of engaged scholarship (see pp. 329–32 below), in the Tenure Team Initiative report (Ellison and Eatman 2008), in the birth of this volume itself, and in other key perspectives and position papers that argue for the place of engagement within graduate programs (e.g., Stanton and Wagner 2006). I honor and am grateful for this work and for this advocacy. But the problem with trajectory thinking is that it implies and relies on a hierarchical understanding of knowledge-building structures that does not accurately or adequately reflect the experiences of many engaged graduate students—nor the ways that knowledge is built in truly public cultural work.

Certainly, it does not explain my own experience. Before I offer an alternative way of thinking about engaged scholarly and professional development, one that seems to me at the moment both more honest and more energizing, I want to pause to explore more deeply why and how "trajectory thinking" has become increasingly uncomfortable for me, even as my own career has indeed taken a distinctly arc-like shape.

Until about a year before I started graduate school, I had no intention of pursuing a Ph.D. *Ever*. In fact, I was actively hostile to the idea. My own very intense liberal arts education—as rich, rewarding, and privileged as it most certainly was—seemed to me enough insularity for one lifetime. I chided my friends who were sending in grad school applications while working on their senior theses. Can't you think of anything better to do? Hooray for the mind—but give me *the world*. Fast forward six years. True love, multiple adventures, and a series of jobs at the margins of various educational institutions (including as after-school and community programs director at a charter high school run by a nonprofit committed to environmental education) led me to my most secure and institutionalized job yet—as the undergraduate advisor in the history department at one of the University of California campuses—significantly, *pre*-California budget crisis. Two surprising things happened there. First, I became intensely jealous of my students. Making a point to start every advising conversation with the question, "So, why history?" I remembered how much I love school. Despite my best efforts at self-education, I began to crave directed learning, mentors, peers, syllabi, and most of all, time. Second, from an institutional position of near powerlessness, I came to appreciate the creative and generative possibilities contained in administrative work. Previously, I had been the nonprofit employee trying to squeeze resources out of whichever institutions of higher education were closest at hand. Please send volunteers, let us use your space, invite our staff to your colloquia. Now (and this is certainly a credit to the candor and leadership of the administrators with whom I worked, if even tangentially) I began to make some structural observations: It is possible to work in a stimulating intellectual context and also to *make things happen*. Big things. Things that matter deeply to people outside the University as well as within it. With the right support, positioning, and experience, this was a site, I realized, where my ideals about the democratic purposes of education could be put into practice.

Within a year, I had embarked on a graduate program in English at the University of Texas at Austin, with the intent to concentrate in rhetoric and composition. This was a disciplinary home that suited me intellectually but that also, I sensed, was one of the few places within the humanities where administration was not a dirty word. Immediately, I set about reconfiguring the standard set of assistantships through which students in my program progressed. Even before I had accepted the offer from my department, I was in touch with the director of the Humanities Institute at UT, feeling out the possibilities of getting involved in the exciting public humanities programs that center was generating. In my first week on campus, I pitched to him my idea for an adult humanities class inspired by a program I had learned about several years earlier and that remained close to my heart—the Clemente Course in the Humanities on the Lower East Side in New York City. This was a humanities seminar taught by top-notch faculty and intended to be as rigorous as any first-year course at an elite university, yet offered to an educationally alienated and economically disadvantaged group of students recruited through a web of social service agencies. I became a program coordinator for the Humanities Institute the following year, a job I held in various forms until my last year in graduate school. After three years of collaborating and coordinating several other public humanities programs, we launched, and I directed, an Austin version of the Clemente Course, called the Free Minds Project (http://www.utexas.edu/diversity/ddce/freeminds).

In my final year of graduate school, I passed on my various

programming responsibilities in order to accept a dissertation fellowship. The following fall, several weeks after my first baby was born, I embarked on an extremely limited job search, applying half-heartedly to a few assistant professorships in rhetoric and composition, jobs that spoke only weakly to my real aspirations, while continuing to pay the bills with a patchwork of administrative and teaching responsibilities. That spring, a colleague forwarded me a job posting that promised precisely the hybrid role I'd imagined inhabiting: public programming; curricular development in the broadest sense; undergraduate teaching as desired; working collaboratively with students, faculty, and community partners. Within two months of applying, my family and I had moved across the country for me to begin the job I hold now, as associate director of a Center for Civic Engagement at a small liberal arts college in the Southeast, a position I have often described in the past year as "very, very nearly my dream job."

Certainly, this story represents a trajectory of public engagement, one that started with my observations about the possibilities contained by administrative work in higher education and augmented through the experiences I was able to find and cultivate support for while in graduate school, positions that allowed me to continue to expand my skills in designing and implementing public humanities programs. But I have told the story with a focus on the structural realities of my engagement as a graduate student—where and how I found the room to be both publicly active and a student—in order to highlight one of the key deficiencies of trajectory thinking. When we think about the "stages of professional development" for engaged scholars, and when we map these stages into a progression that leads to some ideal professional outcome, it is all too easy to come up with a picture of success that looks decidedly like the traditional academic pathway—with an engaged twist. Consider, for example, the chart of "Pathways for Public Engagement at Five Career Stages" included in Imagining America's report on tenure policy in the engaged university, *Scholarship in Public* (Ellison and Eatman 2008, 21; reprinted on p. 34 above). While the chart's framing reminds us that these stages are "recurring" (19), the chart's progression "deciding to be a public scholar" (applicable to grad students and assistant professors) to a climax of "serv[ing] as chair or dean" (available to full professors) implies that knowledge building via publicly oriented scholarship is a linear experience involving the accumulation of credentials that allow us to participate in ever more complex and legitimate forms of scholarly and public production.

Of course, this chart is offered in a report about crafting tenure and promotion policies that recognize and reward engaged scholarship. It is necessarily concerned with legitimation within traditional and hierarchical academic structures. But what my own story illustrates are the ways that publicly engaged work upends those hierarchies. Like many of my peers, I came to graduate school with public commitments, program-building skills, and a vision for the ways that my education in graduate school might fit into a larger sense of momentum and purpose. These commitments and skills clarified and expanded while I was in school, but very little about this process was linear, at least not in the ordered, skill-gathering sense that the chart conveys. As a graduate student with public roles and commitments, I acquired the skills I needed to carry out the projects at hand as I needed them, learning from and with those around me. Commitments and projects unfolded one from the other. In the process, I found myself engaging in many of the "exercising leadership" responsibilities described on the "pathways" chart (writing grant proposals, speaking out for public scholarship) long before I had earned my Ph.D. All of this involved less a progression from one phase or stage of engagement to another than a constant shifting of the weight among the various concurrent roles I inhabited.

Increasingly, it is this imagery and terminology of "roles" that I find most useful as a framework for engaged professional development. The challenge for any engaged scholar (or citizen, activist, advocate), wherever we are in our journey through professional training, is to balance the many roles we play. As many of us know well, this juggling act can feel, and be, desperate. It is often quite literally an act of survival, since no one role can easily be lopped off or put on hold, and each role demands our fullest involvement. At every PAGE conversation I have facilitated, someone has asked a version of the question, "How do I do this work and survive?" Surviving—and thriving—as an engaged scholar, is not, I have come to believe, a matter of accumulating the right skills or the right status. It is a matter of locating our multiple roles around our own central and driving commitment(s). Often these are the commitments that brought us into graduate school in the first place, and they are the commitments that lead us to maintain and initiate our connections with communities outside graduate school while we are there.

Recently, I have been exploring this way of thinking about engagement and professional development through a workshop exercise that asks participants to physically represent the many roles they inhabit—and the connections and disconnections between them (see p. 322). This exercise asks participants to identify, first, the central commitment or passion at the heart of their work ("the thing that you are *for*") and then to depict the various roles they play in and out of relation to that commitment, producing a graphic image of the reasons so many of us feel overwhelmed. It gives us a visual language for the juggling act that makes up the engaged scholar's weeks, months, and years, and dramatizes the ways that our roles may create friction and outright conflict with one another. But the real impact of this exercise comes, for me, in the later steps, where participants are asked to name the projects, programs, and activities with which they fulfill or have fulfilled the roles that are most important to them—and to pay special attention to the connections between them. The exploration truly begins when participants are asked to "think about the projects and activities that stretch between two or more roles and add these to the map."

In producing my own roles map (Figure 17.1) as I developed the exercise, it was this step that brought my current public scholarship projects into focus. The projects that live wholly within *one* of my roles were not nodes of excitement for me. For example, the paper I will present based on my dissertation research at an upcoming conference in my field fits securely in the "Researcher" role, and I could slot the curriculum I wrote for a site-based orientation program for first-year students neatly in the "Teacher" role. These projects were certainly interesting, potentially fruitful, and hopefully worthwhile—but I did not see them brimming with energy and waiting to unfold. In contrast, the projects—or in some cases shades of projects—that stretched across multiple roles seemed to me vibrant, bold, even risky. They were intimately, wholly connected to my driving commitment, which I named at the center of my map as "access to transformational learning." Here, in dotted lines and triangles and highlighted words legible only to me, an undercurrent of projects and potential began to emerge. Exploring the connections between the college access program I help to direct for local high school students and my research into eighteenth- and nineteenth-century vocational schools inspired my aspirations to be involved in our local workforce investment board—and now leads me to think about writing curricular and policy recommendations, not self-contained curricula or historical scholarship per se. Another example: At the intersections between my role as an advocate for civic engagement in higher education ("board member" role) and my responsibilities as a creator and evaluator of programs that bridge our campus and our city ("program administrator" role), I am contributing to a strange, highly collaborative, vision/policy document about assessing engaged academic work in the arts and humanities. The same kinds of connections, overlaps, and intersections can be glimpsed—more readily, perhaps—in the maps produced by students in Julie Ellison and Kristin Hass's Fall 2010 Rackham Public Humanities Institute course at the University of Michigan, where I piloted this roles workshop (Figure 17.2).

ROLES OF ENGAGEMENT: A WORKSHOP EXERCISE

What you need:

- a blank piece of paper, 8.5" × 11" or larger
- a pen or pencil
- crayons, highlighters, and/or markers

Instructions:

1. In the center of your blank piece of paper, write the thing that you are *for*. This is your central commitment. The exercise works best if you express this in the simplest, most general terms possible.
2. Around this central commitment, name the roles that you currently inhabit in relationship to this commitment. You can think in terms of category (Teacher, Researcher, Writer, etc.) or be more specific. Arrange these like spokes on a wheel around the central commitment you have identified.
3. Now identify the roles you don't yet inhabit with respect to this commitment, but want to; differentiate these in some way graphically (using a dotted line, a different color, etc.).
4. Add the roles that fill a significant part of your life but that do not feel connected to your central commitment. Differentiate these graphically as well.
5. Draw circles around the roles that are most important to you right now.
6. Inside these circles, add the current (and, if you'd like, past) projects, programs, activities with which you fulfill or have fulfilled these roles. Be specific. Add the activities you want or intend to undertake within these roles but have not yet. You may also want to circle the roles you have not begun to inhabit yet and indicate what activities, projects, etc., you imagine and anticipate occurring there.
7. Think about the projects and activities that stretch between two or more roles and add these to the map. Differentiate these with shape and/or color so that they stand out.
8. Indicate, in whatever way you like, the pressures that pull you away from the roles that are most important to you. Likewise, indicate the supports that encourage you in these roles. Be specific.
9. Sit back, pause, reflect, add color, and study what you have created. What surprises you about what you produced? What information has emerged for you here?

NOTE: I am grateful to the students in Julie Ellison and Kristin Hass's Fall 2010 Public Humanities Institute course, sponsored by the Rackham Graduate School at the University of Michigan, for being such willing and reflective participants in my pilot version of this workshop. This exercise is a work in progress. I welcome comments and suggestions from those who try it, adapt it, and inevitably improve upon it.

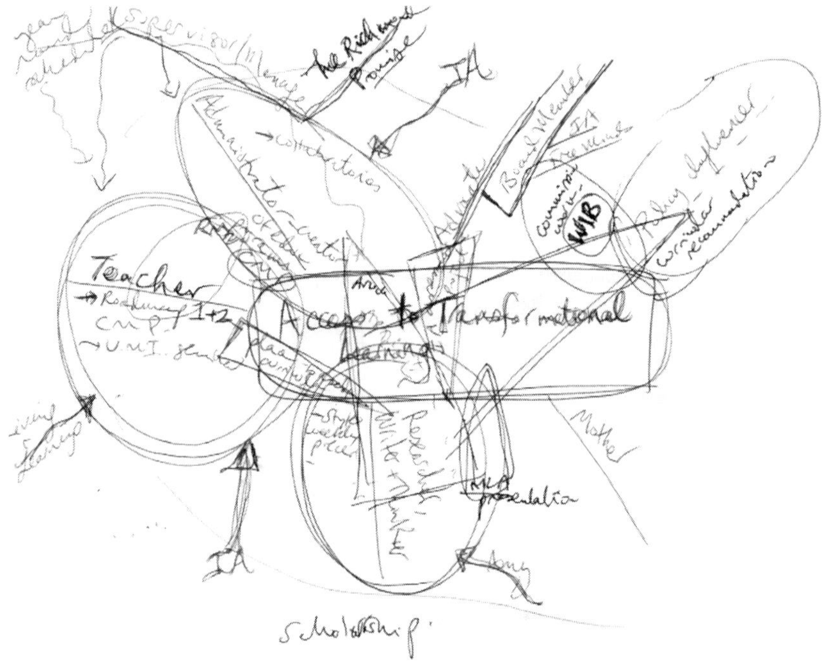

FIGURE 17.1. "Roles of engagement" roles map, by Sylvia Gale. Courtesy of the author.

It is not news that public scholarship emerges out of intersecting interests and commitments and calls upon us to embrace nontraditional (at least in an academic sense) forms, venues, and audiences. The newness that emerges in this kind of "roles thinking," however, is that the juice lies *in the intersections* themselves; the projects literally take shape in the spaces between roles. If this is so, then perhaps the highest goal of the engaged public scholar—the end state of the professional trajectory—is not the integration of roles but an ongoing and dynamic multiplicity. This will not be surprising to publicly engaged scholars who are also associate and full professors and who know that overcommitment doesn't end with tenure. But I am not talking about accepting fragmentation and exhaustion as the status quo. Nor am I disagreeing with assertions, like Timothy Stanton and Jon Wagner's, that cultivating a culture of engaged graduate education requires our institutions to make "deliberate efforts to link engagement … to pedagogical or professional ideals" (22). I am, though, suggesting that innovative public scholarship resists integration and unification.

This recognition changes the questions we ask about supporting engaged scholars at the start of their careers and it also changes the frameworks we use for envisioning the institutional change necessary

FIGURE 17.2. Roles maps by graduate students Lorelie Blackburn (top) and Antonette Adiova (bottom). Used with permission.

to encourage a culture of engagement within our schools, departments, and fields. "Trajectory thinking" causes us to ask, as I did of graduate students from around the country for many years, What do graduate students need in order to *become* publicly engaged scholars? "Roles thinking," in contrast, causes us to ask instead, What do you need to fully activate the roles and the projects that really matter to you?

Lest the significance of this shift be lost, let me illustrate its impact by recalling my graduate school orientation. On the very first day of our new careers as graduate students, within the very first hour of arriving on our new campus and, for most of us, within only days of moving to our new city, our department's then-graduate chair "welcomed" us with a speech delineating the various hurdles and barriers awaiting us in our passage to the Ph.D.—comps, quals, prospecti, assistantships, a race against the funding clock, etc. When he finished, one bold new recruit asked, shakily, "Does anyone ever do this in five years?" The answer was a resounding No. The rest of us were silent, perhaps not sure how to follow up either the diatribe or the question, both of which seemed, at least to me, to diminish our forecasted intellectual journeys. In the years since, I have often imagined an alternate kind of welcome, one that, like the roles exercise I have been experimenting with recently, might have asked us to put our reasons for being—at least for being in graduate school, if not for being at large—at the center of our narrative, inviting us to see how the trappings of disciplinary training would push, pull, propel, and possibly impede us along the way.

This is the radical vision of professional training that roles thinking allows: When we put our driving commitments at the center of our trajectories, we *de*-center the highly professionalized, hierarchical pathway that most disciplinary training reinforces. What my graduate orientation did was put the progression itself at the center of my graduate career, a move that involved assuming a great deal about where my new colleagues and I thought we were headed. Roles thinking opens this landscape up, allowing us to see that the "real work" is happening here and now in the interstices between the various ways we fulfill our central commitments—and opening up the possibility, too, that we really don't know where we are headed. What we learn in the process can be surprising, and unsettling. While discussing my roles exercise with a group recently, one student confessed that his map did not include, anywhere, the role of teacher. "This is very strange," he said. "Before this I would have said that is absolutely where I am headed, that it's one of my primary professional identities."

I love insights like that because they remind me that when we focus closely on the work that feels most urgent to us, the institutions that otherwise might seem to be dictating our passage take a back seat, become witnesses—sometimes useful, sometimes harmful—to a larger unfolding. No doubt, though, my cavalier approach to disciplinary hurdles and professionalized goals will bother some. I recognize that this attitude reflects, for one thing, my own deep privileges, like the privilege to have had several mentors while in graduate school who affirmed my alternately developing path—including a dissertation advisor who deeply valued administrative work. And certainly, my eagerness to embrace professional training that devalues the self-replication of the academy reflects my own choice not to pursue the tenure-track professoriate as my highest goal. For me, the answer to the question of how I could best support my continued commitment to provide, explore, and think deeply about access to transformational learning led me away from a tenure-track job and towards a staff position with "faculty privileges." This choice has, of course, its own deficits and challenges. But in it I find a tremendous amount of freedom to multiply the roles that matter to me and to continue to explore and renew the spaces between the roles I inhabit, rather than subordinating the roles to the spaces my trajectory tells me I should inhabit next.

At the 2010 Imagining America National Conference in Seattle, I heard Julie Ellison reflect on the kind of "meta-analysis of complex roles grounded in public cultural work" that I am exhibiting here, a trend that makes visible, in Ellison's words, "the discontinuity of the so-called spiral, arc, or continuum." Ellison was responding to a presentation of data emergent in a study by Imagining America on "Career Aspirations and Pathways of Graduate Students and Early Career Scholars," a project that emerged out of the PAGE initiative and that focused on identifying several prototypes of publicly engaged scholars, focusing on the lives, aspirations, and decisions that led them to and through graduate school. At the end of the presentation and Ellison's response, one audience member asked bluntly, "Are you going to go farther than this? Hearing *why* my graduate students engage is not nearly as helpful to me as knowing *how* I can be of use to them."

I understood both the agitation and the tenderness embedded in his question. He wanted to know what to do *now* to support the graduate students in his program whose professional lives seemed so fragmented. It was that desire to articulate how to support engaged graduate education and to see the effects of those conversations implemented in the interests of survival that drove my own leadership of the PAGE initiative for so long. I remain as interested in proactive restructurings, radical revisionings, and holistic experiences of graduate education as ever. But the problem, I would submit to the questioner and to myself six years ago, if I could revisit those early conversations I facilitated as director of PAGE, lies not in having multiple roles; it lies in expecting this state to dissolve and resolve into some unified, integrated, coherent whole, that steady state somewhere just over the arc's horizon. To avoid that, and to relish the engaged and artful multiplicity of our roles, we do, most definitely, need to understand the *why* that is at the center of each of our journeys.

References

Ellison, J., and T. K. Eatman. 2008. *Scholarship in public: Knowledge creation and tenure policy in the engaged university.* Syracuse, NY: Imagining America. http://www.imaginingamerica.org/TTI/TTI_FINAL.pdf.

Stanton, T. K., and J. W. Wagner. 2006. *Educating for democratic citizenship: Renewing the civic mission of graduate and professional education at research universities.* San Francisco: California Campus Compact.

INTERCHAPTER

Specifying the Scholarship of Engagement: Skills for Community-Based Projects in the Arts, Humanities, and Design

*Imagining America**

I. SCHOLARSHIP AND CREATIVITY IN THE REAL WORLD

Skills of Place

- Ability to read and to map natural and built environments and people's experience of them
- Sense of the layered histories of places, including their simultaneously local and global meanings and their potential to become "historic sites of conscience"
- Willingness to ask, "where is a discipline" as well as "what is a discipline"

Interpretive and Critical Skills

- Skill in the close reading of words and things
- Ability to use the tools of textual and cultural criticism in unpacking how meaning is constructed, both verbally and visually
- Understanding of genre and form

Creative and Aesthetic Skills

- Poetic, visual, musical, dance, theatrical, craft, or other artistic literacies
- Ability to describe aesthetic experience
- Grasp of where, by whom, and for whom art is made

Research Skills

- Understanding of the principles and methods of participatory action research
- Overview of where knowledge is located, for example, in

---

* Available at https://www.aacu.org/meetings/annualmeeting/AM07/documents/SpecifyingtheScholarshipofEngagement.pdf

document archives, organizational records, census data, published scholarship, Web resources, personal and group memory, museums
- Knowing what methods are suited to finding and understanding these diverse materials
- Familiarity with standards of ethical research practices

Theoretical Skills

- Ability to read and understand theoretical and philosophical reflections relevant to the project
- Capacity to think and talk about concepts and ideas, and about why they matter
- Openness to the manifold forms of explanatory systems created by different cultures and societies
- Ability to revise theoretical frameworks on the basis of experience

II. NEGOTIATING COLLABORATIVE WORK

Intercultural Skills

- Ability to reflect openly on and work across social and cultural differences, including those of race, ethnicity, nationality, age, sexual orientation, language, region, and gender

Political Skills

- Ability to define the public good, the public domain, "the commons" in the context of the project
- Ability to reflect on and raise questions about what democracy, citizenship, 'publicness,' and agency mean in and for one's work
- Understanding how to map power of different kinds and manifestations
- Ability to claim legitimacy for the project and public agency for oneself
- Capacity to change minds, other people's and one's own, and to disagree
- Ability to build alliances among people and groups with diverse interests

Group Skills

- Capacity to form purposeful relationships and networks; to sustain them through inclusive and democratic planning; to negotiate difficulties with transparency in meetings, over the phone, and by email; to reflect together on the import of the project; and to assess its successes and failures

Project Management Skills

- Ability to organize and monitor multi-partner projects that may involve several sites and different types of organizations and groups, as well as multiple timelines, tasks, and products

Resource Skills

- Knowing how to calculate the human effort that it will take to get collaborative work done, taking into account the variables of, for example, time, space, academic credit hours, and funding
- Ability to construct and read a budget
- Ability to talk to people about money and resources

III. REFLECTION IN CONTEXT

Skills Relating to Cultural Institutions

- Understanding of the organizational character of collaborating entities, such as public cultural institutions, nonprofits, NGOs, and for-profit enterprises such as cultural tourism, entertainment, and new media

Skills Relating to Community Engagement

- Familiarity with the practices and histories of activism, public service, advocacy, associations, volunteerism, and other forms of engagement, understood in cultural terms

Skills Relating to Educational Institutions

- Grasp of educational systems—both K–12 and higher education—their historical outlines and recent trends
- Understanding of the defining character, place, and context of one's own education
- Historical map of the disciplines and professions, including one's own

Policy Skills

- Overview of cultural policy as a field
- Ability to locate and use cultural policy resources

IV. COMMUNICATING WITH OTHERS

Listening and Speaking Skills

- Ability to listen to and absorb ideas from a wide variety of perspectives, fields, professional practices
- Speaking abilities adequate to the purposes of introduction, presentation, persuasion, debate, critique, praise, and

intergroup dialogue

- Capacity to negotiate multilingual groups and occasions, including the presence of multiple U.S. and foreign languages other than English, American Sign Language, regional and ethnic dialects and accents, and different professional terminologies
- Grasp of the varieties and purposes of performative or bodily speech, such as song, gesture, ritual

Writing Skills

- Ability to write accessible prose in multiple genres for various audiences, including personal reflection, research reports, persuasive and critical essays, proposals, accurate summaries, life stories, pedagogical materials
- Ability to write individually and collaboratively, and to write under the just-in-time conditions of project-based work
- Understanding of the significance of the look and feel of texts, arising from the choices made in publishing and disseminating the written word

Ethnographic, Documentary, and Oral History Skills

- Understanding of different forms of quantitative and qualitative information, and of the uses of ethnographic and survey research
- Ability to develop the questions for, conduct, and edit an interview
- Familiarity with modes of exchanging and documenting people's stories, including, for example, video and audio recording, Photo Voice, and story circles

18

Leveraging the Academy: Suggestions for Radical Grad Students and Radicals Considering Grad School

*Chris Dixon and Alexis Shotwell**

ROMANTICIZED, demonized, celebrated, denounced—among activists in the United States and Canada, academia is all of these things. It is a gate-keeping institution that shapes and is shaped by relations of power and privilege. It is a site of intense struggle: those who are structurally excluded battle for access, while those who study there fight for affordable and relevant education, and those who work there demand dignity, respect, and living wages. It is a place both where people develop radical politics and transformative visions, and where people seclude themselves in insular, disconnected ivory towers. These contradictions are stark. Yet radicals have tried to make use of the academy. Since the 1960s, in particular, graduate school has become an attractive pathway for many activists, but also often an isolating and depoliticizing one. This is still true today, as radicals active in a variety of movements are choosing to go to grad school.

The questions bound up in this choice are urgent ones: How might activist grad students concerned with fundamentally transforming this society make sense of the university? How might radicals involved in the university relate to it, evading its pitfalls and exploiting its openings? And most importantly, how can the space of the university be made useful for building broad-based radical left movements? We aim to approach these questions by offering some suggestions based in our own experiences of ambivalently occupying the university as graduate students with the hopes of using it to advance political work.

We are fortunate to be thinking about these issues from a site that has shown us many of the possibilities and perils of the academy. We are both graduate students at the University of California, Santa Cruz, in the History of Consciousness Department. UCSC has a distinguished

* An earlier version of this article was published in *MRZine*, January 12, 2007 (http://mrzine.monthlyreview.org/ds120107.html).

history of student, worker, and faculty struggle. During our tenure there this history bloomed into vibrant coalitional work linking low-wage workers in union struggles with direct-action counter-recruitment manifestations, rank-and-file militancy in the teaching assistant union, and lively struggles around access and retention for traditionally marginalized students. Being at UCSC also taught us a lot about how much work is still to be done in university settings: we witnessed deep racial divides among UCSC's activist communities, "radical" faculty unwilling to step up to support low-wage immigrant workers, and a troubling tendency to forget even recent campus organizing history.

Our trajectories also shape our thinking on these matters. Chris, currently in the fifth year of his Ph.D., came to grad school out of a long engagement with anti-authoritarian politics and direct-action organizing. Alexis came to grad school with a background in feminist politics and community radio, and has just completed her doctorate. Both of us worked on rank-and-file organizing with and against our own union (UAW Local 2865), struggled in solidarity with campus service workers as part of a student-worker coalition, participated in counter-recruitment work, assisted with immigrant justice organizing, and worked on an annual Disorientation Guide. We engaged in many of these activities through a political collective made up of six grad students.

Our experience of doing political work as grad students is obviously partial. We don't think we have definitive answers. But we've tried to approach our work experimentally, and we'd like to share some results. Our hope is to open some conceptual terrain for expanded discussion and imagination about academe as a resource for change. We know that, as individuals, graduate students can and do play important activist roles outside the academy. In fact, we think that sort of work is vital. However, we want to examine some of the ways that we can do political work in university settings as well. We address these thoughts primarily to radical grad students and activists considering grad school, but we believe they are relevant for anyone concerned with making use of the academy to further movement-building and social transformation.

But First, a Reality Check

Grad school is sometimes compared to sweatshops, factories, and the military. We are troubled by these comparisons because they erase real differences of racialization and class, in particular, and the exploitation and violence bound up in them. When people make such comparisons, however, they are trying to push back against a competing narrative: that grad school is a cushy, delightful experience, or that grad students should just be quietly grateful for their good luck and not make any waves.

Pushing back against this narrative isn't just whining: it's personally and politically important. Grad students frequently characterize their experience as marked by humiliation, arbitrary rules, a pervasive anxiety about their self-worth, dictatorial superiors wielding life-changing power, and grinding routines that wear down their ability to resist. In our view, grad school often creates exhausted, insecure, status-conscious people who distrust their own judgments and are thus more susceptible to the prevailing norms and styles of the academy.[1] Perhaps the most pernicious norm is an individualistic and isolated mode of intellectual engagement, cutting grad students off from the very work that we think they are uniquely situated to take up.

On top of all this, being a graduate student is genuinely hard. We plunge into an area of study because we feel some passion for it, we spend years learning its vocabulary and methods, and we try to formulate research projects that will sustain our passion while allowing us to survive. Frequently our families of origin, and our nonacademic friends, don't understand what we're doing, why we're doing it, or why it would be worthwhile. And even unionized grad students don't make much money, so we often come out of grad school with big debts and slim job prospects.

These features have been exacerbated by the neoliberalization of the university and the increased casualization of its workforce. That is, universities are increasingly run on a profit-making model, and a rapidly growing number of university employees are part-time, contingent workers with few rights. Campus workers—from custodians and dining hall workers to clericals and non-tenure-track faculty—are doing more labor for less pay in more precarious circumstances. Marc Bousquet has beautifully analyzed the place of graduate employee labor in this context. In "The Waste Product of Graduate Education: Toward a Dictatorship of the Flexible" (2002), Bousquet argues that the grad school system isn't primarily about producing Ph.D.'s for an imagined market in tenure-track jobs. Rather, it is aimed at extracting teaching labor from not-yet-degreed graduate student employees, who will too often later become part of the casualized adjunct pool.[2]

These challenging circumstances also point to opportunities. Each site of exploitation and misery in the lives of grad students is also a site for struggle. And because there are so many of these sites, grad students are uniquely positioned to help build connections among widely varied communities. Graduate students are workers: as teaching assistants, instructors of record, lab assistants, and research assistants, we can struggle for workplace justice and in solidarity with other workers. Graduate students are teachers: as teaching assistants and instructors, we can enact liberatory pedagogical methods, introduce oppositional knowledge and histories, support marginalized undergraduates in their university education, and more. Graduate students are students: as learners and researchers, we can help develop ideas that are relevant for changing the world. And graduate students are located in academic institutions: as members of university communities, we can participate in broader struggles to demilitarize university research, support outreach and retention, challenge funding and curricular priorities, fight sweatshop sourcing of food and university-branded clothing, and more.

Many grad students are uniquely situated in one other way: we come to grad school with movement backgrounds and activist commitments or develop political commitments through grad school. We should be nurturing and drawing on these experiences and commitments, perhaps with the help of some of the following suggestions. These things not only help to leverage the academy for changing the world, but can also help combat some of the soul-destroying features of academe we talked about above. Indeed, it is precisely this work that might move the grad school experience toward something meaningful and politically useful.

Suggestion One: Understand the Academy as a Nexus for Organizing and Capacity-Building

The university is by no means the most important site of social struggle today. Though radical ideas sometimes show up in academic discourse, they almost always originate elsewhere. Still, in the spirit of recognizing where we're located and trying to work from there, we think it is important to appreciate features of academe that make it ripe for political work. For one thing, though we can rightly critique the ivory tower, we can just as easily understand how universities are situated in dense webs of interconnection. The university, in fact, is a nexus through which systems of power manifest. For example, universities frequently replicate frameworks of access based on race and class. Organizing efforts for outreach and retention programs, or for various "ethnic studies" departments, are vibrant challenges on these grounds. Similarly, many universities are connected in significant ways to the military-industrial-complex; campaigns to keep recruiters off campuses and to demilitarize university funding are making crucial interventions in military-university relationships. Universities are major employers and buyers of goods and services; pro-union, living-wage, and anti-sweatshop struggles on campuses can thus have important catalyst effects. Universities have also been important loci for divestment campaigns, and might be again. Because campuses concentrate large numbers of energetic, exploratory young people in one place, there is a lot of potential for mobilization. In many ways, then, the university is an appropriate site for organizing, and political work there can have broader effects.

One especially significant effect of organizing in the university is a different kind of education, one that students gain not primarily through classrooms or books but through activism. Many undergrad activists develop skills and analysis as they work in student organizations; plan events, actions, and campaigns; face hostile administrators; contend with apathetic peers; try to understand and describe the systems they seek to change; experiment with organizing techniques; write and design flyers, websites, and publications; and engage in many other aspects of activist work. This is capacity-building: growing the sensibilities and competencies to do movement work. And graduate students can help in this process. We can share our own experiences as organizers (mistakes included). We can spark reflection and long-term strategic thinking. We can share our resources for political education. We can encourage student organizers to take care of themselves. We can use our positions to help student activists navigate tensions between their academic and political work (not necessarily mutually exclusive). We can ourselves remain (or become) lively, engaged participants in social struggles.

When we see the university as a nexus for struggle and capacity-building, we expand opportunities for social transformation.

Suggestion Two: Work with Undergraduates

What successful grad student organizing we did included significant work alongside and with undergraduate activist groups and involved bridging a pervasive grad-undergrad divide. In general, grad students rarely get involved in student activist groups—as though "student" means "undergrad." Frequently, grad students are scared of large groups of undergrads, feel silly and awkward engaging with undergrad organizing, or feel like we're older, superior, and in a different place in our lives. And often undergrads don't think of inviting grad students to meetings or actions because we're perceived as disengaged and disinterested, or just intimidating. Sometimes these sorts of worries are accurate; addressing them can even be useful on both sides, since they involve broader questions about being welcoming and legible. It is true that graduate students and undergraduates are frequently in different places of their lives, and will sometimes have different organizing priorities and internal cultures. But undergraduate student organizers are often the major motor of campus struggle. Also, with few exceptions, they're really fun.

Graduate students can contribute substantially to the campaigns and political work in which undergrads are involved. In 2004, for example, a student-worker coalition at UCSC initiated a year-long organizing campaign in support of low-wage and predominately Latino/a campus workers. As part of this coalition, graduate students made weekly classroom announcements about upcoming events and the ongoing campaign; wrote and distributed informational materials; drafted and circulated petitions and letters; helped to write press releases; used our access to faculty to advance organizing objectives; agitated with our union to get support for the coalition's goals; and mobilized grad students and other members of the campus community for pickets and direct actions. We've also seen grad students effectively supporting undergraduate work by helping with student publications, mentoring individual undergrad organizers, and providing some institutional memory. But we don't have to just play support roles; we can also initiate campaigns and work as full partners in ongoing organizing. In order to do any of this, however, grad students must build real relationships with undergraduates on a basis of equality and respect. This usually requires facing up to some of the ingrained teacher-student hierarchies we tend to manifest.

When collaborative undergrad-grad organizing happens, it is powerful and energizing.

Suggestion Three: Organize Grad Students

Organizing grad students, as the saying goes, is like herding cats (for all the reasons we talked about in our "reality check"). And often active grad students get isolated and drained by working hard in ineffective or retrograde institutional structures, or by immersion in the political infighting and posturing typical of many academic departments. And yet, it is not impossible to organize grad students in ways that sidestep these dangers and advance positive change. Institutional positions and good departmental cultures can have important activist potential, particularly if they are connected to broader organizing.

Probably the single most common vehicle for organizing grad students is around workplace issues. After all, the main thing we share as grad students, other than doing lots of research, is our wages and working conditions as teaching and research assistants. Such organizing usually results in an attempt to form a union. Sometimes these efforts win formal union recognition by university administrations, often not. (Sometimes, as in the case of New York University, grad students win recognition and the university repeals it through legal machinations; that fight is ongoing.)[3] If you are not a member of a union, it is definitely worth organizing to form one and have it formally (legally) recognized. If you are part of a union, you'll face different challenges. Most unions big enough to run university organizing campaigns follow a business union model, usually resulting in formally democratic structures that are not in fact very responsive to popular rank-and-file initiatives. These unions also tend to resist any response to workplace injustice other than contract enforcements narrowly defined. Opportunities for solidarity work are likewise narrowly understood. In short, a TA union itself is a site of struggle. It's important for us to fight collectively to improve our working conditions, but we can't stop there.

We can work with and against our unions in ways that hold true to the ideal of worker solidarity and challenge a business union model. For example, we were inspired in the early 2000s by grad students at York University in Toronto, who brought their union (CUPE Local 3903) under rank-and-file control, in line with participatory democratic functioning, militant solidarity action, and broader social justice work. Even if our union is really messed up, we can follow Local 3903's example and form "flying squads," in which grad student workers actively mobilize to support other unions' pickets and other community initiatives (Shantz 2009). At UCSC, we developed a graduate-student solidarity network to organize and mobilize grad students to join other workers, on and off campus, for labor actions, and to address some of the failings we saw in our own union. This network developed into a kind of reform caucus, UAW Members for Quality Education and Democracy, which sought to support labor struggles and draw connections between workplace conditions and accessible, quality education. This is an example that we think resonates with many other rank-and-file initiatives and aspirations, not only in the graduate-student union realm.

It is also important to nurture lively political communities among grad students beyond the limited goal of a single campaign, strike, or event. Union culture, for example, requires much more than just mobilization and meetings; it needs a sense of comradeship, a collective practice of caring about what happens to other people. In our experience, when people work together on specific projects over time, they come to trust each other personally and politically. This trust is essential to grounded political community. The tightrope we walk here, of course, is difficult since cliquishness and insularity often result from close organizing ties. And so we think it is important to create structures that people can easily access without already being linked to existing social-political networks. One experiment we tried in this vein, still ongoing, is a non-university-based email listserv for communication among radical grad students at UCSC; we called it "radgrads." At the beginning of each school year, an announcement goes out on the grad email lists, explaining the purpose of radgrads and inviting people to join it. The list serves as a vehicle for informing grad students of events and campaigns on and off campus, a site for discussion among students from very different departments, and occasionally a means for organizing social events and in-person discussions. We've also seen the success of, for example, a women-of-color grad research and action collective and queer grad groups in creating supportive institutional cultures for political work.

When grad students come together, we are formidable.

Suggestion Four: Question Professionalization and Individualism

Perhaps one of the starkest differences between undergrads and grads is that while the university is often a place of politicization for undergraduates, it is more often a place of depoliticization for grad students. Aside from time and money pressures, two of the main depoliticizing forces we encounter are professionalization and individualism, as they are engrained in academic culture. Professionalization is the process of learning and adopting the "rules of the game" of academic life. Usually, these are middle- and upper-middle-class coded ways of talking, dressing, and socializing. They have historically been most comfortably deployed by men, and they are very white. Professionalization includes a set of academic behaviors and accomplishments, like publishing papers, presenting work at conferences, applying for grants and fellowships, and successfully conducting a job search. Individualism is a trait that fits neatly into academic professionalization; individual achievement and brilliance are highly praised, almost defining characteristics of academe. Academics are supposed to live the life of the mind, immune to bodily needs and relational connections. Thus, genuinely collaborative work is not taken as seriously as solitary genius, even in the sciences, and we are expected to diligently pursue our individual "careers." As a result, academic life is often deeply isolating, both in terms of how we conceptualize our work and how our work process is structured.

It might be tempting to throw professionalization out entirely. After all, it brings together many of the most rage-inspiring aspects of academic culture. We call for a questioning of professionalization, however, because there are times when understanding and mindfully deploying norms of the profession is useful. People who come into the academy from working-class backgrounds, people who live with disabilities, or who are racialized, or fat, or otherwise "inappropriate" in the ivory tower's halls, can benefit from a careful investigation into the norms of professional life. Using these norms can be key to infiltrating and surviving academe. Even for the relatively privileged, understanding professionalization is important in refusing to internalize its imperatives. At the same time, we think it is crucial to develop alternatives to professionalization. In particular, a prevailing myth supporting the professionalization imperative is the idea that every worthy Ph.D. student should expect to land a tenure-track job. But this has never been the case. And as universities shift more and more teaching onto contingent labor, it looks very likely that it never will be. As graduate students, we must imagine life beyond the tenure carrot and the adjunct stick. There are, as far as we know, no maps laid out for this work, but we think it's worth exploring.

Collaborative work, in our experience, offers a way to simultaneously challenge professionalization and refuse depoliticization. This alternative to the individualist model can be practiced among academics and also with and among activists outside of academic contexts. For those engaged in movements, this mode should be familiar. Activist intellectual work is often collaborative; it seeks clarity and refinement through the process of conversation and collaboration. We noticed the promise of this kind of approach in our political collective, particularly as we wrote a social-economic analysis of our university's priorities and practices. In general, we found working collaboratively as graduate students outside of academically sanctioned settings to be both challenging and exciting. Often in our lives as grad students we relate to one another as colleagues, interlocutors, or rivals, but usually our work is our own. Politically motivated, shared work is a powerful antidote to these relationships. In our case, we also discovered that it gave us more ground to stand on in our broader organizing work. We experienced this, in a different way, when we assembled an all-graduate-student affinity group for street actions in San Francisco after the ground invasion of Iraq in 2003. Integrating these sorts of approaches into our academic work can have similarly profound effects. And more fundamentally, such approaches can challenge and change the ways we presently think about our day-to-day work routines and ourselves as intellectuals.

Critically approaching professionalization and developing collaborative means of doing activist intellectual work opens surprising and liberating spaces.

Suggestion Five: Build Accountability to Movements into Research and Teaching

The question of accountability is a crucial way to frame and understand our work. We can approach it, among other ways, in terms of how knowledge itself is produced. Veteran activist and academic Richard Flacks nicely illustrates this, recalling that a central slogan among radical sociologists in the late sixties was "knowledge for whom?" The question remains pressing, and it begs another: accountability to whom? One way to answer this question is to think about the communities that validate and thus structure our scholarship. With whom is our work in conversation? To whom is it accountable? How are the answers to these questions related to each other?

Some of us have managed to find ways of sustaining political relationships with activists in a variety of movement contexts. Often, these relationships even become an inspiration for or the focus of our academic work. This is good and useful. But there are many open questions about what accountability is and how we should enact it. Of course, in this case, accountability would involve explicit negotiation with research "subjects" and some account of how the research will come back to the community. But such a mode of accountability will always be dissatisfying and partial—it will always fail. In general, we think of accountability as involving far more than a basic attention to research ethics. It is a relationship that orients our attention, commitments, and research questions. When, as academics, we think of ourselves as standing in solidarity with movements as equal participants in struggles for social transformation, our relationship to what work we do, how we share it, and for whom we're doing it might fundamentally change. This is how we understand accountability.[4]

Issues of accountability are also central to teaching. After all, most of us will teach, sometimes a lot, during graduate school. It is not uncommon to have the chance to design and teach one's own class, and almost everyone works as a teaching assistant at some point. There is no way that we can overview here all of the useful work on radical pedagogy—work on canons, how knowledge is formed in relation to power, how we can use the classroom as a place to teach for liberation, and how our teaching selves can be fully integrated and present beings. There are excellent and important resources out there.[5] But we do want to note the difficulty of bringing activist commitments and sensibilities into the classroom. Teaching is some of the most fulfilling work either of us has done. It is also the most challenging. We have encountered both of these most strongly when we have tried to directly bring our political commitments into our teaching. And so we maintain that teaching is immeasurably strengthened when it is accountable to movements. In our experience, this means facilitating ways for students to not only think critically about the world but to develop means of actively engaging it. It means finding ways to both support and challenge student activists. It means challenging social hierarchies as they manifest in teaching spaces. It means seeing even very politically problematic students as utterly worth working with. It means understanding the classroom as a space that is densely interwoven with the rest of the world.

Developing accountability in our research and teaching helps us make genuine contributions to movements.

Toward Discussion and Collective Strategizing

When we started graduate school, we were searching for models for how to do activist intellectual work in the academy while also sustaining strong connections to movements. We were able to identify individual professors and grad students who seemed to be successfully navigating some of these tensions, but we found little in the way of explicit discussion and collective strategizing. And so we have tried to build some of our own models, always incomplete, at the same time that we have attempted to develop political practice appropriate to our situation. Perhaps the hardest part has been finding ways to generate the discussion and strategizing that we couldn't find but urgently need. We have been fortunate to participate in a lively political community at UCSC, but we have always felt that activist grad students in many other places would have crucial insights to offer to these conversations. In our view, we especially need discussion that evades political posturing and realistically engages with the question of sustainable organizing in unsustainable circumstances. We hope, then, that these suggestions might help spark serious and ongoing reflection and dialogue. We hope too that they might serve as a support of some kind for radical grad student activity. Grad students, as we have argued, are in a unique structural location where political work can have powerful effects. We must develop ways of collectively sustaining and strengthening that work. Doing so will help move us from ineffectiveness and isolation to meaningful and strategic activist intellectual work. It will help us leverage the academy for movement-building.

Postscript

We wrote this piece in late 2006, during our first year living away from Santa Cruz and the graduate student culture we described. We stand behind what we wrote here, but we have a few thoughts to add based on our experiences since then.

First, the economic crisis of the late 2000s has deepened and accelerated the neoliberalization of universities, especially public ones. This is not news for anyone who lives or works on a campus in North America. Although it would have been difficult for us to imagine this while we were in grad school, budget cuts, tuition hikes, furloughs, and other kinds of austerity measures are now even more widespread and aggressive. They are creating more precarity—more of a squeeze—in the lives of university workers and students. This squeeze makes it harder to organize resistance. Still, we've been inspired by the rise of campus-based movements fighting austerity. Some of these movements add new dimensions to what we write here while others challenge some of our assumptions. Since we haven't been directly involved in these movements, we look to others to help us understand the lessons and effects of these struggles.

Second, in the years since this article came out online, we've had lots of feedback from other grad students. Many people pointed out how very rare and precious it was for us to have a lively undergraduate organizing culture to connect with, a broad-enough coalition of activist grad students across the disciplines, and sympathetic professors as mentors and collaborators. Although we thought we understood a wide range of grad school experiences, it became clear to us that we were generalizing from a fortunate institutional context. However, we continue to think that our context was fortunate in part because of the political work we undertook there; although we benefited from certain features of UCSC, we also struggled to actively shape our context. This is what we tried to describe above. Some of the lessons we learned in a reasonably hospitable situation may be applicable on other scales in more embattled contexts. Alexis has seen some of this from the point of view of a job in a university without an active student movement and with very limited faculty support for progressive (much less radical) politics: less hospitable contexts require that we think more strategically, marshal our energy for smaller-scale "wins," and spend more time nurturing what political space there is.

Third, we've reflected a lot on the transition from grad school to life after grad school. For some of the people we did political work with, grad school ended without a degree. Indeed, 50% of people who start Ph.D. programs don't finish them. We also have friends who have completed doctoral programs and either opted out of pursuing tenure-track work or have been unable to find secure academic employment. And we know some people who have found tenure-track jobs—both those who are happy and those who find themselves contemplating leaving academe even though they've supposedly "succeeded." We realize that although we did a good job thinking collectively while we were in grad school, we haven't done this as well since we started moving out of grad school. The professionalizing and individualizing dynamics we talk about above seem to gain power the closer one gets to obtaining a doctorate. We, and many people we know, are still trying to imagine life beyond the tenure carrot and the adjunct/nonacademic stick, but for the most part we're still doing this in highly individualized ways.

Finally, as we attempted to emphasize throughout our discussion, grad students in particular and university-based activists in general are not going to single-handedly generate the mass movements that we need in order to fundamentally transform society. These movements have to come from dedicated organizing in many social sectors. Our hope remains for radical graduate students to contribute to this process.

Notes

1. For more on this process, see Schmidt 2000.

2. See also Bousquet 2008.

3. On the struggle at NYU, see Krause et al. 2008.

4. Three recent collections have influenced how we think about these issues: Frampton et al. 2006, Hale 2008, and Shukaitis and Graeber 2007.

5. For an excellent primer, we recommend hooks 1994.

References

Bousquet, Marc. 2002. The waste product of graduate education: Toward a dictatorship of the flexible. *Social Text* 70 (1): 81–104.

Bousquet, Marc. 2008. *How the university works: Higher education and the low-wage nation.* New York: New York University Press.

Frampton, Caelie, Gary Kinsman, A. K. Thompson, and Kate Tilleczek, eds. 2006. *Sociology for changing the world: Social movements/social research.* Halifax, NS: Fernwood Publishing.

Hale, Charles, ed. 2008. *Engaging contradictions: Theory, politics, and methods of activist scholarship.* Berkeley and Los Angeles: University of California Press.

hooks, bell. 1994. *Teaching to transgress: Education as the practice of freedom.* New York: Routledge.

Krause, Monika, Mary Nolan, Michael Palm, and Andrew Ross, eds. 2008. *The university against itself: The NYU strike and the future of the academic workplace.* Philadelphia: Temple University Press.

Schmidt, Jeff. 2000. *Disciplined minds: A critical look at salaried professionals and the soul-battering system that shapes their lives.* Lanham, MD: Rowman & Littlefield.

Shantz, Jeffrey. 2009. Anarchy in the unions: Contemporary anarchists at work. *WorkingUSA* 12 (3): 371–85.

Shukaitis, Stevphen, and David Graeber, eds. 2007. *Constituent imagination: Militant investigations, collective theorization.* Oakland, CA: AK Press.

19

Collaboration Conversation: Collaborative Ethnography as Engaged Scholarship

Ali Colleen Neff

> Don't stress, innovate.
>
> —Jerome "TopNotch the Villain" Williams

MY MASTER'S DEGREE is thumbtacked to the wall at eye level, just to the left of my bathroom mirror, and set against its cardboard mailer. I can't afford to have it framed, and anyway, I'm hoping to have a nice assemblage of parchment pages to hang in a fresh academic office before too many years pass. It will be another grad-school day: rushing, teaching, sitting, reading, discussing, thinking, filing, learning, typing. I am always a couple of minutes late for each of these activities, which overlap at the edges in order to fit into my waking hours. I think over my daily schedule as I brush my teeth, and my hard-won slip of beige paper, balanced precariously on the edge of my vision, catches my eye. In between parking-spot calculations and mental lists of e-mails to be sent, I always seem to hang on the same calligraphed line:

> Having completed the studies and fulfilled the requirements of the Faculty ... has accordingly been admitted to that degree, with all the rights, honors, responsibilities and privileges thereunto appertaining....

Whatever academic field our earned or in-process degrees claim, and however murky the list of rights, honors, and privileges afforded by our graduate work may be, it's the question of responsibilities that is most challenging to graduate students committed to engaged public scholarship. More precisely, the question of to whom we are responsible sets into motion a series of ethical challenges. What we choose to study, who funds and benefits from our work, what research methodologies we employ, and how our research extends to new possibilities and interventions are in themselves complex considerations. This edited volume invites us to suggest ways in which academic practice translates, through creative, innovative, and committed public engagement, into positive social transformation. Through the channels of academic discourses, resources, projects, and methodologies, we as engaged graduate scholars locate unique possibilities for public collaboration and change.[1]

Ethnography, literally the practice of "writing culture," has become a widely used methodology by cultural researchers, qualitative analysts, oral historians, activists and artists in all corners of academic work. This methodology demands both a public engagement with a community in the "field" of study (for example, a neighborhood, region, school, or musical group) and critical work in the process of representation. The ethnographic process holds the positive potential to bring awareness to community issues, to shape new understandings of what that community does, and to redistribute resources toward the things that community does best. As a dissertating Ph.D. student, my communities of study have involved the singers, musicians, poets, and teachers of the Mississippi Delta and Dakar, Senegal. As I move into an extensive ethnographic dissertation project with women praise-poets and hip-hop artists in Senegal, I draw from the lessons I learned in five years of fieldwork with gospel, blues, and hip-hop musicians and poets in Mississippi. This piece is a reflection on the teachings of that work, and on how this kind of contemporary ethnographic practice, woven from the deep-rooted intellectual discourses and radical political interventions of academic work on culture, promises a medium of social transformation. I will trace the routes by which collaborations between engaged graduate students and their communities of research might change the very ground upon which the academic community imagines and fulfills its public responsibilities. In the space of critical and collaborative ethnography, the study of culture and the work of activism merge in a series of projects by which social transformation is possible. We enact our life's work in our fields of study; in our crafting of critical cultural representation, and in the ways we direct our work into practices of pedagogy, collaboration, and conversation.

Improvisation

I have been tracing a well-worn 13-hour drive between the musical communities of the Mississippi Delta and my home in North Carolina over the past five years. Sometimes I spend a summer month or two working on a short video documentary or recording gospel singing practice; during the school year, I try to spend one long weekend a month following up on conversations with certain artists, gathering signatures for photo permissions and fact-checking, or dining on green bean casserole and spaghetti with the families with whom I work and live. This travel not only offers me an opportunity to learn and create in partnership with the Delta community, it also offers a familiar space of friendship, conversation, and music that sustains me through my pressing academic life. When I am immersed in my coursework at the university, my cell phone emits a muffled beep when someone's calling: I've set it that way so I can ignore it if a call threatens to impose untimely work. But sometimes I see a 662 area code and know it's someone from the Delta calling with an idea, a request, a greeting, or a question. I always pick up the phone in this case, pressing the "send" button on my e-mail manager with my pinky as I answer. "I'm coming to visit next weekend," I say to a Mississippi friend, excited to meet the new baby niece. To another: "Yes, I'll be sure to print the photos we took and to bring you a copy of our film. Did you decide how you want to spell the name of your new song for this article I'm working on?"

The crossover between my professional research and my creative and political commitments traces the same path that brought me to graduate school. At the outset of my work in Mississippi, I had never heard of ethnography, even as I counted ethnographers Zora Neale Hurston and Robert Cantwell among my inspirations in cultural studies and writing.[2] After five years of post-college work as a music journalist, service worker, and literacy volunteer on the West Coast, and in the wake of the War in Iraq, I found myself contemplating the relationship between musical creativity and political change. As my activist friends translated their frustration with the political situation into positive projects involving volunteering, political journalism, and international service work, I sought to understand better the deep roots of global social inequality and the ways in which cultural practitioners shaped poetry, sound, and movement into tools of protest and renewal.

Inspired by the work of folklorist, historian, and ethnographer William R. Ferris, whose lifetime of research with artists in the Delta celebrates the vibrant political possibilities of blues and spiritual music (e.g., Ferris 1998), and who later became my graduate school mentor, I moved to the Mississippi Delta to weave these strands together into a series of writing and multimedia documentary projects that would allow me to write in depth about these cultural practitioners' often widely unrecognized political importance to resource-poor communities as leaders, teachers, poets, and artists. Ferris and his academic contemporaries in the post-Vietnam, civil rights, and feminist eras of the 1970s and '80s, extended the threads of anthropological discourses surrounding the complexity of the field researcher's involvement in her field of study into activist projects. The globally lauded blues musicians of his native Mississippi allowed Ferris to tell the story of the Delta's intense poverty, high mortality, and illiteracy rates while celebrating the artists whose work helped to bring money, attention, and festivity to the community table. The "representational" and "performative" turns brought about by the efforts of feminist, critical, and radical ethnographers have given us space to question the boundaries divide our academic projects from the goals, values and positionalities of the communities and people with whom we work.[3]

Ethnography, arising from Continental "ethnology," folklore, and travel writing, emerged as the medium for social-anthropological data collection in the late nineteeth century. Obsessed with the tropes of primitivism and orientalism, ethnographic fieldwork was a point of cultural contact that satisfied the project of first-generation researchers to freeze cultural specimens in time, and to isolate and make strange the Western academy's Southern, Eastern, or minority "Others" for further study. But along the way, many anthropological fieldworkers found that these Other communities were, in fact, complex, peaceful, and artistically bountiful, and that they offered important pedagogical, medicinal, communicative, or philosophical lessons for humanity. Ethnographers began to take responsibility for the effects that their representations had on public policy toward minority, poor, and marginalized groups. They sought to change, rather than reproduce, uncritical attitudes toward the ethnic-minority, resource-poor, and/or geographically remote communities in which ethnography is often performed.

A new generation of ethnographers saw as well that authentic cross-cultural conversation and understanding could give rise to life-affirming educational, social, and artistic projects.[4] An ethnographic representation of a community in the form of a book, article, lecture, newspaper column, or lesson plan can perpetuate dangerous and disempowering stereotypes; it can also result in an increase of funding toward a community, drawing attention to the effects of social injustice by allowing politicians, scientists, and the general public to encounter Other cultures through ethnography. Critical ethnographers from across the academy began to recognize transdisciplinary kinship, publishing their unguarded stories from the field, discussing the ethical trickiness of involving oneself in another culture, and imagining what social-scientific research based on spiritual belief or artistic practice might look like.[5] In the century since the first ethnographic writings in social anthropology, the communities with whom collaborative ethnographers work in the field have emerged from their status as "subjects" of observation and study to become consultants, partners, and teachers with whom researchers engage in dialogue (Madison 2005). Many contemporary ethnographers come from or identify with the communities they study.[6]

A methodology that was meant to capture "strange" cultures was in fact a ready tool for coming into critical dialogue with them, and as progressive ethnographers learned how to listen as communities spoke back into these projects, the ethnographic encounter between researcher and "researched" often merged in a two-way conversation, prompting researchers to rethink the possibilities of cultural fieldwork and the consequences of their representations.[7] The interdisciplinary ethnographic turn of the post-Vietnam academy fostered the development of new college classes in cultural studies and oral history that promised a new generation of student ethnographers. The ethnographic method of participant observation, in which the researcher maintains an omniscient position as she observes a person or group and makes strategic contact with those subjects, is now giving way to models of mutual "observation" and conversation, as ethnographers ask their would-be subjects (or are asked by them) to take them on as students, to collaborate in artistic and/or political performances, or to help them shape community projects. In this sense, the critical ethnographic "field" is no longer a place distant from the academy, where the researcher observes and comes to know her Others: it is an intercultural space that allows the cultural "data" used by the academy to be shaped by the ideas, understandings, and projects of extra-academic communities of study. Many ethnographic researchers trace interdisciplinary paths, seeking to contextualize their historical, literary, sociological, or documentary work in the kind of depth that necessitates conversation, apprenticeship, witnessing, or in many cases living in and becoming part of a particular community.

One of my most important teachers in these lessons is Jerome "TopNotch the Villain" Williams, a young Mississippi rapper with whom I have worked closely throughout my five years of fieldwork with contemporary musical artists in the Delta. After a few months of freelance journalism and odd jobs in the Delta, I had come to know the regional blues scene and many of its most brilliant practitioners, and I was coming to understand the ways in which positive, contextualized, and well-researched representations of their work could help bring attention, artistic resources, and tourist dollars into the community. I enrolled in an M.A. program at the University of North Carolina at Chapel Hill that would allow me to build these relationships into a research agenda. As I sought out interviews and recordings with blues artists in preparation for my coursework, Jerome introduced himself to me in a little blues juke joint off a Mississippi back road. He is a well-known Delta rapper with deep ties to the blues community and had heard about my interest in learning about the music of young Mississippians from other local artists. He asked me to join him out front and commenced a time-stopping improvised hip-hop poem that drew a crowd of local bluesmen. Like the Delta blues that were his musical bedrock, TopNotch's poem circled his dreams of musical success, his economic desires, and his pride in his local community, much like this freestyle I recorded in an interview with him a week later (September 3, 2005, in Clarksdale, Mississippi):

> Took it down from priceless killings
> And it's killing your soul
> And now I see the cats here
> They all out of control
> Now let me grab hold of respect
> And then put it to paper
> But I call collect for fear that
> Life is spectacular
> Words from the Dracula but don't have them fangs
> The only things that I have
> Is my pain
>
> So I spit this
> From the outside of my heart
> To the inside of my lungs
> And that the last breath that I spit it
> You will hear this song
>
> And every words that I'm copywritin'
> they will receive
> That it's the knowledge, top dog
> From your boy, T.O.P.

I knew at that moment that my ethnographic work was taking an unexpected turn, and with TopNotch as a guide, I tuned my ear to the emerging hip-hop styles of young people of the Delta. I wondered what this new blues might teach me and my readers about the registers of community engagement and activism in a region that has historically gone unremarked in the national news.

That September, TopNotch invited me to spend a weekend in his life, riding low in his Oldsmobile through his old neighborhoods, greeting his cousins, watching him practice his rhymes with friends. We spent our last night together praying with his childhood church choir director, Miss Martha Raybon, who told us of the relationship of the voice of Delta hip-hop to local religious practice, and who traced the history of Delta musical activism to the spirituals of enslaved peoples in the local cotton fields. It was through song, she said, that they learned where to meet for secret worship and how to join the Underground Railroad to freedom. After I returned to class the following week, I called Jerome to tell him that I would be presenting my work in class later that semester. He asked if he could join me, and I in turn asked my professor if I could bend the assignment and present my work with a guest. I was able to find funding for Jerome's flight and managed a colloquium and a small concert to celebrate our first co-presentation.[8] As we stood together in the conference room, TopNotch, dressed in a bright new set of dress clothes, looked at me as I clutched my notes nervously and reminded me of the mantra he continues to repeat as we work together: "Don't stress. Innovate."

In this spirit of innovation, collaboration—and a little rule-stretching—TopNotch and I have made this co-presentation a yearly ritual, and Jerome returns to Chapel Hill time and again to co-present our work. Our partnership bends ears: with TopNotch's intercultural knowledge and ability to weave complex poems about the situation at hand, and my research into the historical, aesthetic, and critical contexts of TopNotch's community work, we've been invited as NPR radio guests and interviewed together for numerous feature articles. In fulfillment of my original goals and the demands of my graduate program, I translated our work into a thesis (later published as a book) filled with TopNotch's story and my own telling of the story of blues, spirituality, and social policy in the Mississippi Delta. TopNotch suggested that, as my slow-moving academic book project did little to contribute to the immediate need for national attention to the current wave of Delta rappers, we work together on a short documentary. With the help of Brian Graves, a graduate colleague in UNC's Media Department, and a limited grant budget, TopNotch and I co-directed a half-hour piece that was available for free streaming online (www.folkstreams.net) by the end of that summer. Our film double-premiered at my university and at the once-segregated little movie theater in TopNotch's hometown. Hip-hop fans, researchers, other artists, curious blues buffs, and family members alike packed both houses. For his part, TopNotch has translated our work into greater community recognition, a new album, and entrance into a four-year private college in hopes of developing new resources he can bring to his community leadership in the Delta.

My book project, presentations, and documentary are directed to different audiences, and each involves a different kind of collaboration and conversation. Much of this work was enriched and enabled by my status as a graduate student. My access to multimedia equipment and people who could teach me how to use it, my classes in ethnographic theory, the mentorship of professors who had done similar work and who could sympathize with the ups and downs of being so involved in a community of struggle, made this work possible. We might do well to begin an ethnographic project not with a definite idea of what form it will take, but instead with a critical survey of what our ethnographic representations might do. When I first started to interview blues musicians and frequent the juke joints of the Delta, I imagined that I would be able to use my journalistic practice to learn and teach about the persistence of domestic racism and poverty, and to publicize the work of Delta musicians to sustain and affirm life above this hardship. In the process, my consultants taught me that, by using my education improvisationally and imaginatively, I could contribute resources toward that change.

My ethnographic commitment requires more than dialogic work on the ground. In the course of my research, I must assure the people whose songs, biographies, and photos I collect that I will preserve these materials, reciprocate their efforts with CDs and prints of our work, and ultimately benefit the community through education and resources. In a process that began as a series of term papers and transcriptions, TopNotch, his Mississippi community, and I have worked together to shape new discourses on the importance of youth culture and musical creativity in the American South. We have found ways to weave together resources from "the field" and from the academy to help amplify the often marginalized voices of these musical practitioners. Our collaboration emerged from my circumstances as a researcher, the critical imaginations of my consultants, and our mutual desire to teach, learn, and create. The book, films, and presentations provide material documentation of Delta hip-hop as a viable, skillful, and life-affirming practice in conversation with traditional blues and gospel forms, and offer a platform by which artists can seek public grants, have access to community space, and claim expertise. This music's powerful depictions of economic hardship and rich portraits of family and friendship promise a broader listenership, allowing artists the chance to break stereotypes of their community and gain positive attention for their cultural work. For this reason, Jerome says, he chose the name of my book about his life and practice: *Let the World Listen Right: The Mississippi Delta Hip-Hop Story* (2008).

Representation: Bringing the Field and the Academy Together

We as engaged graduate scholars are often led to academic study by our life's work as artists, activists, or teachers (to name a few possibilities). Many of us set out to study communities in which we are already a part or with whom we identify. Ethnographers' necessarily thick engagements with the people with whom we work in "the field" entails blurry spatial, affective, temporal, disciplinary, and political boundaries; we find ourselves as not only participant-observers, but also interlocutors who "speak between" shifting and contingent cultural groups to whom we have an (often personal) commitment. Ethnography allows researchers to open up space for powerful new understandings and to materially work upon the distribution of resources (education, research interest, arts grants, poverty programs, medical research) to and within those communities. The possibilities to effect change and the ethical considerations involved in doing so are equally complex. This is why our generation of engaged graduate scholars, across academic disciplines, so often integrates ethnographic projects or components into our work: we realize the practice of ethnography as a space of possibility in which research and community work meet.

For all their intellectual, creative, and transformative promise, the commitments ethnography entails do not come easily. Ethnographic research involves a jarring series of movements between what has been traditionally called in the social sciences "the field" and the academy, where the raw materials of collection are ordered and processed. This kind of work requires a double life: engaged graduate ethnographers must represent (and be present in) the very real lives and communities of the people with whom we work, even while maintaining our full-to-the-brim academic loads and schedules. Our ethnographic consultants often invite us into their homes, their work and performance spaces, their families and their community lives, in order to share their knowledge and work with a greater public. We do our best to hold together two aspects of our lives that feel worlds apart: our ethnographic, community-based, improvisatory, engaged and/or public work in the field, and the linear timeline of graduate school, which pushes forever forward even as we wish to pause, to learn more, to undo and remake the things we thought we knew. The false dualities of this split between our selves-in-the-field and our selves-in-the-academy are sutured together by the powerful continuities we re-present in the books, films, presentations, and classes we create throughout our careers. But the fit, always challenging and full of possibility, is never perfect. We make strategic choices as we attempt to strike a balance between our commitments to our careers and to our consultants, and to do our best to articulate these objectives together.

From the shifting, uneven, and often cloudy space of possibility that is graduate education, those of us who maintain a sincere commitment to the communities whom we study form a community of our own. We, as engaged graduate scholars, strive to deconstruct, trouble, and reconfigure the structures of power upon which the academic world—and the complex of investments that intersect within it—rests. Our academic toolkits for this purpose are manifold: theories and methodologies, our individual talents and passions, public resources, computers and handheld recorders. We also call to our projects a series of emerging practices, poetries, and performances that resonate not only within the brick walls of the campus, but across and beyond them. In fact, even when we are ensconced in the officialdom of the academy, those boundaries can be transgressed by a single, muffled cell phone beep from our consultants in the field.

Graduate students are in a unique position to contribute to the contemporary movement toward ethnographic collaboration following the experimental work of the 1970s and '80s. Poetic, multimedia, filmic, performative, and dialogic ethnographic representations have become a site of creativity and possibility available to contemporary ethnographers. With our shoestring budgets and commitment to extensive time with our research, many of us find ourselves as I did in the Delta: immersed in the daily life of the community as a neighbor, friend, and confidante. Sometimes (as I often was) we are looked upon as the local documentarian who is expected to arrive at a performance recorder- or camera-ready, or as an interlocuting "expert" for official events and journalistic article. Often our roles in the community are chosen for us and reflect the resources we bring to the table, and we in this sense serve as we learn.

As emerging scholars, we are encouraged by our experienced mentors to think in new directions and to perform our work in creative complexity. We experiment with methodologies and theories in our fields and in our classrooms, embodying overlapping intellectual spheres of contestation and struggle, but also realms of possibility, movement, and change. We have the hindsight to trace the trajectories of established cultural representations, noting missteps and misinterpretations and celebrating work that has resulted in more positive attention, reform, or resources. As our mentors publish and present the research they enacted in earlier phases of their careers, we enact our deepest phases of fieldwork "on the ground." This is the space in which we will set courses for the research questions, themes, methodologies, and styles that will last throughout our careers.

We recognize the situatedness of our own knowledge and make legible the crucial work of community members who guide us through their cultural lives. As we experience the perspectives and contingencies of moving in, through, and with a group of people, we take note of the interlocuting voices and guiding hands of those who offer us a seat at their community table. There has been too much good work in critical ethnography for us to think of ourselves as omniscient and impartial researchers, or to maintain the illusion that we alone possess an enlightened insight, or to claim that the guides, friends, performances, community groups, and cultural practices that constitute our "field" freeze idly in time while we diagram the styles and structures of the problematic at hand. In the ethnographic register, we understand that these processes of change and learning are neither linear nor neatly bound; rather, they tangle together in a mutual bond between public, academy, researcher, and collaborating community that, even across the thin connections of the cellular phone or the paper trail of a stuffed field notebook, is never unraveled.

We recognize, further, that we do not always know best what to do with our work, or what it should look like, or where it should emerge. Upon our return to the academy, we struggle to articulate our research within the familiar sites of the classroom, the conference center, the publication venue. Even as we engaged scholars work across institutional boundaries, issues of difference and disciplinarity threaten to slash lines through our representations. In the critical space of good ethnographic work, the "researcher" and "researched" become intellectual partners, working together to build powerful creative relationships that surmount the walls of the academy to celebrate (and redirect resources to support) the educational importance of creative community life.

I did not enter my fieldwork knowing how to nurture a collaborative project. Rather, my consultants, friends, guides, and teachers in the Delta taught me how to perform engaged scholarship: relationships grounded in the mutually beneficial projects of teaching, learning, and understanding. Just as TopNotch insisted on making the film about the work of young Delta artists as a public intervention, the artists of the Delta have been telling me how my work might best benefit their community from my first days on the ground: the opportunity to have their lyrics heard by a wider audience and the visual representation of the poverty and creativity of their neighborhoods through the media of documentary film and new media publicity ; the use of project websites to deconstruct stereotypes of people of the Mississippi Delta; or the interpersonal collaboration that is good friendship. In this sense, ethnographic reciprocity—a concept traditionally framed in social sciences literature as "subject remuneration," or payment—means that we must account for the needs and interests of the researched community. This is not an endeavor that claims to charitably "give voice" to underrepresented communities. Rather, it removes the stifling centrality of the "expert" researcher and allows community members to shape the cultural conversation in collaboration with the researcher and a series of audiences. These collaborative practices also call into question the supremacy of academic expertise by demanding openness and vulnerability on the part of the researcher, labors normally reserved for the ethnographic "subject."

Collaboration and Conversation

We begin with the recognition that our best ethnographic work is instead a co-movement, an unfolding conversation, in which we work not as the Svengali who gives voice to the Other, but as a practitioner of critical cultural assemblage, who uses a series of tools and materials to craft representational works from a multitude of voices. These in turn invite further negotiation, questioning, new contributions, and critical rethinking. In this sense, ethnographic collection becomes a richer activity for all involved: no longer simply spoken about, our consultants in the field find space to speak back through our work. In her *Critical Ethnography*, Soyini Madison (2005) outlines the task of cultural representation as one of dialogue—of an open conversation between the researcher, the ethnographic Other, and the many groups of people who gather in the space of cultural interlocution. Drawing from the work of anthropologist, activist, and performer Dwight D. Conquergood, Madison finds that

> [d]ialogue resists conclusions. It is intensely committed to keeping the meanings between and the conversations with the researcher and the Other open and ongoing. It is a reciprocal giving and receiving rather than a timeless resolve. The dialogical stance is situated in multiple expressions that transgress, collide and embellish realms of meaning. (9)

In this sense, ethnography becomes an open-ended space for conversation, negotiation, and praxis as it comports itself toward transformation rather than static authoritative knowledge. Such methodologies are gaining traction in the humanities, the social sciences, and the arts as researchers move away from the fixity of the ethnographic monograph to engage the discourses that ethnographic writing, documentary, presentation, pedagogy, and multimedia activate. Emerging scholars are engaging new methodologies of research and representation in three performative registers:

In the "field"

While we enter our research sites according to our own research interests and backgrounds and choose the projects for which we are best equipped, we also recognize the act of framing—a research field, guiding questions, or potential collaborators—as full of political potential. The friends, contacts, leaders, practitioners, and guides who help us to become situated within our ethnographic fields orient us in new directions with our projects and reshape preconceived understandings of what is important to know about the community in question. We can trace these points of mutuality and contingency out in our work by keeping ourselves open to connections that we may not have recognized in our planning phases. This process is critical to the practice of embodied fieldwork, through which our research investigates the answers to our research questions, but is also open to those unpredictable moments in which those elements that lay beyond our frame become present to us. When we attend to those moments of unexpectedness, discomfort, challenge, and decentering, we find our richest ethnographic work.

As we move through the communities that are our "field sites" of research, critical ethnographers challenge the standard research performances that have troubled the history of cultural representation. We are critiquing the ethnographic dichotomy of the "knower" and "known" as depicted in the iconic photographic image of seminal ethnographer Bronislaw Malinowski writing in his tent while puzzled and curious Trobriand Islanders look on (Figure 19.1).

FIGURE 19.1. Bronislaw Malinowski in his tent, observed by Trobriand Islanders. Library of the London School of Economics and Political Science, Malinowski3/18/7. © London School of Economics and Political Science. Used with permission.

The fieldworker's tent itself is as an experiential filter, a constructed boundary between researcher and researched that is less likely to be transgressed by half-hearted gestures of participant observation than with active, vulnerable, radical methodologies. In this space, the ethnographer and the people with whom she works speak across difference to craft a moving partnership—a common project activated not in difference, but in confluence.

In the crafting of representation

As we gather and assemble documentary artifacts: field notes, photos, recordings, memories and sensations, ethnographers are challenged to put it all together in a sensible whole. As we use our representational media (writing, teaching, performance, interview) to trace the complex cultural maps that are our fields of study, we necessarily privilege some kinds of information and modes of knowledge over others. Critical ethnography challenges us to craft our representations both as "sense-making" articulations of bodies of cultural understanding and as an invitation to further dialogic complexity through a deconstruction of textual finality and authority. As ethnographic theorist James Clifford writes,

> [c]ultures do not hold still for their portraits. Attempts to make them do so always involve simplification and exclusion, selection of a temporal focus, the construction of a self-other relationship, and the imposition or negotiation of a power relationship. (Clifford and Marcus 1986, 10)

From co-presentation and conversational writing, we assemble legible bodies of work, including articles, books, films, stories, and curricula. As we frame our work, we also call attention to the contingencies, lapses, and complexities of the project at hand and open space for conversation, negotiation, and dialogue. What we sacrifice in terms of exclusive authoritaty, we gain in our ability to open up new, inclusive discourses in cultural representation.

Each aspect of our research calls up a series of literatures and contexts—archives, or bodies of understanding—through which we can assemble, interpret, and represent the project at hand. Many academic traditions work within a set of theories—often those produced within the academy itself—that help to explain and assemble ethnographic materials. Our richest work, however, also draws from what bell hooks calls "unconventional ways of knowing" (1990, 103), or the critical understandings generated in the spaces of community learning and discourse. These range from poetry and historical work done by community members to unpublished verbal texts in which cultural ideas are engaged: from sermons, conversations, songs, and performances to the deeply signified visual arts of communicative dance, gesture, and movement.[9] As we negotiate and arrange our field experiences according to our own academically honed theoretical stances, we also consider the local, unpublished, performative or hidden ways our consultants understand the world and the project at hand.

In the performative extension of our representations

Critical theoretical turns in performance, representation, and context allow us to question the wholeness of cultural representations. We no longer conceive of our work as a single, static academic product or publication, but as a performance that, like the cultures we represent, is always in motion through presentation, performance, and dialogue.[10] It is important that we perform our work in a way that opens it up to a wider series of publics. Although our position in the academy means that our first obligation is to publish academic work, we might also think about subsequent, ongoing projects that are accessible to the extra-academic communities with whom we work, as well as to students, museumgoers, Web surfers, lawmakers, community leaders, and more. A book might have a companion documentary and curriculum guide for grade-schoolers, or a deeply nuanced theoretical investigation might be paired with a website through which the collected materials are made accessible to the broader public.[11] This multiplicity of representation mirrors the complexities both of culture itself and of the publics involved, directly or otherwise, in our work.

Conquergood (2002) suggests that ethnographic research holds the potential to flip the scripts of power, difference, and social inequality by recognizing its own poetic possibilities and inherent performativity. This ethnographic kinesis works not by rethinking pre-existing notions of social relations and modes of representation, but by using performance to move radically between worlds in partnership with our communities of research, shaking the foundations of a social status quo that would separate a (thinking) academic life from a (working or doing) extra-academic one. He calls these destratifying performances "interventions," and they take the form of radical ethnographic/activist projects, including polyvocal writing styles, activist multimedia work, educational theatre, deconstructed documentaries, and longstanding commitments to social change. These also often entail longstanding engagements with the people and communities with whom we work; eight years after my first days in the field, I continue to celebrate with TopNotch as we receive our very modest book royalties (we split the profits 50/50) and make yearly rounds to visit his other friends from the field. We continue to seek out opportunities for him to visit my classes at the university and perform. He checks in for news of what music I'm listening to or to ask about my friends and family. As ethnographers, our academic commitments and research interests lead us to new phases, projects, and fields. Our ethnographic projects continue to shape our future work and to unfold in the lives of those with whom we have worked.

Transformation

Like our hectic morning rituals, we negotiate a graduate school gamut (classes, learning to teach, exams, research, dissertation) that requires a kind of momentum to keep us from toppling as we work progressively through lists of academic requirements and duties. Those of us whose research is motivated by personal values and interests find the strength to move forward in our passion for our work, which wavers but does not wane even as it drags through stacks of white printer paper, or as it pushes far beyond the edges of the documents we display proudly on our desks or bathroom walls. As critical students of culture, we are challenged to remain acutely aware of what cultural representations—and the practices that their craft entails—*do*. They work as a medium for us to manage complex socioeconomic ideas and give traction to the narratives we weave into academic and public discourse. At our best, we find in our work rich threads that rejoin the conversations that have been torn in the separation between the academic world and its peripheral Others, and we weave together the dualities that circumscribe the potential of this work and pull us in conflicting directions. In the process, we work to create a richer and more tangible intellectual fabric of transformation.

Through an increasingly open and organized critical dialogue surrounding what scholarship can *do*, engaged graduate students are committed the larger project of working beyond documentation and analysis to transform their worlds—both in the academy and "the field." Critical to this effort is a willingness to decenter our own ideological authority, and to recognize our shifting and incomprehensibly complex investments in the utopian academic project as only part of our ethnographic potential. While we go about filling in the blanks left by the projects of our predecessors, we also activate emergent representations that allow for richer dialogue across the lines that artificially divide academy from community. We strategically move the centrality of our authority aside (as TopNotch asked me to do) so that our consultants can also be heard in the spaces of their generative power, and speak for themselves in radically creative arenas, rather than relying on the illusory generosity of our "empowerment." These conversations might also take place across disciplinary lines and boundaries that separate the academy from its "others." We ask ourselves how we might rise to the ethnographic occasion through public presentation, performance, and multimedia work that, ultimately, will not only benefit ourselves, the academy, and the communities in which we choose to work, but will also contribute to the larger projects of social equality and structural change.

As graduate students, we must maintain a certain forward focus in order to locate and complete each step toward our degrees. But when we also allow our movements to expand outward and mix radically with the trajectories of our consultants, we engage in a co-movement toward complexity and fullness rather than a lonely forward trajectory. There is no ready-made path, no carved-out space for this kind of work: it requires ear-bending, boundary-pushing, and the deterritorialization of zones of knowledge and power. This often means that we must piece together funding from handfuls of sources rather than carry out a prefabricated research model or paradigm. We might just have to get back into—or leave—the sites of research that complicate our plans of study when we least expect it, moving into new possibilities and brandishing ethnographic innovation as our brightest tool.

As I write this essay, a recording of Robert Belfour, one of the blues musicians who shared his wit and wisdom with me in the course of my research in the Delta, happens to be playing on the coffee-shop speakers, reminding me again that the intersections between my work and the lives of my friends a thousand miles away in "the field" are always more complex than I can ever understand. We are connected, not by degrees and genres and taxonomies of separation, but by lines of possibility. As engaged graduate scholars, we are committed to letting these moments, these unexpected harmonizations and dissonances, resonate through our work.

Notes

1. My thanks to the editors of this volume for shaping this piece into a fuller study. Thanks also to William Ferris, Mark Anthony Neal, and James Peacock for guiding me through my work in the Delta as thesis committee members and mentors, and to Jerome "TopNotch the Villain" Williams and the communities of the Mississippi Delta for their invaluable contributions.

2. Formative texts for me included Hurston's *Mules and Men* (1998) and Cantwell's *When We Were Good* (1997).

3. See Conquergood (2002) for a contemporary exploration of this movement, and the work of José Limon (1994), Barbara Kirshenblatt-

Gimblett (Kirshenblatt-Gimblett and Kirshenblatt 2007), and Kathleen Stewart (1996) for examples of ethnographers who have followed the work of the Boasnian school in engaging the methodology as an activist medium connecting minority communities and greater publics.

4. For instance, the work of academic ethnographers in the African American communities of the Delta and other regions of the American South have contributed to both successful literacy programs and unsuccessful social services projects, as represented by the Moynihan Report (1965). The success of these programs often depends on the register, length, and critical nature of the ethnographers' involvement in their communities of research.

5. In my department (Communication Studies) at the University of North Carolina, Professor Della Pollock's ethnographic/activist performance work and Dr. Patricia Parker's fusion of organizational analysis with ethnographic intervention manifest this interdisciplinary conversation in work with communities surrounding the Chapel Hill campus; see Parker, Oceguera, and Sánchez (2011). For an excellent example of aesthetically inventive ethnographic representation, see Taussig (1992).

6. An early pioneer in native anthropology, Jomo Kenyatta supplanted colonial anthropology in performing ethnographic work in his own Kikuyu community in Kenya, beginning with his 1938 *Facing Mount Kenya*, and Barbara Kirschenblatt-Gimblett draws from her own heritage as the daughter of Jewish immigrants in her ongoing, performance-centered work with immigrants in New York, including interviews with her parents and work in her own neighborhood (co-authoring a book with her immigrant father, Mayer Kirshenblatt).

7. The experiences of college students involved in the civil rights movement, for instance, overwrote previous anthropological depictions of Southern African American communities as pathologically unable to function in a contemporary context, and demonstrated that when given the opportunity and resources to transform their communities peacefully, even the poorest of such communities were instead pedagogically active, politically engaged, and overwhelmingly willing to work to improve community infrastructures.

8. Thanks to the generosity of UNC's interdisciplinary Center for the Study of the American South and the work of Barbara Call and Ayse Erginer.

9. The dramatic works of Bertolt Brecht and the theatre interventions of the late Dwight Conquergood and his student Soyini Madison at Northwestern University's Department of Performance Studies offer critical examples.

10. Techniques for dialectic ethnographic research include the

presentation of one's work in the community of research, invited feedback, collaborative performance, research community roundtables, and making recorded interviews available to consultants for the sake of further critical conversation and revision.

11. The ever-emerging multimedia projects of Steven Feld and Aaron Fox, formerly affiliated with the University of Texas at Austin, are germinal in this regard. My emerging website on musical ethnography (www.ethnolyrical.org) follows the representational creativity of that anthropological/folkloristic research school.

References

Cantwell, Robert. 1997. *When we were good: The folk revival.* Cambridge, MA: Harvard University Press.

Clifford, James E., and George E. Marcus, eds. 1986. *Writing culture: The poetics and politics of ethnography*. Berkeley and Los Angeles: University of California Press.

Conquergood, Dwight. 2002. Performance studies: Interventions and radical research. *The Drama Review* 46 (2): 145–156.

Ferris, William R. 1998. *Blues from the Delta*. New York: Da Capo Press.

hooks, bell. 1990. An aesthetic of Blackness: Strange and oppositional. In *Yearning: Race, gender, and cultural politics*. Boston: South End Press.

Hurston, Zora Neale. 1998. *Mules and men*. 1935. Reprint, New York: Harper Perennial.

Kenyatta, Jomo. 1962. *Facing Mount Kenya*. New York: Vintage.

Kirshenblatt-Gimblett, Barbara and Mayer Kirshenblatt. 2007. *They called me Mayer July: Painted memories of a Jewish childhood in Poland before the Holocaust*. Berkeley and Los Angeles: University of California Press.

Limón, José. 1994. *Dancing with the devil: Society and cultural poetics in Mexican-American South Texas.* Madison, WI: University of Wisconsin Press.

Madison, Soyini. 2005. *Critical ethnography: Method, ethics, and performance.* Thousand Oaks, CA: Sage.

Moynihan, Daniel Patrick, et al. 1965. *The Negro family: The case for national action* [The Moynihan Report]. Washington, DC: U.S. Department of Labor, Office of Policy Planning and Research.

Neff, Ali Colleen. 2008. *Let the world listen right: The Mississippi Delta hip-hop story*. Jackson: University Press of Mississippi.

Parker, Patricia S., Elisa Oceguera, and Joaquín Sánchez, Jr.,

2011. Intersecting differences: Organizing (ourselves) for social justice research with people in vulnerable communities. In *Reframing difference in organizational communication studies: Research, pedagogy, practice,* edited by Dennis K. Mumby. Thousand Oaks, CA: Sage.

Stewart, Kathleen. 1996. *A space on the side of the road*. Princeton, NJ: Princeton University Press.

Taussig, Michael. 1992. *Mimesis and alterity: A particular theory of the senses.* New York: Routledge.

20

Reality Is Stranger than Fiction: The Politics of Race and Belonging in Los Angeles, California

Damien M. Schnyder

I COMPLETED the first year of the Ph.D. program in anthropology at the University of Texas with the confidence of Muhammad Ali following his defeat of Sonny Liston. I was not only equipped to the hilt with Karl Marx, Edmund Leach, Claude Lévi-Strauss, and Franz Boas, but I also had had a serious introduction to the likes of Cedric Robinson, Patricia Hill Collins, Faye Harrison, and Robin D. G. Kelley. It was now the summer, and I headed back to Los Angeles to conduct anthropological research on the so-called tension between African Americans and Latinos in my own backyard. Yet, when I was finally settled after my two-and-a-half-hour flight into LAX, having stopped by relatives' homes to say my obligatory hellos and got down in the "field," there I was again: it was the first day of school.

After a short two-year stint on 75th Street and San Pedro Avenue in South Central Los Angeles, my parents had moved our family ten minutes down the 110 Freeway to the city of Carson. Now, I hesitate to call Carson a suburb of Los Angeles, because the urban sprawl design of Los Angeles and Los Angeles County makes for a hard distinction between city and suburb, and more importantly the word suburb has come to imply some aloof periphery distant from the "city." However, Carson, which is snuggled right in between Compton and Long Beach, does not possess any of those aloof characteristics of a distant utopian oasis. As a matter of fact, Carson is built upon a huge oil wasteland that provided the economic and political basis for some of Los Angeles's premier power brokers. Sitting on a foundation of toxic landfills, and serving as refinery capital of the world to petroleum giants like BP/ARCO and Shell, Carson offered cheap single-family housing to many of the Black civil rights babies and skilled defense industry workers who were looking for a slice of the American pie during the 1970s and early '80s.

From my childhood until my late adolescence, my father and mother would pack my sister and me into the car to traverse the short distance up the Harbor Freeway to make our ritual weekend trips to see our grandparents, aunts, and multitude of cousins in South Central. As I grew older, I began to loathe these trips, for the handgun and rifle shells found in the front yard of my grandparents' house were indicators to them that we should be in before dusk. It would be years before I found out that the outburst in violence was due in large part to the introduction of crack cocaine to the streets of Los Angeles by the CIA and LA Police Department, coupled with mysterious train cars filled with military assault rifles left unattended on railroads adjacent to housing projects in Watts (Holland 1994).

The late '80s and early '90s brought significant change in my life. When I entered middle school in Long Beach, I was introduced to local street organizations in a very visceral manner. There had always been banter about the Grape Street Crips or the Bloods in the Scottsdale housing projects in Carson, but it was in sixth grade that these organizations became more than a myth. The Rollin' 20 Crips, the West Side Longos, and the Islanders were no longer just iconic names; there were now faces behind them. Unlike the invincible army of "deviant youth" I had imagined, the Longos ate processed chicken strips with me in the cafeteria, and I waged verbal confrontations on the basketball court with members of the Rollin' 20s.

When I entered high school, I realized that the terms of the debate had changed drastically again. My high school pushed a mantra of "Each One, Teach One," as a means to deal with what was described as rampant violence in the school and immediate neighborhood. I am pretty sure that this was fueled by the public relations disaster that accompanied a *Newsweek* cover story on "gang violence" in Long Beach, on my school in particular, and on the general problems of racialized urban youth run amuck (Leland and Holmes 1993). Rather than address the issue through an interrogation of race, class, and gender, the school pushed a multicultural paradigm wherein the perceived problem was to be solved through dance celebrations and buffet-style ethnic lunches, all mitigated by the increased presence of the police.

These experiences growing up informed my decision to undertake a summer research project to analyze race and class in Los Angeles County. It was time to put to use the academic training that I had received in my one year at Austin. As a member of the African Diaspora cohort (a specialization within the Anthropology Department), I learned that theory does not come from the top and seep down. Rather, theoretical postulations within the social sciences have to be derived from the people who live within the social conditions being studied. Thus, as ethnographers, it was our job not merely to study the people on the ground. We had to work with people in their daily struggles in order to comprehend the complexity with which race, class, gender, and sexuality operated within particular geographic sites. It was with this academic backing that I re-entered my city of birth and attempted to see past the media's smoke-and-mirrors racialized portrayal of Black and Brown youth engaged in urban warfare.

Race in the Melting Pot

> Racism is the state-sanctioned and/or extra-legal production and exploitation of group-differentiated vulnerabilities to premature death, in distinct yet densely interconnected political geographies.
>
> —Ruth Wilson Gilmore, "Race and Globalization"

I merged onto the 110 Freeway and made my way north to South Central Los Angeles. It is incredible what city and state officials have done through the marvels of freeway construction to temper the urban scenery that outlines Compton and South Central. As the Harbor Freeway twists through East Compton, it is impossible for the millions of commuters and tourists to even see what is above and beside them. Like a trench, the freeway burrows through Compton, and right at the Century Freeway junction it magically ascends above South Central to give the commuter a glorious, smog-ridden view of downtown Los Angeles. Now on a beeline towards downtown, there is a noticeable difference from the many miles of freeway that stretch through Orange County, West Los Angeles, and the San Fernando Valley. There are no signs that read "Library Next Right" or "Museum 2 Miles, Next Exit." Instead, only residents of South Central recognize the posted destinations of Century, Gage, Florence, Manchester, and Slauson, which have no significance to the millions of commuters on their way to anywhere but there.

I turn left onto Slauson Avenue and make my way down Figueroa. I know that I can take Slauson down to Crenshaw, but I also know that too many times down Slauson and your car will need a new alignment. So I take a shortcut and follow Figueroa north to 54th Street and shoot west toward Crenshaw. The South Central that I see now is vastly different from the one I knew as a child. The street, laden with imported palm trees, is occupied by several "mom and pop" mechanic shops and convenience stores. However, gone are the Southern Black faces that used to operate them. It is foot-trafficked primarily by Latino immigrants, especially from Mexico, El Salvador and Guatemala. Although there are sprinkles of Blackness in the area, there has been a drastic demographic change since my grandparents first migrated to Los Angeles from Louisiana and Texas over fifty years ago.[1]

My arrival in Los Angeles coincided with an event considered a marker of the racial shift there. The residents of Los Angeles had elected their first Latino mayor, the Mexican American Antonio Villaraigosa. Mayor Villaraigosa's tenure was off to a rocky start. *The Los Angeles Times* ran a front-page story about the release of Mexico's new stamp featuring the comic-book character Memín Pinguín, depicted in racialized terms as a dark-skinned, big-lipped, wide-eyed monkey (Kraul and Johnson 2005). On July 10, 2005, shortly after the article ran, Los Angeles police fatally shot Nicaraguan toddler Suzie Peña and her father Jose Raul Peña, following a standoff in which the elder Peña allegedly used his daughter as a shield (Pelisek 2005).

Villaraigosa was initially mute about the stamp. Rather than discuss the racial politics involved, he deflected any questions about the stamp onto the Mexican government. In contrast, he was very quick to act upon the death of Suzie Peña, attempting to please both his liberal supporters and LA's conservative political establishment. Immediately following Peña's death, the LAPD, under the direction of Chief William Bratton, issued the kind of routine statement that usually follows when the LAPD kills Black or Brown folks. On a typical sunny Southern California afternoon, he stood outside, stern and focused before the flashing bulbs of a sensationalistic media. Chief Bratton implored the citizens of Los Angeles to stay calm and allow the process of an internal investigation to run its course. Befitting his proximity to Hollywood, Villaraigosa offered his own statement the next evening, during a highly staged and rehearsed press conference. In a somber suit matching the deep earth tones of the mayor's formal press room, Villaraigosa expressed sadness at the loss of young life but urged the citizens of Los Angeles to allow the internal investigation to turn the wheels of justice (Associated Press 2005; Muhammad 2005).

Having pleased the conservatives, he had to address the concerns of his liberal supporters. On a bright clear morning in front of the palm-tree-encircled pond that highlights the docile beauty of MacArthur Park, the television cameras stood in place. Here Villaraigosa introduced the members of the committee he had named to investigate the events that led to the Peñas' death. The politically savvy Villaraigosa appointed to the committee high-profile members of the African American and Latino community, such as past Urban League president John Mack and former federal prosecutor Anthony Pacheco. In a quiet but still effective move, he attended the Peña funeral to show support for the bereaved family.

While some members of the Black community where pleased by his support of the Peña family and his selection of Mack for the committee, many within the activist community read the mayor's actions in a different light. Rather than view the stamp and the police shooting as different incidents, activists saw the two issues as complimentary acts of violence, manifestations of a complex set of racial and economic factors at the root of the racial tension between African Americans and Mexicans. To many Black activists, Villaraigosa's silence about the stamp indicated his true position on the issue of racial and economic inequality.

On an unusually hot afternoon, I sat adjacent to Malcolm Rapp at the headquarters for the Coalition Against Police Abuse (CAPA). A well-informed young African American man of my own "high yellow" skin complexion, Rapp was a long-term member both of CAPA and of the Bloods. In the neighborhood, he was seen primarily as an activist rather than a menace (as the Bloods are portrayed by both news and entertainment media). We folded and placed stamps on CAPA's August newsletter, battling the heat with the assistance of a long-since-worn-out floor fan that would shut off after 15 minutes and restart of its own volition. Rapp insightfully detailed his concern with Villaraigosa's lack of racial sensitivity in regards to the Mexican stamp.

> Look at the stamps, has he [Villaraigosa] said anything about the stamps, the stamps that ... are degrading to our people, to our ancestors, that are a form of degradation, that are demeaning to us, that ridicule us, that exaggerate our features...? Come on, man, what do you think would happen if a Black country put out some stamps like that about white people ... He's [Villaraigosa] gotta make up his mind who his allegiance is with. He should have been like, "You know what, we're going to have to boycott all of their products." Or speak about it at least, put it out on the table 'cause I think that all the products that come from Mexico should be banned and boycotted and an apology ain't enough for me, 'cause the damage has been done you can't unring a bell. I like to see you try; once it's been rung, it's been rung. You can't unsing a song. So what he needs to do, that president needs to set aside some money for reparations 'cause those stamps go all over the world. It perpetuates the myths about us; it furthers the system of white supremacy, which is used to dehumanize us. And once people are dehumanized then it's easier to commit crimes against them because you don't see them as being equal to you if you're a human and they are less than human. (Rapp 2005)

Central to Rapp's critique of Villaraigosa is an examination of the nature of politics within a racial capitalist state (Robinson 1983). Just as Manning Marable argues that once a "Black politician accepts the legitimacy of the State ... his/her critical faculties are destroyed permanently, and all that follows are absurdities" (Marable 1999, 171), Rapp argues that Villaraigosa's apparent lack of a stance in fact has serious political implications. His silence reinforces the status quo and legitimates a global racial hierarchy that utilizes historic archetypes to maintain power.

Rapp's claims about the dehumanization of Black people are elucidated by an analysis of the treatment of race within Mexico. In an official statement released by the Mexican postal service, director Gustavo Islas stated, "Whoever sees the character as something offensive is looking at things completely wrongly." He insisted that Memín Pinguín was "a beautiful personage with no importance given to color" (Kraul and Johnson 2005). This reinforces Mexican racial politics, in which voices of power assert that class, not race, dictates social, economic, and political outcomes. However, careful examination of Mexico reveals a society fraught with racial motivations. According to newspaper columnist Guadalupe Loaeza, "The color of your skin is a key that either opens of shuts doors. The lighter your skin, the more doors open to you." Likewise, José Luis Guitérrez Espíndola of the National Council to Prevent Discrimination claims that Blacks in Mexico "don't feel integrated into the country," as evidenced by their marginal economic, educational, and social standing (qtd. in Kraul and Johnson 2005).

Memín Pinguín resembles the Sambo and Tambo characters of American minstrelsy. All are products of racial projects that are dictated by the particular social, economic, gender, and political history of specific nation-states. Rapp articulated that the constant reinforcement of white supremacy serves to further dehumanize those defined as Other. With an understanding of the historic racist systems in Los Angeles and Mexico, the connection between the shooting death of Suzie Peña and the distribution of the Mexican stamp becomes clear. As Rapp later explained to me in our conversation, it was quite easy for African Americans and Latinos to rally around issues of police abuse, because the two communities have a common experience of being defined as less than human under a social system of white supremacy. In a white supremacist state that does not believe that African Americans or Latinos are human, it is justifiable to unload over 300 rounds of ammunition at a Latino man and his 19-month-old daughter. The police did not heed the pleas of José Peña's wife, who stressed to the police that her husband battled with psychological trauma. Nor did they obey the code of a hostage situation, which states that the use of force is the last option after all possible negotiation efforts have failed.[2] Witnesses testified instead that the area near 104th Street and Avalon Boulevard in Watts, where the shooting occurred, sounded like a war zone, with members of the LAPD's SWAT unit blockading the area. Only through a dehumanization process can such actions become normalized and Chief Bratton's claim that the younger Peña's life was taken while officers "engaged in their lawful duty" become an acceptable response to the loss of life (Garvey and Leovy 2005).

Rather than a static conception of race, Rapp's analysis elucidates the fluidity of racist systems across borders within a global racial economy. His position is further reinforced by the commentary offered by then Mexican president Vicente Fox, who claimed that Mexican migrants in the United States do jobs "that even blacks do not want to do" (Kraul and Johnson 2005). Fox's interpellation of Black people reinforces their subterranean position within the global racial capitalist hierarchy, while at the same time maintaining white supremacy through his normalization of Black labor in a static position of subjugation. As played out on the streets of Los Angeles, Mexican and Central American migrant workers are forced to live in substandard housing conditions due to the extremely low wages that they receive. They are denied health benefits and lack job security. Black workers in Los Angeles have a recent history of receiving union-based wages, and they justifiably will not accept subpar wages in order to live in subpar living conditions. Unquestioned in the official international dialogues of state is the resulting increased profit margin for majority-white-governed corporate bodies, reaping which reap the benefits of white supremacy's twisted logic.

One must understand Los Angeles as a major economic force within a global racial paradigm to fully understand Rapp's demand that Villaraigosa to "choose his allegiance"; Rapp is critiquing politicians who choose to work within the racial confines outlined by a modern capitalist framework, echoing Marable's claim that as long as Black politicians operate within the sphere of capitalism, they will always be the pawn of white supremacist ideology. These institutional limits are in fact "boundaries of Blackness" that dehumanize Blacks and reinforce white supremacy.

Just as Rapp describes race as a fluid entity, Howard Winant argues that "race must be grasped as a fundamental condition of individual and collective identity, a permanent, although tremendously flexible, dimension of the modern global social structure" (Winant 2002, 3). Both Rapp and Winant postulate the flexibility of race; missing this crucial intervention prevents a comprehensive analysis of racial formations throughout the world. Specifically within Latin America, the issue of race is a taboo subject that inspires fervent reaction. Race is often discussed as an issue that only affects the United States, as reflected in the historical legacy of the civil rights era and the Black Power movement. In Mexico, a racial analysis is complicated by the remarks of prominent Black Mexicans, who claim that racism does not exist. Black Mexican singer Johnny Laboriel stated in an interview, "I was born in Mexico, and I have never been discriminated against because of my color. They discriminate more because of one's economic standing" (Samuels 2005).

In Mexico, unlike the United States, there has not been a well-documented struggle over civil and human rights (i.e. constitutional evidence) pertaining to Black liberation, and as a consequence it is claimed that anti-Black racism does not exist. Yet further examination proves the contrary; in fact, race permeates so deeply within the fabric of the Mexican collective memory so deeply that a complete normalization of Black subjugation has occurred. Despite the fact that hundreds of thousands of African slaves were brought to Mexico, the narrative of the nation-state has had a strict, narrow focus upon the European and Indigenous cultures that produced the *mestizaje* blend that currently populates Mexico. Mexico's census bureau, the National Institute of Geography and Statistics, keeps no records on the existence of Black Mexicans (Samuels 2005). The political, economic, and social contributions of Blacks to Mexican society have been omitted from the vast majority of Mexican history textbooks. On the popular culture front, the face of the Mexican television and cinema is white. According to self-identified mestizo actor Bernardo Hernandez, "The degree to which this country adores fair skin and blondes is amazing" (qtd. in Samuels 2005). Outside of strictly subservient roles such as a domestic workers or servants, representations of Black Mexicans do not exist.

Only through the effort of the *tercera raiz* ("third root"), a government-sponsored program initiated under the Fox administration to study and bring attention to Blacks in Mexico, has their plight been brought into the national dialogue.[3] Yet the narrative of *mestizaje* still dominates the collective consciousness of Mexico. In the city of Cuanjinicuilapa in Costa Chica, populated by an estimated 500,000 Black Mexicans, the former mayor Gilberto Garcia, an elderly gentleman of dark complexion, stated, "Now there is no discrimination.... [P]reviously there was a lot of discrimination. Little by little it has changed, and now there's more respect between the races" (qtd. in Samuels 2005). Further examination reveals that Garcia's articulation of "respect between the races" is in fact a reinforcement of the *mestizaje* narrative that devalues/deplores Blackness while promoting the whitening process. Questioned about racial intermarriage, Garcia very frankly stated, "Pure black blood is lazy; I think that pure blacks, they compare with animals."

Garcia's statement highlights the inherent white supremacism that is often not addressed in discussions regarding Mexico's narrative of *mestizaje*. Garcia's claim that discrimination has dissipated is directly correlated with the belief that as Blackness disappears through the process of intermarriage the problems of discrimination will also disappear. His attribution of laziness to "black blood" is a local articulation of a global racial stereotype that correlates skin color with aptitude and morality. Further, the pervasive trope of Blackness as animalistic was used to justify such historical acts as the categorization of African slaves as chattel labor for hundreds of years.

The local racial formation processes in Mexico plays a significant role in the development of racial projects in the United States. I assert that the frequently tense interactions between Black Americans and Mexican Americans are not only tied to issues of economic empowerment, but are also fraught with racism originating outside the United States. The incorporation of local Mexican racial ideologies into another social context that has historically displayed open racism (re)produces notions of white supremacy and Black degradation. This claim is supported by my ethnographic research, which reveals that, in addition to racialized interactions with African Americans, there is an active awareness of the significance of skin color within Mexican American group identity formation. This awareness is intensified in encounters with African Americans. In attempting to place distance between a Mexican American identity and an African American identity, this racist posturing reinforces white supremacy.

Pushing Black

My first encounter with Hector Chavez caught me off guard. My sister, who put me in contact with him, told me that he was a young Mexican American student-activist who was instrumental in trying to assist Mexican, Mexican American, and Black American high school students in Inglewood during a time of grave racial tensions. I was caught off guard because despite all of my theoretical coursework, instruction from professors, and discussions with activists, my own ingrained racial consciousness still connected "Mexican" with phenotypically light skin. As a result, I had to quickly readjust my racial sensibility upon meeting Hector. His complexion a shade lighter than mine when I have not seen the sun in a few weeks, Hector had a closely shaved head, was physically fit, and walked with a self-assured glide. As I walked to our agreed-upon meeting place, I thought, for just a second, that Hector was Black and that I had the approached the wrong person. I was in for some additional education.

Hector explained to me the complexities of race within his predominately Mexican community and how those changed as he navigated through culturally diverse spaces.

> The place where I stayed at [Southeast Los Angeles County] is Latino and I'd say majority Mexican.... [The way] we view phenotype is completely different. By Black standards I'm not dark at all, but back at home, I am considered a darker shade. That has to do with the history of Mexico and how indigenous people are viewed as having a darker complexion and different phenotypical features ... how they were racialized in society and how they were treated in society. And so coming out here [West Los Angeles], when we talk about a Black and white paradigm, I'm kind of in the middle. (Chavez 2005)

Hector analyzes the racialization projects in his community as manifestations of the racial formation process within Mexican society. Hectors acknowledges the historical legacy of race in Mexico and how that legacy is marked in the consciousness of Mexican Americans. Hector's analysis of race emphasizes the normalization of whiteness within Mexican identity formation. He explains that within his predominantly Mexican community he is seen as having as dark skin. Hector's insight draws the conclusion that within predominantly Mexican communities in the United States, the smallest deviation from a white norm marks one as racially "Other."

The effect of this active racial consciousness within Mexican identity formation in the United States is to strengthen notions of white supremacy. Hector told me of the common practices that Latino communities employ in an effort to attain white status: "It's easier for these communities to be assimilated into mainstream America and pass off for being white because there is a lot of Latinos who can pass off into the white community due to a loss of accent or what not." The process of assimilation that Hector refers to, while a move toward whiteness, is also critically a move away from Blackness. The historical negative/positive racial binary formation between Black and white has developed a racial structure by which any negative attributes or behaviors, such as "nonstandard" grammatical structure, laziness, and criminality, are associated with Blackness, whereas the direct converse holds for white. As a consequence, any attempt to "improve" lexicon, grammatical structures, or dialect to "standard" is viewed as a move toward whiteness. However, in order to fully complete the transition all traits of phenotypical Blackness must be deleted.

Perhaps nowhere else is the interaction between local Mexican racial identity formation and racial formation processes in the United

States better exemplified than within the California prison system. Although African Americans represent less than 7% of California's state population, they constitute over 28% of its male prison population and an estimated 32% of Black men born in Los Angeles will be incarcerated (Human Rights Watch 2003; Rivera 2005).[4] As explained to me by a Los Angeles County Sheriff's Department officer, the male prison population is broken down into three strict categories: Blacks, Mexicans, and whites. These categories represent life and death within prison, in the sense that they represent individual protection from other racial groups. As a result, California's prison population is a perfect testing ground to analyze the effects of racial formation. Malcolm Rapp, who has experienced the rigors of California's prison industrial complex, explained the manner in which racial politics unfold on a daily level:

> Inside jail … the Hispanic gang members will not even allow [a Hispanic] to smoke a cigarette behind a Black dude, so if me and you in jail and we cellies and we cool and you smoke a cigarette after I hit it, and the others Hispanics find out, they will beat your ass. And you will have to roll it up and go to another tier or another cell block, 'cause they don't want that. Which is a form of racism, you know, and degradation. (Rapp 2005)

From an insider perspective, the racial politics of California's prison industrial complex are dictated by white supremacy. Many of California's prisons promote racial segregation as an active form of control. Through this lens it is understood that the racial formation process in the California prison industrial complex is not merely an aberration or an extreme form of Foucaldian control, but rather an example of a racial structure that needs a racial hierarchy to maintain white supremacy.

As I was told by an older African American Angelino who had also faced California's prison industrial complex, this politics, as it is called on the prison yard, is easily integrated onto the streets of Los Angeles. The incorporation of "politics" into the racial social structure of Los Angeles parallels the racial formation processes that continue to define the power dynamics of the city. As a result, white supremacist ideology fuels the deadly tension between African Americans and Mexicans in Los Angeles.

The race-based tension within California's prison system and on the streets of Los Angeles is not purely a form of hate against African Americans as a racial group; rather, the logic behind the actions of Latino and white prisoners derives from an anti-Black ideology. As the conversation between Rapp and me proceeded, he explained the process by which dark-skinned Latinos must "prove" themselves.

> In jail, especially if he's in a gang, to prove his allegiance to other Hispanics he has be the first one out to attack other Blacks, to verbally use the word *maits,* which means little black bug or nigger, or *niggrito,* you know stuff like, to just keep showing that he doesn't associate with Blacks, he doesn't identify with blacks, you know. You know that's when you have the term *blacksikins,* or most people prefer the term "traitor to race" – you know, a disgrace to the race, "race traitor." You know it's sad, because when a Hispanic person joins a Black gang we don't make him stop saying that he's Hispanic, we don't make [him] change his name and stop speaking Spanish and send him out to go assassinate or assault other Hispanics, you know what I mean. But that's what happens when a Black person joins a Hispanic gang. You know it's crazy, by the time a lot of them see what they're doing, you know, they come to realize that [they] got so much self-hate inside of them 'cause of what they done, that they wind up self-loathing. They wind up turning to a world of drugs and suicidal thoughts start going through their head, just a whole circle of self-destructive actions. And it's really a shame because a lot of people have wasted so much of their energy and time on racism.

Rapp's articulation of the racial politics between African Americans and Mexicans is a reflection of a social structure dominated by white supremacy. However, the inner dynamics of such processes are far too often displaced by a crude representation of "Black-on-Brown violence." Yet Rapp and Hector both argued that a deeper analysis of race has to occur. Once this became clear, I immediately reflected on conversations that I had with my colleagues and professors in Texas about the issues of race throughout the African Diaspora.

The Politics of Race

Racial imperialism was a term that I heard thrown around quite a bit during my first year at the University of Texas at Austin. The basic premise was that Black American scholars were being charged with going into "nonracialized" spaces and constructing a false paradigm of racial subjugation. The issue became very contested during an ongoing debate between American political scientist Michael Hanchard and European-born social theorists Pierre Bourdieu and Loïc Wacquant over race in Brazil.[5] During our class seminars and reading through the classic anthropological texts, it became quite evident that the issue of race was pushed to the extreme margins in anthropology. However, the irony was that race was always present in the form of the anthropologist's racialized narrative of "Other" communities. Counter to the approach of the expert anthropologist in the field, we were being trained in a different manner.

Specifically, we posited that patterns of racialization occurred throughout the world, with variations according to locale. Given this orientation, my attempt to understand the position of Black people in Mexico and Central America was severely limited by the fact that race in the anthropological imagination, with regard to these regions, negated the experience of Black people. As a budding Black anthropologist, I risked being labeled a racial imperialist for bringing to attention the subjugation of Blacks in Mexico. However, it was quite evident from my conversations with both Hector and Rapp that in fact a long history of anti-Black racism has been central to the development of Mexican identity formation. It was also evident that the struggle to undo these practices has a long history, yet the stories of people who have fought for liberation have been ignored. Thus, as in a moment of clarity, I understood the significance of my training in the African Diaspora program.

Rather than undertaking formal exercises in ethnographic methods, exploring cultural formations, or analyzing kinship ties, we were being trained to work on behalf of those whose voices had continued to be marginalized. We understood that this was a radically different form of anthropology from that on which the discipline was founded. Our research projects carried greater ambitions than simply to be granted legitimacy within academia. In addition to scholarly pursuits, we were charged with the responsibility of serving the communities whom we studied. It was not lost on us that our presence was both a gift and a curse. On the one hand, we provided an extra body to assist those who sought to undo various processes of racial and gender oppression. On the other hand, our presence could very well place in jeopardy the efforts of those from whom we were supposedly there to study and learn. Yet, as I discovered during my time in Los Angeles, this liminal space affords a unique perspective on the particular challenges that Black people have faced all over the globe. In order to tell the untold story, we had to acknowledge the multifaceted natures of white supremacy and anti-Blackness, and remain highly cognizant of the precarious positions of the activists with whom we worked. Just as important was a comprehension that our position as graduate students was twofold: we needed to learn the issues and bring forth indigenous knowledges for incorporation within the canon, and we needed to create possibilities for social change.

It was at this point that I began to understand why the public discourses regarding Blacks and Latinos in Los Angeles were loaded with violent euphemisms. I could only imagine how different my high school experience would have been had we been able to conduct real conversations or read from books that addressed hard-hitting issues of race, gender, and sexuality. A real analysis and discussion of the root causes of perceived cases of racial antagonism might have upended the racial hierarchies and power relations that dominated the school. Further, such acts might have aligned particular communities whose visions of the world have consistently differed from a Western viewpoint. I originally thought that I was moving to Austin to get an education. During this research, I realized that the greatest learning took place back from whence I had come. In a sense, the classroom walls had been extended some two thousand miles—but more importantly, the walls in my mind had been permanently broken down.

Notes

1. World War II, Southern mechanization, and torrid racism were the great catalysts that pushed Blacks from Texas and Louisiana into Los Angeles. However, these Black migrants ran into the same white supremacist ideology that had stalked them in the Jim Crow South. Homeowner's associations such as the Anti-African Housing Association banded together to enforce restrictive covenants that denied residential ownership to nonwhites, while some white residents resorted to such extralegal measures as firebombing Black homes (Davis 1992, 162, 400). The brutality of the LAPD under Chief William Parker, who saw his force as a "thin blue line" protecting white residents from criminal-minded Blacks and Latinos "not too far removed from the wild tribes ... of Mexico" (Davis 1992, 295), culminated in the 1965 Watts Riots. President Reagan's cuts to the Comprehensive Employment and Training Act (CETA) and Job Corps, combined with his funding of a civil war in El Salvador, eliminated jobs for Blacks and forced hundreds of thousands of El Salvadorians into Mexico and eventually into low-wage private jobs in Los Angeles (Kelley 1996; Vigil 2002). Coupled with the explicit police targeting of Black communities, mandatory-sentencing drug laws and gang injunction legislation passed in the 1980s and '90s led to the massive incarceration of Black men and women (Gilmore and Pyle 2005).

2. Information obtained through conversations with community activists.

3. It is of note that the program was initiated after decades' worth of pressure by Black movements within Mexico and following inter-

national scholarship and popular accounts that illustrated the dire situation of Blacks in Mexico (Pérez-Sarduy and Stubbs 1995).

4. Figures are calculated on the basis of U.S. Census Bureau data from 2000.

5. At issue was Hanchard's study of the Movimento Negro Unificado in Brazil, which has been at the center of a growing controversy about the study of race in Latin America. Peter Fry, Pierre Bourdieu, and Loïc Wacquant have attacked Hanchard's work as imposing an African American racial perspective on the politics of Brazil. Bourdieu and Wacquant further attacked the work of philanthropic organizations and NGOs on similar grounds. In particular, they argue that U.S. foundations have wrongly forced affirmative action upon Brazil (Sawyer 2008, 138).

References

Associated Press. 2005. War of words escalates in deadly L.A. shooting. Associated Press, July 14. http://www.msnbc.msn.com/id/8567717/.

Chavez, Hector. 2005. Interview with by the author. Los Angeles, July 15.

Davis, Mike. 1992. *City of quartz: Excavating the future in Los Angeles.* New York: Vintage Books.

Garvey, Megan, and Jill Leovy. 2005. LAPD bullet killed girl in clash. *Los Angeles Times,* July 14.

Gilmore, Craig, and Kevin Pyle. 2005. *Prison Town: Paying the price.* Washington, DC: Real Cost of Prison Project.

Holland, Randy, dir. 1994. *The fire this time: Why Los Angeles burned.* 90 min. Rhino. Videocassette.

Human Rights Watch. 2003. Incarcerated America. Human Rights Watch Backgrounder. April.

Kelley, Robin D. G. 1996. *Race rebels: Culture, politics and the Black working class.* New York: Free Press.

Kraul, Chris, and Reed Johnson. 2005. Mexican postage stamp pushes racial envelope. *Los Angeles Times,* June 20.

Leland, John, and Stanley Holmes. 1993. Criminal records. *Newsweek,* November 29.

Marable, Manning. 1999. *How capitalism underdeveloped Black America: Problems in race, political economy, and society.* 2nd ed. Cambridge, MA: South End Press.

Muhammad, Charlene. 2005. Police kill 19-month-old baby during L.A.

standoff. *The Final Call*, July 27. http://www.finalcall.com/artman/publish/article_2115.shtml.

Pelisek, Christine. 2005. LAPD's half-open book. *LA Weekly*, July 21.

Pérez-Sarduy, Pedro, and Jean Stubbs, eds. 1995. *No longer invisible: Afro-Latin Americans today*. London: Minority Rights Group Publications.

Rapp, Malcolm. 2005. Interview by the author. Los Angeles, July 7.

Rivera, Carla. 2005. Years have done little to help local Blacks. *Los Angeles Times*, July 14.

Robinson, Cedric J. 1983. *Black Marxism: The making of the Black radical tradition*. London: Zed Press.

Samuels, Lennox. 2005. Which face represents Mexico?—Some deny bias against Blacks; others say it's hard to miss. *Dallas Morning News*, July 19.

Sawyer, Mark. 2008. DuBois's double consciousness versus Latin American exceptionalism: Joe Arroyo, salsa, and Negritude. In *Transnational Blackness: navigating the global color line*, edited by Manning Marable and Vanessa Agard-Jones. New York: Palgrave.

Vigil, James Diego. 2002. *A rainbow of gangs: Street cultures in the Mega City*. Austin: University of Texas Press.

Winant, Howard. 2002. *The world is a ghetto: Race and democracy since World War II*. New York: Basic Books, 2002.

21

Participatory Art, Engaged Scholarship: The Embedded Critic in Nadia Myre's *Scar Project*

Amanda Jane Graham

IN AN EFFORT to better comprehend her own scars, artist Nadia Myre began collecting scars belonging to others. Myre started her collection in 2005 and it presently consists of over 800 10" × 10" canvas representations of physical and emotional scars. The small square renderings in neutral-colored string, thread, and twine have been displayed on gallery and museum walls across North America. Wherever Myre exhibits her scar archive, she facilitates an interactive workshop during which participants are invited to create artistic portrayals of their scars using materials provided by the artist. Thereafter these scars, along with the participants' accompanying scar stories and reflections, are catalogued by Myre and become a part of the collective work entitled *The Scar Project* (Figure 21.1).

While the collection of scars illustrates the artist's creative ingenuity and conceptual complexity, the most compelling aspect of Myre's project is that of participation, which art theorist and curator Suzana Milevska defines as "the activation of certain relations that is initiated and directed by the [artist] and often encouraged by art institutions, and that sometimes becomes the sole goal of certain art projects" (2006). As a participatory and ongoing work of art, Myre's project is produced as much by the invisible accrual of personal interactions in and outside of the workshop setting as it is by the visible accumulation of material scars produced within that space.

It is difficult, as contemporary art and social theorist Grant Kester points out in *Art, Activism, and Oppositionality*, to write about art such as Myre's, which does not lend itself to traditional formalist critique "premised on a clear separation … between the artist as a private, expressive subject and the domain of social exchange and collective will formation" (1998, 8). Considering this, how do emerging scholars like me, who are invested in participant-driven art, pursue their analyses in an academic environment dominated by thinkers who favor a more formal approach? Does a different kind of art call for new types of art theory? If so, what form does this scholarship take?

Although numerous theorists, including Milevska, Kester, and Nicolas Bourriaud, describe a paradigm shift in art-making and theory that involves a movement from an object- to a subject-based approach, their work lacks an extensive consideration of the art theorist as one of these subjects (Milevska 2006). If the theorist of what Bourriaud calls "relational aesthetics"—an art theory premised on contemplating "social bonds" (2002, 36)—does not acknowledge her positionality, and thus camouflages her stake in her study, how can she honestly discuss the work in which she is implicated? By consciously or unconsciously removing her subjectivity from her discussion of participatory artwork, she discursively eliminates the social bonds and erases the personal negotiations constitutive to the success of the work itself. She writes herself out of the artwork, and out of the public with whom it is associated. Conversely, a central premise of the present chapter is that by employing discursive strategies utilized by publicly engaged scholars, she can write herself into the art public and speak as both critic and participant. Engaged scholarship authorizes the obvious: research and writing, scholarly or otherwise, begins with a personal investment. The publicly engaged scholar of contemporary art celebrates hybrid roles and discourses, fosters a belief in creating new modes of practice, and invites the personal and experimental into the realm of research.

FIGURE 21.1. Nadia Myre, *The Scar Project*, Smithsonian National Museum of the American Indian, New York, NY, 2010. Photo: Alan Wiener. Courtesy of Art Mûr Gallery.

My aims in this essay are tripartite and closely related. First, I will present single authorship as a persistent and problematic norm for art-making and art criticism and, in particular, for *The Scar Project*. Secondly, I will contend that participation—as a method of art creation—is resistant to sole authorship, but that its critical dialogic intervention is conventionally subsumed and anesthetized in a totalizing frame when analyzed. Lastly, I will propose that being a self-reflexive publicly engaged intellectual, open to sharing personal narratives in the critical context, is one possible way to uncover these relations and realize the work's ongoing dialogical possibilities in the space of writing. My arguments for publicly engaged scholarship are informed by my participation in Myre's *Scar Project* workshop at the National Museum of the American Indian in New York City that took place on March 6, 2010. My intent in broaching these aims is in part to continue the conversations that I began about my scars and those of others in that scar workshop. By continuing this discourse within the context of my writing I hope to share this discussion with a public of readers invested in theories and practices of engaged scholarship.

Part I: Subject to Participation

I contacted Myre months before we met in person and long before I created a canvas representation of a personal scar. I had been directed to her website by a colleague who knew my theoretical and aesthetic interest in scars. As soon as I saw her work I began to imagine collaborative possibilities. Shortly thereafter Myre and I started an e-mail correspondence. My initial e-mail to Myre (June 4, 2009) reads, in part:

> I believe, as it appears you do, that each of us has stories of our encounters written upon our surfaces. Discussing these memory-marks calls forth a psycho-social healing. But how can this trauma and healing be visually manifested? Perhaps re-creating our scars on canvas or with string does just that. Sufficed to say, your work moves me, but more than moving me I see in it the potential to address necessary issues of identity, place, politics, history and the body. It feels important.

In my introductory note to Myre, I hoped to express the parallel between my scholarly writings on scars and her artistic pursuits. As I had anticipated, we quickly came to the conclusion that we shared many of the same convictions, including the belief that participatory art is regenerative and that scars are literal and metaphoric signifiers of traumatic encounters that shape individuals and communities. As Dennis Patrick Slattery poetically expresses in *The Wounded Body*, "To be wounded is to be opened up to the world; it is to be pushed off the straight, fixed, and predictable path of certainty and thrown into ambiguity, or on a circuitous path, and into the unseen and unforeseen" (2000, 13). Slattery's characterization of the wound and its repercussions offers both insight into why Myre is interested in wounds and the scars they become and a compelling parallel to her explanation of the participatory art form she utilizes in the development of *The Scar Project*.

Myre claims that the way in which she "constructed the confines of the project" forced her to give up much artistic decision-making power (2009). When she steps into the role of facilitator, Myre purposively surrenders some of her authorial control. Her work is porous to possibility, or as art theorist Dorothea von Hantelmann writes, convention is "durably rupture[d]" by art that requires interaction and lacks a singular closed material object (2010, 16). The content of Myre's work and its participatory form are linked by uncertainty. The body of the work is punctured by participation, yet like the wound that becomes a scar upon the subject's body or mind, these participatory interventions open the work up in order to incorporate encounters into its very being.

The Scar Project is alive: always becoming more than it formerly was, continually transforming into a new version of itself. Every time Myre facilitates a scar workshop, the project is re-created by the addition of new material canvases and stories as well as through further ephemeral social discourse and silent interaction. The unpredictability of *The Scar Project* imbues it with a dynamism lacking in an artwork created, and completed, by a singular artist. In literary philosopher Mikhail Bakhtin's terms, the form of Myre's artwork allows the scar to be polyphonically defined. Each scar and story remains distinct but converges in the space provided by the artist. What a scar means, and how it can be represented, is determined by the collective.

If every scar and story represents an individual's experience of being marked, then each is a tactile or written reenactment of that experience—a performance of a moment sealed to the participant's memory, and perhaps her body as well. When she enacts her scar by slashing the canvas and sewing the breach to the point that she sees fit, she is performing her wound and her healing. Hers is a public performance of a private memory, as particular as it is universal. Although her product remains unique after she has finished the embodied mimetic encounter with her canvas, Myre does not ask the participant to write her name on the creation or correlating story. Each story is dated, and every canvas designated by a stamped number. These are Myre's methods for ensuring that the pieces are sequentially cataloged. The number protects the anonymity of the artist, but it concurrently prevents the visibility of the distinct participant's subjectivity from being associated with her work. Every individual scar and story is submerged by the total work of art, singularly titled and affiliated with Myre's name alone. Like the novel that Bakhtin describes in *The Dialogic Imagination*, in which utterance and dialogue appropriated from varying texts and cultures are folded into the pages of a book, the particular creative acts executed by each of the participants in the scar workshops are "reconceptualized" through the art form (Bakhtin 1981, 326). Each scar is distinctive, but distinctively one of many.

After participants leave the scar workshop their scars and stories are emptied of origin. As anonymous canvases on the gallery wall and authorless stories compiled into the artist's book, the multitude of voices lose their subjectivity. The scars that compose Myre's project are orphaned. Subsequent to the scar's birth at the participant's hand it is detached from its subject and attached to a "constantly evolving ... heteroglossia" (Bakhtin 1981, 60).[1] The individual scars, stories, and discourse between participants comprise the project and demarcate its boundaries. Without participant involvement, *The Scar Project* would have no beginning or end. But, under the title designated by Myre and her curatorial guidance, the individual participation of project volunteers is erased as often as it is acknowledged.

By framing *The Scar Project* as an artistic version of Bakhtin's heteroglossia, I intend to point out two things. First, engaged scholarship in a participatory artwork can effectively reveal anonymous creative labor and return subjectivity to at least one individual involved—the participatory critic. Second, the lack of recognition for participant authorship in participatory art pieces has ramifications for how *The Scar Project* has been interpreted by curators, critics, and the public. Individual scar pieces remain distinctive on the wall and Myre is forthcoming about the collaborative nature of the project in artist statements and interviews, but ultimately the singular subjectivities of the persons who contributed their time and imagination are swallowed up by the authorial expectations of the art world and its attachment to traditional formalist critique. Although this is a valid participatory art-making practice that can be interpreted as protecting artists' privacy, it is symptomatic of the expectations institutions, not to mention the art-going public, have in regards to the presentation of artworks.

According to Kester, the formalist critical approach is "postulated on the belief that art can retain its authenticity only by remaining in the charmed circle of social disengagement" (1998, 8). Hence, Myre's effort to relinquish her authorial control of the project is limited by the cultural politics of the institutions in which she facilitates her workshops and displays the scars. She remains reliant on formalism, even when the work of art clearly necessitates social engagement. As Kester argues in reference to relational works of art, conversation is an "integral part of the work itself" (2004, 8). But how do scholars who write about relational artworks include this conversation in their theoretical analysis of the work without becoming a part of it? Should this conversation include the dialogue between the artist and participatory critic, since she is both a member of and engaged with the art-making, museum-going public that creates the work? Can publicly engaged scholarship on participatory art, premised on discursive practice, be considered an extension of the work of art?

In order to explore these questions, and concomitantly contend with the problem of participatory art situated by formalist approaches, it is helpful to turn to Bourriaud's foundational book, *Relational Aesthetics,* in which "relational art" is defined as "an art taking as its theoretical horizon the realm of human interactions and its social context, rather than the assertion of an independent and *private* symbolic space." Art, for Bourriaud, is at the "interstice" of communication (2002, 14). Artworks are not singular, but associative. In the relational model proposed by Bourriaud, all art is generated and sustained by linkages; participatory art, especially, is founded upon generative bonds.

Drawing upon the interstitial theory of art proposed by Bourriaud and conceding that relational art is an art of producing social bonds, we may conclude that the critic's relationships with artist and participants, her research, and her writing are constituents of these social bonds. Through writing, the ephemeral discursive connections between the formerly autonomous and disparate parts of the work are codified. Conversations between and among participants, the artist, and the critic are recorded by means of written representation. Like the psychic scars I tactilely confirmed with thread and needle during a scar workshop, intangible discourse is established and recognized on the page. In both instances, the abstract is made concrete.

Bourriaud's conception of art that generates social bonds paints a highly favorable—even utopian—picture of participation. But not all art theorists share his enthusiasm for artworks premised upon human interaction. In her article "Participatory Art: A Paradigm Shift from Objects to Subjects" (2006), Milevska outlines why participatory art has been severely criticized by theorists. She offers two arguments especially relevant to *The Scar Project.* First, much critical response to participatory practice highlights the practical and theoretical implications of artists and institutions creating temporary participant-publics whilst ignoring the possibility of enfranchising stable publics—permanent communities autonomous of institutional affiliations. Artists and the institutions that support them promote, through participatory art projects, the development of new publics that will not maintain their network of connections outside of their brief foray into the participatory project.[2] Is it productive to generate new communities, and inspire temporary bonds, when there are an abundance of individuals within stable community networks for whom the participatory art project might serve as a means of strengthening preexisting bonds? Should that be the artist's or the institution's concern?

A second prevalent judgment of participatory art projects iterated by Milevska is that they can serve as a means of addressing or placating the artist's or institution's concern over a "neglected other"—an apparently disenfranchised public that would, without artistic intervention, have little to no access to a particular institutionally sanctioned contemporary art world (2006). The participatory project, in this instance, becomes a type of outreach that gives a semblance of narrowly perceived and short-lived agency to the "marginalized" masses (2006).[3] In terms of Myre's project, the "participatory art as social work" model may have less relevance because of the heterogeneity of her participants and the longevity of her involvement with multiple publics. The goal of Myre's project never included empowering any one group or type of person; she is committed to facilitating scar workshops, in part, to break down racial, ethnic, national, socioeconomic, and gender borders between and among large and diverse populations.[4] The conversations that take place during the workshop between seemingly vastly different kinds of participants are a testament to the universal nature of scars. Myre chose to focus on scars, in part, because of their universal translatability. Everyone has physical and metaphorical scars, or has scarred another. Each of us knows what it means to feel pain and undergo healing.

While Myre's project is as inclusive as a participatory art project affiliated with institutions can be, the community she creates in her workshops is generally ephemeral. Participants share conversation and materials at tables in the gallery for an hour or two. Their anonymous scars and stories are all that is left behind of the temporary communal public. Myre does not record participant reactions. She has designed her project so that the canvas scars and scar narratives are the time capsule of a moment during which individuals forged temporary bonds. Through encounters in *Scar Project* workshops participants, including me, learn that they have more in common with the public inside and outside of the workshop than they previously believed. While Myre facilitates a space for catharsis, I believe it is the participant's responsibility to continue her healing through an ongoing sharing—a conversation that transcends the designated space of the workshop into everyday life.

Part II. Writing Myself In

My participation, like that of every participant in Myre's project, was initially twofold. I created a canvas scar partnered with a scar story, and I discussed the project with fellow participants at one of Myre's workshops, at the National Museum of the American Indian in New York. When I finished with my scar it was hung on the wall of the museum, in close proximity to other scars belonging to a few participants with whom I conversed and many more whom I never met and may never meet. The bonds enacted by the visual juxtaposition of the scars on display pick up where the discursive bonds between participants in the workshop setting end. They are the result of collectively remembering personal trauma and healing in a public space, and sharing the narratives associated with these memories. The scars and stories are evidence of the conversation. They are the marks of encounter left behind in order to create a new collective body that performs a visual discourse with present and future viewers.

My participation in Myre's project does not end with my engagement in the workshop public, or with the creation of my material scar and story. I continue to engage with Myre's work through my writing. I am participating in her project as I type these words upon the page. That is, the third way I participate in *The Scar Project* is through scholarly discourse that resolves to elucidate the blurred boundaries between analytic and autobiographic writing while creating a blueprint for art theory premised on the intersections of life experience and scholarly inquiry.

Myre's project requires participants to create scars of any sort. However, most participants, including me, choose scars representative of personal histories. Most, including me, choose to represent scars that continue to inform our lives. My participation in Myre's project began before I knew I was participating in any project. My scar and story came into existence when I was engaged with a different sort of public, a public that would forever define what scars mean to me. By sharing the scar story I wrote for *The Scar Project* here, I hope to reveal the layers of engagement I have in Myre's work, situate myself as a visible participant with motivations and interests that inform my scholarly practice, and illustrate that formal public engagement is entangled with personal engagement.

Prior to entering the doctoral program in Visual and Cultural Studies at The University of Rochester, I was an art teacher at an inner-city public school in Brownsville, Brooklyn. There, I encountered a profusion of scars. Physical scars littered the surface of my students' bodies. One boy wore a glove on his right hand for months after punching in a window on the fourth floor of the school during an afternoon rage. His classmate who dressed in long sleeves, even on hot June days, concealed iron burns that could have been minimized if she had received proper medical treatment. After allegedly stealing a few items from a bodega, a former student was bludgeoned in the head with a hammer by an angry store clerk and ended up in a coma. My mom called from New Jersey to inform me that his story was on the five o'clock news. A number of my students' traumas were visible, but the majority remained invisibly inscribed—traumatic remainders that appeared symptomatically as anger, depression, and low self-esteem. These traumas were hardly scars, for they had not healed. Rather, they were open wounds—breaches in the psychic fabric—that emanated intangible but overwhelming pain.

The symptoms of my students' psychic wounds impacted me. I dealt with fights, tears, and extreme apathy on a weekly basis. I think many teachers experience trauma vicariously, through their students—but never diagnose it in those terms. My students' emotional lacerations defined my days, as did the accrual of my own. I experienced my first lockdown midway through my inaugural year as a teacher. Before becoming a New York City public school educator, I believed that lockdowns only occurred in jails. I was naive. Lockdowns were so common at my public school that lockdown procedure was regularly reviewed at faculty meetings: tell students to stay away from the windows, lock the doors, stay calm, and listen for announcements. What administrators neglected to mention during procedural explanations was that many students chose not to comply with the rules.

One day during eighth period some shots were fired outside the school's front entrance. Before I could lock the classroom door, half of the students in the room abandoned their self-portraits and ran to the window to get a better look. Even as I turned off the lights and screamed to gain some semblance of control, I realized the futility of my actions. Many of my students were so desensitized to violence that it had become a game for them. They had witnessed so many traumatic incidents, and had so many wounds, that they had begun to seek them out. Wounds, for them, were normalized.

Later that day, I took the subway home in a stupor. As soon as I entered my apartment I got into bed, fully clothed, and cried until I fell asleep. When I got out of bed the next morning I showered, stopped for coffee, and went to work. I tried not to think about what had happened, and what would happen. In order to work in a culture defined by its wounds, I had to become a part of that culture. After my lockdown initiation I self-anaesthetized; I *saw* violence without *feeling* it.

All wounds are a product of their environment, as are the scars they become with time. If a physical or psychic wound is dressed or addressed, the resulting mark is less severe. Its aesthetic or emotional impact is mitigated. But a wound ignored, denied, and repressed causes lasting psychic or physical damage. We are all in varied states of disrepair. Traumatic incidents occur in every environment, public and private, and inform our actions and interactions within those spaces and for the rest of our lives.

My ongoing concern with the psychic and physical scars in Brownsville is not their presence but their prevalence. A concentration of wounds in any arena propagates more wounds within that space. Trauma, if neglected, is like a disease that spreads. It is a disease of the mind, and leaves its trace on the body, but the core of the collective crisis can only be properly confronted and averted socioeconomically. The reactionary rather than preventative approach of social services, law enforcement, the housing authority, and the educational system fosters fresh wounds in Brownsville, while ignoring the malformed scars of the recent past. After my experience in Brownsville I do not doubt that trauma is, in part, government-sanctioned.

Denying the needs, and even the existence, of "peripheral" communities has been, through official and unofficial oversight, cyclically formalized. A *New York Times* article by Randal C. Archibold (1999) describes a day in the life of summer school students and their teacher, Mrs. Hunt, at a Brownsville elementary school, P.S. 41. The reporter notes the obstacles the group must face daily, including a lack of necessary teaching materials—"Mrs. Hunt had to bring in her own reading books because supplies had not yet arrived"—and oppressive July heat in a classroom without air conditioning: "The Board of Education has begun putting fans in all classrooms. Only a fifth of classrooms in the school system are air-conditioned.[5]" This is not a productive environment for teaching and learning, but the dictates of the New York City Board of Education, including mandatory lesson plans based on the chancellor of education's guidelines and "closely linked to the city's reading and math tests," make educating in low-income New York City public schools almost impossible (Archibold 1999). The personal, social, and academic needs of individual students are overlooked so that teachers can keep to a stringent schedule of test preparation—and ultimately keep their jobs.

The scene Archibold depicts is familiar to me. I remember rooms on the fourth floor of the school where I taught, full of teenagers, with the windows painted shut for security reasons. I remember that a few of those teenagers were still learning to read. There were verbal fights between teachers over copy paper and physical fights between students over pencils. My school was not unique for Brownsville, and nor is P.S. 41. Teachers are frustrated and exhausted, and administrators are without recourse and support. Although complaining has been ritualized in the classroom and community, everyone is relatively complacent because the challenges appear insurmountable. Higher test scores will not address systemic deficiencies, nor will superficial attention to the Brownsville community's safety, health, or housing needs. Change requires acknowledging past failures in education and social services, and addressing them. But that would necessitate time, money, and a plan tailored to the needs of the neighborhood (which requires an intimate knowledge of that neighborhood). Most of the time "bad neighborhoods" stay bad; they live up to their social stigma daily.

As urban historian Wendell Pritchett explains in *Brownsville, Brooklyn: Blacks, Jews, and the Changing Face of the Ghetto* (2002), Brownsville's problems are hardly new. The Brownsville community, generally associated with urban blight today, has long struggled with issues of affordable housing, sustainable businesses, geographic and financial segregation, educational support, and preemptive as well as proscriptive responses to crime. Brownsville has suffered from a lack of resources since the 1940s. This lack has resulted in, among other things, high population turnover and a general atmosphere of disempowerment. Although, as Pritchett points out, Brownsville community activists as well as a handful of city and national government officials have consistently and frequently advocated for change (and have, in general, met with nominal success),[6] the neighborhood remains a focal point of urban crisis, a place on the outskirts of Brooklyn that visitors to New York City (to say nothing of residents) rarely pass through except in a taxi on the way to JFK airport. But why is this acceptable? Why does society contend with certain wounds and render others invisible?

The psychic wounds that I suffered in Brownsville, on the day of my first lockdown and countless days thereafter, traveled with me upstate to graduate school. During my first year in Rochester I had time and perspective to begin to comprehend my wounds, and the violence to which I had borne witness. While I appreciated this time to heal, it was not easy.

When I was a public school teacher, I often gathered with a few colleagues after our students had gone home and shared the day's brutal highlights. One afternoon, a friend recounted a chaotic incident during which a desk was hurled toward her head, and another described the gang symbols inscribed in her classroom wall. We survived our days, weeks, and years because we constructed a community in which wounds were regularly exchanged through conversation. When I began graduate school, it quickly became apparent that the academic colleagues in my new community were excited to trade books and theories, but less interested in sharing stories from our respective personal lives—especially within the classroom setting. Could I blame them? I too enjoyed discussing philosophy, film, and historical movements in art practice and theory. Nonetheless, I felt isolated by the nature of this discourse because the wounds of my former life were relegated to silence. I experienced what artist David Garneau calls "logophobia" and "logophilia," or the simultaneous drive to speak and fear of saying the wrong thing (2009, 11). I longed to express my former experiences but worried these expressions were not suitable in the academic setting.

As my wounds from Brownsville transformed into scars, a new wound developed out of my inability to express my old wounds. The scar I created for Myre's project is representative of both of these wounds. Through my participation in *The Scar Project,* I came to realize that my frustration with discourse, whether academic art criticism or more casual conversation, was not unique. Numerous project participants, as well as Myre, have contended with the limits of language following traumatic incidents. How can anyone say what she is still learning to feel?

While the wounds I imported from Brooklyn slowly became scars, I worried that the same time and distance that facilitated my healing inevitably encouraged forgetting. I wanted to remember where and how I received my wounds and subsequent scars because each of these moments taught me something invaluable about marks that constitute difference. Scars have been a means for me to contend with abstract notions of societal demarcation, a lens through which I come to comprehend how communities and identities are at the same time both internally constituted and externally constructed. These scars have informed my scholarship as much as they have my life. My interests in Bourriaud's theories of relational art, participatory art in general, and publicly engaged scholarship all find their origin in my scars. I want my scholarship to address the gaps in artistic, social, and cultural intersections by revealing the breakdown of bonds and their regeneration. By considering scars in my work, I am able to broach social traumas through art criticism, and demonstrate the relevance of contemporary participatory art to the infrastructure of society.

As a result of participation in Myre's project, I recalled the value and consequence of my psychic scars, as well as the related traumatic traces, emotional and physical, embodied by my former students. I saw that scars had the potential to be used as a means for communication, rather than isolating the scarred. The scars that define me were given form, by my own hand, upon a canvas provided by Myre. This form transformed the invisible and unsayable—the scar stories from Brooklyn that I seldom recounted—into something conspicuous and tangible. After creating my scar with needle and thread, I could thereafter point to its picture. Realized upon the canvas, my scar became part of a community of scars produced by relative strangers, and united by Myre's project. My thin vertical slit of absence, sutured by short horizontal dashes of thread, is one of over 800 scars collectively composing Myre's project.

When I was stitching my scar at the National Museum of the American Indian, I sat across the table from a man in his seventies who was patiently waiting for his wife to complete a canvas scar. While he waited, we began a conversation about urban education during which he recounted his experiences teaching in a New Orleans public high school. He remembered police raids in his classroom. "They'd line all the students up against the wall and search them for drugs," he said, "It came as quite a surprise." After chatting for a few minutes, I asked him to read my scar story. He happily agreed, afterward telling me he identified with my scars; they resembled his own. Meanwhile, this participant's wife created her scar in the shape of a sun, with rays of varying length. She told the table of participants that her scar represented the union between herself and her husband: the most valuable relationship of her life. The woman's remarks inspired a group of us to discuss the regenerative possibility of scars, and the experiences that have marked us positively—like the experience of participating in *The Scar Project.*

Conclusion

When I began to write about *The Scar Project,* I believed that sharing the history of my psychic wounds and the emotional and physical marks that decorated the minds and bodies of my former students would produce discomfort for some within my scholarly setting. I was afraid of my colleagues' reactions. I was scared of my reaction to their reactions. Getting personal in academia, I have come to realize, makes everyone a little uneasy. It disrupts the clean professionalism of the work place and forces us to realize that the divisions between life experiences and professional interests are arbitrary and permeable. As the publicly engaged feminist scholar Sally Kimpson writes, "by transgress[ing] academic and disciplinary expectations about 'acceptable' research topics" we "violate norms about how research is 'supposed' to be conducted" and leave ourselves open to criticism concerning the rigor and credibility of our scholarship (2005, 73). But our theories do not exist in a vacuum. The academic's bonds within social and cultural arenas outside of the university setting inform the direction of her scholarly work. They are *fundamental* to this work.

Publicly engaged scholars intellectually labor to expand academic debates in order to include larger and more diverse publics. Part of expanding the debate involves including new voices—in and outside of academia—but another part of it necessitates uniting the divided voices of scholars, voices that have been split into official and unofficial, professional and personal.[7] Anthropologists have long trumpeted a methodology of participant observation that "focuses on the meaning of human existence as seen from the standpoint of insiders" (Jorgensen 1989, 14) and feminists have argued that the personal is political, and the borders between public and private life are amorphous. As Martha Rosler stated in 1980, "if one exposes to view the socially constrained elements within the supposed realm of freedom of action—namely, 'the personal'" then the personal becomes political (2001, 96). Yet these theories, which have informed contemporary publicly engaged scholarship, continue to be met with resistance by art theorists who predominately maintain a critical distance and voice in reference to their objects and subjects of study.

Ignoring personal influences and discourse, by way of claiming objectivity or out of simple inconsideration, denies the personal stake in academic undertakings. Proponents of self-reflexivity believe "concrete action, emotion, embodiment, self-consciousness, and introspection" enrich scholarship (Ellis 2004, xix). Being forthright about our personal stake in the academic arguments we construct gives them a personality and origin. As Katherine Allen and Fred Piercy state in reference to feminist autoethnography, when we "tell and analyze our own stories, we begin to see how their content is derived from our culture" (2005, 159). No wonder, when we are part and product of that culture.

In this essay, I have tried to elucidate links between diverse publics and *The Scar Project* by illustrating how a single individual—the participatory scholar—can act as a fulcrum for these relations. My argument is premised on the notion that subjectivity is always relational; who we are and how each of us is perceived has everything to do with our actual and discursive connection to others. Although the scholar can serve as a nexus for relations—past, present and future—these relations are impossible without a multiplicity of actors, most notably the artist who initiates the participatory work.

Days after I contacted Myre with my initial e-mail she responded. Her reply reads, in part:

> Your timing is quite beautiful as I find myself a little exasperated with the Scar Project. In 2005 when I first started this investigation I saw it as a first step to mining how we interpret our pain. In observation through this project, our scars and stories simultaneously shape us, divide us and unite us. Now

that I have close to 500 hundred scars and stories of varying depth I am having a hard time determining what the next step is.[8]

What Myre did not realize was that, with this response, she was taking a "next step." Through her discursive exchange with me she was participating in her own participatory project. The discourse that transpired between Myre and me, first through e-mail, then over the phone, and eventually in person, united her art and my scholarship. We related professionally. But inevitably, in the midst of discussing *The Scar Project* we connected personally; we spoke about exhibitions that influenced us, the cities we have lived in, and our respective scar stories. Recognizing our professional and personal discursive interchange here, upon the page, is a means of revealing what always exists within, but often invisibly behind, every scholarly essay: relationships between people and the ongoing conversations they foster. These conversations form and transform the scholarly argument, even after it appears to come to a close.

Notes

1. Heteroglossia is Bakhtin's designation for the internal dialogic quality of a singularly authored work that appropriates multiple voices and presents them as if they were unitary.

2. Contemporary participatory art projects are as ubiquitous as they are varied. For Sonya Clarke's *Beaded Prayers Project,* participants created over 4,000 beaded prayers influenced by African amulet traditions. Rikrit Tiravanija transformed his *Dinner Party* into a performance comprised of producing and consuming a meal. As his guests conversed, the artist cooked and served food, thereafter requesting his dinner guests/participants leave their dirty dishes behind as the proof of the event. Kester and Bourriaud as well as Claire Bishop (2006) and Miwon Kwon (2004) discuss participant-based artists and art projects in detail.

3. Milevska takes a purely theoretical approach in her essay and therefore does not cite any examples of "outreach art," but this topic is taken up with specificity by Kester (1999/2000). In his analysis of participatory art Kester considers a project called *Soul Shadows: Urban Warrior Myths,* produced by an artist from New Orleans named Dawn Dedeaux in 1993. He writes, "It began as part of an 'art in the prisons' program in Louisiana and eventually mushroomed into a traveling multi-media installation with sculptural elements, multiple video monitors, fabricated rooms, large photo-based images, a sound track and so

on." Dedeaux intended to, "help white viewers 'empathize' with the conditions faced by young black men, at the same time that she hoped the piece would act as a kind of moral prophylactic for young black men who came to see it, who would presumably mend their ways after witnessing the contrition expressed by a number of imprisoned figures." The piece was contentious and Dedeaux faced criticism from audiences and critics who felt her class (upper middle) and race (white) problematically highlighted difference rather than productively fostered understanding.

4. Myre has held scar workshops in a variety of settings including museums, galleries, universities, and drop-in centers. Her workshops are always free and open to the public.

5. Although this article was written in 1999 it reflects the current condition in many Brownsville public schools. In fact, recent budget cuts have aggravated these issues and forced schools to let valuable faculty and staff go, thereby increasing class size.

6. Local activist organizations that advocated for change in Brownsville with some success include the Brownsville Neighborhood Council (BNC), the Brownsville Boys Club (BBC) and the Brownsville Community Congress of Industrial Organizations (Brownsville CIO). These groups campaigned for a variety of issues over the years, including better and more affordable housing, safer schools, and regular trash collection.

7. One contemporary scholar who considers personal narratives and trauma within her work is Sophie Tamas. With sensitivity and insight, Tamas writes, "I find [reflexive scholarship] exciting to read and frightening to produce. I am worried, however, by its ethical trespass. While our obligation to the other has been much discussed, there are also important ethical problems in how we present and represent ourselves. I am not worried about what we are saying, but rather by how we speak" (2009). I concur with Tamas; how we write about our own experiences is as important an ethical concern as how we represent the lives of others. Presenting ourselves as doubly or multiply voiced requires a constant balancing of perspectives, and critically conscious awareness of what Tamas, and Carolyn Ellis (1991) before her, calls "sociological introspection."

8. Correspondence with Nadia Myre, June 8, 2009. Since Myre wrote this e-mail she has collected over 300 additional scars.

References

Allen, Katherine, and Fred Piercy. 2005. Feminist autoethnography. In *Research methods in family therapy*, edited by D. Sprenkle and S.

Moon. New York: Guilford Press.

Archibold, Randal C. 1999. In season of play, daunting struggle to learn; CATCHING UP—summer at P.S. 41. *New York Times*, July 18.

Bakhtin, Mikhail. 1981. *The dialogic imagination.* Austin: University of Texas Press.

Bishop, Claire, ed. 2006. *Participation*. Cambridge, MA: MIT Press.

Bourriaud, Nicolas. 2002. *Relational aesthetics*. Dijon, France: Presses Du Réel.

Ellis, Carolyn. 1991. Sociological introspection and emotional experience. *Symbolic Interaction* 14 (1): 23–50.

Ellis, Carolyn. 2004. *The ethnographic I: A methodological novel about teaching and doing autoethnography.* Walnut Creek, CA: AltaMira.

Garneau, David. 2009. Landscape of Sorrow and other new work by Nadia Myre. *Art Mûr Invitation* (exhibition catalogue) 4 (5): 11–13.

Jorgensen, Danny L. 1989. *Participant observation: A methodology for human studies.* Thousand Oaks, CA: Sage.

Kester, Grant. 1998. *Art, activism, and oppositionality: Essays from* Afterimage. Durham: Duke University Press.

Kester, Grant. 1999/2000. Dialogical aesthetics: A critical framework for littoral art. *Variant*, no. 9 (Winter). http://www.variant.org.uk/9texts/KesterSupplement.html.

Kester, Grant. 2004. *Conversation pieces: Community and communication in modern art.* Berkeley and Los Angeles: University of California Press.

Kimpson, Sally. 2005. Stepping off the road: A narrative (of) inquiry. In *Research as resistance: Critical, indigenous and anti-oppressive approaches*, edited by L. Brown and S. Strega. Toronto: Canadian Scholars Press.

Kwon, Miwon. 2004. *One place after another: Site-specific art and locational identity.* Cambridge, MA: MIT Press.

Milevska, Suzana. 2006. Participatory art: A paradigm shift from objects to subjects. *Springerin*, no. 2. http://www.springerin.at/dyn/heft.php?id=47&pos=0&textid=0&lang=en.

Myre, Nadia. 2009. Interview with the author. October 24.

Pritchett, Wendell. 2002. *Brownsville, Brooklyn: Blacks, Jews, and the changing face of the ghetto.* Chicago: University of Chicago Press.

Rosler, Martha. 2001. Well, *is* the personal political? In *Feminism–art–theory: An anthology, 1968–2000*, edited by Hilary Robinson. Malden, MA: Blackwell.

Slattery, Dennis Patrick. 2000. *The wounded body: Remembering the markings of flesh.* Albany: SUNY Press.

Tamas, Sophie. 2009. Writing and righting trauma: Troubling the autoethnographic voice. *Forum: Qualitative Social Research* 10, no. 1, art. 22. http://nbn-resolving.de/urn:nbn:de:0114-fqs0901220

von Hantelmann, Dorothea. 2010. *How to do things with art.* Zurich: JRP Ringier and Presses Du Réel.

RESOURCES

THE FOLLOWING is a concise list of resources that will be of interest to this volume's readers, especially graduate students and faculty mentoring graduate students or directing graduate programs. The list contains general resources, rather than a detailed bibliography of the literature in this area. More detailed bibliographies can be found in the bibliographies of individual chapters or in some of the works below. The first section here concerns public engagement or engaged scholarship in general. The second section focuses more narrowly on publicly active graduate education.

Resources for Engaged Scholars

American Association of State Colleges and Universities Task Force on Public Engagement. 2002. *Stepping forward as stewards of place.* Washington, DC: AASCU.

Campus Compact. http://www.compact.org

Community-Campus Partnerships for Health. http://www.ccph.info

Edufactory: Conflicts and Transformation of the University. http://www.edu-factory.org/wp

Ellison, J., and T. K. Eatman. 2008. *Scholarship in public: Knowledge creation and tenure policy in the engaged university.* Syracuse, NY: Imagining America.

Engagement Scholarship Consortium. http://outreachscholarship.org

Fitzgerald, Hiram E., Cathy Burack, and Sarena D. Seifer, eds. 2010. *Handbook of engaged scholarship: Contemporary landscapes, future directions.* 2 vols. East Lansing: Michigan State University Press.

Imagining America: Artists and Scholars in Public Life. http://imaginingamerica.org

Jordan, Cathy. 2009. Practical tools for overcoming the challenges of advancing your career as a community-engaged scholar. Campus Compact. http://www.compact.org/wp-content/uploads/2009/04/jordan-final1.pdf

Journal of Community Engagement and Scholarship. University of Alabama. http://www.jces.ua.edu

Journal of Higher Education Outreach and Engagement. University of Georgia. http://openjournals.libs.uga.edu/index.php/jheoe

Kellogg Commission on the Future of State and Land-Grant Universities. 1999. *Returning to our roots: The engaged institution.* Washington, DC: National Association of State Universities and Land-Grant Colleges.

Van de Ven, Andrew H. 2007. *Engaged scholarship: A guide for organizational and social research.* Oxford: Oxford University Press.

Resources on Publicly Active Graduate Education

Blee, Lisa, Caley Horan, Jeffrey T. Manuel, Brian Tochterman, Andrew Urban, and Julie M. Weiskopf. 2008. Engaging with public engagement: Public history and graduate pedagogy. (2008). *Radical History Review* 102: 73–89.

Bloomfield, Victor. 2005. Civic engagement and graduate education. *CGS Communicator* 38 (3): 1–2, 6.

Day, Catherine Reid, Pamela Proulx-Curry, and Sandra Hansen. Civic engagement in graduate education: Preparing the next generation of engaged scholars. Wingspread Conference Report, Upper Midwest Campus Compact Consortium.

Gaff, Jerry G. 2005. Preparing future faculty and multiple forms of scholarship. In *Faculty priorities reconsidered: Rewarding multiple forms of scholarship*, edited by KerryAnn O'Meara and R. Eugene Rice. San Francisco: Jossey-Bass.

Golde, Chris M., and George E. Walker, eds. 2006. *Envisioning the future of doctoral education: Preparing stewards of the discipline.* San Francisco: Jossey-Bass.

O'Meara, KerryAnn. 2007. Graduate education and civic engagement. *NERCHE Brief* 20 (February). http://www.nerche.org/images/stories/publications/NERCHE_Briefs/Brief_20_Graduate_Education_and_Civic_Engagement.pdf

O'Meara, KerryAnn, and Audrey J. Jaeger. 2006. Preparing future faculty for community engagement: Barriers, facilitators, models, and recommendations. *Journal of Higher Education Outreach and Engagement* 11 (4): 3–26.

Index